Postcolonial Urbanism

SOUTHEAST ASIAN CITIES
AND GLOBAL PROCESSES

EDITED BY

Ryan Bishop

John Phillips

Wei-Wei Yeo

Routledge
New York • London

WITHDRAWN
UTSA LIBRARIES

Library
University of Texas
at San Antonio

Published in 2003 by
Routledge
29 West 35th Street
New York, NY 10001
www.routledge-ny.com

Published in Great Britain by
Routledge
11 New Fetter Lane
London EC4P 4EE
www.routledge.co.uk

Copyright © 2003 by Taylor & Francis Books, Inc.

Routledge is an imprint of the Taylor & Francis Group.
Printed in the United States of America on acid-free paper.

All rights reserved. No part of this book may be reprinted or reproduced or utilized in
any form or by any electronic, mechanical, or other means, now known or hereafter
invented, including photocopying and recording, or in any information storage or retrieval
system without permission in writing from the publishers.

10 9 8 7 6 5 4 3 2 1

Library of Congress Cataloging-in-Publication Data

Postcolonial urbanism: Southeast Asian cities and global processes / edited by Ryan Bishop, John Phillips,
and Wei-Wei Yeo.
    p. cm.
  Includes bibliographical references and index.
  ISBN 0-415-93249-1 (Hardback) — ISBN 0-415-93250-5 (Paperback)
    1. Urbanization—Asia, Southeastern. 2. Cities and towns—Asia, Southeastern. 3. Globalization.
  I. Bishop, Ryan. II. Phillips, John. III. Yeo, Wei-Wei.

  HT384.A78 P67 2003
  307.76'0959—dc21

                                                                        2002012440

Contents

Acknowledgments

The editors would like to acknowledge a number of people and institutions that have provided logistical, material, and intellectual support for this project: the Faculty Research Committee for the Faculty of Arts and Social Sciences at the National University of Singapore; Lily S. Kong, dean of the FASS; the Urban Studies Research Project at NUS; Brenda Yeoh, former head of the Centre of Advanced Studies at NUS; our many terrific colleagues in the departments of English, history, sociology, architecture, geography, Southeast Asian studies, and the American studies program at NUS, who have lent intellectual and emotional encouragement to this project; Tom Gradisher and his staff at the U.S. embassy in Singapore; Anne Pakir, former head of the Department of English and the American Studies Centre at NUS; John Richardson, head of the Department of English; Alan Chan, head of research in the dean's office; our stellar students who helped in numerous ways: Irving Goh, Wee Liang Tong, Paul Yeoh, Sheri K. Goh, Carolyn Chan, Cohen Tan, and Allan Tan; the ever resourceful George at CAS; Maria Balshaw, Liam Kennedy, and Douglas Tallack of the "Three Cities Project" at the Universities of Birmingham and Nottingham, United Kingdom; Dave McBride, our supportive and insightful editor at Routledge; Ban Kan Choon, Carole Faucher, Philip Holden, Goh Beng Lan, Li Shi Qiao, William Lim, Srilata Ravi, Trent Smith, and Wong Chong Thi; Bobby, who contributed significantly to the intellectual program of the project; a slightly different version of Rajeev Patke's article appeared in *Diacritics* vol. 30 no. 4 winter 2000; and finally our families, without whose love and patience none of this would have been possible or have any meaning.

1

Perpetuating Cities: Excepting Globalization and the Southeast Asia Supplement

RYAN BISHOP, JOHN PHILLIPS, AND WEI-WEI YEO

Contributors from a wide range of disciplinary and interdisciplinary backgrounds were asked by the editors of this volume to explore what we hope will prove to be a unique and productive means for addressing issues of urbanism, globalization, postcolonialism, historicity, and space, as well as the roles that cities in Southeast Asia play in (or are elided from) knowledge production about and legitimization of these phenomena. This introduction seeks to place the other articles in relation to a number of theoretical and disciplinary models related to these various phenomena. As such, we are not proposing a new theory or model or method, but rather a field of potential modes of analysis that could lead to a more qualitatively rigorous set of engagements with the processes usually labeled as global or postcolonial city formation.

The title of the book, *Postcolonial Urbanism: Southeast Asian Cities and Global Processes,* indicates its topicality and the focus of its general concerns. By focusing on cities in Asia, and particularly in Southeast Asia, this volume addresses the need for an in-depth, geographically specific study of urbanism in the region. However, it also fulfills another urgently felt need in urban and postcolonial scholarship: to address the development and structures of global urbanism generally. The perpetuation of cities, understood in their industrial and postindustrial incarnations, has always been linked to the spread of urban capitalism, which largely determined the unprecedented growth, rebuilding, reconstruction, and reconfiguration of cities around the globe during the late nineteenth and early twentieth centuries. It has become increasingly necessary to emphasize the global nature of this growth and to stress the international and nearly contemporaneous development of

1

cities as truly diverse as Glasgow, Manchester, Chicago, Buenos Aires, Melbourne, Calcutta, Hong Kong, and Singapore alongside New York, London, Paris, and Vienna. The city as such is so diversified a phenomenon that commentators are often constrained to use the terms *urban* or *suburban* where the notion of *the city* no longer applies. Urban processes, then, are perpetuated by a number of forces underpinned by the fundamentally economic ones that govern modern existence, the locus of which is always the city, where labor, ownership, and government coexist often uneasily and where goods and services circulate in systems that are rarely if ever wholly visible. Similarly, the cities in the region exist uneasily within current studies of global urbanism and are rarely visible within them. A comparable situation applies in studies of postcolonialism. The cities in the region have a unique relation to each area of inquiry insofar as they went from being colonial cities serving the material, bureaucratic, technical, ideological, and imaginative needs of distant and varied cosmopolitan sites to explicitly modern, international cities in a matter of years, with the concept of the national playing an important, but oddly peripheral, role in city development, self-imaging, and structuring.

A clear signal that there is a need for a collection of this kind can be found in the editors' introduction to the new edition of the prestigious *The City Reader.* The editors make the following observation:

> This is an *international* anthology. In an increasingly global world, students must learn from writers beyond the borders of their country of origin. In addition to writers from the United States, the second edition now contains writings by scholars from Austria, Australia, Belgium, Canada, England, France, Germany, Greece, Scotland and Spain. Some of the writers included are world citizens whose countries of birth, academic training, and current residence are all different and whose perspective is truly global. Space limitations preclude including material whose primary focus is on African, Asian or South American cities, but many of the urban realities and urban processes are applicable everywhere precisely because they have become internationalized.[1]

There are two striking assumptions in this statement: The first is that global urbanism can be regarded as a uniform or homogeneous outgrowth from Europe and America, belatedly affecting Africa, Asia, and South America; and the second is that cities in Africa, Asia, or South America can be understood on the model of cities in Europe, Australia, or the United States. These assumptions implicitly carry over into the notion of what it is to be truly "global," suggesting that world citizenship erases essential differences between residents of, say, Hong Kong and New York. This collection, in providing a forum that allows experts from various disciplines to address the specificity of urbanism in Southeast Asia, contests assumptions of this kind. Our collection reflects critically on the limits and applicability of theoretical paradigms generally, and represents new types of responses to urban realities and urban processes. Purposeful deviation from canonized views and comfortable patterns of thought together with renewed attention to specificity, no matter how unwieldy the particulars—this constitutes the striking commonality within this volume.

What emerges is that it is *because* urbanism tends to be regarded as international that radical differences between urban sites need to be addressed when considering the nature of any urban reality or process. Moreover, the history of urbanism in Southeast Asia provides a particular register of change. Although precolonial cities existed such as Yogyakarta, a political and spiritual capital where the god-king resided, colonialism marginalized such cities through its absorption of the entire region as an outpost to the West. Indeed, it gave birth to a new kind of Southeast Asian city, one that is characterized paradoxically by its resistance to definition. Attention to the cultural diversity and social heterogeneity *within* locales leads to unconventional formulations of the ways in which Southeast Asian cities are placed in relation to the "global," as is seen in the articles by Shirley Geoklin Lim, Steve Pile, and Wei-Wei Yeo found in this volume.

The region's cultures are irreducibly various. To engage with the question of "globalization" while taking such specificities into full account, one might start with the reminder of exceptions, which are exemplified in both argument and example in George Marcus and Angela Rivas Gamboa's piece on Bogotá in this collection. In Lim's piece, heterogeneity is found in configurations of the relation of Singapore to the region through the markedly different accents on the Southeast Asian context for Singapore's self-reflections in regional politics and Singaporean English narrative.

The repeated emergence of concerns with the historicity and space of the local in the many approaches found here suggests perhaps an inescapable condition, implying that globalization itself is structured by what appears to be inexhaustible variety. Variety—or at least diversity (which need not be simply the commodity friendly term it has become)—would be better considered as a structural condition that underlies processes that are normally described as either global *or* local. Global diversification and local diversity would be more or less the same thing from different perspectives unless we were able to sharpen our sense of how diversity helps produce the cultural, economic, political, and personal contexts that interest us.

Our introduction focuses on the intrinsic complexity of processes of globalization and of urbanism. We begin by drawing attention to two distinct needs within current urban and postcolonial scholarship. First, despite the fact that the Southeast Asian region has been heavily colonized in the past, it has, with a few outstanding exceptions, been largely neglected in postcolonial theory and in discussions of global urbanism. This collection helps to address this situation. Second, we wish to draw attention to aspects of these areas, as well as of globalization, that still need serious critical reflection. Not only do we resist the notion that Southeast Asian urban sites can be studied on the basis of established knowledge about urbanization processes generally (i.e., as just more of the same), but we also claim that the conditions that resist this secondary status have implications for the study of urban processes everywhere. The cities in the region, therefore, serve as a supplement to assumptions about global cities, both in the ordinary sense, by which they must be added to current knowledge for a truer picture to emerge, and in the sense by which the supplement changes—qualifies or even disqualifies—the earlier assumptions, opening the global whole to parts of it that must be considered as simultaneously inside and outside so that the notion of the whole is itself irremediably fissured.

Two very basic assumptions form the grounds for our theoretical framework. The first accepts that processes such as urbanization, internationalization, and modernization should be grasped in terms of complex and often conflicting historical conditions, which, in this region especially, are tied up with various different manifestations of the transition from colonial to postcolonial rule. The differences in the urbanism of Bangkok, Kuala Lumpur, Jakarta, Manila, Ho Chi Minh City, Hanoi, Phnom Penh, and Vientiane, for instance, indicate diverse relationships to disparate histories. The only directly uncolonized city in this list, Bangkok, in its past and current relations with the United States, France, and England intimates something of this diversity when compared to Kuala Lumpur's relations with Britain, Jakarta's with Holland, and Manila's with the United States. Ho Chi Minh City, Phnom Penh, and Vientiane each also manifest a complex Eurasian historicity. When we add similar relations with countries such as China, Japan, and India, including their diaspora, the region emerges in even more profound complexity. Further, Southeast Asia has often served as the conduit, or the space between, the pulls of Europe/North America and Asia writ large during the colonial, postcolonial, Cold War, and post–Cold War eras. Much of this volume's work excavates the patterns of historicity that characterize given urban sites.

The second assumption recognizes the importance of conflicting interests and trends in contemporary geopolitical relations and rapid teletechnological developments. Although the rhetoric of globalization, teletechnology, and economic commodity diversification claims to have rendered the tensions of these histories irrelevant, if not obsolete, studies in the region reveal that the rhetoric is not grounded in a rigorous understanding of the situation, a point Marcus and Rivas Gamboa, John Armitage and Joanne Roberts, as well as others in this collection make. Furthermore, the geopolitical situation, which for more than two hundred years has been subject to drastic changes resulting from developments in mass rapid transit and communications media, can now no longer be considered independently of the effects of real-time electronic technology. Much of the region's financial success, for instance, must be understood in terms of the intensification of vastly unequal distribution of wealth across geographically very proximal territories, made possible by patterns of exclusion and inclusion largely manifested, if not produced, electronically.

The two main foci of the book, global urbanism and postcolonialism, are treated as concomitant phenomena that require simultaneous study. Before going into the discussion of the way these foci operate for us, we need to explore the issues and concepts that underlie these notions in some depth, because there remains some confusion over how these terms can or should be used, and within the confusion are productive possibilities. For this reason what follows does not constitute a conventional introduction to a volume of essays but rather is intended to demarcate the theoretical terrain that the volume represents.

CONCEIVING THE GLOBAL AND ITS METAPHORICITY

The first task is to deconstruct the "chaotic concept" of globalisation. The latter is often treated in both theoretical and empirical studies as if it were a distinctive and singular causal process in its own right.   *—Bob Jessop*[2]

I intend to deconstruct the universalizing propensities of post-colonial theorizing in order to warn against the danger of dismissing the significance of history.   *—Azzedine Haddour*[3]

To date, the most decisive and effective attempt to construct the global city as a theoretical object of study would arguably be by Saskia Sassen.[4] The strength of her intervention undoubtedly lies in her persistent attempts to root out the conditions of possibility that underlie the evident emergences of global economies. On this basis she has been able to establish not only theoretically sound hypotheses on which much discussion of the global city can securely depend, but also empirical criteria for discussing specific urban sites. The distinction between world city and global city establishes what she describes as "the specificity of the global as it gets structured in the contemporary period."[5] In other words, while world cities have been in existence for hundreds if not thousands of years in many regions of the globe, accounting for a mere fraction of the world population during this time, the global city is a relatively recent phenomenon intrinsically connected with economic developments of modernity and accounting for massively increased numbers of the world population.[6]

Many of the great world cities are, therefore, now global cities (like London, Chicago, Amsterdam, Paris, and Geneva), which were actively transformed during the crucial years from the mid-nineteenth century and into the twentieth century. These economic centers of international commerce and exchange undergo extreme makeovers on many levels to incorporate the demands of a developing global economy independent of any state-specific central organization. With the geographic dispersal of global economies, the notion of "global city functions" emerges, allowing us to account for those cities that may have developed certain functions of the global city without necessarily being world cities as such. This way of conceptualizing the global city, in terms of functions rather than sites, allows us to consider how different cities gain access to and are accessed by, or even constructed in accordance with, a relatively heterogeneous set of global city functions. Not all global cities access globalization functions in the same way and, according to the same logic, globalization functions through global cities in diverse ways.

The analysis of globalization that Sassen performs, and about which we are generally empathetic, emerges from the world-system models that Immanuel Wallerstein developed out of the work of Fernand Braudel and others. George Marcus and Michael M. J. Fischer influentially theorized the impact of Wallerstein's models for disciplines traditionally engaged in the study of political and economic systems, exploring how the models met the needs of social science and humanities scholars who, typical of the 1950s and 1960s, saw not only the failure of old paradigms to explain global conditions and processes, but also the failure of the reign of paradigms themselves.[7] In addition to this theorization, they explored how interpretative anthropological concerns could help broaden and enrich the enterprise of world-system analyses while also addressing how world-systems models shaped the ethnographic enterprise. As such, the kinds of theorization proposed by Marcus and Fischer provided a productive middle ground between the earlier Wallersteinian inquiries and Sassen's movement beyond them. Marcus has reengaged the trajectory of his initial interventions in the 1980s, and with his article in this volume he has modified Sassen's project by looking explicitly at a "global city" that is *not* a global city, but merely one determined in manifold ways by globalization processes and functions over which it has little influence.

One intriguing promise suggested by thinking of global cities in terms of functions would be the possibility of theoretical coherence and relevance when dealing with what Bob Jessop, against the idea of globalization, describes as its "diverse multitude of contested meanings."[8] Jessop argues that "globalisation is a complex, chaotic, and overdetermined outcome of a multi-scalar, multi-temporal, and multi-centric series of processes operating in specific structural contexts," and he suggests that it is just one of several phenomena that have helped to shape recent developments in social, political, and economic life.[9] There is some comfort in this view, which attempts simultaneously to undermine the international *rhetoric* of globalization and to deflate the theoretical *notion* of globalization as the key problematic issue in contemporary economic, social, and political studies. If the rhetoric of globalization supports what Jessop calls "attacks on economic, political and social rights in the name of enhanced international competitiveness,"[10] then the central concern with globalization in academic discourse indicates a failure to see that globalization processes are not necessarily among the main problems or obstacles to socialist or democratic movements. We are too obsessed with the logic (or, as Jessop calls it, the "illogic") of globalization.[11]

Taking Jessop's line of argument a little farther, we suggest that academic discourses of globalization tend to support by repeating—even if in a negative way—the central claims of the rhetoric of globalization itself, in which case the rhetoric might be seen as one of the main problems. So Sassen's establishment of a theoretical object, based on the hypothesis of specific functions and conditions of possibility, while useful, remains open to objections of the kind indicated by Jessop. Although their complementary aims and intentions belong to a political perspective broadly in line with socialist or democratic principles of social organization, their conclusions and modes of proceeding remain fundamentally split.

Against the subtle differences between the positions of Sassen and Jessop, it is possible to locate some theoretical horizons they share but that provoke some critical questions. First, there is an implicit assumption that whatever we one day decide about what can and cannot be said about processes of globalization, they will nonetheless succumb to what we would broadly understand as a *predicative logic.* In Jessop's case this would be along the lines of his thoroughly determinate economic and historical relativity, according to which "globalization is better interpreted as the most inclusive structural context in which processes on other economic scales could be identified and interrelated and/or as the broadest horizon of action to which accumulation strategies and economic projects can be directed."[12] The hypothesis of what Jessop calls the multiscalar nature of economic processes allows him to derive (again in an apparently inductive way on the basis of specific cases) a further implication "that globalization is best seen as an emergent, over-determined phenomenon rather than as a *sui generis* causal mechanism."[13] In other, simpler terms, Jessop is claiming an inductive gathering of scaling particulars against a deductive inclusion of particulars under a generic class or law. So what he means when he says his first task is to "deconstruct the 'chaotic concept' of globalization" is that he must first contest the notion according to which globalization embodies or implies "a singular causal process in its own right."[14] To all appearances then Jessop's case would fit with our own claims about the constitutive exceptionality of Southeast Asian cities.

But despite appearances, this is not quite the case. Looking back at the terms of Jessop's argument, it is tempting to argue that, although the familiar poststructuralist and postmodernist vocabulary of continental philosophy and critical and cultural theory permeates his texts and those of the social sciences generally, the arguments from which that vocabulary is derived seem to have had little impact. The pattern, predictably enough, almost exactly replicates the problems identified as those of globalization (whether conceived as capital, culture, or rhetoric), in which a flattening out or opacity afflicts a concept that, given enough global repetition, becomes naturalized to the extent that everybody uses the term without really thinking about what it means. So despite Jessop's admirable revisionist and somewhat iconoclastic engagement with the notion of globalization, his own rhetoric suggests to us some further steps that would be required to mobilize the strategies and arguments suggested by his terms (like "overdetermined," "deconstruct," "multiple"). However, the problem here would be that, by mobilizing the full force of these arguments, one risks losing the grounds upon which the social sciences claim to or hope to one day stand—the grounds of an objective predicative logic. Taking the side of the particular, the local, the multiple, the inductively arrived at law, against the claims of the general, the global, the singular, and the deductively given law *would not ever be to alter the horizon of thought that identifies these positions in opposition to each other in the first place.* Causality, whether considered as singular or multiple, remains (as a leading a priori concept) at the ground of all predicative discussion of global processes and phenomena, whether considered empirical or theoretical (predicative logic, in fact, must maintain that distinction absolutely).

But overdetermination—which in its most basic sense means multiple causation—actually implies something more fundamental. Overdetermination signals a concern with the conditions of possibility for how an apparently singular phenomenon emerges from multiple determinations. A condition of possibility would not be equivalent to a cause (which would now have to be relegated as an instance in a general field of possibility). So, accordingly, to "deconstruct" the notion of globalization would not simply be to subvert what in that notion gestures to singularity by asserting multiplicity in its place. Deconstruction, in a more powerful formulation, would not be something one *does* to a notion, but rather it would name what can happen in situations on the basis of their conditions of possibility. In this sense, deconstruction *applies* when the conditions that allow globalization to be determined at all can be affirmed beyond existing determinations, thus indicating how certain kinds of possibility remain to be taken up. Here we confront the inevitable yet incalculable future of these processes. In other words, every time a determination occurs (e.g., a government decision, a business proposition, a military mobilization, media intervention, or cultural movement), it inevitably betrays its own conditions of possibility, creating further, potentially unsettling, possibilities and determinations without end. Peter Jackson's article in this volume begins with an account of how in Bangkok, "in a relatively brief two decade period, a society that previously had had a quite limited range of explicitly differentiated forms of gender and eroticism became much more highly differentiated, not only in terms of discourses, but also in terms of gender and sexual cultures." Jackson's careful study shows how surface similarities between Bangkok cultures and those in the West "mask the persistence of different worlds of meaning between culturally distinct societies." Two types of process are implied. Although global gay fashion styles and the internationalization of the originally English identity label "gay" have clearly contributed in some way to the widening and differentiating not only of discourses but also of cultures of gender and sexuality in Thailand, the meanings of these labels and categories have succumbed to new determinations that emerge from historical conditions that are quite distinct from those of the West. Clearly the potential inherent in the possibilities of labeling derived from global fashion includes as yet undetermined aspects that allow radically different kinds of classification and cultural identification to occur under a global, deceptively homogeneous label.[15]

Take the concept of globalization, as Jessop does: "Globalisation has a multitude of contested meanings."[16] The predicative statement—suggesting a polysemy—remains vulnerable. If a word is determined in different ways in different contexts, then this does not automatically imply polysemy. A meaning is, or many meanings are, predicated of a word, perhaps. The word no doubt may be determined differently each time according to some law, but this need not be the law of polysemia (which is still a law of predication). In the case of globalization, it might make more sense to say that it gestures to the possibility of determinations that each time and at the same time open it to the possibility of further determinations, *potentially ad infinitum*. In which case, for once in our discussions, we recognize a certain continuity between the notion of globalization and the state of affairs it is supposed to account for—if only at the level of conditions of possibility. If we consider the possibilities implied by the restless repetition, replication, displacement, and diversification of a notion that is supposed to account for the incessant repetition, replication, displacement, and diversification of labor, capital, commodities, and culture on a global level, then we may be encouraged to begin to see specific sites in terms of specific engagements, actions, and responses to these conditions of possibility. Globalization would not so much be regarded in terms of *flows*—as in Sassen's hypothetical discussion of the flows of capital and labor between Third World countries and global American cities[17]—but in terms of patterns of repetition that differ significantly through often simultaneous temporal and spatial displacements.

A remark by Jessop indicates the extent to which the metaphor of flow requires further examination. In a brief reference to the way capital can be "disembedded from specific places and thereby enabled to 'flow' freely through space and time," he adds that "the temporal dimension of flow is captured by the metaphors of 'liquidity' and 'stickiness.' "[18] By drawing attention here to the narrowly metaphorical nature of the available theoretical vocabulary (and thus sneaking a suspicious rhetorical distance) Jessop has unintentionally raised a profound difficulty with the logic of predication itself. So long as notions like "flow," "liquidity," and "stickiness" can be maintained as metaphorical supplements, helping to "capture" what is otherwise well understood in more literal and empirical terms (transfer and increase of liquid assets), then they need not be regarded as anything more than elegant rhetorical embellishments, helping to lighten up an otherwise dry scientific discourse. However, this is distinctly not the case. These metaphors and others are already grounding the whole explanation. The metaphors of flow and liquidity already contain the predicates for whole explanatory apparatuses of global processes, which thus assume some continuity across spatial and temporal dimensions.

But what is it exactly that these metaphors are being used to explain? If globalization involves the disembedding and transfer of some material or content across spatial and temporal dimensions, as Jessop affirms, then this is exactly the fate of the metaphors used to explain these processes. At the level of their enunciation the discourses of the social sciences and humanities unwittingly behave in the same way as the processes they are attempting to comprehend. But the discourses have been betrayed by their metaphors—which demonstrate in their metaphoricity a different kind of explanation. If metaphoricity allows the transfer from one context or class to another, Jessop's discussion of global disembedding and transfer (whether goods, capital, or labor) replicates the conditions general metaphoricity implies. Now approaching a continuity of discourse and event at the levels of enunciation and performance requires us to acknowledge a loss of a sovereign subject position that would be capable of grasping, as if from outside, the movements we are trying to describe.

The problem lies in the presupposition of predication. In terms of the historicity of modern global and urban processes, it is possible to argue that the dominant trend is toward an increasingly narrow concept of causality, implying notions of origin and cause that are not remotely affected by the assertion of multiplicity against singularity.[19] In fact, if the multinational mantras of commodity diversification show some relish in the idea of multiplicity, then the same idea underlies the discourses of the social sciences in their most institutionalized forms, because the logic seems to apply particularly well to institutions that must simultaneously maintain and play down the role of sovereignty in their marketing of knowledge-based systems (commodity-based knowledge). A narrow notion does not imply a singular notion of cause but is rather capable of giving rise to all manner of complicated explanatory procedures. But so long as some attribute can be predicated of some thing (subject or substance) and some process attributed with some cause, then a fully functional technological discourse will be ensured. We would not deny this, because the logics of causation, predication, and function can produce powerful effects, as the rapid development of modern technologies and urban processes demonstrate. But the implication may be this: that the social sciences function as an effect— a function—of the processes they are attempting to comprehend.[20] To acknowledge this would be to acknowledge a loss of grounds in the predicative logic of explanation. However, without losing the power of predication itself, it might be worth attempting to come to terms with what could not be comprehended within such logic—that is, the conditions of possibility according to which such a logic emerges. The aim would then be at least provisionally to open up the kind of mechanical perpetuation of global processes at all levels (including academic discourse) to questions of conditions of possibility and thus emphasizing *possibility* with a view to alternative ways of engagement.

One way to begin thinking through the aporias posited by predicative logic (which is not necessarily to suggest a way beyond them) is to consider the gestures provided by the middle voice, a voice that echoes throughout this volume. The middle voice offers a place of enunciation that is not necessarily spatially or temporally privileged, as is the case with predicative logic, for it speaks from the space at which the grammar of causation turns on itself. The middle voice allows us to understand that the ends of the continuum posited by Sassen and Jessop are just that, a continuum. The model of "the global city" posited by Sassen is no more idealized than the extreme relativism posited by Jessop that seeks to overturn singular models; for the radical relativism, paradoxically, requires a fixed temporal or spatial position from which the relativism is projected.[21] The middle voice gestures toward a horizon of thought that does not privilege the present moment or space of enunciation as a time and site from which a judgment, or law, emanates, be it Platonic model or manifold empirical exceptions to the model. Rather, the middle voice evokes a "landscape of events"[22] that preceeds the distinction between the Platonic model and empirical exception and makes them necessary for one another. Marcus and Rivas Gamboa's dual emphases on the idealized, external global model discussed by Sassen, and the diverse, chaotic particulars of this (or any) specific cityscape, for example, allow their study to address concerns articulated by both Sassen and Jessop without falling prey to all the trappings of predicative logic. As such, Marcus and Rivas Gamboa carve out a middle voice–inflected examination of the institutional and enunciative space of the public sphere of local politics in a city defined by historical specificities and globalization processes in which it does not necessarily participate.

The middle voice elements of the introductory essay's title, "Perpetuating Cities," indicates the combination of empirical, discursive, material, and imaginative dimensions of postcolonial urbanism that this volume addresses. Cities indeed perpetuate notions of urban space and urban existence, just as our collective imaginations about cities perpetuate various empirical and corporeal interactions with them and with other people. Similarly, postcolonial cities perpetuate an array of complementary and contending ideological, intellectual, social, cultural, and material systems integral to a collective that always exceeds its limits (the city, per se, and its physical and political boundaries). This excess spills over and is sometimes contained by that administrative embrace called globalization, which is itself perpetuated by these local excesses.

Indeed, the middle voice's inherent ambiguity about transitivity and its direction proves useful in thinking through a number of concerns addressed in this volume: the supposed temporal lag between colonized and colonizing sites (as well as between global and globalizing cities), the directions of influence in colonial and current moments, and the aporia of the example that is also an exception. This latter dimension emerges in the notion of the exception (signaled by our subtitle, "excepting Southeast Asia") in which the cities in the region exemplify specific standard qualities of "global cities" while being exceptions to the rule in an equal number of ways. In this manner they play a role similar to that of the metaphoricity of academic discourses, insofar as they tend to be taken for granted at the level of statements about global processes, while illustrating or demonstrating alternative explanations at the level of enunciation. Singapore, in fact, might be the only truly global city in the region, but that is only by dint of its explicit desire to be so—complete with coordinated governmental schemes and plans to become such.[23] Yet other cities certainly tap into the global networks that mark the postcolonial/Cold War/post–Cold War eras and serve as nodes of said networks, many of these the direct result of technologies developed for Cold War military applications, as discussed by Ryan Bishop and Gregory Clancey, and John Armitage and Joanne Roberts in this volume.

COLONIZING THE POST

If various fields have worked hard to justify consensual notions of the global city, then the notion of postcoloniality remains more fraught than ever. Certainly, the historical transitions designated by the word "postcolonialism" determine current conditions to varying degrees, but the extent to which this actually happens often remains obscure or subject to odd displacements. One apparently very simple problem, which is nonetheless a real sticking point, is that the ordinary or commonsense meaning of the term post-colonial (as with all such terms) is helpful only as a starting point, which all discourses must inevitably leave. The historical, cultural, and intellectual currents associated with the term oblige us to use it as a key to understanding very specific critical attitudes, trends, and problems.

We should also note that *post* (after) doesn't necessarily indicate either that the colonizers have gone away (literally or in terms of cultural or political influence) or that the conditions of postcolonialism have necessarily changed much from those of colonialism, despite appearances. In the first case a strong imperial presence might remain in the form of a "metropolitan-periphery" hierarchy so that the colonial hierarchy is simply repeated in a different way. In the second case (not unrelated to the first) the systems of administration (legal, educational, sanitary, etc.) are often kept in place. It is well understood that you cannot simply replace one system with another without serious or even catastrophic results (tending to reinforce the inevitable powerful resurgence of the replaced system). In general (and still obviously predicative) terms, then, a postcolonial situation always involves a relation (often if not always in terms of repetition) at once to its colonial history and to its current geopolitical and economic dependencies (which might always be the same thing).

The relationship, as it is mapped out in different ways around the larger part of the globe is extremely complex and obliges us to take into consideration an attention to specific and particular details that would threaten to break down any sense of generality concerning the notion *postcolonialism*. But certain generalities do emerge. These involve the recent historical conditions that many critical commentators have been studying in terms of the word *modernity,* as well as more recently powerful phenomena associated with modernity, particularly *global modernity.* The latter is in its turn often simplified correctly, yet not without gross error too, as *Western modernity.* Rajeev Patke's article in this volume draws attention to the way a more critical notion of modernity derived from Walter Benjamin can help to elaborate the complex relationships between modernity and postcolonialism.

Given the simultaneous generality of the notion and the extreme diversity of the situations supposedly designated by it, we might wonder at the very general failure to recognize the nature or manner of the attempts, especially in their earlier versions, to intervene through the mediated discourse of academic study. If work by Gayatri Chakravorty Spivak, Homi Bhabha, and others, appearing in the late 1970s and throughout the 1980s on the heels of more directly historicizing works by Franz Fanon and Edward Said, has quickly become the foundation of a kind of theoretical canon in the arts and humanities, especially in literary theory, then this is at the cost of a clear sense of the *manner* or *mode* of their intervention. The influence of contemporary continental thought, critical theory, twentieth century Marxism, and literary poststructuralism is evident throughout this discourse; but, once again, the specific nature of the arguments seems to be lost on many of their followers, critics, and commentators. This is partly the fault of the writers themselves and may be built into the structure of this still minor discourse, which is constrained to explore the disturbing conditions of possibility beneath a modernity that takes in both urbanism, globalization, colonialism, and postcolonialism (in the ordinary senses) while at the same time anchoring that discourse of *possibility* to specific historical geographical sites and experiences.[24] The paper by Tony King in this collection provides an excellent and nuanced overview of the routes postcolonial studies have taken and could take farther. While acknowledging the enunciative force of theoretical, and specifically literary, postcolonialism, King then turns to a number of recent works that engage with the geographical and political specificities of what he calls "actually existing postcolonialisms." King's identification of two significantly different streams of thinking about postcolonialism helps illustrate one of the main problems that we are engaging in this introduction and this volume: a credulity to the theory–empiricism distinction that serves as a kind of axiom for the humanities and the social sciences.

Postcolonialism, in the genre defining work of Bhabha and Spivak, attempts to intervene at the level of the modalities of enunciation. Their work defines the genre as a specific kind of critical intervention within various fields of culture and in disciplines of literary and cultural studies. Modalities of enunciation can be considered as sites of discourse, modes of saying or writing constituted by the simultaneous influences of various determinations (historical, political, economic, imaginary, or cultural) and what always remains undetermined, as constituent possibility of determination per se. In other words, the modality of enunciation suggests the possibility of acknowledging the conditions of emergence and perpetuation of the patterns that particular sites and struggles reproduce, in terms of the determinations (which may be regarded as limits) as well as the indeterminacy (which converts limits to resources) without which there would be no particulars whatsoever. But, postcolonialism—which is obliged to deal with

specific historical situations if only by the connotations of its own name—tends to isolate this "undetermined" as the *Other* and, having found a suitable name, has little trouble identifying concrete historical *Others*.[25]

The problem, which in this sense almost exactly replicates that of the social sciences addressed above, is signaled clearly in an article by Azzedine Haddour, whose title alone marks out the specific subgenre of discourse he participates in: "Citing Difference: Vagrancy, Nomadism, and the Site of the Colonial and Post-Colonial." He begins with a distinction between the theoretical invention of "post-colonialism—arguably a British invention—a discourse which emerges from the experience of a British settler society," and what he calls "colonial vagrancy," by which he means "the dispossessed colonized Algerians who are turned by French colonialism into a vagrant people, disenfranchised, denied the rights which political citizenship bestows on subjects of law."[26] At this stage, the terms of the debate fold over almost exactly onto those we discussed earlier under the rubric of globalization. Haddour argues that this disjunction "adumbrates a gap between history and theory," and then proceeds to make a move that is probably necessary, though quite typical and very like the one made by Jessop. He writes, "I intend to deconstruct the universalizing propensities of post-colonial theorizing in order to warn against the danger of dismissing the significance of history."[27]

Haddour's article makes a number of points that we would support unreservedly. His observation, for example, that a number of influential writers use notions of foreignness, nomadism, and vagrancy in idealized ways (he cites Julia Kristeva, Stuart Hall, and Iain Chambers at length) is an indication of a vast problem for cultural studies generally. In Southeast Asia—perhaps more than in any other region—the figure of the refugee, the transmigrant, the homeless wanderers of several different diasporas emerge in situations that at the same time represent not only extreme attempts to establish and maintain modern state nationalism but also entrenched social and cultural division and opposition based on traditional values or assertions of indigenous ethnicity. Here the relationship between national or ethnic identity and vagrancy clearly gestures to deeper political conditions that cannot be restricted to the region. The tendency to idealize the wanderer or hybrid identity in support of some spurious origin-free postmodern subject can therefore be seen as a way of containing or disavowing the larger political forces that help to determine phenomena of this kind.[28]

But Haddour, in his rigor and vigilance against these "universalizing propensities," may himself be indicating a different kind of danger. First, the sense of the word "deconstruct" that Haddour uses is, as he acknowledges, derived from the arguments of Jacques Derrida, whose "Plato's Pharmacy" serves as an epigraph for the article. Haddour reads a passage

whereby, in describing the attitude typical of Western thought to the written mark, Derrida discovers a comparison, according to which writing is

> like all ghosts: errant . . . like someone who has lost his rights, an outlaw,
> a pervert, a bad seed, a vagrant, an adventurer, a bum. Wandering in the
> streets, he does not even know who he is, what his identity . . . what his
> name is . . . but he can no longer repeat his origin. Not to know where one
> comes from or where one is going, for a discourse with no guarantor, is not
> to know how to speak at all, to be in a state of infancy. Uprooted, anony-
> mous, unattached to any house or country, this almost insignificant signifier
> is at everyone's disposal.[29]

If Haddour had attempted a more sustained reading of this text, he would
perhaps have been less tempted to read it in the following way. He writes,
"Derrida overcomes, by idealizing, the reality of the errant vagrant. There
is a gap between the existence of the expropriated vagrant and the notion of
writing conceived as democracy at everyone's disposal."[30]

The first thing we might question in Haddour's reading is the notion
of "democracy" at everyone's disposal. In the context of Derrida's reading
of Plato, this would be difficult to uphold. To say that the insignificant mark
is at everyone's disposal is not to say that the insignificant mark is a democracy exactly, but more powerfully to suggest that without knowing how to
speak at all the insignificant mark is what allows anyone (everyone) to speak.
So long as we can speak, this would be by virtue of the mark that is at
everyone's disposal.[31] In other words, Derrida is outlining the conditions
of possibility for speaking—and thus he is gesturing to the modality of
enunciation—and, in the context of his reading of Plato here, his main
focus is on assertions (like Plato's) of a priori conditions for all experience
whatsoever. The insignificant mark, it turns out, only disrupts the traditional
notions of ideal or transcendental determination by implicating those determinations inextricably with what they oppose themselves to—in Plato's
case, of course, writing. So the insignificant mark implicates all determinations of experience with an undetermined aspect a priori.

In this light, the comparison between Plato's characterization of writing and the homeless vagrant may be more interesting than Haddour seems
to think. The impoverishment of writing and the impoverishment of the
errant vagrant may not, after all, be considered as a mere simile. Rather, we
might see them as related not as synecdoche to synecdoche but *outside the
rhetoric of predication according to which parts must add up to a whole.*
Instead, they may be related as specifically different examples of a pattern
of historicity that ensures the impoverishment of some essential aspect without which some valued ideal would not be what it is. So the more obviously
political dimension here might serve to expose the notions of belonging,

property, attachment, and home (each of which play privileged roles in the establishment and perpetuation of modern nation-states and the notions of human rights that go with them) as rigorously dependent upon aspects of existence from which they are distinguished rhetorically. You would not have a home at all if it was not for a priori infantile wandering: the errant ghost of the nation-state in its tactics of inclusion and exclusion. There is no contradiction between this view and the actual impoverishment of colonized people, who are regularly forced into dispossession to guarantee the rhetoric of possession and the notions of origin, presence, and propriety that support it.[32]

But more critical than this already critical issue—not many issues could be more critical than homelessness in contemporary political thought— would be the foreshadowing of the *gap* itself in the Derrida quotation. Haddour's easy identification of the differences between history and theory or reality and ideality betrays a too easy readiness to validate an empirical present and to valorize experience as some kind of unquestionable beginning or starting point—the same impulse to the sovereign position we discussed earlier. Without wanting to lessen the sense of political urgency clearly expressed by Haddour, and while in support of his own vigilant readings of less meticulous postcolonial theorists, we would question the notion of experience that takes pride of place in his discussions. In a thoroughly dismissive gesture—arguing that postcolonialism is "a discourse which emerges from the experience of a British settler society"—he explicitly opposes "the errant nomads of postcolonialism" to an identification of "the dispossessed colonized Algerians."[33] The opposition does the work of "intersection" that he claims it does, showing that it is based on fundamentally different experiences of "people on the move." So the *gap* (and its adumbration) would thus not be between an experience and a theory but between two different kinds of experience.

However, even if this were the case, it remains unclear from Haddour's article how he grounds this notion of experience as empirical history without reproducing exactly those universalizing propensities he charges postcolonialism with. Postcolonialism in its arguably most interesting aspects attempts to address this question of the enunciative grounds of experience and culture. As Bhabha writes, in justification of his own method, "My shift from the cultural as an epistemological object to culture as an enactive, enunciatory site opens up possibilities for other 'times' of cultural meaning (retroactive, prefigurative) and other narrative spaces (fantasmatic, metaphorical)."[34] Although Bhabha's work remains difficult, and, in the eyes of his critics at least, not always clearly formulated, there's no denying the boldness of this intention, which mobilizes, by acknowledging, the *gap* that Haddour can only thematize in the impoverished terms of failure. At the level of enunciation, the moment is fundamentally fissured by incalculable future events and the absolute past of unrealized possibility. Only in the face of these impossible presentiments could a determination have had a chance of being made at all. To conceive of the present as irremediably disjunct, or "out of joint," is to acknowledge the impossibility of the purely empirical, and it hints at the potential damage this implies to all the presumed horizons of our thought. "Theory," in this case, is already the mobile engagement with the world that "empirical history" was supposed to be, without theory. But instead of resting with the blunt statement of the determined historical, postcolonialism promises to go further in its questions about the *historicity* of the historical—the conditions on which a historical determination could ever have come about at all. And it does so without the hypostatization of a transcendental or final cause.

Despite this, we'd have to admit that the promise suggested by Bhabha, and to a certain extent by others, has not been developed much beyond a narrow field of the humanities and, even then, in a way that suggests an implicit return to the epistemological object. In this introduction, through our readings of the humanities and the social sciences, and in what follows, we have tried to outline an *institutional,* and by that we mean an *enunciative,* modality according to which the application of instrumental rationality and predicative logic tends to replicate itself in attempts to engage and comprehend processes like colonialism and globalization, which themselves operate almost entirely according to the application of instrumental rationality and predicative logic.

By exposing the enunciative modality of institutional practices, however, we now find ourselves in a potentially disturbing place, no longer able to fall back into the security of a simple epistemological statement but not wishing to confine ourselves to the relativity of perspectivism or, worse, indeterminacy. Rather, in what follows, we attempt to outline the conditions as they pertain to urban processes in Southeast Asia by attending as rigorously as possible to the relationships between determinate conditions and the historicity out of which they inevitably emerge. We stress, as is signaled in the term *perpetuating,* the futural direction of global urbanism, a dimension that at once gives itself to current determinations (global trade and regional strategy) yet which perpetually withdraws from calculation, thus allowing further determinations. It is on this level that the exceptionality of the Southeast Asian city at once establishes the global condition of general substitutability (every global city can represent every other global city) yet simultaneously marks each global city as absolutely different from the others. Only on this basis is it now possible to establish specific ways in which particular Southeast Asian cities demonstrate responses to these conditions.

Patke indicates, with considerable subtlety and complexity, how this might be achieved when he explores simultaneously two discursive worlds that are rather different at first sight: Walter Benjamin's unclassifiable engagement with the cities of modernity in the form of the posthumously published and unfinished *Arcades Project,* and the Asian and Southeast Asian postcolonial city. Patke begins by acknowledging that there are "several Benjamins to be conjured from the *Arcades Project,*" and he takes this opportunity to emphasize "the one who invites speculative discourse on the idea of the postcolonial city." Benjamin's *plurality* would not be an excuse for *pluralism,* but an indication of the grounds of theoretical application generally, on which it is possible for a certain kind of singular response to operate differently in numberless contexts. These "Benjamins" would be understood neither as the plural use of an empty signifier nor as a signifier with multiple meanings but more as the repeatability and differences of the singular mark or signature in its potential to connect with unheard of future contexts. The "speculative discourse" of Patke's article demonstrates a clear alternative to the predicative logic of the social sciences as well as to the use of theoretical models in most engagements with contemporary urban processes. An alternative, as we see, need not be impressionistic, subjective, or vague, but like Patke's, subtly grounded in an undeniably rigorous response to complex conditions.

There are two inheritances implied here and a kind of praxis that connects them. Modernity tends to advance through repetitions of its patterns of inclusion and exclusion—patterns that none of the writers we discuss in this introduction fail to pick up on. The risk in attempting to distance oneself from these patterns of repetition, attempting to locate the unrepeatable particularity of a historical experience, for instance, lies in failing to see how that gesture itself perpetuates the repetitions of modernity, which globalizes by particularizing and diversifying. Benjamin's suggestive power lies in his meticulous and faithful reproduction of the patterns of history—the historicity of modernity—to the extent that his repetition begins to exceed the possibilities we cannot avoid inheriting. Patke's Benjaminian intervention does similar work, by repeating Benjamin's own response to modernity in the context of a response to Asian urbanism (an urbanism of remarkable exceptions). So Benjamin is seen to differ from himself in Patke's subtle mimesis, and we are reminded that while we are unlikely to escape repetition, we nonetheless need not be restricted to the mechanical repetitions of global urbanism, but, by focusing painstakingly on details and threshold experiences, we find that possibilities emerge that would otherwise have been excluded from view.

THE *EMPIRIAL*

To help structure our sense of institutional or enunciative modality, we take our focus from two assumptions, which, in shorthand, we have designated

"the *empirial*" and "stereoscopy." The terms indicate sites of intense interaction. Electromagnetic systems interact with geopolitical systems in a city's
attempts to make itself postcolonial and global. The electromagnetic realm
has had profound effects on the notions of public space and public discourse, which were once the domain of the urban *agora,* as Marcus and
Rivas Gamboa explicitly explore in this volume.

The notion of the empirial, introduced by John Phillips, can be regarded
as a conceptual resource for outlining the conditions of the possibility of
urbanism in Southeast Asia.[35] While it outlines the constraints that help to
determine the relative successes and failures of urbanism in the region, the
stress is more on the possibilities and impossibilities that are produced and
perpetuated by those constraints. The notion was developed to help account
for what remains of the multiple histories that can be read back into cities
like Bangkok, Kuala Lumpur, and Singapore, some of which are more insistent, more seemingly permanent, than others. The Southeast Asian city
emerges out of a number of different heritages. The empirial has no single
source but rather is the upshot of a series of tensions, struggles, and formations of compromise. Emerging in a dispersed and often quite discrete way,
it has a consistency that characterizes its many forms. The following is a
schematic account of this phenomenon. 1) In part it is derived from imperialism, the form of centralized government common to the great empires
of the East, the forbidden cities of the powerful Chinese dynasties, as well
as the great Roman Empire preceding and inspiring European imperialism
and its colonial fulfillment. The imperial in each case serves the interests
of a centralized state power, its military supremacy and the maintenance of
economic monopoly. 2) A second aspect is derived from empiricism, its
focus on the sensible object and, its correlate, the subject of experience, the
figure par excellence of early modern urbanism with its democratic pretensions and its developing technology. The need to link these two tendencies (imperialism and empiricism) emerges in the attempt to understand
the various forces that overdetermine (a term we are using advisedly)
Southeast Asian cities like Singapore and Bangkok. The first thing to note
is that the tension indicated by these two tendencies cannot be reduced to
the simple opposition between West and East, but that, while much of
Western modernity can be grasped in terms of the productive tension
between state imperialism and urban or civic expansion, the long-term historical situation in Asia shows a powerful resistance by imperial powers to
any other kind of political organization that might have arisen as a viable or
powerful alternative. In other words, empires come and go, but the imperial *mode* of government remains the only viable system.

The result in the West of the tension between civic and imperial modes
of organization leads, as has been well documented, to an economic mode of

production—fully mobilized by Western states—based on the expansion of capital. With the development of capitalist multinationals occupying transnational economic spaces within expanding urban global networks not reducible to nation-states, global diversification knows no bounds. In Southeast Asia, where many of the earliest experiments in *modern* urbanism were made, the relative weakness or even absence of a critical or democratic tradition drastically alters the development and the structure of urban space. Controlled much more severely by imperial styled bureaucracies, Southeast Asian cities must welcome the fruits of global capitalism but within spaces sharply controlled by state interests. This is the broad political situation designated by the term *empirial*. Matters become more complex when we begin to consider, as we must, the range of conditions that together overdetermine phenomenal aspects, which include the institutional, historical, cultural, imaginary, and emotive forces that at any time structure experience.

So the *empirial* is not the culmination of a historical progress or development but the result of specific patterns that manifest compromised economies, insofar as global exchange serves functions indifferent to the specific interests of national organizations, and despite the fact that these operate within the same systems of exchange. For Southeast Asian global cities, in which radical capitalism coexists with often rigid governmentality, the need to operate a fully free market economy (the success of the city depends upon its function as a nodal point facilitating financial exchange, electronic media, and cultural and geographical paths between other cities) cannot be separated from the need to maintain an actually very rigid bureaucratic administration. If, as has been often noted, the two needs complement each other perfectly in terms of selective economic success, then this is in spite of considerable if not always visible tension at the social level, because both needs run counter to each other. That is, global capitalism surpasses the economic interests of the nation, traditionally conceived, unless nation is refigured—as is entirely possible—along the lines of international business, with the citizen reconstrued on the model of the global employee. In this sense the imperial pattern works in support of tendencies within global urbanism that subordinate national identity—even under the sign of the most strident nationalism—to international economic interests. The first need opens a city as a nodal point in the network of international cities, facilitating (if only blandly) social, cultural, cosmopolitan, religious, and financial exchange—a fully translatable currency. The second imposes the need for rigid rules, regulations, and laws, as the manifestation of cultural, social, and governmental constraint in the hands of decision-making governmental elites. The global city in Southeast Asia, while maintaining the legal structures of democracy, simultaneously negates complementary democratic institutions. These conflicting but synchronous conditions provide the possibility of abstracting aspects of both egalitarianism and imperialism as functions of the empirial.

STEREOSCOPY

Our second focus is the phenomenon of stereoscopy, the simultaneity of virtual and real environments. Taking Paul Virilio's attempt to cast our contemporary moment as bounded by two global networks, the geopolitical and the electromagnetic, we observe that many of us, especially those in postcolonial urban sites, spend our day-to-day lives *between* these two networks. The rapid increase in, for instance, real-time teletechnologies can be situated as a development within traditions of modern urbanization, which have always had a powerful effect on social experience in its production of urban subjects. To the familiar technology of telephony and television, we must now add opto-electronic, electro-acoustic, and even teletactile technologies to the list of profoundly influential conditions of modern urban life. The role of the independent geopolitical realm is severely weakened in this respect, as the two networks do not correspond isometrically. One cannot understand the electromagnetic realm as having been superimposed upon geographical space, as if a virtual superstructure had been built upon a real base. The virtual impacts actual conditions of both experience and political economy no less than geopolitical conditions do, leaving us radically divided between two powerful yet relatively heterogeneous worlds.

These networks are simultaneously a part of us and apart from us, phenomena we respond to and react against. This *betweenness,* as physical and intellectual space, provides an area of inquiry that repays careful study as it brings to light the very conditions that help to determine our experience of the shapes and manifestations of a specifically postcolonial urbanism. The role of teletechnologies, in this respect, is as potent when it concerns those excluded from their reach as it is when it concerns those who have been entirely taken up into the communication networks they govern.

Virilio has described the situation as a stereoscopy, where the human being is increasingly caught between two worlds, stuck simultaneously in the "real" space of an increasingly limited environment and real-time relations at a distance, to the extent that the human experience of the world and of the world's horizon is becoming, in Virilio's terms, irretrievably polluted (provocatively, perhaps, he argues that this pollution by the electromagnetic sphere is every bit as devastating as the more commonly documented forms of ecological pollution).[36] If this is a consequence of the electromagnetic sweep of global networks, then the postcolonial city can be taken as a cutting edge exemplar of a worldwide phenomenon, because at the same time much of the region is apparently untouched by the most advanced electronic media. The borders between the urban and its others are perhaps sharper in Southeast Asia than anywhere else in the globe, as whole populations are exiled to its immediate outside—often within the city itself—but nonetheless inescapably shaped by it, regulated by it, watched over by it in a way neatly encapsulated by the flickering screens that appear with increasing frequency on the outsides of high buildings, sending their silent messages across miles of cityscape.

(POST)COLONIAL EXPERIMENTATION

There is always and inevitably a sense of evanescence in the notion of historicity, which must be regarded as both hidden but also susceptible to analysis, as in the ways in which Cold War policies and strategies interact with postcolonial sites. Globalization's current manifestations relate in some direct ways to Cold War policies. This has special salience in the region, as its historicity is profoundly marked by various catastrophic effects of Cold War policy played out, for instance, on the fields and cities of Southeast Asia. In fact, both colonial and postcolonial situations in Southeast Asia are often revealed as sites for experimentation and appropriation, which produce different kinds of feedback effect: The colonial site can be seen as an ideal space for all kinds of experimentation, including, civic, military, ideological, technological, and scientific. There are botany, social/class containments, human resource management, and developments in biology, physics, and chemistry. Colonial urban space (from the beginning global) has been used in different ways as space for urban experimentation. Economic (the autonomous meltdown) and military uses involve experiments with civilian targeting, riot control, penalization, and policing. Southeast Asia begins to look like an intense and multidisciplinary laboratory in which some of the great developments of urban modernity (in anthropology, technology, visual culture, and mass media not least) were developed, to be returned to European and American urban state centers, often in unexpected ways.

Despite the fact that the emergence of major cities in colonized regions was virtually synchronous with those in the colonizing countries, most models of "development" and "progress" cast colonized sites as lagging behind their cosmopolitan counterparts in substantial ways. The same assumptions of delayed modernization underpin current thinking about urban sites in "developing" countries in contrast to "developed" ones. In a sense, then, these assumptions project and perpetuate a temporal dimension of the past onto both colonized cities during the colonial era and postcolonial cities in the post–WW II world. But the more accurate temporal relation between colonized and colonizing cities (or global and postcolonial cities) might be futural insofar as the colonized site by virtue of its very nature required experimentation on the part of administrators and commercial ventures. The history of colonization, in fact, belies a latent modernization and reveals an extended engagement with potential futures for the cosmopolitan cities of the colonizers as those experiments in science, technology, social control, labor practices, and knowledge formation that proved successful in the colonies were often exported home for application there. This transfer can be found in a diverse range of areas. For example, William Marsden's introduction to his 1812 *Dictionary of Malayan Language* delineates the parameters for dictionaries adapted by James A. H. Murray and his project that resulted in the *Oxford English Dictionary;* identity cards and other forms of population control got their start in Asian and Southeast Asian colonies; fingerprinting made its initial appearances in South American colonial sites; penal colonies and penal systems developed there provided models for punishment and incarceration used in European cities; the telegraph networks linking remote sites within colonies, as well as to Europe for commodities trading purposes, predated their application and integration in Europe or North America; laboratories for studying and treating an array of contagious diseases sprang up in India and Southeast Asia, as did quarantining practices; and the botanical knowledge that shaped Linnaeus's taxonomy emerged from the work of Garcia da Orta in colonial botanical gardens. These are just a few examples that mark flow from the colonized city back to the colonizing capital, thus overturning the temporal lag that supposedly hindered the enterprises of "progress" in nineteenth century Asia, Africa, and South America.

The complexities of urban colonized/colonizing relations offer a myriad of potential ways for critically engaging current globalization practices and the assumptions upon which they are engaged in public discourse. The biotechnical laboratories that were the botanical gardens of the colonial era, as Emma Reisz discusses in this collection, served not only scientific but also explicitly commercial purposes. Further they played a role in urban planning back at the cosmopolitan site by experimentations with the construction of recreational, "green" space within the heart of the city. In a darker vein, Richard Derderian (included here), Gwendolyn Wright, and Nicola Cooper have explored how urban designers for the French imperial administration in Indochina experimented with various theories and material designs for the management of urban space and crowd control later deployed in Paris.[37] The increasing militarization of society in the late nineteenth and twentieth centuries additionally has a range of imperial roots. Bishop and Clancey (in this volume), H. Bruce Franklin, and Sven Lindquist have all explored the colonial legacy of aerial bombing of civilian populations. Accords reached by the European powers at the turn of the twentieth century that sought to forestall the potential threat from the sky posed by flight agreed to ban all bombing of civilian populations; such bans did not extend to colonized peoples, as they did not count as civilians.[38] The efficacy with which air power could contain, control, and decimate large numbers of people in colonial sites proved too seductive for military and political planners. Once the notion of "total war" became the operating principle of World War II, the tactics deployed on the enemy in the colonies were applied to the enemies in the heart of civilized Europe.

But if the postcolonial often reiterates colonial structures, networks, relations, and technicities, then certain contemporary trends in Southeast Asian urbanization and globalization processes are worth watching out for, as Armitage and Roberts reveal. The Export Processing Zones in the Southeast Asian region, especially those in the Philippines, might be the futural avatars of Tax Free Zones, or Enterprise and Incentive Zones, which emerged in rural centers of North America and the United Kingdom during the 1990s. The militarization of labor and the tax incentives that encourage corporations to do so find full form in the mobile EPZ of Cavite, currently anchored off Manila. If the labor conditions and tax(less) structures of Cavite attract adequate capital, then its mobile enterprise and enterprise of mobility might well be circulated back to production and consumption sites of current global cities. The "archaeology of the future" delineated by Armitage and Roberts contains within its "hypermodern" trajectories vestiges of colonial practices past. In this way, the Southeast Asian global cities of the postcolonial moment might foretell, once again, what laborers and investors in cosmopolitan cities will see in their own neighborhoods and city centers.

THE COLD WAR VERSUS POSTCOLONIALISM

The eras demarcated as colonialism, postcolonialism, the Cold War, and the post–Cold War eras in the region have curious overlaps, reiterations, redundancies, and developments. Because the postcolonial moment in Southeast Asia is inextricable from the Cold War, these two eras prove remarkably difficult to differentiate. Virtually simultaneous but having been constituted in elaborately different ways by various disciplines, the two eras, or networks, are not related isometrically, as we have indicated with other networks. Rather they interact in a much more complex and problematic way than is accounted for by current dominant discourses about either one or the other. Similarly, the emergence of "globalization" in popular discourse along with the post–Cold War moment further blurs trajectories and temporalities that need to be distinguished while reifying divisions that require less solid delineation.

Postcolonialism has largely ignored the role of the Cold War in the formation of postcolonial nation-states, especially in Southeast Asia. The myriad ways in which various countries in the region encountered the post–WW II moment, as both emergent or emerging postcolonial nation and player in the new Cold War global ideological jockeying of superpowers, have largely been addressed as separate phenomena or as one subsuming the others, especially the narrative of nation-building taking precedence over other concerns. If one were to consider Indonesia's Sukarno or Suharto, for instance, as postcolonial political figures of vastly different nationalist stripes, the myriad ways in which U.S., Chinese, British, and Japanese policies in the region kept corrupt regimes in power from the moment of autonomous statehood would largely be ignored.

Although Sukarno used the rhetoric of postcolonialism, and probably envisioned his anti-Western enterprise as such, the United States, China, and the Soviet Union viewed him and his policies in distinctly Cold War ideological terms that were completely indifferent to colonial relations. The struggles most Indonesians faced were not ones of forming a national identity in the sun of independent sovereignty once the Dutch had left, but rather ones of how to make ends meet under the shadow of dictatorial administrations that waged direct and indirect war on their populations. The struggles were not over conceptions of autonomy and self-rule but to get rice on the plate and shelter over one's head. However, to hear Postcolonial Studies speak of the situation, which it rarely does, one would think that national identity as an equal among the global family of nations occupied the consciousness of all citizens.

As far as urban space is concerned, neither postcolonialism nor most theories of globalization come close to evoking the heaving chaos and complexities posed by Jakarta, as made evident in the work by Abidin Kusno, as well as James Rosenau and Diane Wildsmith in this volume.[39] The heterogeneity of that city's engagement with history, geopolitics, teletechnologies, global capital, and ideology provides an exemplary case for the excesses that any one discipline, or set of disciplines, encounters when attempting to examine how urban space aligns with historicity—a point exemplified by "fragmegration," Rosenau's portmanteau term for varied and various urban alignments with globalization processes.

The conflicts in the Southeast Asian region were central to U.S. foreign policy during the Cold War. But in the post–Cold War era, when new nodal networks of interest were drawn, some of the nations that had warranted the various superpowers' policy attention disappeared from view. The nodes constructed in the neoliberal interventions of the current "global" moment did not often align with centers related to "domino theories" or communist anxieties. Cambodia provides particularly vivid example. Because Cambodia did not seem to fit neatly into the networked nodes of capital, production, and labor that mark the post–Cold War world of globalization processes, it has been allowed to lapse into civil war and mine clearance at the expense of developing any sustainable infrastructure after being decimated by the U.S.–Vietnam war. The danger of having been placed in the ideological spotlight of the Cold War has given way to the danger of having fallen into the post–Cold War darkness, a periphery that can only glimpse the larger networks from a distance.

An interesting juncture at which both Cold War and postcolonial trajectories met in ways that marks both overlaps and disconnects is tourism, the single largest industry in the world. Tourism's place of prominence in the production and circulation of wealth flies in under the power of the jet engine at the dawn of mass jet age travel. Tourism has played an especially important role in the development strategies for Southeast Asia, from Bangkok to Bali,[40] just as the region has played a special role in superpower negotiation of global ideological balance. At the height of the Cold War, John F. Kennedy famously dubbed each tourist a cultural ambassador, and the UN held its first conference on International Travel and Tourism (1963). The rhetoric that tourism broke down cross-cultural ignorance and biases while simultaneously stimulating developing economies was furthered by the massive influx of funds from international institutions such as the UN, UNESCO, the WTO, and the World Bank for tourism development. The Hilton Hotel chain coined a slogan that succinctly articulated the commercial endeavor of international prosperity and safety through tourism: "World Peace through World Travel." Such assumptions fit neatly with early 1950s U.S. Cold War policies, as well as later "hearts and minds" strategies played out in the Southeast Asian region. As a result, the cities in the region, in a postcolonial/Cold War environment, found themselves actively engaged in the formal construction of a nation-state and a national culture that were at once geopolitical/ideological entities and international commodities; that is, a national culture that both justified autonomous statehood *and* could attract the funds for tourist development as well tourists themselves.

Further, if the generalized relations between colonized and colonizing sites, or globalized and globalizing ones, does not necessarily reveal a lag between the latter and the former, as we have argued, but rather a relation of experimentation, then Kathleen Adams's article on "danger tourism," included here, reveals a trend as disturbing as the one pointed out by Armitage and Roberts. In a move as chaotic and violent as the one from colonial to postcolonial status, the move from Cold War networks to neoliberal ones has generated the commodification of intranational violence as spectacle. The tourists who sport T-shirts that proclaim "Danger!! Mines!! Cambodia!!" now travel to Jakarta and Dili to witness revolution and economic-political violence—albeit one step removed. Such tourism is almost like real-time TV but unfolding in the "here" of spatial proximity and not the "there" of teletechnologies while simultaneously providing the distance of economic advantage. Such tourism traffics in a currency of death, destruction, and war that danger tourists feel is the domain of Southeast Asian (and Middle Eastern or Central African) cities and not that of their own "global" homes.

The dangers in danger tourism evoke all the other dangers involved with being brought into any given network, be it colonialism, post-colonialism, Cold War, post–Cold War, or neoliberal "free markets" of globalization—and perhaps this accounts for the wary and varied ways "global cities" that are not global cities engage with these processes in the current moment. Cambodia, the Philippines, Malaysia, Burma—the entire region—provide cautionary tales of this sort of interaction, especially in the current forms of the global. The discourse of the neoliberal market claims to provide open borders to allow the free flow of technology, capital, ideas, goods, and information. These are all part and parcel of the modernity's discourse too, and, as explored by Patke, are open to being recast (as Benjamin did) as "the three satanic promises" found in "the illusion of freedom, the illusion of independence," and "the illusion of infinity"—infinite growth, potential, and wealth. Hidden in the discourse is the fact that "flow" assumes the hierarchy of the natural phenomenon of gravity required to make something flow, which in many cases accurately portrays the events, despite other emancipatory assumptions operative in this pervasive "commonsense" discourse. But, as argued in a number of pieces in this collection, networks circulate, as well as flow, with no fewer dangers as Steve Pile reminds us in this volume. Brushing up against these powerful (almost supernaturally so) networks promises immortality but can leave the city's corpus with gashes in its neck and drained of its life-giving substance, as Cambodia, Burma, large chunks of Indonesia, the Philippines, and Thailand know all too well. These are the lesson the most recent emerging "global cities" in the region, those in Vietnam, have before them, as well as their own draining and drained past encounters with the global networks of the Cold War.

The Cold War evokes scenes of death on a cosmological, unimaginable scale, as does the historicity of colonialism. The prevalence of certain issues associated with death in this volume is notable. The extent to which death is associated in consistently precise ways with cities remains one of the most interesting aspects of global urbanism. The recurrence of spectral figures, whether they take the form of the supersensible in the sensible field (as ghosts or spectres) or whether they emerge through electronic and mass media (as spectral and displaced urban memories, for instance) has also been remarkable. The obvious connections of death and spectral figures to history and historicity seems particularly worth considering in light of the "future"-oriented trajectories of global cities, especially postcolonial urban cities.

HISTORICITY

We have used the term *historicity* in this introduction already in reference to what we have tried to excavate as the grounds or conditions of the phenomena of globalization and postcolonialism. Reasoning from phenomena, we have attempted to ask the question, what makes such situations *possible?* (This is not the same as asking what are their causes.) Sassen's attempt to construct the global city as an object of study follows a similar procedure. But we are attempting a yet more basic strategy, which is to establish the conditions not only for the phenomena as such but also for our being able to theorize them. As we observed in our discussion of Patke's paper, if modernity is to be understood as the application of reason, then to understand the conditions of that application would already be to grasp something of the object itself. But the means of understanding how we understand (the basic grounds of theory) have been reduced by modernity to the distinction between a subject of knowledge and an object of enquiry, according to which by turning the intentionality of subjective knowledge back onto itself the subject is thrust irremediably into self-reflexive paradox.[41] This need only be regarded as an impediment to theory by those who are committed to a ground in the sovereign subject of modern rationalism or empiricism. The paradox neither disallows the findings of objective science nor disqualifies the apparatuses of causal and predicative logic. Rather it exposes their conditions of possibility while at the same time hinting at what is excluded when those conditions are taken as the truth itself—even if this is given in terms of a more subjective and thus relative notion of a horizon of cultural assumptions.

At the heart of these conditions is a certain profound operation on the spatiality and temporality of experience, and it is on that level that some of the articles in the collection attempt to intervene. Wei-Wei Yeo's "City as Theatre: Singapore, State of Distraction" maintains a close focus on conditions that pertain to Singapore, but her conclusions point to some wide-ranging implications. First there is a consistent awareness of the mediated status of experience, acknowledging, in the rigorously cautious practice of reading, an experience that can only be derived through diffused or refracted versions of it. So the article begins with an account of Singapore's hyper-reality through Lau Siew Mei's novelistic evocation of it, according to which, as Yeo affirms, "Life in the city moves in fixed cycles like the endless repeat performances of [a] play. . . . A collective amnesia seems to hold the city under its spell: lives within it press on with an ever increasing sense of urgency about the present, not having time or space for thinking about the past." By observing a range of city phenomena that manifest or provoke a "state of distraction" and linking these to the growing practice in Singaporean drama to reproduce distraction, Yeo has identified a way of understanding the role that distraction plays in making sense of the city's overwhelming overload of external stimuli: "Constructive distraction is crucial to the audience's capacity for making sense of what they see before them, just as it is essential in the keeping of one's balance in everyday city life."

It is probably not by chance that the term *distraction* would adequately translate the Greek *ekstasis,* which is the term that Martin Heidegger uses in *Being and Time* to denote what he calls "the ecstatic unity of temporality" according to which it is possible for us to experience other beings.[42] The unity describes the way that time is constantly "outside itself," insofar as the present must be regarded as derived from a combination of having-been, and the future. *Ekstasis* denotes how a unity of future, having-been, and present allows the human being to be "cleared." It provides a spatial and temporal present that is only authentically arrived at through this state of *ekstasis* (in Yeo's terms, *distraction*). The city increases the demand on existential functions like *ekstasis,* provoking an escalation of the repetitiveness and intensity of the acts or performances of presencing (which allows beings to present themselves in particular times and spaces). Heidegger's radio broadcast from 1934 defending his decision not to come back to Berlin to take up the prestigious post offered to him gives us a sense of how he felt about this: "The world of the city," he said, "runs the risk of falling into destructive error," and he identifies "a very loud and very active and very fashionable obtrusiveness."[43]

Heidegger's roots as he evokes them lie in deeply conservative rural Southern Germany. His lifelong suspicion of modernity, machinery, democracy, liberalism, and the forms of commoditized style (like journalism and mass culture) certainly contributed to his radical critiques of the productivity and efficiency that are valorized by forms of modern urbanism, its bland cosmopolitanism, and its perpetually seductive novelty. But, alongside this, Heidegger's untiring philosophical questing was able to disclose a deep complicity between the tradition he was committed to preserve (i.e., Western metaphysics) and the conditions he found around him in the modern technological world. An acknowledged and powerful alternative to predicative logic, Heidegger's thought opens with the way beings are revealed through what he called "the question of being," which he formulates as follows: "why are there beings at all, and not rather nothing?"[44] The "why" in this case would not be a question about the *cause* of beings but something more like a celebration of the wonder that anything exists at all, thus revealing beings in hitherto unthinkable ways—for instance, opening experience up to the indeterminacy of its future and the disjunctive quality of temporality. Heidegger's critique of Western metaphysics lies in his discovery that these constitutive aspects of experience have been systematically excluded by the metaphysical tradition, which privileges predicative logic and the correspondence theory of truth, and which reaches its ultimate form as technologizing rationality. Modern urbanism, then, can be revealed as both in part a consequence of as well as a main contribution to the historical forgetting of *being* and of historicity. But the articles in this collection have shown that a careful engagement with specific forms of urbanism reveals specific responses to historicity. Southeast Asian urbanism reveals itself as something quite exceptional and irreducible to any notion of a general urbanism, thus suspending the notion of a general urbanism leaving us only with examples, but ones that cannot be used as paradigms to explain other examples.

So modern urbanism can nevertheless be opened up to just this kind of questioning, and perhaps urbanism is the mode of contemporary existence that most demands it. Robbie Goh's article for this collection, "Deus ex Machina: Evangelical Sites, Urbanism, and the Construction of Social Identities," establishes a number of connections that are crucial in this respect. If, as Goh demonstrates, Christian culture thrives in Asian urban contexts like Singapore through "flexible and adaptive uses of space and its symbolisms, media texts, Internet resources, international networking systems, and other strategies,"then this is both a phenomenon of information implosion generally and something specific to the relation between Christianity and urbanism. What we find takes the form of an extremely uncanny repetition, similar to the kind we find at work in Patke's analysis of modernity and postcolonial urbanism, according to which, as Heidegger shows, *being* is determined as presence. The determination of being as presence finds its most consistent formulation in the division between the empirical (e.g., the perpetual presence of urban distraction) and the transcendental—the radical absence or placing beyond of an eternal and fundamental ground. So the coexistence of the modernity of urban processes and a thriving institutional Christian culture would not only follow as a probability, but the intensification of modernity could predictably imply the intensification, in certain Southeast Asian cities, of Christian culture. This point is thoroughly worked out in Armitage and Roberts's arguments about hypermodernity. But the precise reasons why this probability is realized in Southeast Asian urban sites more than others has to do with the historicity of the region. Goh suggests that "Christian culture corresponds with some of the significant ideological and technological currents of the present era," owing to its ability to adapt to the "exploitation and manipulation of shared spaces and discourses." Thus, the collusion between global urbanism and Christian culture would be perpetuated by the apparent contradictions between them.

Heidegger, who derives alterity from finitude as the undetermined future of a determined heritage, seems to have arrived at his position through his own radical critique of the Christian tradition, and it would be worth exploring this aspect of historicity further in relation to current phenomena of global urbanism.[45] We would find, as many of the articles in this collection show, an alternative to the classical division between the empirical and the transcendental in the uncanny repetitions that are produced through perpetuating cities.

The amnesia that Yeo discusses in her article can also be connected with Heidegger's worry about the "forgetting of Being," if we bear in mind that Heidegger's analysis of temporality in *Being and Time* ground to a halt unfinished and would thereafter take an increasingly less metaphysical and more poetic route. To witness the performance of our everyday raptures (distractions, ecstasies) is to begin to excavate and to open up the grounds of our quotidian forgetting. But if, as Heidegger's analyses suggest, the experience of the temporal modality of the future (which can only be experienced as perpetually "coming") adds to our experience the past of a future that was never anybody's present, then this also opens up a past that carries forward, in its own being, toward a future, an undetermined possibility in the form of a historicity that we can always forget or ignore—which is what aspects of modern urban life encourage us to do. This combination of past and future grounds history, certainly, but it grounds us in an uncertain relation to it, which can be taken up or disavowed.

We have explored in some detail how various responses within academic study attempt to resolve this uncertain relation, which we may or may not acknowledge as the conditions that help to structure our awareness generally. In these cases, the attempt to solve the problem perpetuates it. Once we recognize our ways of thinking and acting as a kind of *dwelling*—so that living in the dwelling would be to take shelter within its threshold—then our attempts to grasp the processes of urbanization and globalization would become attempts to grasp our own mode of dwelling. As we have argued, most attempts to step outside the mode of dwelling, whether by constructing theoretical paradigms or by keeping on the side of the brutally empirical, lead to paradox. As the articles in this volume collectively show, there are alternatives. By taking the example of Southeast Asia we find that the examples must be considered as exceptional. Yet it is the exceptionality of our examples that is suggestive of the grounds of the global itself. Here the dwelling itself begins to shake.

NOTES

1. Richard T. LeGates and Frederic Stout, eds. *The City Reader* (New York: Routledge, 2000), xvi.
2. Bob Jessop, "Globalisation, Entrepreneurial Cities and the Social Economy," in *Urban Movements in a Globalising World,* ed. Pierre Hamel, Henri Lustiger-Thaler, and Margit Mayer (London: Routledge, 2000), 82.

3. Azzedine Haddour, "Citing Difference: Vagrancy, Nomadism and the Site of the Colonial and Post-Colonial," in *City Visions,* ed. David Bell and Azzedine Haddour (Harlow, U.K.: Longman, 2000), 45.

4. Saskia Sassen, *The Global City: New York, London, Tokyo* (Princeton: Princeton University Press, 1991); *Cities in a World Economy* (Thousand Oaks, Calif.: Sage Press, 1994/2000); *Globalization and Its Discontents* (New York: New Press, 1998).

5. Saskia Sassen, "The Global City: Introducing a Concept and Its History," in *Mutations,* ed. Rem Koolhaas, Stefano Boeri, and Sandford Kwinter (Bordeaux: Actar, 2000).

6. Kingsley Davis charts the increase in urbanized populations in his 1965 article "The Urbanization of the Human Population," *The City Reader,* ed. Richard T. Gates and Frederic Stout (New York: Routledge, 2000). Céline Rozenblat charts the phenomenon through statistics derived from the Global Urban Observatory in *Mutations* (2–7) where they serve as a kind of stark facticity for the studies that follow.

7. George E. Marcus and Michael M. J. Fischer, *Anthropology as Cultural Critique* (Chicago: University of Chicago Press, 1986), 77–110.

8. Jessop, "Globalisation," 97.

9. Ibid.

10. Ibid.

11. Zygmunt Bauman, in his *Globalization: The Human Consequences* (Cambridge, Mass.: Polity, 1998), begins by drawing attention to the recent fate of the word "globalization," pointing out that "all vogue words" like globalization "tend to share a similar fate: the more experiences they pretend to make transparent, the more they themselves become opaque" (1). It is not certain that Bauman is aware of the irony according to which if, as he claims, the word "globalization" is "no exception to the rule" that governs the naturalization and generalization of questionable terms in repetition, then the fate of the word itself embodies in the broadest sense its own meaning. The book, as is the case with most recent interventions in the field, sets out to engage with the processes of globalization by questioning the meaning of the word.

12. Jessop, "Globalisation," 84.

13. Ibid.

14. Ibid., 81.

15. Clearly, then, our own claims for a notion of deconstruction that differs from most current usages in the humanities and social sciences must succumb to exactly the fate that these different usages imply, so it would be foolish for us to try to lay down the law on this. The best we can do is try to expose these conditions, according to which even the use of a word like "deconstruction" must be able to succumb to its own deconstruction.

16. Jessop, "Globalisation," 81.

17. Saskia Sassen, *the Mobility of Labour and Capital: A Study in International Investment and Labor Flows* (Cambridge, U.K.: Cambridge University Press, 1988).

18. Jessop, "Globalisation," 92.

19. Martin Heidegger, "The Question Concerning Technology," in *The Question Concerning Technology and Other Essays,* trans. William Lovitt (New York: Harper and Row, 1977); *The Principle of Reason,* trans. Reginald Lilly (Bloomington and Indianapolis: Indiana University Press, 1996); *The Dialectic of Enlightenment* by Theodor Adorno and Max Horkheimer, trans. John Cumming (London: Verso, 1972).

20. Significantly, many academics in the social sciences envisage their role as a potentially advisory one, justifying a narrow focus on causal aspects of the processes under study. Janet Lippman Abu-Lughod, for instance, states that "Causal comparative analysis can not only deepen our understanding of world cities in the world system but potentially can offer some helpful guidelines for making realistic policy recommendations." From "Comparing Chicago, New York and Los Angeles: Testing Some World Cities Hypotheses," in *World Cities in a World System,* ed. Paul L. Knox and Peter J. Taylor (Cambridge, U.K.: Cambridge University Press, 1995), 186. The fraught relationship between academic study and public policy does indeed indicate some unrealized potential, but the relation itself requires further investigation, given that policy-derived funding for academic institutions is overwhelmingly on the side of professional or technological services whose impact is directly functional. The potential that Abu-Lughod identifies here would be inversely proportional to the degree of critical engagement underpinning her work.

21. We are indebted to Stephen A. Tyler, "The Middle Voice: The Influence of Postmodernism on Empirical Research in Anthropology," in *Postmodernism in Anthropology: Theory and Practice,* ed. K. Geuijen, D. Raven, and J. deWolf (Amsterdam: van Gorcum, 1995), 77–88, for various insights into the functions of the middle voice.

22. See Paul Virilio, *A Landscape of Events,* trans. Julie Rose (Cambridge, Mass.: MIT Press, 2000).
23. See Dean Forbes, *Asian Metropolis: Urbanisation and the Southeast Asian City* (Melbourne: Oxford University Press, 1996), 51–54.
24. See John Phillips, "Lagging Behind: Bhabha, Theory and the Future," in *Travel Writing and Empire,* ed. Steve Clark (London: Zed, 1999), for an attempt to disclose the aporia of post-colonial theory.
25. See Ryan Bishop and John Phillips, "Diasporic Communities and Identity Politics: Containing the Political," in *Asian Diasporas and Cultures: Globalization, Hybridity, Intertextuality,* ed. Robbie Goh and Shawn Wong, under consideration University of Washington Press.
26. Haddour, "Citing Difference."
27. Ibid., 45.
28. See Bishop and Phillips, "Diasporic Communities," for a more complete discussion of these issues.
29. Quoted in Haddour, "Citing Difference," 44; with his ellipses.
30. Ibid., 45.
31. Another way of putting this, which connects the present discussion with our earlier reading of Jessop, would be to say that only on the basis of an undetermined aspect of the signifying unit could a determination (some meaningful statement, class or category) be possible.
32. See Bishop and Phillips, "Diasporic Communities," for a discussion of these issues.
33. Haddour, "Citing Difference," 45.
34. Homi Bhabha, *The Location of Culture* (London: Routledge, 1994), 178.
35. John Phillips, "Singapore Soil: A Completely Different Organization of Space," in *Representations of Urban Space,* eds. Liam Kennedy and Maria Balshaw (Cambridge, U.K.: Pluto, 1998).
36. For Virilio's clearest statement on electronic pollution see *Open Sky,* trans. Julie Rose (London: Verso, 1997).
37. See Gwendolyn Wright, *The Politics of Design in French Colonial Urbanism* (Chicago: University of Chicago Press, 1991), and Nicole Cooper, *France in Indochina: Colonial Encounters* (Oxford: Berg, 2001).
38. See H. Bruce Franklin, *War Stars: The Superweapon and the American Imagination* (New York: Oxford University Press, 1988), and Sven Lindqvist, *The History of Bombing* (New York: New Press, 2001).
39. See Abidin Kusno, *Behind the Postcolonial: Architecture, Urban Space, and Political Architectures in Indonesia* (London: Routledge, 2000).
40. See Ryan Bishop and Lillian S. Robinson, *Night Market: Sexual Cultures and the Thai Economic Miracle* (New York: Routledge, 1998), 6–91.
41. The consequences and implications of self-reflexive paradoxes have been well documented in the critical tradition of continental philosophy but remain safely domesticated under the banner of postmodernism when it comes to the mainstream of the humanities and social sciences.
42. Martin Heidegger, *Being and Time,* trans. Joan Stambaugh (New York: SUNY, 1996).
43. Martin Heidegger, "Why I Stay in the Provinces," in *Heidegger: The Man and the Thinker,* ed. Thomas Sheehan (Chicago: Precedent, 1981), 27.
44. Martin Heidegger, *Introduction to Metaphysics,* trans. Gregory Fried and Richard Polt New Haven: Yale University Press, 2000), 1.
45. Jean Genet in his 1968 article, "L'étrange mot d'urbanisme" [The strange word of 'urbanism'], already highly suggestively connects the city of Rome (and thus the Roman Empire) to the city per se (through Pope Urbain) and then to theatre and to death. *Oeuvres complètes IV* (Paris: Gallimard, 1968), 9–18.

In the simultaneously emergent postcolonial and Cold War worlds, tourism played an important role in the establishment of Southeast Asian nation-states and economies. Similarly, the post–Cold War/neoliberal globalizing networks have placed nation-states once important to Cold War struggles in peculiar positions, some within the new networks' concerns and some outside of them. Internal issues squelched by nationalist agendas and Cold War policing have now emerged in nations such as Indonesia, Cambodia, Burma, and the Philippines. Tourism, however, remains a constant appeal within this complex historicity, with a peculiar trend that partakes of exoticism and spectacle: "urban danger-zone tourism" is what Adams calls it here. Shirley Geok-lin Lim has called the region a "third space of the imagination," and the imaginary Adams delineates is one that uses inequitable economic power relations to fulfill the desires of tourists to "experience" politics—resistance, revolution, and war—in distant places such as Southeast Asia and feel as if they are removed from and protected from the events themselves. These tourists target specific cities in the region, especially now Dili, and are targeted by North American and indigenous tourist organizations (echoing targeting strategies discussed by Bishop and Clancey) that play up or play down the "danger" dimensions of the tourist package as it suits their target audience. As Adams negotiates the historicity of colonialism, postcolonialism, Cold War, and post–Cold War globalizing processes through tourism, she also bears in mind the futural dimensions of experimentation the region has long played, and ends by linking Dili to "the mobile city" of un-nationed labor and production discussed by Armitage and Roberts, presenting a grim urban scene that plays well in media and pays well in global bank accounts with dire results for tens of thousands whose past and present violence has been commodified and spectaclized.

2

Global Cities, Terror, and Tourism: The Ambivalent Allure of the Urban Jungle

KATHLEEN M. ADAMS

In the early 1960s, *National Geographic* magazine commissioned a series of articles from a California couple exploring the roadways and waterways of Asia on *Tortuga II,* an amphibious jeep purchased from a WW II surplus depot. The couple's first installment recounts their floating and driving adventures on and along the Ganges, where *Tortuga* would sometimes carry them "to venerable cities and princely palaces" and other times serve as their "campsite in the countryside, where the only wealth was in the stars."[1] Their next installment, published in May 1961, chronicles the couple's travels through Indonesia. As the article's subtitle heralds, this leg of their *Tortuga* adventure transpires in a "young and troubled island nation": Their essay opens dramatically, with their arrival in the capital city of Jakarta, a little over a decade after Indonesia's independence from the Netherlands:

> Djakarta's traffic swarmed around us: I made my turn with more than usual caution. Crack! A rifle flashed close by, and a cordon of soldiers materialized. In minutes we stood in the office of an army commandant. "But all I did was make a wrong turn," I protested. "Your sentry could have blown his whistle—he didn't have to shoot!"
> The commandant smiled in apology.
> "Forgive us," he said, "but Indonesia is in a state of emergency. Even here in the capital, one sometimes shoots first and asks later."[2]

Encapsulated in the opening paragraph of this Indonesia travelogue is a theme central to this article, namely, the imaging in global travel media of certain insular Southeast Asian cities as danger zones, inspiring aversion and allure for armchair travelers and intrepid adventurers. This article is broadly concerned with danger zone travel to insular Southeast Asian cities. Whereas safaris to untamed wildernesses caught the fancy of elite thrill-seekers in colonial times, in the contemporary postcolonial era "urban jungles" are developing a new allure for a certain breed of Euro-American adventurers. In the pages that follow, I examine the touristic imagery and cybercelebrity of these postcolonial urban jungles.

Much has been written on the ways in which Southeast Asian cities have been undergoing touristic (re)imagining, (re)structuring, and (re)framing in the postcolonial era, as nations once relegated to the fringes of Euro-American consciousness now pursue a dual quest for foreign capital and global celebrity.[3] With cities such as Paris, London, and New York hailed as central nodes in transnational economic, technological, and media net-works, some Southeast Asian governments have begun strategizing to add their capitals to the list of "preeminent global cities," with the aim of thereby infusing these capitals with a different sort of capital. As governments and planners strive to transform their Southeast Asian cities into international "command posts" for finance, technology, markets, media, and creative genius, a relatively consistent theme has been the reimaging and touristic promotion of these cities. For a number of Southeast Asian cities, then, becoming a destination for international tourists appears to simultaneously contribute to and underscore one's status as a so-called global city. Witness Singapore's recent campaign to transform itself into a "Global City for the Arts," capable of attracting and retaining foreign businesses as well as inter-national tourists.[4] Likewise, Indon.com (a leading Internet company rep-resenting Indonesia in the international Internet community) celebrates Indonesia's capital with a "Welcome to Jakarta" webpage:

> Home to over 10 million people, Jakarta is always bustling, from the sound of the wheel of government turning to the sight of the economy churning. Skyscrapers, single story residential houses, modern apartment complexes, survivalists' shanties—all coexist in this city. So why should you visit Jakarta? Well, for the same reasons you would visit New York, or London, or Paris, or Singapore or any other big city. Because you can find everything there![5]

In short, for some, a city's touristic magnetism underscores its status as a so-called global city, worthy of joining the ranks of New York, London, or other global cities. That is, the ability to transmit an alluring image as a cultural center and draw international tourists can be seen as an accou-trement of a global city. But what of the dynamics in tumultuous times, when images of these cities as sites of rioting and violence are projected around the globe on nightly CNN reports? How do mayhem and the threat of urban violence unsettle conventional assumptions about the trajectory to global city status?

There is a growing literature on the effects of political instability and violence on tourism to urban Asian destinations.[6] To date, the predominant focus of research on tourism and political instability has examined political unrest in destination cities in terms of tourist flows, economic impact, or image management.[7] However, surprisingly little scholarly attention has been directed to the ways in which urban violence rearticulates touristic images, conceptions, and fantasies about postcolonial Southeast Asian cities. Moreover, the forms of urban tourism that thrive in tumultuous times have been largely ignored. This article explores these themes in Indonesia and East Timor, drawing on ethnographic data collected in Indonesia in the 1990s, interviews with returning "danger-zone tourists" encountered in Singapore and the United States, and postings to travel-oriented Internet sites. I suggest that this underexplored genre of tourism has the potential to reconfigure perceptions of Southeast Asian cities: Danger-zone travelers are not merely innocuous observers of political clashes, but can play a role in the reshaping of sensibilities about urban sites. I argue that the narratives and electromagnetic images produced by urban danger-zone travelers both inscribe cities such as Dili and Jakarta as global metropoles, and simultaneously mark them as wild urban jungles. Tracing the specific historicity of travelers' images of Dili underscores the centrality of the electromagnetic sphere in concomitantly globalizing *and* disenfranchising Dili as a ruinous city scarred by its legacy of violence. Finally, I suggest that urban danger-zone travel offers a lens for understanding Dili and other tumultuous urban Southeast Asian destinations as "futural cities," harbingers of the total urban mobilization depicted by Armitage and Roberts in this volume.

First, I delineate the category of "danger-zone tourist," and outline the imagery of danger-zone tourism in postcolonial Southeast Asian cities. As I examine the context for urban danger-zone tourism in Indonesia, and sketch the array of images motivating this genre of tourist, it will become apparent that these images are both self-images and city images. My focus will be on the case of the city of Dili, capital of East Timor, one of the newest postcolonial cities on the globe. With historic roots in the spice trade, years of Portuguese and Indonesian colonialism, and, more recently, much-televised urban turbulence, suffering, and destruction, Dili offers a unique lens for viewing the interplay between historicity, geopolitics, and global communications networks. Whereas in colonial days, Dili drew traders seeking Timor's sandalwood and offered a stopover for vessels en route to the Spice Islands, today's postcolonial Dili has become an urban magnet for not only reporters and international aid workers, but also a particular breed of danger-zone tourist, who chronicle their adventures on the web. Images of the war-scarred city have entered the global electro-magnetic stream.

DEFINING DANGER-ZONE TOURISTS

As Malcolm Crick observed, sun, sand, sea, and sex are the four "S"s often perceived as the essence of a developing nation's touristic appeal.[8] And as Linda Richter added, "a fifth 's' is even more critical: security."[9] However, these ingredients tend to be irrelevant or even antithetical to one genre of tourist generally overlooked in the tourism literature. While tumultuous Southeast Asian cities have frightened off many package tourists, they have emerged as alluring destinations for what I term "danger-zone tourists."[10] Danger-zone tourists are travelers who are drawn to areas of political tur-moil. Their pilgrimages to strife-torn destinations are not for professional purposes but rather for leisure, although in some cases the professional iden-tities of danger-zone tourists are related to their leisure pursuits.[11] The back-packer traveler in Thailand featured in Alex Garland's 1997 novel *The Beach*[12] captures the mindset of many danger-zone tourists:

> I wanted to witness extreme poverty. I saw it as a necessary experience for anyone who wanted to appear worldly and interesting. Of course witnessing poverty was the first to be ticked off the list. Then I had to graduate to the more obscure stuff. Being in a riot was something I pursued with a truly obsessive zeal, along with being tear-gassed and hearing gunshots fired in anger. Another list item was having a brush with my own death.[13]

A similar mentality pervades Fielding's Black Flag Café, a website devoted to travelers returning from and planning visits to dangerous places. The site's byline explains its unique orientation:

> Looking for fun in all the wrong places? Well you've found the nets [sic] only hangout for hardcore adventurers, travel junkies, DP'ers [dangerous placers] and just about anyone who runs screaming from glossy brochures, backpacker guidebooks and Robin Leach. So let's get busy. Got a tip? Just came back from the Congo, just heading off to Albania? Let us know and don't be surprised if the staff of Fielding, the authors of DP [Dangerous Places] or the CIA drops you a line.[14]

Black Flag Café frequenters appear to have varying levels of experience with danger-zone travel, though all seem to share an intense interest in "adrenalin-rush" travel. Although some of the Black Flag Café visitors are armchair danger-zone travelers, others are actively engaged in touring the world's hot spots, often beginning with risky off-the-beaten-track destina-

tions and working their way up to battlefields and war zones. As one recent
Black Flag Café posting reads,

> A traveller in many "soft" DP [dangerous place] countries over the past ten
> years, I have decided it is time to go for my first war zone. Armed with my
> clippings, letters of intro and mas bullsh**, where should I go for my
> first ringside view of armed conflict? Should I dive into the thick of it
> "Chechnya?" or should I find a good "intro" hotspot?[15]

Among the Asian destinations suggested by repliers were sites of civil strife
in Indonesia and the war zone in Afghanistan.

The Black Flag Café website is an outgrowth of the popular travel guide
Fielding's The World's Most Dangerous Places,[16] by Robert Young Pelton,
Coskun Aral, and Wink Dulles. Hailed by the *New York Times* as "one of
the oddest and most fascinating travel books to appear in a long time,"[17] the
1998 edition of this volume features chapters on Cambodia, Myanmar, the
Philippines, as well as shorter entries on Indonesia (Timor) and Laos. With
its fourth edition in press, the book has enjoyed cult popularity among both
armchair travelers and American danger-zone tourists. The brisk sales of this
and other related guidebooks, as well as the touristic popularity of T-shirts
with slogans such as "Danger!! Mines!! Cambodia!!"[18] not only suggest the
allure of danger-zone travel but also demonstrate that some entrepreneurial
individuals have begun to capitalize on this emerging genre of travel.

While the numbers of danger-zone tourists appear to be rising, the
allure of touristic forays into politically risky regions has a long history, as
do danger-zone travel entrepreneurs. According to Mitchell,[19] as early as
1830 French entrepreneurs were ferrying tourists to North Africa to witness
the French bombardment of Algiers. In more contemporary times, educational tour organizers have marketed trips to Indonesia to explore the
religious strife between Christians and Muslims in Indonesia and the U.S.-
based Reality Tours has offered group trips to politically volatile events and
destinations in Latin America and Southeast Asia. Likewise, an Italian travel
agency has organized groups equipped with doctors, guards, and combat
gear to usher tourists to the edges of battle zones in places like Dubrovnik
and the south of Lebanon.[20] Such touristic expeditions to "the places shown
on the television news" can have hefty pricetags: The aforementioned Italian tours were sold at U.S.$25,000 per person.[21] Many danger-zone
tourists are low-budget travelers; however, the fact that some are willing
to spend extravagant amounts for their travels prompts questions concerning the compelling allure of this genre of travel.

Wayne Pitts is one of the few scholars to have made passing note of this
genre of tourist, which he terms "war tourists."[22] In his discussion of the
impact of uprisings in Chiapas (Mexico) on the tourist economy, he com-

ments, "Just like drivers on the interstate stretching their necks trying to get a glimpse of 'what happened' at a wreck scene, these individuals [war tourists] wanted to be a part of the action."[23] As Pitts later adds, the "war tourists" in Chiapas were there "to experience the thrill of political violence." One magazine reported a Canadian woman explaining her reasons for visiting Chiapas were "journalism, a tan and a revolution."[24] Likewise, while researching the broader topic of risk creation in travel narratives, Torun Elsrud reports that she has come across interviewees who say they are looking forward to riots in Indonesia as it is "cool to have seen/been in one."[25] These descriptions hint at some of the varied activities and motivations of the tourist who is drawn to tumultuous urban sites in Southeast Asia.

In spite of the precedent set by Pitts, I prefer to employ the term "danger-zone tourists" instead of "war tourists," as I believe this particular form of tourism necessitates distinction from the broader category of "war tourism" discussed by Valene Smith.[26] In her path-breaking exploration of war tourism, Smith focuses on the commemorative dimension of tourism to the sites of *past* wars—battlefields, cemeteries, military reenactments, monuments, and so forth.[27] My interest here, however, is not tourism pertaining to *past* wars, but rather tourism to tumultuous urban locales, cities that are not necessarily the sites of declared wars but are nevertheless sites of *ongoing* political instability, sites where there is at least an imagined potentiality of violent eruptions. Likewise, I have not adopted the term "risk tourism" embraced by some writers,[28] as this term covers a broader array of activities including physically challenging hinterland enterprises such as whitewater rafting in Sarawak. For these reasons pertaining to precision, in this article I adopt the expression "urban danger-zone tourism." One final point merits emphasis: A wide array of motives and interests fall under the heading "danger-zone tourist"—from humanitarian/activist tourists, to adrenalin-rush pursuers and those seeking firsthand journalistic experiences—as shall become evident in our discussion of urban danger-zone tourism in Indonesia. In discussing urban danger-zone tourism, I am not arguing for an essentialism of this genre of tourism, but rather an advocating of the need to attend to the image-trafficking manifest in urban danger-zone travel.

THE IMAGERY OF URBAN SOUTHEAST ASIAN DANGER-ZONE TOURISM

Fielding's The World's Most Dangerous Places,[29] the definitive guidebook for danger-zone tourists, devotes chapters to several Southeast Asian nations and their cities. In the 1998 version of this handbook, as on the corresponding website, Cambodia and Myanmar (Burma) figure prominently. Through media images and guidebooks, tourists develop images of their vacation destinations long before they depart: because they draw on these glossy images to assess experiences in these destinations,[30] our discussion should begin with an examination of the urban danger-zone imagery found in such guidebooks and travel advice websites.

In logging on to Fielding's website devoted to dangerous places (www.fieldingtravel.com), one immediately knows one is in a different sort of travel zone. The background wallpaper for pages devoted to Cambodia, Myanmar, and the Philippines features cartoon-like images of rifles, shields, and spears in crossbones positions, and ignited time bombs. Likewise, each chapter of the book version of *Fielding's The World's Most Dangerous Places* is decorated with a comic image of a sunglass-sporting skull toting a base-ball cap adorned with the DP logo. The chapters themselves are illustrated with smaller cartoons of exploding demonstrators, bazooka-carrying troops, burning dynamite sticks, and fierce killer bees. These comic images seem-ingly "tame" the terrors of riots and warfare, offering the subliminal message that dangerous travel can be something entertaining. Even the danger-themed photographs accompanying each chapter have lulling dimensions. The Myanmar chapter, for instance, opens with a shot of artificial limbs dangling decoratively from tropical vegetation. Other images in this chapter include two plump toddlers holding whimsically decorated guns, and troops trot-ting in front of a thatched-roofed pavilion. Smiling gunmen and helicopters make frequent appearances in the pages of this book, but there are no images of corpses or actual warfare. This and other similar books render danger-zone travel inviting yet thrilling.

The narrative "Cambodia—In a Dangerous Place" underscores these themes of unpredictable danger for the unaware and excitement for the savvy traveler. As the writers recount,

> We went to Cambodia on a lark. These days, Cambodia is not necessarily the most dangerous place in the world, or even a nasty place, but it is an exotic, very inexpensive stop that every traveler to Asia should make. Is it safe? Well, if you stay inside the tourist ruts (literally), don't venture outside the ill-defined "safety" zone and watch where you step, Cambodia can be safe. Cambodia can also be brutal if you pass through the invisible safety barrier and end up in the hands of the Khmer Rouge. Just remember the advice of your first grade teacher, "Don't color outside the lines. . . ." One tourist can fly into Phnom Penh and Siem Reap on a modern jet, stay in a five star hotel, and see the temple complex, complete with cold Pepsis, an air-conditioned car and a good meal, followed by an ice-cold beer at one of the many nightclubs the U.N. soldiers used to frequent. Another tourist can find himself kneeling at the edge of a shallow, hastily dug grave, waiting for the rifle butt that will slam into his cortex, ending his brief but adventurous life. The difference between the two scenarios might be 10 km or lingering a few too many minutes along the road.[31]

Southeast Asian cities in Cambodia and Myanmar, in particular, receive dramatic danger-zone profiling in the 1998 edition of Robert Young Pelton's book. In a section of the Cambodia chapter titled "In a Dangerous Place," Pelton devotes two pages to describing a typical evening in Siem Reap. His narrative could easily have been drawn from the script of a Chuck Norris film, encompassing guns, seedy discotheques, insipient violence, a brutalized police officer, and danger-habituated bar hostesses:

> That night back in Siem Reap we go to a nightclub. The sign outside says "no guns or explosives." The music is pure sing-song Khmer played at ear-damaging levels. . . . Wink [Pelton's fellow danger-zone traveler and co-contributor to the volume] decides to get up and jam with the band. The audience is dumbstruck and stares open-mouthed for two songs. The dance floor clears out and the Cambodians don't know if they should clap or cover their ears. Wink finishes up to a round of applause. After Wink sits down, it seems not everyone is thrilled with the impromptu jam session. We are challenged to a fight in a less than sensitive manner. An elbow not once, not twice, but three times in the back—hard. We decide to split. This would not be a John Wayne punch 'em up. But probably a good ole' sloppy burst of gunfire.[32]

They change venues and have yet another close call with the nightly violence of Siem Reap:

> Sitting outside to avoid the chilling air conditioning and deafening noise inside, we are interrupted as a Cambodian cop comes flying out of the glass entry doors, followed by shouting, punching and kicking patrons. The girls sitting with us immediately react, jump up and drag us around the corner and down an alley. They plead with us to "Go, go, run! Please, before you are shot! . . ." We push past them and are in time to watch the cop being kicked and beaten and slammed unconsciously [sic] into the back of a pickup truck. The girls explain that we are lucky (a term we are hearing a lot here). Usually, there is gunfire . . . I laugh. . . . The sad look in her eyes tells me I am being far too casual about a very real threat. With a sense of resignation, she says, "This is a dangerous place. You should not be here."[33]

By 2000, Siem Reap has begun to lose its cachet for danger-zone travelers. One returnee from a trip to Siem Reap posts his advice on Pelton's Black Flag Café website, warning other danger-zone travelers to give Siem Reap a pass, as it had ceased to be a danger-zone destination—it had become a "TOURIST TRAP." As he grumbles, "Its [sic] no longer adventurous, dangerous, fun etc. to go there—every tourist in Cambodia goes there. Go to Burma. . . ."[34]

As such postings hint, danger-zone tourism has fickle tendencies: As destinations become perceived to be calmer and draw growing numbers of "ordinary" travelers, danger-zone pilgrims move on to new sites of tumult. The various editions of *Fielding's The World's Most Dangerous Places* attest to the rapidity with which destinations move in and out of vogue with this genre of traveler. Dangerous cities spotlighted in one edition are often absent from the next, replaced by new war-torn sites currently featured on CNN reports. When the *Fielding's* volume includes dangerous destinations that are not active war sites, they are often depicted as camouflaged tinderboxes. For instance, the 1998 edition of the book devotes copious pages to Burma/Myanmar and includes a lengthy section on the city of Yangon. Here, as elsewhere, we find the theme of superficially "normal" urban scenery masking lurking dangers:

> Yangon has a slightly cosmopolitan feel. The sidewalks are packed with a mish-mash of races in the colorful garb denoting their ethnic blueprints: Indian, Burmese, Balgladeshi, Chinese, Shan. They stroll past the washed-out aqua, yellow and pink pastels of apartment buildings and businesses and the restored, grand buildings of British colonial days.
>
> During rush hours, Yangon's streets rival those of any other Southeast Asian capital; traffic crawls at the pace of democratic reforms here. But not at the pace of hotel construction; five-star caravanseries are shooting skyward in all parts of the city like a seismograph in Riverside County, California. . . . The streets of Yangon are clean, curbs freshly painted . . . lawns, parks and even road medians are meticulously manicured and landscaped. There are few beggars. People dress remarkably well. . . . Comparisons with Singapore come to mind. In fact, a visitor here is struck with an indelible sense of Yangon being a prosperous city-state rather than a Third World capital.
>
> Unless one is accustomed to hanging around dictatorships, the causal visitor won't get it. . . . But dig a little deeper and the observer will be shocked. . . .[35]

The contributing author, Wink Dulles, goes on to compare the city of Yangon to a library, where if one talks at all, it is in hushed voices. Noting that the topic of politics will instantly clear a room, he adds, "Ask a shopkeeper in Yangon why barbed-wire barricades have been set up on the street in front of his establishment and he'll answer 'to slow traffic.' Ask what kind of traffic and you'll be asked to leave."[36] Dulles proceeds to chronicle his evening adventures in the streets of Yangon, the time most favored for observing the "viscera" of this particular urban danger zone.

> I picked a delightful March evening for a stroll through the capital. . . . I first dined on curried roadkill down the street. . . . A troop transport truck rolled

up to the corner; a half dozen rifle-toting soldiers jumped to the street and made themselves conspicuous. The rest of the patronage paid their bills.

I did so as well and headed in the direction of the mosque, where three other troop transport trucks, packed to the stakes with soldiers, had set up shop for the night. I walked past; the soldiers all wore the same expression—like the way the Green Beret guy with the bloody hands stares at Martin Sheen when he arrives at Col. Kurtz's kingdom in "Apocalypse Now."[37]

Eventually Dulles finds himself questioned by a sinister character in charge of the troop movements. He claims to be merely a tourist out for a smoke, and his disbelieving interrogator gruffly sends him back to the confines of his hotel. Noteworthy here, as at the Black Flag Café website, is the allusion to Hollywood images as prior texts for processing travelers' adventures in dangerous destinations. Peppering the narratives of some danger-zone travelers are references to *Apocalypse Now, The Year of Living Dangerously,* and *The Beach.*

Having briefly surveyed some of the pretravel Southeast Asian urban imagery offered to budding danger-zone tourists, I turn now to examine danger-zone tourism in the urban Indonesian context. As the Indonesian case will illustrate, the range of urban danger-zone tourists is varied, as are the images they produce of Indonesian cities.

URBAN DANGER-ZONE TOURISM IN INDONESIA

Since mid-1998, Indonesian tourism promoters have struggled against mounting negative imagery due to political, economic, ethnic, and religious unrest. As a September 1999 online article headlined "Indonesian Tourism Industry Battered by Images of Violence" reports, "Indonesia has been plagued by image-problems in recent times—from last year's economic crisis and related unrest to this year's militia rampage in East Timor and riots in Jakarta."[38] Likewise, increasing numbers of independent travelers sharing advice on the web are painting a tableau of Indonesia as a land of travel traumas, urging fellow travelers to opt for Thailand or Malaysia's more predictably peaceful isles. Such negative imagery has taken its toll: In 1998 the number of foreign visitors to Indonesia shrunk by 18.6 percent (to 14.4 million), with Bali being the sole Indonesian destination to record an increase in foreign visitors. It is precisely in this sort of context that danger-zone tourism emerges.

Indonesian danger-zone tourism comes in various forms, reflecting the varied orientations and motivations of danger-zone tourists. At one end of the continuum are the independent budget travelers who make their way to cities like Dili and Banda Aceh, priding themselves on slipping into off-limits destinations. At the other end of the spectrum are the "reality tours" packaged by operations such as Global Exchange and even Indonesian travel houses. Interviews with independent travelers, examinations of danger-zone travel narratives, and perusal of advertisements for Indonesia "reality tours" suggest a number of themes in the imagery of urban danger-zone travel. These include the promise of having authentic encounters with grassroots actors, the potential for enhancing one's personal identity as an activist or humanitarian, and the allure of a unique, "exciting" travel experience that will distinguish the traveler from the growing hoards of ethnic and cultural tourists that now voyage to most corners of the globe. Let us examine this imagery.

My awareness of danger-zone group tours to urban destinations in Indonesia was first prompted by a newspaper advertisement for a planned March 1998 "reality tour" to Java billed as "Democracy and Culture of Resistance in Indonesia: Suharto's Last Term?" The tour was organized by Global Exchange, a San Francisco–based group. The imagery of authentic grassroots encounters is a recurrent theme in their webpage. As it explains, their "reality tours" are designed "to give people in the U.S. a chance to see firsthand how people facing immense challenges are finding grassroots solutions in their daily lives."[39] Moreover, "Reality Tours provide North Americans with a true understanding of a country's internal dynamic through socially responsible travel."[40] Here, then, we find the image of the politically correct traveler. For U.S.$2,150, tourists were invited to sign on for a group trip to Jakarta to witness the goings-on of the March 1998 preelections. The initial itinerary promised conversations with former political prisoners (including as a possibility the celebrated Indonesian writer Pramoedya), factory workers, and human rights activists. The pièce de résistance, however, was to "dialogue with Indonesians and observe the election day atmosphere in the capital." The repeated use of the word "resistance" and the emphasis on the tentative nature of the itinerary "due to circumstances beyond our control" offer a subtle background image of potential danger, as befits this particular special-interest market.

I Gede Ardika, Indonesia's Director General for Tourism, was quick to pick up on this special interest market. On March 5, 1999, he told reporters that several parties have welcomed the plan to turn the general election into a tourist attraction. For U.S.$200 a day, three Indonesian travel agencies were selling the "general election tourism package," which promised not only the latest update on the national election process, but a "close look" at the election process.[41] Not surprisingly, the theme of danger receded from the Indonesian packaging of the elections tours; however, the theme of accessing an exciting political event to which only few foreigners are privy remained.

The comingling of politics, idealism, and the rare opportunity for authentic face-to-face dialogues with Indonesians about potentially explosive issues does not only manifest itself in election-watch tours to Indonesia's capital city, but also in a religion-focused tour sponsored by the Hartford Seminary. Titled "With Muslims and Christians in Indonesia," this 1999 tour offered a firsthand experience that would "deepen participants' awareness of the state of Christian–Muslim relations and peace-making in the region by seeing the issues through the eyes of the indigenous communities."[42] Addressing recent upheavals in various cities in Indonesia, the webpage tour advertisement promised that "close attention will be given to the social, economic and ethnic reasons behind the recent unrest, and the role religious communities are playing, especially in relations to dialogue and understanding between Muslims and Christians."[43] As in the election-watch tours, here too we find the imagery of firsthand dialogues with local communities. In this case, however, the imagery of humanitarian and spiritual activism is even stronger.

Such "reality tours" to Indonesia's capital, where participants risk close-up encounters with political riots and religious violence, spotlight Jakarta as a member of the matrix of global cities. In essence, these danger tours underscore Jakarta's position as political center worthy of the world's attention. Moreover, these political and humanitarian tours' web-based imagery of potential urban violence and lurking unrest project perilous images of Indonesia's capital city. These Internet-propelled images, as well as returning participants' slide shows and travel tales, have the potential to subtly shift Euro-American sensibilities concerning the quality of urban Southeast Asian life. Ironically, such danger-zone tours simultaneously herald Jakarta's arrival as a global city and reify it as an unruly urban jungle. Having sketched Jakarta's paradoxical imaging as global city/global jungle, I turn to Southeast Asia's newest postcolonial capital city, Dili (East Timor), where I trace the traffic of danger-zone images of this city.

DILI, EAST TIMOR: A COLLAGE OF TRAVELER'S IMAGES, FROM INSALUBRIOUS FEVER TOWN TO SLEEPY OUTPOST TO SCARRED CITY

Chinese and Javanese traders seeking sandalwood and beeswax visited East Timor from as early as the thirteenth century; however, travelers' mentions of Dili are scant prior to the era of Portuguese colonialism. Portuguese explorers and traders began visiting the island in the early sixteenth century (around A.D. 1515). One of the earliest European maps and accounts of the island derives from Pigafetta, the son of an aristocratic Vicena family who joined Magellan as the chronicler of his voyage.[44] Following Magellan's demise in the Philippines, Pigafetta sailed to the Timor archipelago with Magellan's successor, Captain J. S. de Elcano. They landed in Amaben (on Timor's north coast) in January 1521, seeking provisions. Although Pigafetta recounts learning of Timor's white sandalwood and wax, no mention is made of Dili in this account of their travels. By 1556, a small group of Dominican friars had established Portugal's first outpost at Lifau. It is not until much later, however, that Dili becomes the seat of Portugese Timor and gains a growing place in the imagery of eastern Indonesia.

The English naturalist Alfred Russel Wallace offers one of the first images of Dili to be imparted to a wider European readership. Writing of his visit to Dili in the 1860s he conveys a miserable image of a lonely outpost town:

> Delli [Dili] is a most miserable place compared with even the poorest of the Dutch towns. The houses are all of mud and thatch; the fort is only a mud enclosure; and the custom-house and church are built of the same mean materials, with no attempt at decoration or even neatness. The whole aspect of the place is that of a poor native town, and there is no sign of cultivation or civilization round about it. His Excellency the Governor's house is the only one that makes any pretensions to appearance, and that is merely a low whitewashed cottage or bungalow. Yet there is one thing in which civilization exhibits itself—officials in black and white European costume, and officers in gorgeous uniforms abound in a degree quite disproportionate to the size or appearance of the place. The town being surrounded for some distance by swamps and mudflats is very unhealthy, and a single night often gives a fever to newcomers which not unfrequently proves fatal.[45]

Apparently Wallace's dismal imagery of Dili and Portuguese Timor lodged in the imagination of other nineteenth century British travelers. From 1878 to 1883 the British naturalist Henry Forbes traveled in eastern Indonesia and offers his "field notes made during [his own] wanderings to be considered in light of an *addendum* to . . . [Wallace's] model book of travel."[46] As Forbes submits in his preface, his publication represents the first detailed account of the inhabitants of the interior of Timor. Indeed, it offers not only a wealth of early images of the island's inhabitants but of the town of Dili as well. Accompanied by his wife, Forbes arrives in Dili by steamer in late 1881. His initial impressions are hardly positive:

> Landing [in Dili] later in the day, we perambulated the town, which wanted much before it could be termed neat or clean or other than dilapidated, but when we afterwards came to know how terribly insalubrious it is, we were surprised that the incessant fever and languor which made life on the lowlands an absolute burden left a particle of energy in anybody to care for anything. The supreme evil of Dilly[47] is its having been built on a low morass, when it might have stood far more salubriously on the easily accessible slopes close behind it.[48]

The sapping fever and pestilence of the city are steady themes in Forbes's subsequent commentary on Dili. Upon returning to Dili after a foray to the Moluccas, Forbes is horrified by the emaciated countenances Dili has produced in his European acquaintances.

> In all of them the notorious Dilly fever had killed down the cheerful vivacity, buoyancy of spirit and bright eye with which they had stepped ashore in the month of May. With the utmost kindness commodious apartments were offered to us in the Palace, but it was perfectly evident that if I wished to accomplish any serious work in Timor, it could not be from Dilly as a center, constantly exposed to the pestilence that nightly rises from the marshes surrounding the town.[49]

Forbes's text also offers glimpses into the ways in which his vision of Dili is refracted through Alfred Wallace's prior text:

> The town, though vastly improved since Mr. Wallace's visit, was still disappointing in may respects, and its Hibiscus-lined streets looked poor and uninviting. The lack of money to carry out efficiently the necessary municipal arrangements was painfully evident. . . . had the necessary resources been at [the local officers'] disposal, Portuguese Timor might have caught the tide of prosperity she had long waited for. . . .

Forbes's recordings convey not only his aversions to the city but also some of its appeal to European naturalist-explorers. He is unabashed in his fascination with the city as a crossroads of peoples, languages, and cultures:

> In going into the various offices and shops I was struck to find all business conducted not, as in the Dutch possessions, in the *lingua* franca of the Archipelago, Malay, but in Portuguese. . . . In the different quarters of the town native police posted in little encampments are always on guard, and during the still nights it was curious to hear from Timorese throats the *Alerto sta!* at the stroke of every hour. Besides the official staff very few Europeans live in Dilly; the entire trade of the island being conducted by Arabs and (chiefly) by Chinamen.
>
> The streets of Dilly itself offer to the traveller a fine studio for ethnological investigation, for a curious mixture of nationalities other than European rub shoulders with each other in the town's narrow limits. . . . Tall, erect indigenes mingle with Negroes from the Portuguese possessions of Mozambique and the coasts of Africa, most of them here in the capacity of soldiers or condemned criminals; tall lithe East Indians from Goa and its neighbourhood; Chinese and Bugis of Makassar, with Arabs and Malays and natives from Allor, Savu, Roti, and Flores; besides a crowd in whose veins the degree of comminglement of blood of all these races would defy the acutest compu-

tation. . . . The shop of Ah Ting, Major of the Chinese, was my favorite study-room while in Dilly, for there during the whole day came and went an endless succession of these nationalities for the purpose of barter or simply to lounge.[50]

Forbes's sojourn in Portuguese Timor was ultimately cut short. After several months of ornithological and ethnological work, Forbes's wife became violently ill with "Dilly fever" and, so five months after their arrival, they fled Dili on a mail steamer. For almost a hundred years following Forbes's account, travelers' images of Dili rarely surfaced in widely viewed media. A 1943 *National Geographic* article profiled Timor as a "key to the Indies,"[51] conveying the perception of the island as being of great strategic importance in World War II. However, it is not until 1962 that American readers are treated to a new set of adventurers' images of the city. This time, the images come via a final *National Geographic* installment of the Schreiders' amphibious jeep trip across the Indonesian archipelago.[52] The Schreiders arrive in Dili following a harrowing stormy night crossing the sea between Alor and Timor. Eerily, the tone of their danger-laden arrival in Dili and their description of the city with its "scars of war" foreshadow some contemporary danger-zone travel narratives:

> At the end of nine hours we were desperate to reach land. In spite of the ever-growing metallic cadence from the engine, I again increased our speed. Slowly details became distinct through the binoculars: first a lighthouse, then the red roof of a military post, finally the rows of trees marking the road to Dili, capital of Portuguese Timor.
>
> When the last swell pushed *Tortuga* ashore, we knew how Captain Bligh must have felt when he ended his own small boat journey on this same island 173 years ago.
>
> Dili was still rebuilding from World War II. Despite Portugal's neutrality, Timor had been occupied by the Japanese and had suffered heavy bombardment. By the end of the war its sandalwood—long a lure for traders—was gone, its coffee plantations were overgrown, its cattle herds decimated, and most of its white Portuguese population dead of starvation, sickness or reprisals. Only the newly rebuilt residential area, clinic, church and government building gave evidence of what Dili would become.[53]

In the years until 1974, when images of Dili surface in adventurers' travel accounts, they are generally that of a quiet colonial outpost, or a regional crossroads. It is not until the tumultuous events of the mid-1970s that Dili bursts into global consciousness once again, setting the stage for it to become a magnet city for international danger-zone travelers.

DILI: URBAN DESTINATION FOR DANGER-ZONE TOURISTS

Today, as in the post-WWII period, the dominant image of Dili is once again that of a "scarred" city. Following a military coup in Portugal in 1974, East Timor was poised for independence when Indonesia invaded. An estimated 200,000 people perished in the ensuing battle and famine. By July 1976, amid international controversy, East Timor was declared Indonesia's twenty-seventh province and Dili its capital. For most of the twenty-four years that East Timor was occupied by Indonesia, the area was closed to foreign travelers, as Indonesian troops attempted to suppress the Fretilin[54] resistance movement. However, for a brief period in the late 1980s and 1990s, Indonesia opened the city to foreign tourists. During this window period, Dili becomes a featured city in eastern Indonesian tourist guidebooks and web-based travel accounts. The imagery of these tour books is notably tame in contrast with travelers' Dili diaries. One officially sanctioned guidebook from this period spotlights Dili as "A Slowly Awakening Capital City," "super-clean and yet soul-less"[55]: a city of "ruler-strait one-way streets" boasting the largest cathedral in all of Southeast Asia. Another web-based guide describes Dili as a

> quiet, clean town with a very colonial feel, the long sea front road is littered with old Portuguese mansions and offices. Many of the streets behind are strewn with old bond houses and sailors' quarters and give a quick idea of the large export business the Chinese and Portuguese ran from here. With its large supermarkets, hip clothes' shops, traffic lights and wide streets it exudes a wealth and sophistication unlike any other city in this part of Indonesia.[56]

While this web-based guide to Dili Regency goes on to note the large military and police contingent in Dili, it downplays the theme of touristic danger. Indeed, most Indonesian-government sanctioned guidebooks of this period avoid accentuating that Portuguese colonialism had been replaced by Indonesian colonialism. Instead, the officially approved tour books of the late 1980s and early 1990s touted the colorful vestiges of Dili's Portuguese colonial history, or hailed Dili's recent emergence as an urban hub of eastern Indonesia. Dili is scarcely linked to danger in the pages of these books. In contrast, a number of banned guidebooks and travelers' web-based chronicles of their adventures in Dili draw heavily on the imagery of threat and imperilment. For instance, a Canadian's web journal entry describes his and his wife's trip to Dili as follows:

> At the first road junction we encountered, just before coming into Dili, there was a check point where we had to get out of the bus and go into a police post. The plainclothes man there took down all our particulars. We were on our way back on to the bus when we were called over to the military post on

the other side of the road . . . where we were surrounded by soldiers in full battle dress armed with M16s, while they again took down all our particulars. It was a little tense.[57]

Accompanying this writer's account of this trip are excerpts from the *Jakarta Post* and other newspapers on the violence that had transpired in Dili just weeks before their arrival. The writer's friends at home and other curious web surfers were thus offered journalistic "proof" of these intrepid travelers' brushes with danger.

A New Zealand traveler's web-based account of his 1998 visit to Dili paints a similarly militaristic image of the city. Again, as with some of the entries in *Fielding's The World's Most Dangerous Places,* we find the initial imagery of tranquility yielding to that of insipient violence:

It was a beautiful morning as the boat approached the Dili port. The sea was calm. In the distance stood the prominent Motael Church and other old Portuguese buildings visible through the scattered trees. In the background were the browned hills. All of this created a sense of tranquility. Not exactly the feeling I expected to be having on arrival in East Timor. It was short-lived, as on the wharf stood armed uniformed soldiers and a handful of police. Like thistles on a golf course, soldiers nullify a tranquil environment. For the next eleven days spent in East Timor, I observed how thoroughly permeated the Indonesian military and police force are in East Timorese lives. In the main part of Dili there are several barracks. Out towards the airport in Comoro, two large military trucks full of soldiers from Battalion 744—all wearing bullet-proof vests and guns deliberately visible—came thundering down the main road. . . .

The Indonesian government appear [sic] to be promoting tourism in the country, but in reality they don't want foreigners there. More chance of their crimes being exposed. But it is beneficial for East Timorese that more travelers visit their country. . . . It presents an opportunity to disclose their situation to more foreigners. And also it would make it easier for human rights activists and journalists to enter and move around the country.[58]

By the late 1990s, as global pressure for East Timor's independence intensified, and tensions and violence mounted, Indonesia cracked down on tourist visas to the region. It is in this period that urban danger-zone travelers' interest in Dili intensified. The imagery in the narratives of some of these independently traveling danger-zone tourists parallels that found in the election-watch group tours to Jakarta discussed earlier, where potentially explosive urban destinations commingle with the travelers' self-images as activists, humanitarians, or travelers seeking journalistic firsthand experiences. As one Australian man planning a 1999 adventure in Dili and East Timor explained to me,

> The reason that I'm going [there] is as much for the adrenalin as it is for the ethical side that is if I can do something, anything, to help then I'm obligated to. The crew that I'll be traveling with and myself are all environmental activists in Australia and for me that is my full-time job. Living in and touring the forests of Oz in a kind of bourgeois, middle class, pacifist, guerrilla war gives me as much satisfaction for doing "the right thing" as it does for providing me with the rush of doing illegal stuff in the middle of the night in the forest. You see the same crew at the camps all over Australia, most are transients and all do it for the reasons that I have just mentioned.[59]

Clearly, the allure of urban danger-zone travel is complex. For some, humanitarianism intermingles with addiction to adrenalin rushes while for others the desire to witness news-in-the-making is paramount. As an American applied social science researcher in his mid-30s told me when he learned of my interest in danger travelers and Dili,

> I went to Dili for a long weekend, just to see what was happening there. That's how I spend my vacations, going to places like Kosovo and the Balkans. For a while, a few years back, I even toyed with the idea of starting a hot-spot travel agency. There are a lot of people like me, interested in experiencing these places . . . and understanding firsthand what is going on.[60]

As the news of East Timorese resistance movements became more prominent on the global electromagnetic stream, Dili drew increasing numbers of activists. Their web postings further enhanced Dili's appeal to urban danger-zone travelers. An Australian university student's web-based journal of his early 1998 trip to Dili to meet members of the East Timorese resistance offers a sample of an activist's portrait of the city:

> Thursday. Arrived in Dili. Everything on the ground hot and dry. Taxi driver soothed our jangling nerves with loud Billy Ocean tunes. . . . Stopped in a café for a warm lemonade. Three police armed with automatic rifles sat next to us. Got spooked by the guns and had to leave. Tried to look like bank clerks rather than student activists. . . .
> Friday. . . . Wandered by the University—the scene only two months ago of the shooting of students during their mid-year exams. Made our first contact with clandestine student operatives. Told to return tomorrow. In the afternoon we climbed Christus Raja, the second largest statue of Christ in the world, kindly donated to the "liberated peoples of East Timor" by Suharto. The statue stands 27 metres high (to symbolize East Timor as "Indonesia's 27th province") on an ocean cliff top facing Jakarta with open arms.[61]

In other danger-zone travelers' accounts, activist and humanitarian interests take a backseat to the imagery of fearless ventures to a life-imperiling site. As one Australian man who had visited Dili commented in an e-mail to me,

> I've got some friends over there now in a non-work capacity. They had to sneak in as no tourist visas are being offered. The sh** is really going down there now and caucasion [sic] people are being targeted. The scenary [sic] is great and ordinary people are cool but unless you are like my friends who are there for an adrenalin [sic] rush then your timing sucks. Keep in mind the Indonesian people (yes I know the Timorese are a hugely different ethnic group) invented the word amock [sic] ie. Run amock [sic] and in Indonesian it means to spontaneously lose control in a frenzy. I've been around when this has happened before. . . .[62]

In late August, just days before the above e-mail was sent, a historic election organized by UNAMET (United Nations Mission in East Timor) resulted in 78.5 percent of East Timor's population voting for independence from Indonesia. The celebration was short-lived: Within days of the September 4, 1999, announcement of election results, armed militia groups backed by the Indonesian military had tortured and killed tens of thousands of East Timorese and had torched much of the city of Dili. Eventually, UN forces suppressed the slaughter and the Indonesian government agreed to grant autonomy to East Timor. Through much of late 1999, nightly CNN telecasts transmitted images of the ravaged capital of Dili round the globe, and newspapers worldwide featured front-page accounts of the devastation. By October, the United Nations Transitional Administration in East Timor (UNTAET) was established to oversee East Timor's transition to independence. Foreign aid workers and entrepreneurs flooded into the country, and volunteer political observers and still more danger-zone travelers have followed. Their accounts of their harrowing, haunting, frivolous, and daring experiences are prevalent on the Internet, in the form of diaries, reports, and postings to danger-zone webpages. A sampling of the titles of these postings conveys the predominant themes: "Terror and Fear on the Streets of Dili,"[63] "Dilly Dally,"[64] and "Tempest in Timor."[65] Although it is varied in content, one Australian adventurer's web journal of his April 2000 visit to Dili conveys a number of salient images and offers a new take on the history, layering, and structuring of the global in newly postcolonial Dili:

> We catch a bemo[66] to Dili. After a ten minute ride I'm in one of the most depressing places I have ever seen. I have never been in a war zone before and the sights are quite shocking. Now all the destructions are on a much larger scale, multi-story buildings are deprived of everything but their outer shell, block after block. Only a couple are repaired, one is a huge white palace-like structure, the governor's or government palace, with big UNTAET signs on

it and the roof (corrugated iron) being painted green right now. That's the place that first had the Portuguese in it, then the Indonesians, now the UN. To the average Timorese it's perhaps just the change of some meaningless sign anyway. Soon the CNRT will take residence and the big black Volvos will replace the Landrovers.

At the moment, Dili has probably the population of Darwin and that's the end of the comparison. . . .

We . . . walk around the town a bit. It is not a pretty sight, although most of the rubble has been cleaned up. There is still the occasional rampaged building with all the debris inside, a couple recently renovated— a hotel, a Telstra office, but the overall impression remains. And on top of that there are the vehicles—lots of 4WDs, the ever-present bemos, scooters and bicycles, and occasionally a sedan, usually big ones—Mercedeses, Fords, curiously enough some Lancias, the black Volvos of the CNRT. The plates are a real Babylon, from all over the world, making Dili the most cosmopolitan place to be. If you're a car plate.

It's time to go back to the airport. I'm utterly depressed by the sight-seeing and just want to get out of here.[67]

FINAL RUMINATIONS

A pervasive theme in these Internet diaries and in recent danger-zone travelers' images is that of Dili as a shell of a city—a scarred city. In a physical sense, after the destruction of 1999, Dili is an anti-city, a city of spaces where buildings once were. But these spectral memories lend it all the more salience as a postcolonial global entity. Dili's terror scars have drawn the international media and international curiosity-seekers. The city's scars are filmed, televised, photographed, and reproduced in newspapers and on the Net, transporting the idea of Dili (and independent postcolonial Timor) into living rooms and studies around the world. And yet, ironically, these Dili images circulating through the global electromagnetic stream are only visible in the living rooms of the most privileged of Timorese today. Those Timorese without homes, roofs, or electricity are obliged to haunt actual ruins, rather than view virtual ruins from the comfort of their armchairs.

Meanwhile, entrepreneurs, global marketers, UN staff, international consultants, and danger-zone tourists continue to flock to Dili. The wealthiest among them, however, need no longer stay amid the scars of the city: As of October 2000, a deluxe Thai-owned floating hotel has been docked in the Dili Harbor.[68] The Central Maritime Hotel, a former cruise ship, is outfitted with hundreds of rooms, a swimming pool, speedy Net connections, and other assorted business and leisure services.[69] In essence, this floating hotel (and the floating offices in the white government palace of Dili) may well be harbingers of the "mobile city of hypermodernity."[70] Dili shares traits of what John Armitage and Joanne Roberts have termed a "gray zone of total mobilization,"[71] a city divorced from the temporal and territorial, characterized by "emergency and disintegration" and based on a "mentality of total mobilization." In this sense, danger-zone tourism offers a lens for understanding Dili and other Southeast Asian urban danger destinations as futural cities in other ways.

Urban danger-zone tourism is very much a product of the global era. However, as the examination of earlier imagery of Dili suggests, there is a parallel in earlier colonial eras. Then, as today, adventurers harvested new experiences in what they considered exotic outposts, and marketed these novel tales back in the homeland. Today, CNN news coverage of the world's hot spots, worldwide networks of activists, and Internet danger-zone travel sites have fueled the global traffic in images of postcolonial (and futural) urban jungles such as Dili, facilitating the blossoming of urban danger-zone tourism. Danger-zone tourists are generally fueled by global politics, their itineraries inspired by the imagery of nightly news reports from the world's tumultuous zones. As I have suggested, urban danger-zone tourism has the potential to subtly shift nontravelers' sensibilities concerning the quality of urban Southeast Asian life. Their adventure tales are recounted, and their web-based travelogues with images of urban strife zones are read and amplified by cybervoyagers round the globe. Danger-zone travel, then, both inscribes cities such as Dili and Jakarta as a global metropoles, and simultaneously marks them as wild urban jungles.

NOTES

I wish to thank Peter Sanchez and Ryan Bishop for their encouragement and suggestions. The Centre for Advanced Studies at the National University of Singapore and the Singapore Tourism Board generously provided me with an Isaac Manasseh Meyer Fellowship that facilitated my initial explorations of the topic of danger-zone tourism in Southeast Asia. I am grateful for their support, as well as for thoughtful comments at this earlier stage from colleagues at the National University of Singapore, especially Ryan Bishop and Maribeth Erb. Portions of this work appeared in my 2001 article "Danger-Zone Tourism: Prospects and Problems for Tourism in Tumultuous Times" in *Interconnected Worlds: Tourism in Southeast Asia*, ed. Peggy Teo, T. C. Chang, and K. C. Ho (New York: Pergamon Press, 2001), 265–81.

1. Helen and Frank Schreider, "From the Hair of Siva: *Tortuga II* Explores the Ganges," *National Geographic* 118, no. 4 (October 1960): 445.
2. Helen and Frank Schreider, "Indonesia: The Young and Troubled Island Nation," *National Geographic* 119, no. 5 (May 1961): 579.
3. See Carolyn Cartier, "Megadevelopment in Malaysia: From Heritage Landscapes to 'Leisurescapes' in Melaka's Tourism Sector," *Singapore Journal of Tropical Geography* 19, no. 2 (1998): 151–76; T. C. Chang, "From 'Instant Asia' to 'Multi-faceted Jewel': Urban Imaging Strategies and Tourism Development in Singapore," *Urban Geography* 18, no. 6 (1997): 542–62; Joel Kahn, "Culturalizing Malaysia: Globalism, Tourism, Heritage and the City in Georgetown," in *Tourism, Ethnicity and the State in Asian and Pacific Societies,* ed. Michel Picard and Robert Wood (Honolulu: University of Hawaii Press, 1997), 99–127.
4. Kathleen M. Adams, "Museum/City/Nation: Negotiating Meaning and Identities in Urban Museums in Indonesia and Singapore," in *Theorizing the Asian City as Text,* ed. Robbie Goh and Brenda Yeoh (Singapore: World Scientific Press/Singapore University Press, in press); T. C. Chang, "Renaissance Revisited: Singapore as a 'Global City for the Arts,' " *International Journal of Urban and Regional Research* 24, no. 4 (2000), 818–31.

5. Bali Online, "Welcome to Jakarta," *Jakarta Tourism,* 1995–1997. http://www.indo.com/jakarta/tourism.html Accessed 20 December 2001.
6. Ryan Bishop and Lillian Robinson, *Night Market: Sexual Cultures and the Thai Economic Miracle* (New York: Routledge, 1998); W. C. Gartner and J. Shen, "The Impact of Tiananmen Square on China's Tourism Image," *Journal of Travel Research* 30, no. 4 (1992): 47–52; Linda Richter, "Political Instability and Tourism in the Third World," in *Tourism and the Less Developed Countries,* ed. D. Harrison (London: Belhaven, 1992), 35–46; Michael Parnwell, "Tourism, Globalisation, and Critical Security in Myanmar and Thailand," *Singapore Journal of Tropical Geography* 19, no. 2 (1998): 212–31.
7. A. Pizam and Y. Mansfield, eds., *Tourism, Crime, and International Security Issues* (Chichester: Wiley, 1996); D. Wilson, "Tourism, Public Policy, and the Image of Northern Ireland Since the Troubles," in *Tourism in Ireland: A Critical Analysis,* ed. B. O'Connor and M. Cronin (Cork, Ireland: Cork University Press, 1993), 138–61; Gartner and Shen, "Impact of Tiananmen Square."
8. Malcolm Crick, "Representations of Sun, Sex, Sights, Savings, and Servility: International Tourism in the Social Sciences," *Annual Review of Anthropology* 18 (1989): 309.
9. Richter, "Political Instability," 36.
10. For a fuller exposition of this concept, see Adams's "Danger-Zone Tourism."
11. A number of public policy planners, social science teachers, and activists were also among the danger-zone tourists I interviewed.
12. A. Garland, *The Beach* (London: Penguin, 1997). In the film version of *The Beach,* released with great hoopla in early 2000, the British hero of the novel has been transformed into an American backpacker traveler. In both versions, however, the action is set in Thailand and the hero is a young man who deliberately targets dangerous, off-the-beaten-track destinations believing that risk-packed experiences would make him more worldly and interesting.
13. Ibid., 164.
14. Anon Fielding's Black Flag Café website: http://www.fieldingtravel.com. (2000).
15. Andre, "My First War," posted on *Fielding's Black Flag Adventure Forum,* 20 February 2000. http://www.fieldingtravel.com.
16. Robert Young Pelton, C. Aral, and W. Dulles, *Fielding's The World's Most Dangerous Places* (Redondo Beach, Calif.: Fielding Worldwide, 1998).
17. Cited in Pelton, et al., *Fielding's,* cover.
18. Torun Elsrud notes that, while in Thailand conducting field research, she observed tourists sporting war-related T-shirts with slogans such as "Beware of Mines—Cambodia" or "Saigon" with an image of a gun. As Elsrud comments, "It appeared quite a few travelers and other tourists took a few weeks in Cambodia or Vietnam and at least some returned to Bangkok with these T-shirts as a symbolic expression of their trip" (personal e-mail communication, 1999).
19. T. Mitchell, *Colonising Egypt* (Berkeley: University of California Press, 1991), 57.
20. Diller and Scofidio, *Back to the Front: Tourisms of War* (Basse-Normandie, France: FRANC, 1994), 136. Also cited in P. Phipps, "Tourists, Terrorists, Death, and Value," in *Travel Worlds: Journeys in Contemporary Cultural Politics,* ed. R. Kaur and J. Hutnyk (London and New York: Zed Books, 1999), 83.
21. Phipps, "Tourists, Terrorists," 83.
22. W. J. Pitts, "Uprising in Chiapas, Mexico: Zapata Lives—Tourism Falters," in *Tourism, Crime, and International Security Issues,* ed. A. Pizam and Y. Mansfield (Chicester: Wiley, 1996), 215–27.
23. Ibid., 221.
24. Quoted in Pitts, "Uprising," 224.
25. Torun Elsrud, personal e-mail communication, 1999.
26. Valene Smith, "War and Its Tourist Attractions," in *Tourism, Crime,* 247–64.
27. For related explorations of forms of war tourism, also see C. de Burlo, "Islanders, Soldiers, and Tourists: The War and the Shaping of Tourism in Melanesia," in *The Pacific Theater: Island Representations of World War II,* ed. G. White and L. Lindstrom (Honolulu: University of Hawaii Press, 1989); Geoffrey White, "Museum/Memorial/Shrine: National Narrative in National Spaces," *Museum Anthropology* 21, no. 1 (1997): 8–26; L. Yoneyama, "Memory Matters: Hiroshima's Korean Atom Bomb Memorial and the Politics of Ethnicity," *Public Culture* 7, no. 3 (1995): 499–527; J. E. Young, *The Texture of Memory: Holocaust Memorials and Meaning* (New Haven: Yale University Press, 1995).
28. Torun Elsrud, "Risk Creation in Traveling: Risk-taking as Narrative and Practice in Backpacker Culture," *Annals of Tourism Research* 28, no. 2 (2001): 597–617.
29. Pelton, et al., *Fielding's.*
30. Kathleen M. Adams, " 'Come to Tana Toraja, Land of the Heavenly Kings': Travel Agents as Brokers in Ethnicity," *Annals of Tourism Research* 11, no. 3 (1984): 469–85.

31. Pelton, et al., *Fielding's,* 364.
32. Ibid., 368.
33. Ibid., 369.
34. Mike "Cambodia," posted on *Fielding's Black Flag Café,* 5 February 2000. http://www.fieldingtravel.com.
35. Pelton, et al., *Fielding's,* 613–14.
36. Ibid., 614.
37. Ibid., 614–15.
38. Tom Mintier, "Indonesian Tourism Industry Battered by Images of Violence," *CNN.com,* 26 September 1999, http://www.cnn.com/ASIANOW/southeast/9909/26/indonesian.tourism/.
39. Global Exchange, "Democracy and Culture of Resistance in Indonesia: Suharto's Last Term?" *Global Exchange Reality Tours,* 18 August 1999. http://www.globalexchange.org/tours/indonesiaItin1.html.
40. Ibid.
41. Asia Pulse, 19 August 1999, http://wysiwyg://98/http://www.skali.com/business/eco/199903/05/eco19990305_07.html.
42. Hartford Seminary, http://www.hart.sem.edu/macd/events/Default.htm. (1999).
43. Ibid.
44. Donald Lach, *Asia in the Making of Europe* (Chicago: University of Chicago Press, 1965), 173.
45. Alfred Russel Wallace, *The Malay Archipelago* (London: Macmillan and Co., 1869).
46. Henry O. Forbes, *A Naturalist's Wanderings in the Eastern Archipelago: A Narrative of Travel and Exploration from 1978 to 1883* (New York: Harper & Brothers, 1885), 286.
47. The older orthography of Dili.
48. Forbes, *Naturalist's,* 286.
49. Ibid., 415.
50. Ibid., 417–18.
51. Stuart St. Clair, "Timor: A Key to the Indies," *National Geographic,* September 1943, 355–84.
52. Helen and Frank Schreider, "East from Bali by Seagoing Jeep to Timor," *National Geographic* 122, no. 2 (August 1962): 236–79.
53. Ibid., 275–76.
54. The Frente Revolucianario de Este Timor Independente (Revolutionary Front for an Independent East Timor).
55. Kal Muller, *East of Bali: From Lombok to Timor* (Lincolnwood, Ill.: Passport Books, 1995), 230.
56. P. R. Ryan, *Timor: A Traveler's Guide,* 1993, 1998. http://members.tripod.com/balloon_2/.
57. Anon "Part III—Nusa Tenggara Timor 1991–1992 Travel Diary," http://www.infomatch.com/~denysm/indon913.htm.
58. Ian Sugden, "Ian Sugden in East Timor," *Stu Web Site Production,* 1998. http://homepages.ihug.co.nz/~stu/fret/ian_sugden.html.
59. Personal communication, 30 August 1999.
60. Personal interview, 25 August 1999.
61. AVCAT, "A Short Trip to East Timor—Extract from Travel Journal," *Timor Lorosae,* 30 March 1998. http://www.geocities.com/capitolhill/senate/7112/essay_01.htm.
62. Personal e-mail communication, 2 September 1999.
63. Jerald Joseph, "Terror and Fear on the Streets of Dili," *Pax Romana ICMICA,* 2 September 1999. http://www.geocities.com/capitolhill/lobby/9491/pub/etimor/jerald.html.
64. Marie Javins, "Marie's World Tour: Second Installment, Australia to Cambodia, February–March 2001," *GoNOMAD.com,* 2001. http://www.gonomad.com/caravan/0105/javins_worldtour2.html.
65. Louise Chernetz, "Tempest in Timor," *East Timor Alert Network (ETAN) Canada,* October 1998. http://www.etan.ca/winnipeg/louise.html.
66. A minibus often used as a form of public transport in Indonesia and East Timor.
67. G.Y.T., "7: 2/4/2000, Dili–Darwin," *Unfolding Timor,* 2000. http://www.geocities.com/untimor/7/7.html.
68. Scoop: East Timor. "Tourism Gets to Dili," *Lonely Planet,* 6 October 2000. http://www.lonelyplanet.com/scoop/asi/tim.htm.
69. Ibid. As the Lonely Planet Travel News Review notes, the hotel "seems to have a penchant for anchoring luxury tourism in dubious destinations, as it was previously floating in Yangon, Myanmar."
70. See John Armitage and Joanne Roberts, "From the Hypermodern City to the Gray Zone of Total Mobilization in the Philippines," found in this volume.
71. Ibid.

Like Adams, Bishop and Clancey set their sights on an aspect of the global city that is rarely conceptualized in the mainstream literature of global culture, political economy, urbanism, or colonial and postcolonial history: the target. Yet as their painstakingly researched article shows, a global city tends to achieve its status to the extent that it can be regarded as a target of some kind. The targeting of cities would not be simply a matter for civil defense, emergency services, and the military, who are responsible for responding to a variety of disasters, catastrophes, and attacks, but also (and by the same principles) the global city is the target for multinational corporations as well as refugees, immigrants, transmigrants, and settlers of all kinds. The postcolonial city, in this respect, is both exemplary and exceptional. For instance, it was these cities, during the era of European imperialism, that were targeted in early experiments with aerial bombing, marking out these cities as being in a real sense more advanced than cities like London, Berlin, and Paris, which would only later enjoy the expansion to global status by becoming targets during World War I. Bishop and Clancey maintain their focus as they move into a discussion of the intensification of targeting phenomena during the Cold War and post–Cold War eras, observing how increases in speed of targeting, and speed of delivery to the target and impact correspond with the increasing speed of the perpetual cycle of urban destruction, renewal, and reconstruction that dominates global cities. Completed six days before the notorious attacks on the World Trade Center in New York on September 11, 2001, this article need not be considered simply as prophetic. Rather, it is worth acknowledging the extent to which the patterns of historicity it outlines are becoming increasingly intense.

3

The City as Target, or Perpetuation and Death

RYAN BISHOP AND GREGORY CLANCEY

For a child it is extraordinary to see to what degree a city can be obliterated in a single bombardment. For a kid, a city is like the Alps, it's eternal, like the mountains. One single bombardment and all is razed. These are the traumatizing events which shaped my thinking.   —*Paul Virilio*[1]

Life is haunted and filled with the idea of protection.   —*Adolf Hitler*[2]

As the global city emerges ever more hegemonic, the attention it reaps is not always welcome. Attention is another word for targeting. The city is a target for a range of catastrophes from natural disasters (such as earthquakes, floods, tornados, hurricanes, tidal waves, and plagues) to those of more obvious human construction (chemical spills, factory explosions, and mass transit accidents or derailments), strategic geopolitical targeting (official military aggression to terrorist attacks), large-scale macro-investments (International Monetary Fund or World Bank interventionism, UN development schemes), more modest global investing (by multinational corporations, advertising campaigns, Information Technology networks, real estate speculation, global capital maneuvering, currency markets, satellite imaging of neighborhoods for marketing purposes), planned (il)legal immigration (foreign labor for menial tasks), or unplanned illegal immigration (refugees fleeing war, famines, ethnic cleansing). The list hints at the range of the tropological and intellectual terrain proffered by the city-as-target model. Their density of population, material goods, and wealth have made cities, from their inception, simultaneously a given culture's goal (future and potential glory realized) and vulnerability (future and potential destruction of the culture's perceived trajectory).

The city is a lure to both settlers and sackers, something to shoot *for* as well as shoot *at*. In the earliest secular work in the Western intellectual tradition, *The Iliad,* Homer evocatively captures the inescapable duality of the city by exploiting the pun in the Greek word *kredemnon,* which means both veil and battlement. When Andromache watches from the walls of Troy as her husband, Hektor, is dragged in death behind Achilles's chariot, she removes her veil. Both she and the city are undone by the failure of the veil/battlement to protect and by its success in attracting undesired attention. This sense of the city as both stronghold and Achilles's heel, as it were—physically manifested in the walled fortress—was best realized in the collective Western imagination with the metonymies of Rome and Carthage.

As the Enlightenment yielded to Modernity, however, the memory of Carthage receded. Modernity, especially, avoided the confluence of urbanism and catastrophe. We are not just referring to the imaginary of catastrophe, but to the kind that produces bodies that have to be burned or buried and rubble that has to be cleared. Death on this scale was exceptional, exotic, or merely absent in the official and academic literature of the "The City," especially the dominant stream produced by urban theorists in the late nineteenth and twentieth centuries. "Decay" and related disease-terms were common, but these fell short of depicting large-scale destruction and death. The analogies were medical and therefore hopeful, rather than mordant or funereal. Biblical and Classical descriptions/celebrations of urban extinction, in which walled enclosures are entirely wiped out to the last inhabitant, had little counterpart in the The City discourse. Urbicide has been mainly encountered in politico-military histories whose central characters were not cities but armies and nation-states.[3]

Why could catastrophe not be Modern? Beginning with the Bible and then reinforced by the rise of ancient history and archeology in the nineteenth century, the destruction of cities was a theme readily available to academic narratives, in both their religious and secular manifestations; however, the theme grew increasingly attenuated, and eventually petered out. The demarcation between Modern and Ancient, from the perspective of the nineteenth century, was between the time when whole cities were destroyed and their inhabitants slaughtered, and the time when that no longer happened—when cities instead built glass exhibit halls for each other's steam engines and wallpaper. The hinge was perhaps the Napoleanic War, when urban sacking was sporadic and relatively contained. While Europeans continued to raze African and Asian cities, it now came to be reported under words like "retaken," "pacified," or "civilized."[4]

The destruction of cities became a show at the periphery. The non-European world was read as still-Ancient and/or subject to rule by Nature (including human natures in need of taming). Earthquakes, the most newsworthy city-destroyers of the period between the beginning of the Enlightenment and World War II, generally happened far from the North Atlantic power-grid, in a geography largely coterminous with the orientalized world. The most dramatic destruction of a major European city between Lisbon (1755) and Warsaw (1939) was the earthquake-induced disappearance of Reggio/Calabria in 1907, cities on the southern fringe of a metropole that had moved decisively north and out of the seismic zone in the seventeenth to eighteenth centuries. The United States provided more regular examples, such as Chicago in flames, followed by San Francisco. Here it was an East–West axis that projected the images of natural disaster against geographies already considered disordered, violent, and overly spontaneous. Media-centers consumed urban catastrophe as exotic news, safe from any sense of their own vulnerabilities.

In the natural sciences, the nineteenth century replacement of "catastrophism" with "uniformatarianism" made sudden disaster an epiphenomenon of natural history, and rendered steady progress in historical time more natural as a result. Where the destruction of Lisbon had given the Enlightenment pause, the destruction of Chicago (1871) or Tokyo (1923) only accelerated the tempo of nascent global capitalism. In the age of trans-city finance, destruction came to be seen as prelude to a reconstruction synonymous with growth or evolution. Disaster was mitigated for an influential few. The rest suffered as before, but their damage was now collateral.

Yet if the perpetuation of the The City in Modernist discourse was partly conditioned by catastrophe-avoidance, the same cannot be true for The City in its post-WWII, hyper-Modern form. That war was, after all, an absolute orgy of city-killing. The premeditated murder of very large cities was one of its most salient characteristics, Hiroshima and Dresden being only the iconographic examples. The genealogy of catastrophe visited upon ancient cities was consciously articulated in names bestowed on targeting plans; for example, the assault on Hamburg was called "Operation Gomorrah."[5] As in the Old Testament, all cities became potential "cities on the plains," with few fitting another typology found in the Pentateuch: "cities of refuge." The rise of modern architecture and "The Architect" as a god-figure—and of architectural history as about the future more than the past—was partly due to the opportunities to rebuild urban centers laid flat by (mostly) Allied air forces. The modern bomber, a design icon for the prewar Le Corbusier, became a major technological facilitator of his postwar influence. And this was no irony. The master-builders, especially from Hausmann onward, were first master-targeters and master-destroyers, although their acts of ground-clearing have left far fewer traces in the historical record. The bulldozer, was as much a legacy of World War II as penicillin and DDT.

To renew the question, How is it that, in the aftermath of 1940 to 1945, the most sustained period of urban disaster since Tamerlane, and continuing through a period of global targeting for future urban catastrophism on a near-total scale, The City remained a multidisciplinary discourse almost utterly shorn of catastrophic tropes?[6] One reason is The City's heroic status in both capitalist and socialist storytelling. It was not only the actor, but the stage, scenery, and audience in a drama of irreversible world-historical change. The thunderous collapse into one another of modernization and urbanization was one of the few "emperial" spectacles that collectively bound politicians and intellectuals of all persuasions, at least until the final quarter of the twentieth century. More mundanely, urban planning, architecture, art, and journalism—the professions who most controlled the object of The City—were also most dependant on cities as work-sites. The suburb, and all that-was-not-The-City, was often construed as their enemy. Death—centered now in the soul—was relocated outside the city gates. Until Stephen Spielberg's portrayal of the liquidation of the Krakow ghetto in the 1993 film *Schindler's List,* even the Holocaust was presented in media images as mainly a suburban phenomenon. The banality of evil that made Auschwitz possible, from certain abstracting perspectives, can seem akin to the banality of postwar Levittown—better to leave The City out of it.

The absence of death within The City reflected the larger economy of death within the academy: its studied absence from some disciplines and compensatory over-representation in others. History (the discipline) has been left largely by default to animate the city of the dead. It is not just that the dead are the historian's actors. Historians are actively interested in what killed them. They are particularly interested if people have *been* killed, although the killed arrange themselves into hierarchies of historical interest. Murder is more historically fascinating than other forms of death, because it is "social, cultural, and political" (the historian's declaration of solidarity with his social science colleagues). Those who have been killed by Nature, as in earthquakes, have traditionally not been considered to be "historical actors" by a profession whose stage center remains The State (rarely The City) and which shares only a short border with the natural sciences. Tokyo can burn up with most of its inhabitants, for example, and yet barely register as an event(s) in survey history texts of Japan. Epidemics, likewise, seem to come and go like the common flu. Demicide, the murder by a state of its own citizens, ranks high on the list of killings that would attract progressive historical research, as history overlaps with the law and investigative journalism in its studied instinct for the pursuit of justice. The resulting imbalance in how historians arrange and treat their dead sometimes makes them seem sloppy in the eyes of social scientists. To historians, on the other hand, the utter lack of corpses in social science texts on The City is the problem, the puzzle, needing to be explained.

We don't make these observations for the sake of morbidity, or from anti-urban instincts, but to demonstrate that a history of The City as a site of catastrophe—of urban densities as targets—certainly has been constructible from available evidence, particularly in our own time. The failure of Modernism to produce this history—its writing of The City as a site of "processes," development, and yes, perpetuation—is thus worth noticing, especially when its own concentric zone models look so much like bull's-eyes. Evolutionary models of the urban ecologists could not allow for emergency, in the form of the sudden and unpredictable event, a phenomena-set too closely associated with Fascism, the opposite of Planning. The City was, after all, the site of data-gathering and trend-setting par excellence. The principal "event" was growth, or decay. It was all botany. The power of biological metaphors in city development and planning, whether medical or botanical, rest in their ability to avoid agency and responsibility for the way cities have been grown, despite the rhetoric of planning, just as similar metaphors for the marketplace have elided human control over economic forces and conditions.

The city-as-target, a reading long buried under layers of academic Modernism, did find a certain robust expression in popular culture. As Mike Davis and H. Bruce Franklin have recently reminded us, cities have been insistently destroyed, and over a more sustained period, in novels, movies, and comic books.[7] At least in the last two art forms, however, destruction on a truly Judeo-Christian scale was arguably held in check through the end of the Cold War, as Hollywood and the American comic industry are relatively optimistic media. No imagery the West produced (until only very recently) could match that of a fire-breathing atomic-born Godzilla dismantling Tokyo *cho* by *cho*. Americans preferred that their giant screen-creatures live in the jungle or desert, and merely menace nearby cities. King Kong is defeated by The City, not the other way around. The same would generally hold for most of his Cold War permutations.

TARGET PRACTICE: CONSUMING HIROSHIMA, HANOI, PHNOM PENH . . .

The Arab and Kurd . . . now know what real bombing means in casualties and damage; they now know that within 45 minutes a full-sized village (vide attached photos) can be practically wiped out and a third of its inhabitants killed or injured by four or five machines.   —British Wing-Commander
Arthur Harris (later Air Marshall Sir Arthur "Bomber" Harris),
writing of his participation in the aerial bombing of Iraq in 1924[8]

Japan offers an ideal target for air operations. . . . [Its] towns, built largely of
wood and paper, form the greatest aerial targets the world has ever seen. . . .
Incendiary projectiles would burn the cities to the ground in short order.
  —*U.S. General Billy Mitchell, writing in* Liberty *magazine, January 1932*[9]

Because of Picasso's artistry, it is widely believed that the first aerial
bombing of a concentrated civilian target was the Luftwaffe's raid against
Guernica, Spain, in 1934. But the colonized world, more specifically North
Africa and Asia, experienced even earlier aerial bombardments of concentrated populations, beginning with an ineffective but symbolically important raid on Tripoli in 1911 and including some carried out with deadly
effect by the air forces of Spain. Aerial bombing in the twentieth century,
of course, continued an age-old tradition of bombardment by land and sea;
but in seeking to distance it from historic strategies and practices, its earliest advocates continually suggested its use not against walls or fortifications,
but the densities that they contained. The Hague Convention of 1907 pro-
hibited the targeting of civilian populations by airborne weaponry. In colonial territories, however, civilian population didn't necessarily count as a
"civilian population."

Italy, France, Spain, and Britain led the way in the use of aerial attacks
against colonial populations as a means of "pacification." France, in fact,
called their first systemized form of air attack "colonial bombing" and developed a specific plane, *Type Colonial,* for just such a purpose. Anticipating
the benefits of contemporary long-range high-tech weapons, Britain called
its air targeting of colonial cities "control without occupation." The expansion of such bombing to target cities like London, Berlin, and Paris during
World War I constituted an expansion from colonized cities to cosmopolitan ones. In fact, if the "civilizing" of colonial areas occurred through means
of urbanization, then it also converted colonial populations into potential
aerial targets. The colonial city was the paradigm for the city-as-target that
has dominated the military imagination in the twentieth century.[10] Although
countless cities, towns, and villages across Asia have been consumed (literally) in aerial and naval attack, the histories of their destructions have yet to
be consumed (figuratively) through images or even, in many cases, texts.
They have, with few exceptions, lacked their Picassos.[11]

To suggest that Hiroshima and Nagasaki were not fully consumed
seems at first unreasonable. Did not their very names become metaphors for
destruction of the most complete, nearly Carthaginian type? Yet the catastrophism these words evoked was always about the future more than the
past—about your own place rather than their place. Alain Resnais articulated this in his film *Hiroshima Mon Amour,* in its opening sequence and its
sustained meditation on the consistent external construction of the city as

a global metaphor for, of all things, "peace." "Hiroshima" came to mean, for many who deployed it, the possibility of the end of the world in its entirety, an event "beyond history." History (and specificity) often stopped with the towering white cloud that symbolized all nuclear explosions from Hiroshima to the final one(s). How many people could ever pick out Hiroshima's and Nagasaki's unique death-columns from the dozens of mushroom clouds that might merely have been tropical tests? Post-occupied Japan cooperated by reconstituting the victims in universal rather than ethnically specific terms. Whatever the good intentions, moral or geopolitical, the dead of Hiroshima and Nagasaki suffered a second act of disappearance. An image of a little girl, bodily whole and holding her head and arms hopefully aloft, cannot begin to represent what actually happened in both those places. Nor, it seems, is she meant to.

So passionless, disembodied, and consumable was the mushroom cloud image that it became the icon on many American consumer products in the middle to late 1940s, helping flog everything from toothpaste, drive-in movies, and a terrific Count Basie album, to special drinks at bars. Indeed, the U.S. Post Office very nearly issued it as a Hiroshima commemorative stamp in 1995. The stamp was subsequently taken into private production by a group of American veterans angry at its last-minute cancellation, and it is now distributed via the website of Brigadier General (retired) Paul Tibbets, the pilot of the *Enola Gay* and leader of the 509th Composite Group over Hiroshima. According to the same website, the great-grandson of the *Enola Gay* Tibbets is a pilot in the present 509th Bomb Wing, recommissioned in 1993 specifically to receive the new B-2 bombers.[12] It was the 509th, whose shoulder-patch emblem is the Nagasaki mushroom cloud (archivally correct), which flew B-2s against Belgrade. The "509ers have every intention," boasts their own website, "of equaling, if not surpassing, the past accomplishments of the 509th Bomb Wing." The restoration of the 509th, an intentional act of convergence between B-2s and "the story of Hiroshima/Nagasaki" (a story of how the American citizen-army was saved by a *deus ex machina,* which is also "the story of the Gulf War" projected forward and backward in time[13]) was coincident with the restoration of the *Enola Gay* itself for iconographic exhibit at the American National Air and Space Museum.[14]

How little of Hiroshima and Nagasaki had really been consumed became apparent in 1994, when even "liberal" American media like the *Washington Post* worked (successfully) to prevent items such as half-melted lunchboxes and tricycles from being moved into the immediate proximity of a "restored" *Enola Gay.* At stake was the creation, even indirectly, of embodied victims, for the lunchbox's disfigured surface too neatly evoked the flesh of the child who carried it.[15] Compare "Hiroshima" to

"The Holocaust," not in terms of moral equivalence, but economy of images. The Holocaust is all about bodies, violated in every imaginable way. Hiroshima, according to a popular imaginary, is exactly the opposite: a place where bodies simply disappeared ("vaporized"). If not a mushroom cloud, our first image of the city is of a flat and lifeless plain. The most famous Hiroshima "body" might be that of a shadow-figure on a concrete wall, this despite massive documentation by the U.S. Department of Defense that showed burn victims and immediate effects of nuclear radiation. "Vaporization" and even radiation poisoning were bloodless by comparison with the imagined effects of "conventional" aerial bombing. Particularly in the immediate postwar period, they seemed "scientific"—read clean, painless, and uncarnate—ways to die.[16]

Hollywood, despite its remarkable stable of special effects artists, never portrayed the actual bodily horrors of nuclear warfare. Such images exist, however, in the form of often haunting colored drawings by atomic bomb survivors and photographs of horribly disfigured living *hibakusha* (atomic bomb victims), such as the "Hiroshima Maidens." Hiroshima also has its Picassos in Iri Maruki and Toshi Maruki, the artist couple whose series of "Hiroshima Murals," completed over a period of three decades, have been described by historian John Dower as displaying

> . . . (an) anger, complexity, and humanism . . . unparalleled in the Japanese artistic tradition; indeed one is hard pressed to find counterparts in the non-Japanese traditions of high art.

Despite their publication outside Japan, these and other images from ground-level Hiroshima and Nagasaki have yet to find a secure place in the "global" (Western) economy of images of Modern war-related destruction. The perspective of the bombardier, who sees his urban target only as a map through the clouds, became (and arguably still is) the agreed-upon shared perspective of the postwar war-consuming public.

Even in Japan, Hiroshima and Nagusuki have often been made to stand for all the bombing victims, while the more numerous dead of Tokyo and other cities have been less visibly memorialized. The proof is in the comparative anonymity of the firebombing of Tokyo, in which more people were killed than in either atomic blast. Even in Japan, Hiroshima has been made to stand for all bombing victims, while the more numerous dead of Tokyo are scarcely memorialized. Yet the firebombing of Tokyo was in no sense conventional—it was not an episode of factory bombing that got out of hand. Rather, the U.S. Army Air Force constructed an authentic Tokyo neighborhood in the western desert and experimented with various incendiary devices before arriving at the perfect formula for a firestorm. The intentional incineration of whole urban populations was invented there and elsewhere, not at Los Alamos. The technology was napalm, which would become infamous throughout the world only with the Vietnam War.[18]

It was the disembodied, metahistorical reading of Hiroshima that gave aerial bombing depiction its postwar style. Belonging to the realm of "communication" more than atrocity—for the sake of its victims as much as its perpetrators—targeting was invariably depicted from a God's-eye perspective. It took the Vietnam War, uniquely productive of images of death and maiming at ground level, to produce a picture of aerial bombing comparable in its impact to that of the crying Chinese infant alone in the ruins of Shanghai—the little girl running naked down a road was a victim of the same technology that had killed Tokyo. Yet this was, for all its impact, a "rural" scene "explainable" in terms of "collateral damage." This last term would itself have little meaning without the model of Hiroshima, this time as a towering column of intentionality and completeness.

A history of modern urbanization in Indo-China could be written with the B-52 bomber at its center. Political theorist Samuel Huntington made this explicit in coining the phrase "forced-draft urbanization" to describe the twentieth century airborne version of eighteenth century enclosure.[19] Thus did Phnom Penh double in size because of American aerial bombing of the countryside around it. When the peasant-victims of Cambodian carpet-bombing eventually took that city, they forcibly emptied it out in the most infamous deurbanization of modern times. Hanoi also emptied out dramatically, but this time under the direct threat of American bombs. Less is remembered of the dramatic urbanizations/deurbanizations of South Vietnam as a result of military action. The American air force likely killed more urban residents of the southern cities it was "defending," particularly during the Tet Offensive, than it did in campaigns against the urban North. In most filmic and other popular accounts, the Vietnam battlefield is remembered as countryside and jungle, and its cities as the "normative" sector of a hellishly abnormal geography, or as the liminal space between the chaotic jungle and the "normal" U.S. suburbs. Yet there was nothing normative about urban Indo-China during the period of warfare, and the present shape and character of its cities are very much artifacts of sustained military targeting.[20]

RETARGETING THE CITY

Mechanical and electrical engineers destroy targets. Civil engineers build them.   —*Anonymous*

*7. To direct or aim on a course. Freq. const. to; Hence "**targeting**" vbl. n.* **1961** Guardian *24 Oct. 8/4 "Being forced to rely on so much inspection . . . that targeting information would be given away to the other side."* **1963** Newsweek

11 Feb. 23 "Planners have recently put forward the notion of city-avoidance, a tacit agreement between potential enemies to arrange their targeting so that missiles are aimed at military objectives rather than civilian populations." **1968** Economist *8 June 65/2 "A general complaint is that consultants sometimes stick too much to their business precepts, such as 'targeting' and do not bend enough to the particular needs of the company."* **1976** National Observer *(U.S.) 27 Nov. 5/1 "NCEC laid out $350,000 for candidates in 1976. That paid for 64 polls in 32 separate congressional districts and for computerized precinct targeting and analysis in more than 40 districts."* **1977** Time *21 Nov. 24/2 "None of these possess as sophisticated a targeting system as the new Soviet model's [sc. a T-72 tank]."* **1982** Financial Times *13 Mar. 14/1 "In terms of targeting ability."*
—Oxford English Dictionary[21]

The examples of usage for the gerund form of the verb "target" that are found in the *Oxford English Dictionary* unsurprisingly reiterate the city-as-target applications in this essay's opening paragraph. Roughly contemporary with the emergence of postcoloniality and the triumph of global urbanism, the *Oxford English Dictionary* examples range from military, to business, to political notions of targeting, all relevant to how the current global city functions as both imagined and experienced entity. The convergence of military and marketing designs on urban areas, of course, has political implications, but also economic ones, for the technology that makes it possible to so target the city in our current post–Cold War moment results from concerted military-funded research and development that have become the basis for the information technology revolution in the "new economy" of the global order. This same technological revolution remains in military hands, however, and allows us to imagine (and visualize in popular culture and news broadcasts) wholesale urban destruction with ever-greater intimacy. Tripoli, Beirut, Belgrade, Grozney, Sarajevo, and Baghdad have provided recent generations with images of urban targeting altogether more insistent, clear, and technicolored, yet disturbingly adrift from progressive narratives.

Thus with the end of the Cold War, "The Modern City" has begun to be subject to a new kind of catastrophic imaginary, this despite the immediate post–Cold War claim that the targeted city had lost its bull's-eye. The recent intensification and increase in Old Testament–scale images of urban destruction in the convergent realms of journalism, film, military action, telecommunications, government policy-making, computer gaming, and the academic press show no sign of abating, as if the collective sigh of relief of having dodged "the big one" allowed the possibility—and invited the pleasure—of its representation in more "contained" forms. "The Postmodern City" is now visualized more commonly than before as a site of violent, sudden death writ large and small, a new economy of images that makes the old (Modern) one seem tinted and opaque.

This imaginary is still largely absent, however, from current urban plan-ning, theory, and discussion. Current trends in global (read, North Amer-ican and European) urban planning seek to fuse an eclectic, New Age spirituality (emergent from unprecedented privilege that is the result of global exploitation) with notions of "ecology" and "nature" as kindly cor-rective and nurturing—sort of a cybernetic Bambi-ism. The result is a nos-talgic reclamation of community and local color in the face of increasing corporate global homogenization. The fusing of spirituality and nature in constructed urban environments that reclaim "the local" points toward a "Romantic resurgence" by urban theorists and planners.[22] The built envi-ronment in this 1990s reaction against the corporatization of cities and the globe (which, ironically, fuels and drives the very technologies these thinkers claim as emancipatory) means "tribal groups" at spatial, but not temporal, distances can form communities no longer dependent on topographical proximity but rather on the proximity of "shared interests." These interests, of course, are produced on, circulated by, and consumed on "real time" information technologies, themselves increasingly in the control of fewer and fewer multimedia conglomerates—the very organizations these groups wish to eschew while having that eschewal become instrumental in their built environment. Far from being an element in narrowing human and ecological horizons, technological virtualization, from this perspective, has helped us already actualize this delicate balance of urbanism and spiritual fulfillment in tune with ecosystems.

As we have seen, however, the foundation for this global reharmoniza-tion of nature and culture, ecology and city, global and local, is composed of fragile electronic grids that can disappear in the click of a mouse. Silicon Valley residents and the rest of California experienced the many brown-outs and rolling blackouts of 2000 and 2001 as deregulation derailed electrical utilities. The ironies are heavy and manifest. An environmentally driven urban zeitgeist dependent on plundering the earth's natural resources, as in opening Alaskan wildlife and nature preserves to oil drilling, also manifests itself in conflagrations such as the Gulf War. But, as is the case with the long-distance high-tech weaponry now favored by the U.S. military and with the exorbitant inequity of global trade, the Romantic resurgence of contemporary urban planning operates in a mystified and mystifying dis-cursive and epistemological domain that obliterates the relationship between cause and effect.[23]

The Romantic shift in current global urbanism is simultaneously prospective and retrospective, as is all nostalgia. At the same time that the Romantic impulse emerges as a dominant intellectual mode in global urban-ism, with environmental concerns taking a supposedly central role, the city-as-target of human-created disaster, directly or indirectly, is elided from all public discourse and memory of urban trajectories. Human habitats have been, and remain, the total targets of total war in the twentieth century, and, as Paul Virilio reminds us, "scientific arms aim at the volatilization of environmental conditions; what biological warfare accomplished for animal life, ecological warfare did for flora, and nuclear warfare, with its radiation, for the atmosphere."[24] Cold War satellite technology used for urban planning forgets its military origins, just as the earliest uses of aerial photography to plan cities at the turn of the twentieth century forgot its. Yet cities remain targeted sites well within the military's aerial and prosthetically enhanced visual sights.

The retargeting of the city in the post–Cold War era, bearing the full weight of real-time technology's ramifications, is neatly exemplified in both the 1997 Southeast Asian economic crisis and the Gulf War—two events from the past century's last decade that reveal the vulnerability of urban space, urban dwellers, and urban economies locked in the global embrace. The Gulf War marked a return to, or a retargeted application of, "conventional weapons" and "strategic intervention," which could render a city, a nation, and a military immobile. Bombing in the Gulf War took advantage of real-time data transmission, sophisticated information technology systems, and intelligent projectiles to reinvent bombing without Cold War vaporization, Vietnam War sledgehammer bombing, or WWII inaccuracy. This event reopened the city as a viable military target, rendering urban space more vulnerable to airborne attack, because the attack could be "contained." The city was once more a legitimate military option, more so than at any point between 1945 and 1990. Just as the colonial cities of Africa and Asia pointed toward the later aerial targeting of the metropoles that controlled them, the cities of Hanoi and Haiphong pointed toward the potential targeting of other cities. Though no new technology or restraint prevented the wholesale destruction of North Vietnamese provincial capitals, the attacks showed that it was possible to avoid the nuclear annihilation embedded in Cold War policies while avoiding WWII-like practices.

As the Cold War has vanished from our collective screens, Cold War technology transfer to the private sector has spilled over with unintended consequences in a variety of ways. The very same real-time technologies that allowed instantaneous data transfer for identifying military targets during the Gulf War were used to target global capital investments and pullouts during the Southeast Asian economic crisis some seven years later. Technologies designed to take snap-second decisions out of human hands in military situations—taking the human element out of the loop—function similarly with currency exchange markets and other global investment strategies. Maximum control by these technologies led to maximum economic meltdown, leaving urban centers such as Bangkok, Singapore,

Jakarta, and Manila exposed to the vagaries of capital speculation. Investors, or their computer programs, suddenly and dramatically lost confidence in the region in a self-fulfilling prophetic spiral of documented real-time loss of confidence, and capital ran for high ground outside Southeast Asian urban investment schemes.

The targeting can, and does, take on more ominous tones if we consider the Gulf War and the Southeast Asian economic crisis as two sides of the same complex geophysical, ideological, and techno-scientific coin. The globalization thrust that allows for the real-time surveillance of the Earth and its networked nodes also provides the means for homogenizing the Earth into a single market. And if a "rogue nation" refuses to play by the end-of-history political/economic rules, it can be (and has been) targeted for punishment, including strategic bombing. Stereoscopy telescopes the horizon (which has been lost in the vanishing point of perspectival painting and cartography) as well as market, economic, social, and urban choices. The global market consumption predicated on and enacted in the name of "choice" works well enough for urban denizens as long as they (and their nation-states) choose correctly.

Just as currently constituted and understood globalization processes emerged from Cold War policies, practices, and technologies, so too did the interconnected fate of global cities. As nodes in the global, ideological grid of surveillance and intercontinental ballistic missile targeting, each global city was potentially *every other* global city. A nuclear attack of one (which implied direct attack of more because of Mutually Assured Destruction policies) meant radiation fallout and environmental devastation for all others. Global cities became, and remain, global insofar as they are targets for attack. It is their status as targets that renders them, de facto, "global." The conversion of military technology into the bases of the "new economy" merely shifts the targeting from directly geopolitical to indirectly geo-political, while remaining wholly ideological. And as we have seen, this conversion can easily be shifted back to direct military targeting—as the convergence of the Gulf War and Southeast Asian economic crisis attest.

Global cities bear the marks of their global status by virtue of target-ing in myriad ways civil defense plans, emergency operations, and military infrastructure. This manifests itself as their various tools of implementa-tion for these procedures should the city-as-target find itself directly in the crosshairs: bunkers/shelters, evacuation plans, and defensive military hard-ware such as "Star Wars." Many of these plans and the support to put them into practice serve double duty. That is, civil defense and evacuation plans also can provide cleanup for chemical spills or natural disasters. The im-print of the Cold War can be found everywhere in the great global city, in all of its technologies, in all the distributed systems that link cities in nodes—even in office designs of workstations meant to expedite communication and decrease hierarchies, as does that other great Cold War technology: the Internet.[25] Cities bear the mark of their status as target at every level of empirical, quotidian life. This has been true for a long time, as the etymology of city planning terminology reveals. The French "boulevard" is a corruption of the Dutch word for an artillery bastion, "*bolwerk*," while an "*esplanade*" in today's global city forgets its origins as the open space lying before fortifications.[26] Singapore's most recent investment in the arts is a complex called "The Esplanade of Theatres on the Bay." We are constantly reminded of the necessity of city targeting for urban planning, especially when we remember that city planning demands urban destruction before urban reconstruction can occur. The Cold War and its New World Order aftermath have simply upped the ante, through increases in speed of targeting, speed of delivery to the target, and impact.

THE ASIA-PACIFIC AS DISASTER ZONE

Indeed, we are today forced to produce the Metropolis and are given no other choice: it is the savage and meager return for all that has been subtly and ceremoniously expropriated from us.   —*Sanford Kwinter*[27]

I think no power to your refrigerator, no gas to your stove, you can't get to work because the bridge is down—the bridge on which you hold your rock concerts and you all stood with targets on your heads. That needs to disappear at three o'clock in the morning.   —*Lieutenant General Michael Short, NATO's top air-war commander, speaking to the* New York Times[28]

Most of the world's earthquakes occur in a belt that extends from the Mediterranean Sea, across central Asia, through northern India, and around the Pacific Rim: a geography strangely convergent with the map of world power prior to the rise of Protestantism. Cities in this zone are seen to have a fundamentally different relationship with their Earth than those outside it. They can theoretically be brought down without warning at any time, and sometimes are. They thus watch each other's disasters more closely than they are watched outside the region. Because seismology has never evolved into a predictive science, there is nothing that cities in the Eurasia-Pacific earthquake zone can do but fortify themselves and hope for the best. Yet earthquakes come so infrequently, apocalyptic ones may never come at all, and good fortification is so expensive (and surveillance-intensive) that if the great quake is truly unprecedented in its ferocity the city may be destroyed despite everything. Such is the gambler's logic that works against putting too many of one's resources into self-fortification, and makes every new earthquake-disaster an occasion for intense, but temporary, recrimination.

But earthquakes and other potentially city-destroying forms of nature (typhoons, tsunamis, floods, etc.) are not uniform in their effects on Asia, despite the West's historic construction of that continent as peculiarly ruled by superhuman forces. The cities of "Island" Southeast Asia (Indonesia and the Philippines) are within the Trans-Pacific Earthquake zone, for example, while those of "Mainland" Southeast Asia are not. Singapore, despite the occasional tremor telegraphed from Sumatran epicenters, experiences Nature as tamer and less threatening than Amsterdam or Minneapolis do. Of all of the major urban concentrations in the geographies of Pacific Rim and Asia-Pacific, Singapore is arguably least aware of itself as existing in a natural environment that might do it harm. No earthquakes, no typhoons, no volcanoes, no tsunami. Singapore experiences Nature not as threat, but as an absence. The absence of natural resources is what begins to trace the contours of the city's sense of its own vulnerability.

Singapore's self-image as target is a dense collage of memory, geography, and political science. There is its identity as a small city-state between two much larger and resentful neighbors, one of whom controls its water supply. There is its newness, its perceived artificiality—the un-maskable fact of its colonial creation and function (more easily masked in Bangkok and Jakarta) within a region alive with ancient claims and anticolonial mobilizations. It has a Chinese majority far from "home," again between countries that have been accused of persecuting their own Chinese. And marbled through these geopolitical and geolocal awarenesses is the historical memory of what happened after the city fell to the Imperial Japanese Army in 1941.

The *Sook Ching* was a ceremony of concentration and targeting. The majority of the Chinese population was gathered, examined, and some marked—often arbitrarily—for immediate death. It was a moment of intense emergency, from which some members of the later leadership emerged as acci- dental survivors. It arguably set in train a whole series of emergencies, including the unexpected emergence of independence in 1965. Emergency— "a moment of anguish" colored with an acute sense of vulnerability, and even regret—is the story the country chooses to tell about its birth, a narrative relatively rare in the annals of nations. This narrative undergirds a continued sense of mobilization and preparedness, which both integrates Singapore into the grid of global cities while subliminally questioning its purported securities. In different forms, however, emergence/emergency are a not uncommon dualism among global cities in the Asia-Pacific disaster zone. None has ever experienced the "security" of New York, nor can they reasonably expect to.

Singapore's emergence as a "virtual" global city comes with protections and maskings. Because the strength of its geography (as a world-class port) is also its greatest weakness (as the Japanese occupation and proximity to a volatile Indonesia and recalcitrant Malaysia reveal), Singapore's full-bore plunge into the "new economy" has the added advantage of deterritorial-izion. In the contemporary moment, as space yields to time—the world-time of "real-time"—Singapore's economy becomes increasingly spectralized, rendering the nation a less appealing target, at least for aggressive occupa-tion. Why would any potential invader want to possess the intelligent island of Singapore? What gain could be had? The infrastructure, like the Web, is both here and not here; the city has become not-a-city. Virilio could well have been describing Singapore when he discusses a teleoptical sleight-of-hand that also serves as a protective device: "While the topical *City* was once constructed by the 'gate' and the 'port', the teletopical *metacity* is now reconstructed around the 'window' and the teleport, that is to say, around the screen and the time slot."[29] The screen provides a screen for the city-as-target to hide behind, just as the timeslot allows an opening for space to dis-appear into real-time teletechnologies' erasure of here and there. As the virtual replaces the material, as the uncarnate replaces the incarnate, a new type of "protection" coincides with the new economy.

The new protection provided by the new economy is just as illusory, of course, as any old protection ever was, a point the 1997 economic crisis made painfully clear. Just as the mind-body split remains a metaphysical desire always dragged down by inescapable embodiment, so too the virtual metacity functions with the "betweeness" of stereoscopy. In this space be-tween the wired and the geopolitical worlds pulse petrochemical plants, a *real* and *really active* port, and other desiderata of the material world we would rather slough off. The ads for the Home office, painted on double-decker buses with the slogan "there's no place like home," remind us that a potential *Sook Ching* looms ever on the horizon. Similarly, the Civil Defence ads remind us that "there is no place like home" because home cannot ever really be a no-place, a utopia, free from the vagaries of the body and bodies, no matter how neatly or centrally planned.

A mural outside the Civil Defence station near Queenstown makes this point. The mural depicts dedicated Civil Defence workers armored in pro-tective garb from visor to boot clearing some generic toxic spill that never-was but could-be at any moment. The mural, in essence, memorializes a *potential future moment* of the city-as-target that we might not live to memo-rialize once it actually enters the past. At the same time, the mural is meant to instill confidence and well being in the people who pass it, so they can go about their business in the virtual, wired, real-time metacity knowing they are protected from the troubles of other, apparently less-clean and less-safe, industries that are hang-overs from the old economy. But, as with nuclear fallout shelters, the scene smacks of whistling past the graveyard, and that which is meant to comfort can actually prove discomfiting. The new economic order is just as much a target, if not more so, than any past economic order, if for no other reason than it is almost exclusively the result of targeting technologies.

CITY RUINS (TARGETS PAST AND FUTURE)

Ruin is formal.   —*Emily Dickinson*[30]

It is easier to imagine blowing things sky high than to give up homogenized order as a measure of urban success.   —*Herbert Muschamp*[31]

When the architecture of cities sported their target status—when they were fortified with walls—masonry, ironically, marked the shift from "barbarism" to "civilization." Nineteenth century Europe developed an special fondness for the ruins left by cities and empires past. As cities began to shed their walls and camouflage (their potential-target status), artists, historians, writers, urban planners, and a myriad of others found in ruins *memento mori* at individual and collective levels, delineating the deaths of citizens, cities, and states alike. Ruins both humbled and emboldened their viewers. They reminded those who gazed upon their grim visage that no nation or people had defeated the Heraclitian forces of existence, and yet, at the same time, these piles of rubble and graceful dilapidations could also be interpreted as embodying evolutionary theories of science, as purported by Lyell and Darwin. Not only did the earth change, it actually progressed. Ruins, as a result, played a pivotal role in the nineteenth and twentieth century European and North American imaginary, and they did so in ways that had direct effects on the understanding of cities as human habitats freed from the devolutionary ways of the targeting past—or so it was believed. In the process, ruins bespoke the present and future as much as they did the past.

If the Civil Defence mural in Singapore memorializes a potential future moment of the city-as-target and ruin, the 1997 Southeast Asian economic crisis has also bestowed on the urban landscape futural ruins resultant from the city-as-targeted by real-time teletechnologies and the flow of global capital. Bangkok flaunts a number of such ruins: high-rise luxury condos abandoned in mid-flight to the heavens, highways to nowhere ending in steel-cable tatters, unfinished office skyscrapers made ghostly despite never having been inhabited. These ruins house squatters from rural areas, suburbanites tossed out of homes they can no longer afford, and criminals and drug addicts seeking addresses that do not appear on maps, not to mention rats and other such urban vermin. Where residents were once threatened with homelessness because they dwelled in the path of upward mobility's crushing progress and would probably no longer be able to afford to live in their neighborhoods, the ruins of the future left behind by the teletechnologies' targeting now threaten them by driving down (rather than up) property prices and imperiling their daily lives. Joining Bangkok in this opulent display of ruins created by opulence's failures are neighborhoods in Jakarta, Manila, and Bataam, where development and speculation often ended without fulfillment.

Other futural ruins litter the Southeast Asian city horizon. One such example is Singaporean architect Tay Khen Soon's "Tropical City," an imprint of the current Romantic resurgence in urban planning, tinged with nostalgia and "green consciousness." The Tropical City covers its international-style office buildings in vines, foliage, and other indigenous flora, along with running water, in an attempt to take advantage of their properties for functioning in an equatorial climate. Despite a desire to integrate buildings into the unique tropical setting of Southeast Asia, Tay's designs strike one as resembling camouflage of a sort, as deployed in the Pacific theater during World War II and later in the Vietnam War. The buildings that populate Tay's Tropical City can easily be in hiding so that they do not become ruins due to military targeting by hostile forces. As esteemed local architect Bobby Wong reminds us, the only "green areas" remaining in Singapore belong to the military.[32]

Lebbus Woods argues that the current wave of urban planners and architects in the grip of the Romantic resurgence ignore the long-term effects of their building and buildings, not to mention the environmental processes necessary to build in the first place. The delusion operative in "green" building and urban designs manifests itself in environmental consciousness as decoration, not to mention as marketing tool. But the ruin the Tropical City really camouflages is the one that it purports to stave off—that which would result from global warming. That is, the Tropical City camouflages the agency of global cities in the ur-environmental disaster, of which they are both belated victims and perpetrators. As with all of the urban plans swept up in the utopian visions of the Romantic resurgence, the notion of the Tropical City operates with an exceptionally limited view of the interaction between urban planning and ecosystems, as we have discussed earlier.

Vines and gardens no more hide the target that is The City than virtuality does. The city's boundaries are always both veil and battlement. The current discourse about global cities and global urbanism emphasizes the positive elements of the various trajectories that make up its complex existence (what one shoots *for*) at the expense of the negative elements (that which is shot *at*), and the dearth of such discursive interaction and critical engagement must come at a cost. The cost might be found in the futural ruins that haunt our current cityscape today.

NOTES

The bulk of this essay was written in the early spring of 2001. The date of the last substantial draft of this essay was September 5 of that year. Following the September 11 attack on the World Trade Center in New York, the authors considered, but rejected the idea of changing the manuscript to incorporate reflections on that event.

1. The epigram comes from "Is the Author Dead?: An Interview with Paul Virilio," in *The Virilio Reader,* ed. James der Derian (Oxford: Blackwell, 1998), 16.
2. Quoted in Paul Virilio, *Bunker Archeology,* trans. George Collins (New York: Princeton Architectural Press, 1994), 32.
3. Weber, Simmel, Spengler, and the Chicago School almost never addressed the city as a site of conflagration. Although Weber proposed the "garrison theory" for modeling of city development, he concentrated largely on the notion of defense, ignoring the carnage that results when defense fails. Similarly, the "human ecology" model emerges fully with the Chicago School, and the city-as-organism yields to a medical discourse that addresses urban space as a collective corpus, not one in which corpses pile up. When the machine metaphor emerged in the post-WWII moment, the planning of cities merely entailed tinkering with, not accounting for, carnage. The influence of nuclear weapons on this moment cannot be overstated, for population density yielded to population dispersal, and the city became increasingly a site for consumption rather than production. The major postwar texts on urban planning, such as Peter Hall's influential *Cities of Tomorrow* (Oxford: Blackwell, 1988), were mute on the many targets that cities had become. Even in our current, postmodern moment, the role of the city-as-target remains elided. In her excellent overview, *Postmodern Urbanism* (New York: Princeton Architectural Press, 1999), Nan Ellin lists environmentalism as a major influence in contemporary urban planning and architecture, but not environmental disaster. Urban destruction, even today, apparently results only from gentrification, design, and globalization.

   Some notable exceptions exist. In the 1980s, the city-as-target was problematized in a series of articles by geographer Kenneth Hewitt, notably "Place Annihilation: Aerial Bombing and the Fate of Urban Places," *Annals of the Association of American Geographers* 73 (1983): 257–84, and "The Social Space of Terror: Towards a Civil Interpretation of Total War," *Environment and Planning D: Society and Space* 5 (1987): 445–74. See also Wilbur Zelinsky and Leszek A. Kosinski, *The Emergency Evacuation of Cities* (Savage, Md.: Rowman & Littlefield, 1991). G. J. Ashworth's *War and the City* (London and New York: Routledge, 1991) attempts to bring urban studies and military history together. The provocatively titled *Pandemonium: The Rise of Predatory Locales in the Postwar World* (New York: Princeton Architectural Press, 1999) by Branden Hookway usefully explores the influence of military technologies on urban space in the latter part of the past century, with special emphasis on systems designs. Peter Lang's edited collection *Mortal City* (New York: Princeton Architectural Press, 1995) includes a wide range of critical architectural pieces that foreground the interaction of city space and violence. Mike Davis's *Ecology of Fear* (New York: Metropolitan Books, 1998), in its desire to foreground a range of disasters that could befall Los Angeles, speaks in ways familiar to this article. Most recently, Sven Lindqvist's *A History of Bombing* (New York: New Press, 2001) brings a broad historical perspective to bear on a topic normally dealt with as discrete episodes. Finally, Paul Virilio's work on the complex relationships between urbanism, technology, and the military provides an important inspiration for our work here.
4. Engels's comment on the sacking of the Indian city of Lucknow by the British in 1858 remains rare in its lack of varnish: "For twelve days and nights there was no British army at Lucknow— nothing but a lawless, drunken, brutal rabble, dissolved into bands of robbers . . . the sack of Lucknow in 1858 will remain an everlasting disgrace to the British military service." Engels, "The Seige and Storming of Lucknow" in Marx and Engels, *Collected Works,* vol. 15 (Moscow: Progress Publishers, 1975), 419–24. In fact the sacking of Lucknow and similar events were largely ignored and ultimately forgotten outside the memory of the victims. Levels of brutality toward cities in the nineteenth century seem to have been chiefly conditioned by the "racial" identity of conquerors and conquered, or the perception that collective "rebellion" against established authority was being collectively punished (hence the allowable sacking of "white" cities like Atlanta in the American Civil War).
5. Targeted European cities also became "colonial" cities when Allied propaganda described their inhabitants as "The Hun," suggesting that their barbarism had meant a loss of whiteness.
6. The point is brought home by browsing through Lewis Mumford's *The City in History* (New York: Harcourt, Brace & World, 1961), the most ambitious urban history project of the postwar period. If anyone had the vocabulary to confront urbicide, surely it was Mumford, the

fire-breathing critic and polemicist who would cap his career later in the same decade with a jeremiad about the coming destruction of the world. Yet in 657 pages of historical narrative stretching from Babylonia to the present day, Mumford paints not a single word picture of a city destroyed. Tenochtitlan is not razed to the ground, Lisbon and Tokyo are not brought down by earthquakes, and London does not burn (nor, closer to home, do Chicago or San Francisco). Carthage, mentioned once in passing, does not even appear in the index. Photos of Pompeii are used mainly to illustrate Roman architecture. When Mumford arrives at his own time, Hiroshima appears in only a single line (which it shares with London, Tokyo, and Hamburg), and Nagasaki not at all. The wartime destruction of cities made a deeper impression on urbanists from outside the English-speaking world. Wolf Schneider's 1960 *Uberall ist Babylon* includes such chapter titles as "The ABC of Destruction: Jericho and Troy" and "The Death of Lisbon." *Babylon is Everywhere,* trans. Ingeborg Sammet and John Oldenberg (New York: McGraw-Hill, 1963).

7. Mike Davis, *Ecology of Fear: Los Angeles and the Imagination of Disaster* (New York: Henry Holt, Metropolitan Books, 1998); H. Bruce Franklin, *War Stars: The Superweapon and the American Imagination* (New York: Oxford University Press, 1988).
8. Quoted in Geoff Simons, *Iraq: From Sumar to Saddam* (London: MacMillan, 1994), 214.
9. Quoted in Franklin, *War Stars,* 98.
10. For an extended discussion of colonial bombing across multiple empires, see Lindqvist, *History of Bombing.*
11. We do not even know most of their names. In January 1999, Tjeffe van Tijen began "Unbombing the World, 1911–2001" an "imaginary museum project" and Internet database (http://people.a2000.nl/ttijen/ubw/ubw01a.html). His goal was to fully chronicle and record "90 years of aerial bombing of the human habitat," or "the history and future of planned destruction and reconstruction." Van Tijen notes "an inescapable relation between the targeting and destruction of human habitat and the reconstruction afterwards." Surveying the existing literature on aerial bombing, Van Tijen estimates that 400 towns and cities have been the targets over 90 years. He admits, however, that the list is incomplete. In fact, it is grossly so. For Cambodia and Laos he consolidates all the bombing under the heading "communist bases"; North Vietnam, he writes, also "needs further detailing." It is scarcely Van Tijen's fault; he notes that an extreme precision among his historical sources in chronicling European targets gives way to extreme vagueness about targets in Asia.
12. Mid Coast Marketing, "Enola Gay and the Bombing of Hiroshima in World War II," *The Official Website of Brig. Gen. Paul W. Tibbets (USAF Ret.),* 2001. http://www.theenolagay.com/. Individual webpages are indexed as "The Man," "The Plane," "The Decision," "The Event," "Collectibles," and "Appearances." Besides the stamp, the "collectibles" include a framed photograph of the mushroom cloud rising over Hiroshima signed by the three surviving crew members, which sells for $400 plus $4 shipping and handling.
13. The Gulf War, however, despite its postmodern military label, revealed the neatness and precision with which the "new, high-tech" U.S. military could surgically carve up a city, thus avoiding the massive vaporization of Hiroshima or blanket bombing.
14. 509th Bomb Wing Public Affairs Office, "509th Bomb Wing History," *Whiteman AFP.* http://www.whiteman.af.mil/guide/509thist.html. The coproduction in the 1990s of the iconography of the B-2 "stealth" bomber and the *Enola Gay* went largely uncommented during the Smithsonian exhibit scandal of that decade, and in the substantial literature produced around the issue since (see note 15). To the successful opponents of the Smithsonian's "revisionist" exhibit, however—themselves active revisionists—the importance of a consistent narrative linking past, present, and future would not have been obscure.
15. On the battle over the *Enola Gay* exhibit, see Edward T. Linenthal and Tom Engelhardt, eds., *History Wars: The Enola Gay and Other Battles for the American Past* (New York: Henry Holt, 1996); Martin Harwit, *An Exhibit Denied: Lobbying the History of Enola Gay* (New York: Copernicus, 1996); and Phillip Nobile, ed., *Judgment at the Smithsonian* (New York: Marlowe, 1995).
16. The literature on Hiroshima has only grown in size and quality since the end of the Cold War. For a start, see Susan Lindee, *Suffering Made Real: American Science and the Survivors at Hiroshima* (Chicago: University of Chicago Press, 1994); Robert Jay Lifton and Greg Mitchell, *Hiroshima in America: Fifty Years of Denial* (New York: G. P. Putnam and Sons, 1995); Michael J. Hogan, ed., *Hiroshima in History and Memory* (Cambridge, U.K.: Cambridge University Press, 1996).
17. For drawings by survivors of Hiroshima and Nagasaki, see John Dower, "Japanese Artists and the Atomic Bomb" in Dower, *Japan in War and Peace* (New York: New Press, 1993, quotation from page 252) and for reproductions of the Marukis' murals, see Dower and John Junkerman, *The*

Hiroshima Murals: The Art of Iri Muraki and Toshi Muraki (New York: Kodansha International, 1986). Over a hundred of the images drawn by atomic bomb survivors (some of which are reproduced in Dower's article) have been published in Japan National Broadcasting Corporation, ed., *Unforgettable Fire: Pictures Drawn by Atomic Bomb Survivors* (New York: Pantheon, 1981).

18. William A. Remers, *Chemists at War* (Tucson: Clarice Publishers, 2000). Napalm was invented by Dr. Louis Fieser of Harvard while working under a U.S. government contract during World War II. Early tests were performed behind the Harvard Stadium in the center of metropolitan Boston–Cambridge. For the Tokyo bombing, see E. Bartlett Kerr, *Flames over Tokyo: The U.S. Army Air Forces' Incendiary Campaign against Japan 1944–1945* (New York: Donald I. Fine, 1991); Hoito Edoin, *The Night Tokyo Burned* (New York: St. Martin's Press, 1987); Kenneth P. Werrell, *Blankets of Fire: U.S. Bombers over Japan during World War II* (Washington, D.C.: Smithsonian Institution Press, 1996).

19. Quoted in Noam Chomsky, *Radical Priorities* (Montreal: Black Rose, 1981), 158–64.

20. On aerial bombing and the cities of Indo-China, see John T. Smith, *The Linebacker Raids: The Bombing of North Vietnam, 1972* (London: Wellington House, 1998); James William Gibson, *The Perfect War: Technowar in Vietnam* (New York: Atlantic Monthly Press, 1986); Ralph Littauer and Norman Uphoff, eds., *The Air War in Indochina* (Boston: Beacon Press, 1972).

21. Oxford English Dictionary Online. http://dictionary.oed.com.

22. For a discussion of the Romantic resurgence in urban planning, see Nan Ellin, *Postmodern Urbanism,* 12–21.

23. See Ryan Bishop, "Phantom Limbs of the Body Politic," *Lemmata,* vol. 1, 2002, www.lemmata.com, for a discussion on the connections between long-range weaponry and causal relations.

24. Virilio, *Bunker Archeology,* 38.

25. See Hookway, *Pandemonium,* 61–68.

26. Ashworth, *War and the City,* 170.

27. Introduction to Hookway, *Pandemonium,* "War in Peace," 12.

28. Reported in *The International Herald Tribune,* 14 May 1999.

29. Paul Virilio, *Open Sky,* trans. Julie Rose (London: Verso, 1997), 62.

30. "Poem 997," in *The Complete Poems of Emily Dickinson,* ed. Thomas H. Johnson (Boston: Little, Brown, 1960).

31. "Things Generally Wrong in the Universe" in *Mortal City,* 102–107.

32. See Bobby Wong's discussion of this project in *Beyond Description: Space Historicity Singapore,* ed. Ryan Bishop, John Phillips, and Wei-Wei Yeo (London: Routledge, 2003), as well as Abidin Kusno's extended analysis of Tay's work in his *Behind the Postcolonial: Architecture, Urban Space and Political Architectures in Indonesia* (London: Routledge, 2000).

Taking exception with "postmodern" as an adequate term for describing our contemporary moment, Armitage and Roberts proffer "hypermodern" because of its relation to the continued and heightened projects of Modernity being projected in the present toward a future still determined by Modernity (hence, their portmanteau word, "project(ile)s"). Similarly, they eschew "globalization" in favor of Paul Virilio's "globalitarianism," with its implications of totalitarianism lurking in the emancipatory, neoliberal, democratic capitalist discourses and practices in globalization processes. The terms coalesce in the increasing militarization of society, as exemplified in the "deterritorialization" and "reterritorialization" of humanity found in the mobile Export Processing Zone of Cavite, currently anchored off Manila. Cavite, they argue, represents the total mobilization of everyday life that reflects, intensified, the materiality and military mentality of the current global moment. Being disconnected from any territory, society, or culture except the "gray zone" of profit maximizing, Cavite and other mobile EPZs represent a test site for the hypermodern city of the future. Calling their project an "archeology of the future," Armitage and Roberts examine a fundamental dimension of Southeast Asian city formation that this volume seeks to exemplify: the ways in which the region operates as a testing ground for technics later applied to the cosmopolitan/global cities behind which it supposedly lags. The temporal disjuncture embodied in the phrase "archeology of the future" offers a supplement to received notions of globalization processes past and present. As such, this piece is in dialogue with issues specifically raised by Adams, Bishop and Clancey, Derderian, King, Marcus and

Rivas, Patke, Pile, and Reisz in this volume. Perhaps most provocatively, however, Armitage and Roberts reveal how the Southeast Asian post-but-still-neo-colonial region remains a site of experimentation for (hyper) modernity's many projects.

4

From the Hypermodern City to the Gray Zone of Total Mobilization in the Philippines

JOHN ARMITAGE AND JOANNE ROBERTS

I n the hypermodern city, the "project(ile)s" of hypermodernity, namely, hypercapitalism, globalitarianism, and militarization, surround us, generating the "molar-project(ile)" of hypermodernization: the deterritorialization and reterritorialization of humanity. What does this signify for the materiality and mentality of our everyday life in the hypermodern city? According to our hypermodern sociocultural perspective, the changes have been extreme. Indeed, and inspired by Paul Virilio's "archeology of the future," we argue that the hypermodern city and what Albert Einstein called the "military mentality" are ceding to the time-space of Giorgio Agamben's "gray zone" and what we call "total mobilization." A time-space or "mobile city" cut loose from temporal and territorial, social and cultural responsibility, the gray zone is presently effecting a new mentality of total mobilization conditioned by emergency and disintegration.

We suggest that the transformations in the materiality and the military mentality of our everyday life in the hypermodern city are the symbols of our entry into the time-space of the gray zone of total mobilization. We interpret the significance of these changes through a case study of Export Processing Zones (EPZs) in the Philippines, and, in particular, the EPZ of Cavite, a mobile city currently anchored thirty kilometers south of the capital city, Manila.

We begin by defining and discussing the concepts of the hypermodern city and the military mentality before raising the important question of the advent of the time-space of the gray zone and the mentality of total mobilization. EPZs in the Philippines are accordingly considered as mobile cities, as gray zones and sites of total mobilization conditioned by and facilitated through emergency. We then analyze the EPZ of Cavite, its mobilization and disintegration, prior to providing a number of critical and concluding comments.

THE HYPERMODERN CITY

The hypermodern city of the twenty-first century is an outstanding exposition of hypermodernity, a concept that refers to any contemporary social experience containing an excessive or greater than usual amount of various elements relating to the materiality and mood, processes, history, quality, or state of modernity.[1] In our account, it is in the hypermodern city where we find the project(ile)s of hypermodernity. Briefly, we define a project(ile) as "any project or projection that entails physical objects and environments or human subjects being thrown forward in the manner of a self-propelling rocket, especially one that is powered by or fired from business corporations, political organizations, and military institutions."[2] The time-space continuum of the project(ile)s of hypermodernity is characterized by modern capitalism and globalization morphing into a hypercapitalism or "dromo-economics" of excessive speed.[3] Founded on the corporeal and the increasingly ephemeralized commodities provided by information and communications technologies (ICTs) such as the Internet, hypercapitalism and dromo-economics are therefore intimately connected to Virilio's critique of the development of a totalitarian "world time" or what he calls globalitarianism.[4] Similarly, the transformation of the modern military-industrial complex into the "hypermodern military-scientific complex" involves the increasing immersion of people in the project(ile) of militarization.[5] The creation of the molar-project(ile) of hypermodernization, therefore, depends on "rigid sedimentations which function according to laws of statistics, so that the effects of precise details, differences and singularities are cancelled out."[6] The molar-project(ile) of hypermodernization consists of a multitude of economic and social, technological, political, military, and other project(ile)s that create, coincide, collide with, or follow the transition from modernity to hypermodernity, hypercapitalism, globalitarianism, and the hypermodern military-scientific complex. In the context of the project(ile) of deterritorialization ("leaving home and traveling in foreign parts"), a movement away from the settled life of whole populations is coupled with the development of reterritorialization ("making a new dwelling place") and the generalized turbulence of human migration.[7]

What does this denote for the corporeality and mindset of our everyday life in the hypermodern city? This question has become a specific focus of research for hypermodern social and cultural theory, founded on an appreciation of the transmutations of modernity and modernism into the extremes of hypermodernity and hypermodernism. In fact, as archeologists of the future, we want to propose that the hypermodern city and Einstein's military mentality are yielding to the time-space of the gray zone, what we label total mobilization and the emergence of the mobile city.[8]

However, before proceeding with this argument, it might be helpful to clarify what is meant by the methodological tradition of the archeology of the future. The archeology of the future is concerned with the examination of urban and other contemporary innovations in order to indicate the time-spaces of future mutations with a view to signaling to others potential negative effects through the extrapolation and amplification of present tendencies.

Hence, to speak of the hypermodern city is to speak of a city that is no longer governed by capitalism but by hypercapitalism and other globalitarian systems related to the hypermodern military-scientific complex and the perpetual deterritorialization and reterritorialization of people. Moreover, it is within the hypermodern city that the civilian materiality and mentality surrenders to what Einstein labeled the military mentality, that is, the tendency of "people to place the importance of . . . 'naked power' far above all other factors which affect the relations between people."[9]

Yet, within the conventions of the archeology of the future, we believe that the hypermodern city and the military mentality are succumbing to the time-space of the gray zone of total mobilization. To be sure, we want to propose that the original innovation made by business corporations, political organizations, and military institutions in the EPZs of the Philippines requires the construction of new time-spaces or mobile cities. For EPZs are not merely free of almost all temporal and spatial, social, and cultural concerns but are mobile cities in which the new mentality of total mobilization is obtained. The instant of discharge and stimulus for the project(ile) of total mobilization can be designated as the complete and permanent mindset and corporeal preparedness for war or similar emergencies involving the reorganization and disintegration of local, national, and global economic, political, and military rights and resources. In the time-space of the gray zone of total mobilization, the hypercapitalist, globalitarian, and militarized partnership between worker and owner thus becomes a hypermodernized emergency.[10] This partnership is then reorganized to the point of breakdown, as former workers become deterritorialized "contractors" and the reterritorialized transnational corporation (TNC) emerges as a "casualty" of "global competition." The materiality and mentality of everyday life in the hypermodern city is thus transformed under extreme conditions. The archeology of the future accordingly reveals the advent of the time-space of the gray zone of total mobilization in the EPZs of the Philippines and the appearance of the mobile city in the time-space of hypermodernity.

THE GRAY ZONE OF TOTAL MOBILIZATION

From the standpoint of hypermodern social and cultural theory then, our argument is that the metamorphosis of the hypermodern city has been extraordinary. Additionally, and in conformity with the archeology of the future, we argue that it is possible to trace the "disappearance" of the hypermodern city and the military mentality. For the ephemeralization of the hypermodern city and the military mentality converges with the appearance of the gray zone of total mobilization in the cities of the Third World in the 1980s. In brief, we connect the signs of the time-space of the gray zone of total mobilization—the time-space of the mobile city spatial, social, and cultural negligence and the new mentality of exigency and decay—unambiguously with the appearance of EPZs in Mexico, Indonesia, China, Vietnam, and the Philippines.

The hypermodern city is, consequently, in the process of revolutionizing the materiality of our hypermodern everyday lives in the extreme as it becomes no longer a hypermodern city but a gray zone. The time-space of the gray zone is the site of the ceaseless appearance and disappearance of territory, sociality, and cultural responsibility. Here, the rise of hypercapitalism corresponds to the rise of a new mentality disconnected from the social and cultural life of the town and province.

Thus, on the one hand, the hypermodern city presents the tangible representation of a military regime and mentality of naked power. On the other, the time-space of the gray zone is perceived as a zone conditioned by the hypermodern military-scientific complex, the project(ile) of militarization, and the new hypermodern reality. It is a time-space in which the mentality of deterritorialized and reterritorialized total mobilization—or the frame of mind associated with the unbroken and lasting preparation for crisis and decomposure—is all too evident.

Consequently, the architectural conjectures of the Archigram group of the 1960s and contemporary "urbanists" such as Virilio have at last been realized. For, today, the inert hypermodern city and the military mentality of the era of hypermodernism can be contemplated as nothing less than an "instant" or "plug-in" city environment and a mental outlook that can be continually moved around.[11] Indeed, in the present period the gray zones of total mobilization are already executing the practice of the relentless movement of production from EPZs in South Korea to Indonesia and from China to Vietnam. We turn now specifically to an examination of the gray zones of total mobilization evident in the EPZs of the Philippines.

INTO THE PHILIPPINES

Hypermodern EPZs have gained significance during the past three decades as excessive means of achieving greater socioeconomic "openness" and "growth."[12] But what are the connections between the emergence of hypermodern EPZs and the project(iles) of hypermodernity? What projects and projections are business corporations, political organizations, and military institutions currently throwing forward? Clearly, the time-space continuums of EPZs and the project(ile)s of hypermodernity are characterized by hypercapitalism. Originating in the 1960s,[13] there are now well over 850 EPZs operating around the world.[14] An EPZ is, of course, a physical geographic area within the territory of a country where particular kinds of socioeconomic activities and commodities are promoted and produced through political policies that are not generally applicable to the rest of the country. Increasingly built on the transfer of ever more advanced technology, hypercapitalist export-oriented manufacturing activity in the EPZs is conducted by leading and speeding foreign-owned globalitarian firms. Host countries, however, must offer incentives to attract investment into EPZs, including of duty-free status and tax holidays, exemption, and reduction; simplified administrative procedures and fewer regulations; and improved infrastructure and facilities. Benefits to the host countries, meanwhile, include job creation, improved capability of foreign exchange earnings, and trade expansion. Moreover, as we shall see below, EPZs follow a common trajectory that is linked not only to the transformation of the modern military-industrial complex into the hypermodern military-scientific complex but also to the project(ile) of militarization and its increasing integration into the local economy. The typical life cycle of an EPZ is thus marked by a number of features associated with the molar-project(ile) of hypermodernization. These features include the growth of net exports, levels of unionization, and domestic sales alongside the decline of the share of the dominant industry in total employment, of female workers, and of total value added accounted for by fully owned foreign subsidiaries.[15] Additionally, as EPZs rigidify, they become less attractive to the nomadic TNCs that can easily relocate to, or contract out, production to firms in different or newly established EPZs. Characterized by the molar-project(ile) of hypermodernization, EPZs therefore present themselves as important geographical and geopolitical sites for the transition from modernity to hypermodernity, for the transition from the fixity of modern territory to the flux of hypermodern deterritorialization and reterritorialization.

Material necessity and a mental desire to engage in the increasingly globalized everyday life of the gray zone of total mobilization characterizes countries establishing EPZs, and the Philippines is no exception in this regard. Largely resulting from pressure from major international development agencies, including the World Bank, the hypercapitalist transition from modernity to hypermodernity in the Philippines is predicated on the pursuit of "outward looking" development patterns. Indeed, this future-oriented strategy has been the defining feature of the Philippines government's socioeconomic policy since the late 1960s.[16] The aim of this policy is the eventual elimination of the hypermodern cities of the Philippines and their military mentality. Thus, the deregulation of business, trade and investment liberalization, the encouragement of export manufacturing, and the establishment of EPZs all facilitate the introduction of the time-space of the gray zone of total mobilization, the mobile city of tomorrow's fully integrated global economy.[17]

These future-oriented policies have already resulted in significant growth in the inward stock of foreign direct investment in the Philippines, from U.S.$1,281 million in 1980 to U.S.$11,199 million in 1999.[18] According to UNCTAD, of the 110 approved EPZs in the Philippines, 56 are active, offering tax holidays of four to eight years, and duty-free imports and exports. In total, the direct and indirect employment generated by EPZs in the Philippines amounts to 609,000.[19] The main investor countries in these urban innovations are Japan, the Philippines, and the United States, while the main sector is electrical machinery.[20] Not surprisingly, electrical and electronic equipment accounted for 58.2 percent of the country's merchandise exports in 2000.[21] Yet the key questions that arise from within the methodological perspective of the archeology of the future concern the *analysis* of these new urban forms. What kind of innovation is the EPZ? What transformations and negative effects are apparent today or are likely to appear in the future in the Philippines?

In attempting to answer such questions it is important to remember that, quite apart from the contemporary openness to hypercapitalism noted above, the hypermodern cities of the Philippines also have a long history of engagement with globalitarianism and militarization, with deterritorialization and reterritorialization. For example, Kelly notes that the discourse of globalization in the Philippines is "facilitated" by its "colonial history and post-colonial political economy," citing in particular the importance, impact, and "influence of Western, mostly American, media" and the "cultural distinction invested in foreign brands and images."[22]

Engagement with hypercapitalism and globalitarianism in the Philippines is also stimulated by the transition from the modern military-industrial complex to the hypermodern military-scientific complex or the project(ile) of militarization. Throughout the Cold War, for instance, U.S. military bases such as Subic Bay provided a significant economic contribution to the Philippines, accounting for an estimated four percent of the gross domestic product (GDP) and employing some 42,000 people in the 1980s.[23] Indeed, as late as 1989, 15,000 U.S. armed forces personnel were permanently stationed in the Philippines, with visits by aircraft carriers increasing the total number to 25,000.[24] These forces thus provided the local population with jobs directly supporting the modern military-industrial complex as well as employment in the local leisure, sex, and entertainment industries. However, as the modern military-industrial complex gave way to the post–Cold War hypermodern military-scientific complex, the United States withdrew its military presence from the Philippines in 1992. The recent establishment of the Subic Bay Free Port and Special Export Processing Zones are therefore directly connected to the effort to minimize the economic and global impact of the U.S. military withdrawal on the Philippines.

There are, of course, other ways in which the people of the Philippines are attempting to reduce the effects of hypercapitalism, globalitarianism, and militarization on their country. One of these ways is through the dialectic of deterritorialization and reterritorialization. For, as Kelly points out, "the aspiration of working abroad" has not merely been realized by large numbers of Filipinos but has also "served to ensure the continuation of an economy, and a cultural identity, that is firmly grounded in the opportunities that lie, or come from, abroad."[25] Enlisting this deterritorialized cultural identity, the Philippines government encourages the global reterritorialization of its population. Thus, the deterritorialization of Filipinos is facilitated through agencies such as the Philippines Overseas Employment Administration (POEA), established in 1982. Exporting workers and importing remittances are, therefore, important mechanisms to cope with unemployment and foreign debt running at 11.1 percent and U.S.$51 billion, respectively, in 2000.[26] For example, according to Sassen,[27] newly reterritorialized Filipino overseas workers—many of them women working as nurses, maids, or in the sex and entertainment industries of the United States, the Middle East, and Europe—have sent home almost U.S.$1 billion per annum on average in the last few years. The scale and significance of this source of income becomes clear when compared with the Philippines GDP of U.S.$75.2 billion in 2000.[28] In the hypermodern cities and EPZs of the Philippines then, modern capitalism and globalization, together with the modern military-industrial complex and its territories, are ceding to hypercapitalism and globalitarianism, to the hypermodern military-scientific complex, and to the dialectic of deterritorialization and reterritorialization.

In other words, from the standpoint of the archeology of the future, the hypermodern cities of the Philippines and their military mentality are, particularly in the wake of the Asian financial crises of the late 1990s, presently being transformed into new time-spaces or the gray zones of total mobilization. These transformations are being led, of course, by the "entrepreneurial" activities of various business corporations, political institutions, and militarized institutions within the Philippines. Thus, while the Filipino business community makes much of its commitment to "openness," the government's *Medium-Term Philippine Development Plan (MTPDP) 1999–2004,*[29] on the surface at least, promotes a harmonious vision of "sustainable development and growth with social equity" through free competition and integration into the global economy. However, the *MTPDP* is also a plan that openly acknowledges the need for the entire population of the Philippines to prepare itself for militarization. For, as the following quotation from the *MTPDP* makes clear, it is not only the nation's EPZs that require the creation of new time-spaces or mobile cities where the emerging mentality of total mobilization rules. Indeed, according to the *MTPDP*,

> . . . all sectors—social, political, cultural and economic—will help strengthen the foundation and facilitate the mobilization of resources and institutions to pursue the *MTPDP* vision. Thus, the long-enduring Filipino value of *pagkakaisa* or solidarity, reinforced by the people's resiliency to changes remain crucial in uplifting the lives of the poor at the same time that all Filipinos face the challenge of vast and rapid developments in the global economy.[30]

On this account, then, all sectors of society in the Philippines are to become incorporated into the project(ile) of total mobilization. Everyone is expected to prepare for a life lived as if under conditions of war and emergency. That is, they are expected to prepare for a life lived under conditions of permanent reorganization and the disintegration of all social resources and institutions in the pursuit of the *MTPDP*'s "vision." But in the time-space of the gray zone of total mobilization can the values of partnership between worker and owner remain values based on solidarity? Or will they, instead, be transformed into a hypermodernized emergency, a form of social breakdown predicated not on the "people's resiliency to changes" and "uplifting the lives of the poor" but on the relentless dialectic of the deterritorialization of contractors and the reterritorialization of TNCs under the sign of global competition? Let us look at the materiality and mentality of everyday life in an EPZ in the Philippines that is currently being transformed under extreme conditions. One such EPZ is the time-space or mobile city of the gray zone of total mobilization of Cavite.

CAVITE—A MOBILE CITY?

Cavite, which occupies a 276-hectare site located approximately thirty kilometers south of Manila in the town of Rosario, is an excellent example of the hypermodern EPZ. It has grown from just a few factories employing less than 100 people in 1986[31] to a major center for electronics and garment manufacturing comprising over 200 enterprises employing 54,141 people in March 1998.[32] The time-space continuum of the project(ile)s of hypermodernity in this gray zone is one in which factory operatives assemble the finished products of the hypercapitalist and speeding "branded world" of Nike running shoes and Gap pajamas, Old Navy jeans and IBM computer screens. Cavite is one of the few globalitarian places on the planet where those new totalitarians, the superbrands, mark neither world-time nor space. Inside this hypermodern military-scientific complex, however, there is the unmistakable submersion of workers in the project(ile) of militarization. The inception of the molar-project(ile) of hypermodernization in Cavite is contingent upon what Klein calls a type of "pure, 100 percent production" that functions in conformity with the statistical logic of maximal production, work rates, and working hours.[33] In fact, hypermodernization in the time-space of the gray zone of Cavite can, according to Klein, be characterized as nothing short of a "tax free economy, sealed off from the local government of both town and province—a miniature military state inside a democracy."[34] The deterritorialized young workers in the military state of Cavite consequently create their newly reterritorialized dwelling-place in a transit lounge somewhere between a local "here" and the global "now." Employed by migrant contractors and subcontractors from Korea, Taiwan, and Hong Kong, these totally mobilized workers occupy their own space-time completing "orders" for U.S., U.K., and other First World TNCs.

How can we explain the meaning of these developments and their impact upon the bodies and outlook on everyday life of Filipinos? Our answer to this question and the result of analysis within hypermodern social and cultural theory is that the EPZ of Cavite is not merely a gray zone but, equally important, a hypermodern *test site* for the totally mobilized hypermodern cities of the future. Consequently, it is important to show how the disappearance of the hypermodern city and the military mentality are giving way to the appearance of the gray zone of total mobilization in the mobile city of Cavite.

First, the gray zone of Cavite is a new time-space that is ruled by a form of hypercapitalism that has severed almost all connections to the surrounding territory. Here, the globalitarian search for territory is associated with the hypermodern military-scientific complexes and the continuing deterritorialization and reterritorialization of factories and workers. Additionally, it is inside gray zones such as Cavite that the civilian materiality and mentality has capitulated to the military mentality of naked power. As Klein writes, in this "cardboard complex," fear is ever present for, in a climate where the government is afraid of losing foreign factories, "the factories are afraid of losing their brand-name buyers" and "the workers are afraid of losing their unstable jobs."[35]

What, then, of the appearance of the time-space of the gray zone of total mobilization? Our answer is that the ingenious innovation made by hypercapitalist corporations, political agencies, and the military in Cavite and elsewhere in the Philippines is that of the creation of a new time-space: the mobile city. Indeed, as Klein notes, Cavite is "designed as a fantasyland for foreign investors" complete with golf courses and "executive clubs," while "private schools have been built on the outskirts of Rosario to ease the discomforts of Third World life."[36] In the same way, the driving force behind this EPZ is the Philippines federal Department of Trade and Industry, a department that has the power to refuse even the local police and municipal governments the right to cross Cavite's borders. Performing in the manner of a siege warfare-like blockade, Cavite thus functions to keep the possibly unruly masses of Rosario far from the expensive goods being assembled inside the zone and blinds the rest of the population of the Philippines to the activities taking place within it. The EPZ of Cavite is therefore crucially engaged with reinforcing the idea that, from this moment onward, everything is mobile, including the city.

The new mentality of total mobilization accordingly heralds the era in which companies can present themselves as economic tourists while everyone else is "held hostage to the threat of departure."[37] Total mobilization in Cavite, however, is not merely based on the fear of scaring away foreign investors but also on an assault on labor rights and working conditions as well as the introduction of starvation wages and "iron fist rules" of production. In a factory that makes Old Navy jeans, for example, seamstresses, mindful of the perils of "nonproductive time," occasionally have to "resort to urinating in plastic bags under their machines."[38] Likewise, the last bastions of the civilian mentality at work crumble after the introduction of rules against talking or even smiling within some Cavite factories. So, both within and beyond this gray zone, the emergency requires the reorganization and disintegration of local, national, and global economic, political, and military rights and resources.

It is also in the time-space of the gray zone of total mobilization where the partnership between worker and factory owner becomes an emergency. For example, when First World TNCs landed in Taiwan and Korea in the early 1990s, local contractors operated the factories. However, once the TNCs began their flight from one EPZ to the next, the original contractors were left with nothing but empty factories. Since then, though, the contractors have literally learned to move with the times. For now they fly almost alongside the TNCs, opening and closing factories in EPZs all the way to Cavite while the TNCs of the First World focus their attention on "brand management," outsourcing the manufacture of goods and the associated risks to the contractors. As Klein puts it, "maintaining contractors who have had the rug pulled out from under them once before is a stroke of management genius on the part of western multinationals. What better way to keep costs down than to make yesterday's casualties today's wardens?"[39] And, we may add, what better way to transform the materiality and mentality of everyday life in the hypermodern city and prepare for the hypermodern era of the gray zone of total mobilization in the mobile city?

The significance of Cavite consequently lies in the fact that it is a kind of secret state where maximum production and pure work, ID cards, and armed guards discourage all visitors. In contrast to the materiality and military mentality of everyday life in the hypermodern city, Cavite presents an image of the time-space of the gray zone that is distinct from free-trade zones and city-states as well as from free ports and offshore banking zones such as the Cayman Islands. Rather, the gray zone of Cavite is a new, assembly only, state in which all taxes have been abolished and the twelve-hour workday has been normalized through the imposition of military-style management, below subsistence wages, and low skilled work performed by migrants on short-term contracts.[40]

Importantly, such changes are often less concerned with industrialization than with militarization and the elimination of industrial unrest, with the sale of the lowest citizens to the highest bidder in the minimum wage war against the economic tourists presently resident in "Corporate Club Med."[41] However, as noted, the transformation of the Philippines is part of an ongoing First World transformation of the Third World. This transformation necessitates the disintegration of local cultures and economies, the creation of non-unionized workforces, and, above all, severing the link between territory and sovereignty in an effort to introduce and expand the mentality of total mobilization. A state that remains entirely separate from the Philippines, Cavite is the "futuristic industrial suburbia" of hypercapitalist revolutionaries intent on storming and globalizing the gray zone.[42] But it is a state composed of concrete bunkers and overshadowed not only by threats of departure but also of imminent disconnection from the territory, society, and culture of the Philippines, not to mention the town of Rosario.

Gearing up for total mobilization is, as a result, crucially concerned with the removal of unions[43] and the installation of a regime that relies on a fear of questioning authority at work and the introduction of regular threats, forced overtime, and job insecurity. As Klein puts it, what is "happening in the EPZs is a radical alteration in the very nature of factory work."[44] None of this is intended to suggest that the preparations for total mobilization remain unchallenged. Resistance to the removal of unions in Cavite, for example, is coordinated through organizations such as "The Solidarity of Cavite Workers" and the "Workers' Assistance Center."[45] And this resistance takes place despite the best efforts of national and local agencies to extend their factory regime beyond Cavite into the "total reproductive and domestic spheres of their workforce."[46] As one company manager explained, campaigns aimed at workers' compliance with the authority of the supervisor are not only conducted at work but also "through their wives, their children, their mothers . . . so that the people will be told not to go on strike." Forced overtime, job insecurity, and other major changes in the factories of Cavite, meanwhile, are maintained through the elimination of permanent labor, the introduction of temporary working, and the constant churning of the workforce supplied by local employment agencies. Nevertheless, such preparations are actually preparations for life in the mobile city grounded on migration and the desertification of the hypermodern city. Homeless, landless, and often broke, the young workers in Cavite exist in an atmosphere of work-induced delirium, alienation, and fear, in which immobile mothers and pregnant women or those with children, for example, are viewed by the factory owners with contempt.[47]

Creating the gray zone that is the totally mobilized city means destroying the immobility of the inhabitants of the hypermodern city. The era of total mobilization is the era of a new mentality spearheaded by the increasingly mobilized workers and factories of the EPZs and founded on permanent migration and instability, fear, and the wage race to the bottom. Last, it is important to understand that, while Cavite may currently be hypercapitalism's fantasyland in the Third World, it looks set to become the stuff of nightmares in the First World as it too prepares for its entry into the gray zone of total mobilization.

CONCLUSION

Challenging the economic, political, and militarized character of the hypermodern city and its correlation with hypermodernity is, like much of our recent work, chiefly aimed at generating discussion of these important concepts.[48] The essence of any such discussion must begin by considering the usefulness of incorporating the principal ideas we have identified with the hypermodern investigation of the city. For the conceptualization of the project(ile)s of hypermodernity and hypercapitalism, globalitarianism, and militarization—together with their contributions to the molar-project(ile) of hypermodernization, deterritorialization, reterritorialization, and the turmoil of diaspora—gives rise to a number of themes that require further elaboration and debate.

What, for instance, might the concept of the project(ile)s of hypermodernity contribute to our understanding of the significance of the changes to the materiality and mentality of our everyday life in places *beyond* the hypermodern city? Obviously, an important question concerns the identification of the main subjects of any fully developed hypermodern social and cultural theory based on the notion of excess. What can such a theory bring to the contemporary analysis of the hypermodern city or other as yet unexplored spaces? Perhaps Virilio's and our own attempts to apply the methodology of the archeology of the future are an impossible dream, attempting, as they do, to apprehend the present day as well as the future by excavating the here and now.

Despite such conceptual and methodological difficulties, it remains the case that the ideas associated with the hypermodern city and the military mentality are especially relevant to contemporary questions relating to the gray zone structured around the mentality of total mobilization. Of course, it has to be said that it is much too early to speak of the impact of questions and motifs related to the time-space of mobile cities that are autonomous of most social and cultural obligations. Nevertheless, surely it is sometimes just as important to articulate new questions and themes for debate as it is to try and answer old ones. From this vantage, it is clear that conceptualizing the emergent places and mental spaces of the First World and the Third World in the twenty-first century will benefit from an engagement with the concepts of the gray zone and total mobilization. Lütticken, for instance, in a significant article titled "Parklife," has identified hypercapitalism's fantasyland in the First World as a dream world of "fenced-in-spaces" and "gated communities." Invoking the disturbing concept of the "human park"—a kind of menagerie where order and stability must be maintained by the "keepers"—Lütticken makes explicit the "pervasive tendency" in the culture of the First World of the "contemporary fear of social disintegration." Here too "a new kind of urbanism" is at work "in which towns are created as a refuge from the larger community." Split off from society, such "miniature states" or "compounds" are therefore First World gray zones or "parks" that mimic the totally mobilized activities of the country-hopping, nomadic, and deterritorialized TNCs and their contractors that we have been discussing in relation to the Philippines and the EPZ of Cavite.[49]

We have portrayed the twenty-first century hypermodern city propelled by the project(ile)s of hypermodernity as a scene of unprecedented material and mental change. Embracing a hypermodern social and cultural position within the archeology of the future, we have argued that the hypermodern city and the military mentality are acquiescing to the time-space of the gray zone and total mobilization. The concept of the mobile city has confirmed its advantages in conceptualizing spatial, social, and cultural phenomena in the present period of hypermodern emergency and disintegration. The transpositions in the materiality and mentality of everyday life in the hypermodern city described above are significant because they are the most obvious signs of the time-space of the gray zone of total mobilization. The extraordinary changes that these shifts have effected in Third World EPZs are important by virtue of their disconnection from territory, society, and culture and by their relationship to the appearance of the gray zone of total mobilization and the mobile city. The hypermodern Filipino city of Cavite is a key example of the gray zone because, like other EPZs, its total mobilization is a test site for the hypermodern city of the future. Thus, in the new time-spaces of the gray zone, the mobile city has emerged and, with it, a new mentality of emergency and disintegration, transformation, and even revolution—the mentality of total mobilization.

NOTES

1. John Armitage, "Project(ile)s of Hypermodern(organ)ization," *Ephemera: Critical Dialogues on Organization* 1, no. 2 (2001): 131–48.
2. Ibid.
3. See for instance, Phil Graham, "Hypercapitalism: A Political Economy of Informational Idealism," *New Media & Society* 2, no. 2 (2000): 131–56, and John Armitage and Phil Graham, "Dromo-economics: Towards a Political Economy of Speed," *Parallax* 18, no. 1 (2001): 111–23.
4. For a discussion of the term "globalitarianism," see Paul Virilio's interview with John Armitage in *Paul Virilio: From Modernism to Hypermodernism and Beyond,* ed. J. Armitage (London: Sage, 2000), 25–57.
5. See Armitage, "Project(ile)s."
6. See Philip Goodchild, *Deleuze and Guattari: An Introduction to the Politics of Desire* (London: Sage, 1996), 218.
7. Ibid., 218–19; also see Nikos Papastergiadis, *The Turbulence of Migration: Globalization, Deterritorialization, and Hybridity* (Cambridge, Mass.: Polity Press, 2000).
8. Giorgio Agamben, *Remnants of Auschwitz: The Witness and the Archive* (New York: Zone Books, 1999), and Armitage, "Project(ile)s."
9. Albert Einstein, "The Military Mentality," in *Ideas and Opinions* (New York: The Modern Library, 1954/1994), 144–46.
10. Although our work on the gray zone of total mobilization does not draw on the writings of the cultural geographer Nigel Thrift, there are, nevertheless, some important points of convergence between our concept of a "hypermodernized emergency" and Thrift's ideas concerning what he calls the "performing cultures in the new economy." For instance, Thrift argues that "something new is happening to Western capitalism" and that the "something new is preparation for a time that Walter Benjamin once forecast, when the emergency becomes the rule." See Nigel Thrift, "Performing Cultures in the New Economy," *Annals of the Association of American Geographers* 90, no. 4 (2000): 674–92.
11. On Archigram see, for example, Peter Cook, *Archigram* (London: Klotz, 1974). Virilio's thoughts on the mobile city are usefully summarized in his interview with Andreas Ruby, "The Time of the Trajectory," in *Virilio Live: Selected Interviews,* ed. J. Armitage (London: Sage, 2001), 58–65.
12. Wei Ge, *The Dynamics of Export-Processing Zones,* UNCTAD Paper No. 144 (New York: United Nations, 1999).
13. The decline of Shannon International Airport in Ireland, brought about by the jet airline, which, unlike its predecessors, did not require refueling on transatlantic flights led to the establishment of the first EPZ in 1960. The aim of the first EPZ was, therefore, to attract foreign firms and replace the jobs that were lost as a consequence of the airport's decline.
14. International Labour Office, *Labour and Social Issues Relating to Export Processing Zones* (Geneva: International Labour Office, 1998).
15. International Labour Office, *Economic and Social Effects of Multinational Enterprises in Export Processing Zones* (Geneva: International Labour Office, 1988).
16. Sylvia Chant and Cathy Mcilwaine, "Gender and Export Manufacturing in the Philippines: Continuity or Change in Female Employment? The Case of the Mactan Export Processing Zone," *Gender, Place and Culture* 2, no. 2 (1995): 147–76.
17. Philip F. Kelly, "Globalization, Power and the Politics of Scale in the Philippines," *Geoforum* 28, no. 2 (1997): 151–71.
18. UNCTAD, *World Investment Report 2000: Cross-border Mergers and Acquisitions and Development* (New York: United Nations, 2000), 297, Annex table B.3.
19. UNCTAD, *World Investment Report 1999: Foreign Direct Investment and the Challenge of Development* (New York: United Nations, 1999), 453, table A.IX.3.
20. Ibid.
21. The Economist Intelligence Unit, *Country Briefings: Philippines,* [2001]. http://www.economist.com/countries/Philippines.
22. Kelly, "Globalization," 156.

23. Peter J. Rimmer, "US Western Pacific Geostrategy: Subic Bay before and after Withdrawal," *Marine Policy* 21, no. 4 (1997): 333.
24. Ibid., 334.
25. Kelly, "Globalization," 156.
26. Economist Intelligence Unit, *Country Briefings.*
27. Saskia Sassen, "The Excesses of Globalisation and the Feminisation of Survival," *Parallax* 18, no. 1 (2001): 100–10.
28. Economist Intelligence Unit, *Country Briefings.*
29. National Economic Development Authority (NEDA), *Medium-Term Philippine Development Plan, 2001–2004,* [2001]. Available for order via http://www.neda.gov.ph/.
30. Ibid.
31. Philip F. Kelly, "Everyday Urbanization: The Social Dynamics of Development in Manila's Extended Metropolitan Region," *International Journal of Urban and Regional Research* 23 (1999): 293.
32. Philip F. Kelly, "The Political Economy of Local Labour Control in the Philippines," *Economic Geography* 77, no. 1 (2001): 6. A more recent, though perhaps less reliable, set of figures is available from the Rotary Club of Cavite. The Rotary Club states that in 1999 there were 220 actively operating companies, employing a total of 62,000 management and production workers in Cavite. A further estimated 4,500 people were employed by brokers, banks, security agencies, canteens, subcontractors, and other offices doing business inside the zone. For further details see the Rotary Club of Cavite Export Processing Zone Website at http://www.rccepz.org.
33. Naomi Klein, *No Logo* (London: Flamingo, 2001), 203.
34. Ibid., 204.
35. Ibid., 206.
36. Ibid.
37. Ibid., 209–10.
38. Ibid., 211.
39. Ibid., 225.
40. Jean-Paul Marhoz, with Marcela Szymanski, for the ICFTU, "Behind the Wire: Anti-union Repression in the Export Processing Zones," *International Confederation of Free Trade Unions,* April 1996. http://www.itcilo.it/english/actrav/telearn/global/ilo/frame/epzicftu.htm.
41. Klein, *No Logo,* 207.
42. Ibid., 208.
43. Like other EPZs in the Philippines, Cavite operates a "no union no strike" policy. See International Confederation of Free Trade Unions, "Philippines: Annual Survey of Violations of Trade Unions Rights, (2002)," *International Confederation of Free Trade Unions,* [2002]. http://www.icftu.org/displaydocument.asp?Index=991215667&Language=EN.
44. Klein, *No Logo,* 218.
45. The Workers Assistance Center was established in Cavite in 1995 as a socio-pastoral program of the Most Holy Rosary Parish in Rosario. The Inter-Church Action for Development Relief and Justice group supports the center. For further details see "Organizing and Supporting Workers in the Philippines," *Inter-Church Action 1999/2000 Annual Report,* [2001]. http://www.web.net/~icact/9900annual_report/9900ej_philippines.html.
46. This and the following quotation are taken from Kelly, "Political Economy," 11–12.
47. According to the International Confederation of Free Trade Unions, young women in Cavite have to sign a document saying that the employer can dismiss them if they get married. See the ICFTU site at http://www.icftu.org.
48. See, for example, Armitage, "Project(ile)s."
49. Sven Lütticken, "Parklife," *New Left Review,* July/August (2001): 111–18. Interestingly, as evidenced in Kelly's (2001) interviews with them, many of the managers of the factories inside Cavite and other EPZs in the Philippines commonly refer to EPZs as "parks."

By exploring the creative productions of the Vietnamese community in Paris, and contrasting it with those produced by the other substantial postcolonial community in the city, the Algerians, Derderian explores the myriad ways colonial and postcolonial movements of people, ideas, and representations shape the relation of urban space. If the colonial city haunts its temporal coeval, the cosmopolitan site, then the colonial and postcolonial cities similarly haunt the imaginations of diasporic groups in the contemporary moment, and provide a range of ways for thinking through urbanism that flesh out standard concepts in unexpected ways. By exploring current cultural productions in Paris of colonial and postcolonial Saigon and Hanoi, Derderian taps into a spectral mode of collective memory that is oddly complementary with the vampire's presence in empirial cities (as examined by Pile later in this volume), revealing evocative temporalities at play in the historicity of any given urban site. Similarly, the colonial experiment to control populations in the colonies is reiterated in the cosmopolitan site, having profound effects on the boulevard and architecture, as well as on police tactics. In this way, the colonial site inscribes experience at the quotidian and extraordinary levels found in a walk, a film, a piece of music, or a riot. The ebb and flow of influence between city sites that belie narratives of unidirectionality and belatedness addressed in this article complements issues addressed in Adams, Armitage and Roberts, Bishop and Clancey, King, Marcus and Rivas, Patke, and Reisz, just as the connection between historicity and creative productions as a means of negotiating urban space finds resonance with the pieces by Lim and Yeo, all found in this volume.

5

Urban Space in the French Imperial Past and the Postcolonial Present

RICHARD DERDERIAN

U rban space is central to the rich and still largely unexplored corpus of creative works produced by younger generations of Vietnamese and Algerians raised in France. As sites of creativity and loss, desire and decadence, perceptions of urban space in cultural productions by members of France's Vietnamese community echo many older themes from the French imperial past. Comparing the treatment of urban space by Vietnamese and Algerian cultural actors, however, we discover important conceptual differences based on divergent imperial legacies. Very different socioeconomic profiles, housing experiences, wars of decolonization, and stereotypes from the imperial era are key determinants that influence dissimilar visions of urban space.

Yet in the case of both Algerian and Vietnamese cultural actors the urban space is seen and experienced through the lens of past conflicts. For the Vietnamese community, it is the Vietnam War that creates pro- and anti-Hanoi internal divisions that are mapped out within the confines of the center city. For Algerians, it is the still unresolved memories of the Algerian War that pit Algerian youth against French authorities in the urban periphery. However, if in both the French and Algerian perceptions the working-class suburbs or *banlieues* have become the nation's most racially charged sites of conflict, it is because they are fueled by an Algerian past that continues to exert a powerful hold on the present.

What is unique about Paris, explains jazz guitarist Nguyen Le, are the limitless possibilities for exchange and interaction with ethnic minority artists from around the globe. Although he secured his first commercial outlets in Germany with its more developed market for jazz music, he has found it hard to imagine that the kind of collaborative work that has enriched his music could have taken place in any other city than Paris. Discs such as his 1998 *Maghreb & Friends,* which features a blend of Algerian and Moroccan artists, or his earlier ethno-fusion of African sounds with the group Ultramarine, are products of what Nguyen casts as a particularly open and dynamic Parisian environment. He points out that today's world music market dominated by African rhythms still leaves far too little room for Vietnamese sounds, but he acknowledges that the status of Paris as a hub for this burgeoning new genre has been of great benefit to his own career.[1]

At a time when scholars alert us to the rise of cultural racism, which criminalizes cities as lawless sites overrun by dangerous and unmeltable ethnics, Nguyen presents the French urban environment in very different terms. Echoing the views of Paul Gilroy, Nguyen emphasizes the cultural borrowings, fusion, and syncretism that take place in former colonizing capitals like Paris and London.[2] Nguyen's optimism recalls that of French urban designers and administrators who once saw imperial cities in terms of the endless opportunities they presented to advance the conceptualization, construction, and management of complex urban communities. Bringing home the skills and resources acquired overseas was supposed to be the means of breathing life into what they saw as ossified continental cities like Paris. Nguyen voices the same kind of optimism by emphasizing the wealth of creative exchanges between artists from the former imperial periphery who now reside in the metropolitan center. In the postcolonial urban present, Nguyen's example shows us that knowledge, skills, and creativity continue to flow between the old imperial center and its peripheries. It was through his collaboration with traditional Vietnamese musicians and singers in the Paris area that Nguyen made his own artistic return journey to Vietnam in the form of the disc *Tales from Vietnam* (1996), a collection of traditional Vietnamese tales interpreted though a fusion of jazz and Vietnamese sounds.

As the vast majority of Vietnamese refugees or "boat people" settled in the United States, interaction between Vietnamese in France and America has become quite common. Pham Phuong Khanh, long-time member of the General Association of Vietnamese Students in France (AGEVP), commented that her association's newspaper, *Nhanban* (humanism), collaborates from time to time with the radio station Little Saigon in Orange County, California. Interviews conducted with prominent members of the Vietnamese community in Paris or the United States are exchanged and aired over Little Saigon or printed in the pages of *Nhanban.*[3] The future of Vietnamese youth in the diaspora was the subject of a recent conference organized in France with the help of the AGEVP. The Second World Conference of Vietnamese Youth brought together some sixty-three associations from over twelve different countries for six days of meetings and cultural exchanges in the town of Athis-Mons just outside of Paris.[4]

Uprooted by decades of conflict stretching back to the French war in Indochina, it is not surprising that many Vietnamese who settled in France harbor sentiments of loss and a desire to recover elements of their personal or collective past. The yearning for the distant fragments of childhood is particularly strong in the work of movie director Tran Anh Hung. The visual attention devoted to insects, lizards, and the seeds of the green papaya outside the 1950s Saigon home in his debut film, *Scent of the Green Papaya* (1993), echo the memories that continue to resonate most powerfully for the director. Although he left his childhood town of Danang at the age of four, Tran still recalls "the smell of fruit coming in through the window, a woman's voice singing on the radio." He remembers this past as a magical moment in his life. "If I've ever experienced harmony in my life it was then." The main character in the film, the servant girl Mui, played by the director's wife Tran Nu Yen Khe who has starred in all three of his movies, seems to embody the undiminished childhood wonder of the director. Although the movie follows the life of Mui from a ten-year-old girl to a young wife, she never loses her fascination for the natural beauty that surrounds her Saigon homes. Tran has since moved on to films about Vietnam's urban present, but memories of childhood remain an important source of inspiration. Commenting on his third and most recent film, *At the Vertical Edge of the Summer* (2000), Tran remarked that he was struggling with the challenge of "translating that rhythm and that musicality [from his childhood] into the new film."[5]

The recovery of a lost urban landscape is not restricted to the past. In a recent interview, Tran explained that the decision to feature present day Saigon and Hanoi in his last two films, *Cyclo* (1996) and *At the Vertical Edge of the Summer,* was inspired by a desire to recover a more authentic urban present. "When you go to Vietnam today," Tran remarked, "the people who've lived through the war with the Americans don't talk about it. It just doesn't come into their minds to do so. And in some ways, possibly subconsciously, I wanted Vietnam to regain her normality."[6] In light of the preponderance of American war films on Vietnam, or more recent nostalgic French films about the colonial past, Tran's movies can be understood as an effort to restore an appreciation of Vietnamese life in the urban present. Set in the fast-paced, money-driven city of Saigon, *Cyclo* features the desperate plight of the city's working poor to eke out a living without succumbing to the rampant crime and corruption that afflicts the former southern capital. *At the Vertical Edge* takes place in the much more tranquil, leafy neighborhoods of Hanoi. The northern city becomes a colorful backdrop for an exploration of the emotional quandaries of three Vietnamese sisters. The diversity of the physical and human geography of Saigon and Hanoi in Tran's movies defies attempts to restrict Vietnamese urban space to American or French narratives of meaning.

Recovering a lost Vietnamese cultural past is central to the work of choreographer Ea Sola.[7] Fleeing her war ravaged homeland and arriving in Paris at the age of sixteen, Ea Sola turned to dance as a means of reconnecting with her Vietnamese roots. Her performances, which combine elements of modern and traditional Vietnamese dance, can partly be understood as a response to the shock of being uprooted from her childhood home in rural northern Vietnam and transplanted to the alien urban environment of Paris. "Suddenly everything was immense: the people, the streets, the buildings, the system of life were unrecognizable." She found that dance offered a means of reconstructing a lost rural environment. Receiving a grant from the French Ministry of Foreign Affairs in 1989, she returned to northern Vietnam where she spent three years recovering traditional dances lost during the war or banned by the Communist regime after independence. Drawing from the memory and actual talent of older village women still able to recall and perform the dances of their youth, Ea Sola has presented her unique fusion of Vietnamese and modern dance to urban audiences around the world.[8]

Of course, many members of the Vietnamese community in Paris were raised entirely in France with no personal memories of Vietnam. Collective projects such as *Pousse de bambou,* the association newspaper of the Union of Vietnamese Youth from France (UJVF), function as important educational resources for learning about Vietnamese culture, religion, history, and current events. These kinds of shared projects are also helpful in offering a forum to express and constructively reflect on the confusion and mixed emotions that often arise when Vietnamese youth travel to cities like Saigon. *Pousse de bambou* writer Thai-Binh Nguyen's first impression after his much-anticipated arrival in Saigon was the enormous "divide between this country and my life as a young Parisian. I wonder whether I'll ever be able to blend into this other world."[9] The desire to fit in, to experience an authentic Vietnam, and to not be labeled as *Viet kieu* (Vietnamese from the diaspora) are recurring themes in personal accounts appearing in *Pousse de bambou.* "We were attached to this country, to the culture, and our families who stayed in Vietnam," explains Mai Lien after her trip to Saigon. "We wanted to know this country, while realizing that some of us would always be *Viet kieu* and tourists in their eyes."[10]

Journeying to Vietnam in search of an authentic experience, many *Viet kieu* react with shock and dismay to the reality of accelerated development and the spread of Western influences in cities like Saigon. In Tran

Anh Hung's *Cyclo* Saigon is reduced to a cesspit of crime, delinquency, and materialism where survival becomes a daily struggle that overwhelms many residents. Similarly, when Thai-Binh Nguyen arrived in Saigon he experienced a combination of "rage mixed with shame at the sight of all these prostitutes who could have been my own mother." He depicts today's Ho Chi Minh City as a violent place filled with "hoards of Honda motorcycles, a thirst for money, and young girls disfigured by the vulgarity of their Western trappings."[11] Upon her return to her Saigon birthplace Viên Phô is not sure how to react to the proliferation of colonial-style buildings in the city. "It's a new dream we're experiencing: to look as much like the Occident as possible. But for someone like me who comes from the Occident how should I understand a Vietnam that looks like the Occident?"[12]

In his critical reading of the film *Cyclo* J. Paul Narkunas suggests that urban spaces such as Ho Chi Minh City must now be understood in terms of global capital flows. For Narkunas, the artistry of Tran's film accurately captures a new Ho Chi Minh City that is in the process of being homogenized by the forces of global capitalism. Just as Vietnamese authorities recede from the foreground, suggesting a loss of national sovereignty, so do ancestral ties and traditional ways of life diminish in importance. What matters in the global present are exchanges and flows of capital that flatten out the city into a "smooth space" by disconnecting it from larger "historical, cultural or national narratives." Although traces of its layered past remain like those on a palimpsest, Ho Chi Minh City becomes a kind of "any-space-whatever."[13]

Narkunas concludes that global capital flows recolonize places like Ho Chi Minh City by homogenizing them to the point where they look like any Western metropolis.[14] "This could be Los Angeles as readily as Ho Chi Minh City," Narkunas asserts. However, Narkunas's overemphasis on the flattening effect of the global capital highway tends to pave over the complex network of human routes that still connect the former imperial center and its peripheries. Tran's decision to focus on the Vietnamese urban present in *Cyclo* and *At the Vertical Edge* cannot be fully understood without recognizing the director's refusal to take the well-trod routes of nostalgia and trauma omnipresent in French films on Indochina and American movies on Vietnam. Yet one might question whether in his desire to find a way home, to recapture and relive the sights, sounds, and rhythms of his homeland, Tran ends up on the even older Orientalist route leading to the timeless ways of life and natural exoticism of the Far East. Whatever conclusions we may reach, these are routes that have no place in Narkunas's account. By claiming that global capital flows have paved over former imperial cities leaving only barely visible and largely insignificant traces of the past, Narkunas fails to recognize the extent to which older human networks rooted in the imperial past and the legacy of decolonization continue to shape influential representations and presentations of places like Ho Chi Minh City.

Dynamic sites of creative inspiration, corruption, loss, and unfulfilled desire, the urban imaginaries of France's Vietnamese cultural actors mirror the themes used by French writers, artists, and urban designers to depict cities at home and in the empire. Gwendolyn Wright argues that cities in the empire were seen by French urban designers as inspiring sites of opportunity and creativity for experiments in urban planning that were impossible to carry out at home. In a tradition-bound metropolitan France, resistance to innovative urban renewal projects was a source of frustration to French urban designers, Wright explains. Under the patronage of powerful colonial administrators less constrained by metropolitan authorities, urban designers enjoyed far-reaching powers to test out and implement new theories and approaches to the management of urban space. From Africa to Indochina, urban designers saw the empire as a valuable site of experimentation for design strategies that could one day restore life and vigor to metropolitan France.[15]

It was precisely because cities at home and the empire were often regarded as dangerous sites of resistance or political sedition that they became objects of various renewal projects. The period of conquest and pacification in Indochina, according to Nicola Cooper, was marked by the same kinds of urban design measures employed by Haussmann to quell resistance in the French capital. If Saigon's neoclassical architecture and wide boulevards mirrored those of Paris it was because of the same desire to reign in and control populations only recently brought under French rule.[16] Similarly, Zeynep Çelik argues that the erection of massive housing projects by French authorities in Algiers from the 1930s through the end of the Algerian War was partly driven by the desire to neutralize the use of traditional homes as bastions of resistance. Housing policies in Algiers, according to Çelik, were integral to French efforts to reinforce imperial power in the colony and to undermine the traditional use of the home as a sheltered matriarchal domain.[17]

Imperial era critics often lambasted French policies in cities like Algiers and Saigon for stripping these urban centers of their indigenous authenticity. In the works of many imperial-era writers, notes Nicola Cooper, Saigon was above all a city that represented the loss of an earlier, purer, pastoral way of life corrupted by the introduction of metropolitan forms of development. Borrowing from a line of reasoning stretching back as far as the time of Tacitus's *Agricola* and the *Germania,* the city came to symbolize not the benefits of French civilization but rather the depravity, corruption, and immorality associated with urban ways of life.[18]

Saigon, the so-called Paris of the Orient, was particularly troubling for French artists precisely because it replicated the capital city at home. In search of a more authentic Indochina, French artists often avoided depicting Saigon and instead chose more remote areas less touched by visible signs of development. Cambodia was a favored location because of its supposedly timeless patterns of life and the ruins of a once glorious Khmer civilization. The temple ruins of Angkor Wat, a Siamese possession attached by the French to Cambodia, became one of the most popular attractions for French artists and tourists alike. A mammoth replica of Angkor Watt was the centerpiece of the 1931 Colonial Exhibition in Paris, an event that drew several million visitors. The recently restored Musée Guimet in Paris, which houses most of the French art collection from its former colonies in Indochina, is still dominated by works from Cambodia.[19]

The influence of the empire in matters of urban design survived the process of decolonization in numerous ways. Many of the colonial urban specialists repatriated to France after the end of empire eventually played an active role in carrying out social engineering projects unprecedented in their scope and ambition.[20] Ironically, it was partly in response to the increased demand for housing created by the nearly one million Europeans who left Algeria after the Evian Accords in 1962 that urban reform and experimentation opportunities expanded at home. Kristin Ross adds that, in terms of French national identity, the end of the empire made urban forms of modernization and development even more of a priority. If France could no longer bask in its imperial grandeur, if it was denied the status of a civilizing power, then it became even more important to distinguish itself from its former empire by becoming even more modern and civilized than its ex-colonies. It is impossible to understand the French obsession with modernization between the 1950s and 1960s, Ross asserts, without taking into account the psychological need of French administrators and elites to distinguish and distance the nation from its former empire and its now defunct imperial identity.[21]

The very different images of urban space in cultural works by Algerians and Vietnamese raised in France have much to do with the dissimilar implications of modernization in postcolonial France. Although prolonged wars of decolonization and independence displaced both communities, the socioeconomic profile of Algerians and Vietnamese who came to France between 1945 and 1975 was dramatically different. The much larger number of Algerians who arrived in France were predominantly from working-class or peasant origins. They took jobs in factories, mines, and construction sites in response to the demands of modernization and France's perennial shortage of homegrown labor. Few provisions were made for the arrival of Algerian workers and their families. Many were simply relegated to shantytowns or *bidonvilles* on the outskirts of French urban centers like Paris, Lyon, and Marseilles. The smaller numbers of Vietnamese who came to France were mostly students from middle-class or upper-class families. Vietnamese students often came with the intention of acquiring skills they could later use at home and never saw themselves as immigrants. Most had no exposure to the dismal housing conditions experienced by Algerian workers and their families.

It is therefore not surprising that memories of deplorable housing conditions are replete in second-generation Algerian accounts of urban space but completely absent from those of Vietnamese youth raised in France. The *bidonvilles,* for example, are prominently featured in a number of films, novels, songs, and documentaries by Algerian youth. In Bourlem Geurdjou's 1998 *Vivre au paradis* [To live in paradise], for instance, the film centers on the exploits of one Algerian worker during the closing years of the Algerian War who desperately attempts to move his family out of the infamous Nanterre *bidonville* in the northern suburbs of Paris. The debut novels of perhaps the two most successful second-generation writers from the Algerian immigrant community, Mehdi Charef and Azouz Begag, feature the *bidonvilles* of Nanterre and Lyon where each spent the early years of their childhood. "Friends from the bidonville, he recognized them by their dirty shoes," writes Charef in *Le thé au harem d'Archi Ahmed* [Tea in the harem of Archi Ahmed].

> The mud. It was useless to polish your shoes there unless you were an incredible acrobat! As soon as you took two steps you were marked. A great distance separated the *bidonville* and the street and you couldn't cross it on your head.[22]

In *Le gone du Chaâba* [The kid from Chaâba], Begag uses a similar blend of humor and realism to portray the stark conditions of the Chaâba *bidonville* outside Lyon. He describes his own concrete house as being lost in the "geometric disorder of the *bidonville*." "The shacks are stuck together, they hang on to each other and all around them. A strong gust of wind would be enough to sweep them all away."[23]

Algerians frequently gained access to improved housing only through a drawn-out, multistage process. The first stage was the move to prefabricated and often substandard "transit cities" meant to temporarily house former *bidonville* dwellers until more permanent public housing became available. Yet as Yamina Benguigui's television documentary *Mémoires d'immigrés* [Immigrant memories] reveals, immigrant families often found themselves parked in these transit cities for over a decade. Toward the end of the documentary, one interviewee puts the question bluntly to the camera and asks how it would ever be possible for anyone to forget the years of living like prisoners locked away in these transit cities. If the future prospects of a nation are measured in terms of its willingness to look at the darker moments of its past, the refusal of all the major networks to air the documentary does not bode well for France. Only the support of the cable station Canal +, explained Benguigui, allowed her to see the project to completion.[24]

The housing experiences of the Vietnamese community were entirely different. The much more privileged Vietnamese students who arrived in France were never exposed to the *bidonvilles* and the transit cities to the same degree as Algerians. As a result, past housing experiences do not scar the urban imaginary of Vietnamese youth raised in France. Even when less privileged Vietnamese refugees arrived in France beginning in 1975, the *bidonvilles* were finally being torn down and their residents moved to more permanent housing. In fact, Nicola Cooper argues that one of the reasons for the French decision to extend a generous welcome to some 40,000 Vietnamese "boat people" was to mask the concomitant tightening of controls on the North African community.[25]

If divergent housing experiences shape different perceptions of urban space so do the legacies of the wars of independence. Although the vast majority of Vietnamese raised in France are too young to have any memories of the war in Indochina, many Algerian youth who arrived or were born in France in the 1950s retain powerful childhood recollections of the Algerian War. Consequently, references to the war in Indochina are almost entirely absent from the cultural productions of Vietnamese youth while the Algerian War is omnipresent in novels, documentaries, songs, and films by second-generation Algerians.[26] Only the first part of Tran Anh Hung's film *Scent of the Green Papaya* overlaps with the French war in Indochina. Yet even here the film centers on an exclusively middle-class Vietnamese family in Saigon, far from the fighting to the north. Only the infrequent and distant sounds of curfew sirens and jet engines overhead offer vague indications of the ongoing conflict.

Here it is important to note that the absence of Indochina does not necessarily mean that Vietnamese artists from France have escaped French modes of representing Southeast Asia. One might underscore Tran Anh Hung's penchant for foregrounding the same kind of image of Indochina as a site of passionate romance and lavish scenery that Panivong Norindr argues is so pronounced in recent French big budget films on Indochina. The rich colors, exotic beauty, and complicated love affairs found in Tran's films are reminiscent of the kind of lavishness, splendor, and romance that Panivong Norindr finds in French films such as *The Lover* (1992), *Indochine* (1992), and *Dien Bien Phu* (1992).[27] It may be going too far to conclude that Tran's work, like those of French filmmakers, helps sustain and perpetuate traditional myths about France's relationship with Indochina. However, the familiar elements found in Tran's films, all released after the trio of French films on Indochina, do raise questions about the ability of ethnic minority artists to resist dominant modes of representation or commercial pressures to market "exotic" spaces in recognizable forms.

If the French war in Indochina is absent in works by Vietnamese raised in France, the American phase is strikingly visible. Not a single article on the Indochina War appeared in a perusal of over a dozen articles of *Pousse de bambou* spanning the period from 1994 to 2000, but dozens featured the Vietnam War. Former editor Jérôme Tham admitted that shedding light on the past for the paper's Paris-area readers was challenging given the limited historical knowledge of many of the writers. "We had to transmit information about traditions that we didn't really understand. So we had to ask others to help explain them."[28] Pham Phuong Khanh remarked that if the French conflict was left out of the performances organized by the AGEVP it was a question of sensitivity to French viewers in the audience. AGEVP festivals frequently include songs and theatrical performances that evoke the memory of soldiers during the Vietnam War and civilians displaced by the conflict. However, given the French presence at many of these performances, she explained, it is simply too difficult to address the earlier war in Indochina.[29]

The AGEVP is part of a Parisian landscape still charged by memories of the Vietnam War. The principal anti-Hanoi association in France, the AGEVP is located in Paris's thirteenth arrondissement, a focal point for the largely anti-Hanoi refugee community. At the meeting place of the AGEVP on the Avenue d'Italie, red and gold promotional posters recall the colors of the flag of the now defunct Republic of South Vietnam. Hung on a corner wall is a black and white framed picture of former association president Trân Va Ba. Pham explained that the picture was a memorial to Trân, who was captured and executed by the Vietnamese government in 1985 after returning to his homeland to take up arms against the communists.[30]

Pousse de bambou, the association newspaper for the UJVF, is situated in the building that houses the parent association, the General Union of Vietnamese in France (UGVF). The principal pro-Hanoi association in France, the UGVF is located in the fourth arrondissement. A short distance across the Seine is a concentration of establishments in the fifth arrondissement including the Sudestasie bookstore, the University of Paris VII–Jussieu, and the Foyer Vietnam, all regarded as being linked to the pro-Hanoi camp. One senior faculty member at Jussieu remarked that students from the anti-Hanoi segment of Paris's Vietnamese community still avoid enrolling in courses in his Vietnamese studies program because of the university's pro-Hanoi image.[31]

The kind of violence that once characterized relations between Paris's pro- and anti-Hanoi communities in the years immediately following the arrival of the boat people in France does seem to have dissipated.[32] Commemorative ceremonies that mark the "fall" of Saigon no longer draw large crowds from the anti-Hanoi camp, and the fights that once erupted during the respective Têt celebrations are now a memory of the past. Some members of the Paris Vietnamese community were quick to point out that internal conflicts were never as violent as those in the United States. This is because most of the former South Vietnamese military officers went to the United States, explained Nguyen Quoc Nam, cofounder and vice president of the Alliance for Democracy in Vietnam. France's Vietnamese community, he added, which is built on an older core of former students like himself, is more open and less volatile than the younger, predominantly refugee community in the United States.[33]

Although passions have cooled, tensions between the pro- and anti-Hanoi communities have not altogether disappeared. *Pousse de bambou* writer and UJVF member Thai-Binh Nguyen still regards the thirteenth arrondissement as a predominately refugee, anti-Hanoi enclave. "If you're in the thirteenth in a restaurant," he commented, "you don't tell people which association you belong to." Tensions between the pro- and anti-Hanoi camps are particularly evident during the period of Têt, the Vietnamese lunar New Year. Nguyen explained that, whereas the anti-Hanoi associations are free to advertise their Têt events within their geographic space, this is not the case for members of his own association. "We can never put up our posters during the day because we'll be attacked as communists, so we put them up at night."[34] Jazz guitarist Nguyen Le added that Têt celebrations are also problematic for musical artists from the Vietnamese community. By performing traditional Vietnamese music at a Têt celebration organized by one or another segment of the Paris Vietnamese community, artists run the risk of being labeled as pro- or anti-Hanoi supporters. Even within the musical community, he explained, there are some musicians who refuse to perform with certain singers because of their perceived political affiliations.[35]

Divisions within the Paris Vietnamese community have repercussions that go beyond France's national borders. As the vast majority of the some two million refugees who left Vietnam after 1975 settled outside of France, the Parisian anti-Hanoi community tends to be much more plugged into the informational and organizational networks of the predominantly anti-Hanoi diaspora. When I met Nguyen Quoc Mylinh, she was preparing to present a speech at a conference in Boston as the representative of the youth wing of her father's association, the Alliance for Democracy in Vietnam. The goal of the international association, she explained, is to help prepare for the eventual transition to democracy in Vietnam.[36] During that same month the AGEVP was helping to organize the Second World Conference of Vietnamese Youth. The conference, which drew over four hundred participants from sixteen different countries, sought to strengthen ties between Vietnamese youth in the diaspora and in Vietnam.[37]

Whereas the legacy of war in Vietnam divides France's Vietnamese community internally within the bounds of the capital, the Algerian War has transformed the urban periphery into a battle zone, pitting Algerian youth against French authorities. In novels by Nacer Kettane, Mehi Lallaoui, and Ahmed Kalaouaz we find a common vision of racial assaults in the urban present as manifestations of the unhealed wounds of the Algerian past.[38] One Algerian youth interviewed in Yamina Benguigui's *Memoires d'immigrés* explains that you can't understand the bitterness harbored by the children of Algerians toward French authorities in the suburbs today without taking into account the memories of police oppression during the Algerian War. Indeed, the single most prominent reference to the Algerian War appearing in songs, novels, and movies by second-generation Algerians is the massacre of Algerian demonstrators by French police on October 16, 1961.

In the mainstream French imagination the suburbs have become the nation's most demonized space. The image of the suburbs is a racialized one that associates ethnic minorities with crime, delinquency, drugs, violence, and institutional breakdown. Powerfully conveyed in films such as *La Haine* (1996), the suburbs today are cast as dysfunctional sites of misery populated above all by ethnic and religious minorities at odds with the authorities and consumed by a rage that threatens to spill over into the urban center. In keeping with a tradition of pathologizing marginal urban spaces that began with medical specialists in the early nineteenth century, François Dubet describes the suburbs as "neighborhoods of exile" that breed a highly volatile sense of detachment and frustration that he terms *la galère*. *La galère*, according to Dubet, is always at risk of degenerating into *la rage*, a destructive form of explosive anger and the chief trigger of the unsettling urban riots that have periodically erupted across France's suburban landscape since the early 1980s.[39]

Images of riotous, deviant, and violent suburban youths in France have become synonymous with second-generation North Africans and Algerians in particular. The fixation on Algerian youth represents a double association with France's urban and imperial past. Second-generation Algerians have become France's new *apaches* or *blouson noirs*—today's version of the delinquents and hoodlums who terrorized the urban periphery during the late nineteenth and mid-twentieth centuries.[40] They have inherited all the dark images of floating populations, threatening strangers, and dangerous classes whose arrival on the urban fringe in the early nineteenth century struck fear into the hearts of the country's urban elite.[41] At the same time Algerian youth trigger still unresolved memories of a bitter eight-year war of decolonization and the loss of a territory considered as an integral part of France. For Kristin Ross, the inability of the French to address the past openly and the impossibility of forgetting are the causes of the surge of neoracism in the 1980s and 1990s.[42] As Anne Donadely puts it, "the explosion of racist violence in France over the past two decades could well be interpreted as a Freudian return of the repressed."[43]

This double demonization of Algerian youth in contrast with the relative invisibility of the Vietnamese community is also the result of very different stereotypes inherited from the imperial era. Éric Savarèse argues that there is a striking resemblance between the image of North Africans in the 1980s and the stereotypes associated with Arabs from the imperial era. "Dishonest, cruel, criminal, promiscuous, violent, fanatical, dangerous, vain, cowardly: almost nothing is missing from the portrait, established one century earlier by ethnologists and travelers." The bitterness left by the war can be understood as contributing to what Savarèse describes as the "reinvention" or the "rediscovery" of Algerian otherness in the 1980s.[44]

In contrast with North and Sub-Saharan Africans, Asians were admired for their more puritan attitudes about sexual relations, their moderation, the gentleness of their values, and their discretion. The absence of polygamy, the smaller stature of Asians, and their image as a more reserved and self-policed community made them less threatening than North and Sub-Saharan Africans, argues Savarèse.[45] Although Asians may never have been deemed capable of bridging the cultural divide that invited and justified French rule, they were certainly regarded as being far closer to their European overlords than was ever the case with French subjects on the African continent.

If the recycling of imperial stereotypes partly explains the visibility of North Africans today it also helps account for the invisibility of Vietnamese. Thai-Binh Nguyen recalled that the French tended to ignore the violent clashes that erupted within the Parisian Vietnamese community. Fights between members of the pro- and anti-Hanoi camps that took place between 1975 and 1985 were seen as internal and largely self-contained disputes. Nguyen argued that the tendency to play down the significance of these struggles was partly due to the image of Asians as "cute, polite, and hard workers in school—they don't make trouble like blacks and Arabs." Asians are not subject to the same kind of hostility as North and Sub-Saharan Africans, explained Nguyen. Rarely has he been exposed to the kinds of racial slurs that he recognized are routinely leveled at ethnic minorities from Africa.

Nguyen pointed out that stereotypes of ethnic communities also shape very different French perceptions of ethnic neighborhoods in Paris. He argued that the predominantly Asian neighborhood in Paris, located in the thirteenth arrondissement in the vicinity of the Place d'Italie, is seen by French visitors in folkloric, nonthreatening terms. The concentration of North and Sub-Saharan Africans in the northern neighborhoods near Barbès in the eighteenth arrondissement evokes very different reactions: "There they see only Africans and this calls to mind images of clandestine immigration and insecurity." "All this occurs unconsciously," continued Nguyen, "Asians are not considered as immigrants like blacks and Arabs."[46]

A member of the UJVF, Nguyen added that an awareness or internalization of racial stereotypes, particularly among older members of the Vietnamese community, has influenced decisions about political actions in the Paris area. According to Nguyen, younger Vietnamese were discouraged by their elders from participating in the civil-rights-style marches against racism in the early 1980s that were spearheaded by second-generation North African association leaders. "When young people wanted to join in the demonstrations against the rise of racism, Le Pen, and the National Front," Nguyen explained, "they were told by their elders that this was not their concern—Asians were not the targets of Le Pen's racism."[47] If Algerian youth perceive the French urban landscape as a geography of escalating hostility and racial intolerance, many Vietnamese do not share this vision. In the case of initiatives like the marches on Paris against racism, different urban visions clearly work against cooperation across ethnic lines.

Stuart Hall's assertion that we are all indelibly marked by the imperial past, although not necessarily in the same ways, appears particularly true for France's Algerian and Vietnamese communities.[48] Both Algerians and Vietnamese were brought to France and prevented from returning home because of the disruption caused by conflicts that began in response to French imperial rule. Although Vietnamese and Algerians both arrived in larger numbers during the period of decolonization, they hailed from very different socioeconomic horizons and experienced dissimilar urban environments. Vietnamese students from a much more privileged background never experienced the trauma of the *bidonvilles* or transit cities that are so prominently featured in the works of second-generation Algerians. Yet the divisions created by past conflicts in Vietnam continue to separate the Vietnamese community of Paris. From association headquarters to bookstores and university campuses, Paris remains a politically charged landscape that reflects the ongoing tensions between the pro- and anti-Hanoi camps.

The divisions created by the past are more far reaching in the case of the Algerian community. Given the greater impact of the Algerian War—a conflict that affected nearly an entire generation of French youth who did their military service in Algeria, roughly one million *pied-noirs* or former European residents displaced from their ancestral home, tens of thousands of Algerians who fought in the French army, and several hundred thousand Algerians who arrived in France during and shortly after the war—it is not surprising the memory of the Algerian past looms much larger in both the French and Algerian imaginary. If the image of the *banlieues* as a war zone pitting angry Algerian youth against overzealous French police has gained broad currency in the popular imagination, it stems from both the unparalleled magnitude of the Algerian War and the accumulated baggage of fears and stereotypes from the French urban and imperial past. By contrast, the French tendency to ignore the internal strife within the Vietnamese community and to exclude them from racialized fears about the suburbs reflects a largely forgotten war in Indochina and more positive images of Asian populations inherited from the imperial past.

NOTES

1. Interview with Nguyen Le, 15 June 2001.
2. Paul Gilroy, *"There Ain't No Black in the Union Jack": The Cultural Politics of Race and Nation* (Chicago: University of Chicago Press, 1991), chapter 3.
3. Interview with Pham Phuong Khanh, 17 June 2001, Paris.
4. For details see the AGEVP website at www.agevp.com.
5. Trevor Johnston, "Features," *The Independent*, 19 August 2001.
6. Carol Allen, "Reel Lives," *The Times of London*, 23 August 2001.
7. The artist's full name is Ea Sola Nguyen Thuy. See Cressard Armelle, "Carnet de Voyage," *Le Monde*, 26 August 1996.
8. Amy Serafin, "A Trek from War to Liberation," *The New York Times*, 4 July 1999.
9. Thai-Binh Nguyen, "Terre de mes aîné(e)s," *Pousse de bambou*, No. 2 (May–June 1994): 12–13.
10. Mai Lien, "Viêt Nam, pays des espoirs," *Pousse de bambou*, No. 3 (June–July 1994): 9.
11. Thai-Binh Nguyen, "Terre de mes aîné(e)s."
12. Viên Phô, "Saigon d'hier et d'aujourd'hui vu par une Viêt kieu," *Pousse de bambou*, No. 5 (November 1994): 24.
13. J. Paul Narkunas, "Streetwalking in the Cinema of the City: Capital Flows through Saigon," *Cinema and the City: Film and Urban Societies in a Global Context*, ed. Mark Shiel and Tony Fitzmaurice (Oxford: Blackwell, 2001), 156.
14. Ibid.
15. Gwendolyn Wright, *The Politics of Design in French Colonial Urbanism* (Chicago: University of Chicago Press, 1991).
16. Nicola Cooper, *France in Indochina: Colonial Encounters* (Oxford: Berg, 2001), chapter 3.
17. Zeynep Çelik, "Gendered Spaces in Colonial Algiers," *The Sex of Architecture*, ed. Diana Agrerst, Patricia Conway, and Leslie Kanes Weisman (New York: Harry N. Abrams, 1996).
18. Cooper, *France*, chapter 6.
19. Nadine André-Pallois, *L'Indochine, un lieu d'échange culturel?: les peintres français et indochinois, fin XIXe–XXe siècle* (Paris: Presses de l'Ecole française d'Extrême-Orient, 1997); Herman Lebovics, *True France: The Wars over Cultural Identity, 1900–1945* (Ithaca: Cornell University Press, 1992).
20. Paul Rabinow, *French Modern: Norms and Forms of the Social Environment* (Cambridge, Mass.: MIT Press, 1989).
21. Kristin Ross, *Fast Cars, Clean Bodies: Decolonization and the Reordering of French Culture* (Cambridge, Mass.: MIT Press, 1996).
22. Mehdi Charef, *Le thé au harem d'Archi Ahmed* (Paris: Mercure de France, 1983), 117.
23. Azouz Begag, *Le gone du Chaâba* (Paris: Seuil, 1986), 11.
24. Interview with Yamina Benguigui, 14 June 2001, Paris.
25. Cooper, *France*, 196.

26. Richard L. Derderian, "Algeria as a *lieu de mémoire:* Ethnic Minority Memory and National Identity in Contemporary France," *Radical History Review* 83 (2002): 28–43.
27. Panivong Norindr, "Filmic Memorial and Colonial Blues: Indochina in Contemporary French Cinema," *Cinema, Colonialism, Postcolonialism: Perspectives from the French and Francophone World,* ed. Dina Sherzer (Austin: University of Texas Press, 1996), 140–41. I would like to recognize my students for making this observation.
28. Interview with Jérôme Tham.
29. Interview with Pham Phuong Khanh, 17 June 2001, Paris.
30. On the anniversary of his execution, the AGEVP unveiled a special Internet site to commemorate Trân's martyrdom. See www.tranvanbag.org.
31. The University of Paris VII has long had an active exchange program with the University of Hanoi.
32. Gisèle Bousquet already recognized this shift in the course of the 1980s. See Gisèle Bousquet, *Behind the Bamboo Hedge: The Impact of Homeland Politics in the Parisian Vietnamese Community* (Ann Arbor: University of Michigan Press, 1991).
33. Interview with Nguyen Quoc Nam, 4 June 2001, La Courneuve.
34. Interview with Thai-Binh Nguyen.
35. Interview with Ngyuen Le, 15 June 2001, Paris.
36. Interview with Nguyen Quoc Mylinh, 4 June 2001, La Courneuve.
37. See the AGEVP website at www.agevp.com.
38. See Nacer Kettane, *Le Sourire de Brahim* (Paris: Denoël, 1985); Ahmed Kalouaz, *Point kilométrique 190* (Paris: L'Harmattan, 1986); Mehdi Charef, *Le Harki de Meriem* (Paris: Mercure de France, 1989).
39. François Dubet and Didier Lapeyronnie, *Les Quartiers d'exil* (Paris: Seuil, 1988); François Dubet, *La galère: jeunes en survie* (Paris: Fayard, 1987), 23–24.
40. Loïc J. D. Wacquant, "Pour en finir avec le myth des 'cite-ghettos': Les differences entre la France et les Etats-Unis," *Annales de la recherche urbaine* 52 (1992): 20–30.
41. See John M. Merriman, *The Margins of City Life: Explorations on the French Urban Frontier, 1815–1851* (New York: Oxford University Press, 1991).
42. Ross, *Fast Cars,* 8–9.
43. Anne Donadely, " 'Une certaine idée de la France': The Algeria Syndrome and Struggles over 'French' Identity," in *Contested Nationhood in Twentieth-Century France,* ed. Steven Ungar and Tom Conley (Minneapolis: University of Minnesota Press, 1996), 221.
44. Éric Savarèse, *Histoire colonial et immigration: Une invention de l'étranger* (Paris: Séguier, 2000), 214.
45. Ibid., 84.
46. Interview with Thai-Binh Nguyen, 9 June 2001, Paris.
47. Interview with Thai-Binh Nguyen.
48. Stuart Hall, "When Was 'The Post-Colonial'? Thinking at the Limit," in *The Post-Colonial Question: Common Skies, Divided Horizon,* ed. Ian Chambers and Lidia Curti (London/New York: Routledge, 1996).

The agendas that urban botanic gardens can serve range from scientific discovery and taxonomy, public recreation, and economic gains to nationalistic self-creation and affirmation in domestic and global spheres. Reisz shows that different principles of governance from different governments create disparate combinations and permutations in the mixed functions of botanic gardens in Singapore and Malaysia. Once a space where British colonial interests were physically, geographically etched into colonies' natural environments, in present day Kuala Lumpur and Singapore the botanic gardens have become a space where the postcolonial state can develop its international portfolio through participation in regional or global arenas of botanical research. Newly independent Singapore and Malaysia nurtured their gardens for interests beyond the horticultural, following the example of the British Empire. Reisz contends that this pattern highlights the garden's "ambiguity of epistemological and physical position," an ambiguity that seems to stem from the fecund potentiality of the space. The most obvious aspect of this is in the cultivation of plants, but Reisz draws attention to another: the botanic gardens as a space of pre-Information Age stereoscopy. As with many of the other articles in this collection, Reisz provides a complex historicity that uses the various semiotic markings of botanical gardens as embodying colonial mastery, postcolonial nationalist desires, and global era urban lungs. Although largely a study of the history of science, Reisz's article provocatively reveals botanical gardens as sites where science, commerce, constructions of "nature," and regimes of instrumentality contend under and against specific forms of governance.

6

City as Garden: Shared Space in the Urban Botanic Gardens of Singapore and Malaysia, 1786–2000

EMMA REISZ

THE GARDEN IN THE CITY

In the market-driven cities of contemporary Singapore and Malaysia, gardens are usually understood by urban geographers as semiotic voids. Gardens are seen as urban lungs where air can circulate, necessary to the survival of the city as a whole, but deficient in internal structure and divorced from the city's fundamental economic functions—they are located within the physical space of the city, but outside its conceptual space.[1] This view was born during the industrial revolution in Europe, where gardens were intended to be an antidote to the social and environmental pollution of industrialization.[2] From this perspective, gardens package nature as a consumable, a visit to a garden serving as prophylaxis against the degradation of more "unnatural" forms of environmental shaping.[3]

Yet the postcolonial government of Singapore rejected this model, labeling it old-fashioned, and implicitly colonial. In modern Singapore, the "Garden City," the garden has become the city itself rather than an antidote to it. An interweaving of built and grown environments has supplanted the idea of clearly demarcated segments of nature.[4] The principle that the city is intrinsically inharmonious and must be balanced by nature has been abandoned; instead the city itself can be built—or grown—in balance. Dr. Ahmad Mattar said of Marina City Park in 1990 that it would be a "Green Jewel in a Modern City," adding that "alongside the commercial heartland of Singapore City, [it] aims to blend nature, art, and modern innovations that will reflect the many aspects of the city and its relationship with the people."[5] Singapore operates less through green lungs than through "green pores"; nature and the business of the city are intended to form a seamless tapestry.

At once the centerpiece and the antithesis of this conception of Singapore is the Botanic Gardens. Founded in 1859, this colonial institution forms a central part of government policy for a park network across the island, but at the same time its quasi-rural feel (of a very English variety) and its comparative lack of economic productivity recall its colonial function as an antidote to the polluting city, exactly the urban idea from which Singapore has been trying to escape. Small wonder that there have been calls recently for the garden to start charging admission fees; this vast lung can seem gratuitous when the built/grown skin of the city should allow its citizens to breathe freely in any case, and when many of the visitors are tourists and expatriates.[6] Meanwhile the Botanic Gardens endure, apparently little changed in a hundred years, while around it Singapore has been visibly transformed, and while the very idea of Singapore rests on its claim to archetypal newness. Certainly Singapore's botanic garden, like Chinatown and the Raffles Hotel, survives partly as a historical theme park, where the selective packaging and marketing of the past emphasizes the modernity of the present. More important, however, while the garden's place in the scheme of urban planning is no longer as secure as it once was, it fulfils other, less apparent, functions in the city and in the state, and in these areas there is considerable continuity between the colonial past and the postcolonial present.

The garden is not simply part of the urban environmental texture of Singapore; it is also a showcase for what its director thinks is "best" about nature on the island, attempting to capture nature in microcosm. Like all museum-type institutions, the garden both displays its contents (in this case flora), and also implies an intellectual framework within which such objects (plants) can be understood both inside and outside the physical space of the garden.[7] This dual role of presentation and representation applies not just to the plants but also to the ordering of space.[8] The garden presents through its landscaping an interaction between the grown and the built, between the natural and the artificial, and between the wild and the controlled. This ordering represents a way of understanding space that is bigger than the city itself; it raises very general points about the relationship between humans and the natural world. Each of these four types of display—two types of presentation and two of representation—constitutes a function of the botanic garden, which has at some time or all the time been regarded as useful by government, suggesting below that urban geographers should pay more attention than they generally have to the last of the four: the gardens as a symbol of the manipulation of the environment.

More generally, all four of these ways of approaching the botanic garden were themselves represented to a wider world beyond Singapore, both publicly and privately. Tourism has been an important source of garden visitors since the 1880s, providing sense-experience of the garden to many who do not live on the island.[9] A far greater contributor to the garden's international presence has been the transmission of information about it. For over a century, the garden's horticultural and botanical work has been reported in specialist and general publications and discussed in scientific correspondence, while its physical shape has been depicted and described, both for private purposes, for dissemination in tourist literature and post-cards, and today for the Internet as well.[10] Through such information, the Singapore Botanic Gardens has since its inception been known to many influential figures beyond the island. Besides tourists, Singapore's Botanic Gardens are of global interest to those interested in the relationship between humans and nature: scientists, conservationists, environmental planners, and government experts in these fields; and at many times during its history the garden has been, as this article will show, of interest to those working directly in the economic harnessing of nature, namely agriculturists. Consequently, the garden has long had a presence, if only a conceptual one, beyond the physical space that it occupies. In this sense, the garden has long anticipated some of the features of Paul Virilio's "stereoscopy," a theme discussed further below.[11] The garden is not just in the city; it is in the world as well.

The garden forms part of these internationally located groups' conceptualization of the island and of its aims. Contributing to this are both the presentational and representational functions of the garden. The garden projects an image of Singapore as blessed with a verdant, luxurious natural landscape in an urban context, alongside the more predictable downtown skyscrapers; but equally important, the garden also implies a set of values, or rather several overlapping conceptual frameworks, relating to the scientific ordering, management, and conservation of nature. Unfortunately, there is inadequate space here to consider in detail the comparatively subtle evolutions of ideas about botanic gardens over time or to address challenges to dominant colonial and postcolonial conceptions about gardens. For the purpose of this article, the significant point is that the very existence of a botanic garden implies that its proprietor considers the projection of a scientific understanding of the natural world onto the physical landscape to be a useful exercise. A state-owned botanic garden thus reflects back onto the government a glow of enthusiasm for order based on reason and knowledge, so valued in the post-Enlightenment world. The garden's international presence acts as an advertisement for Singapore and for its government.

The Enlightenment triad of absolute reason, knowledge, and order was the ideal (though a hopelessly unrealistic and often actively disingenuous and misleading one) professed by colonial governments, and it continues to exert considerable sway in the postcolonial world.[12] While architecturally

Singapore may be questioning the neat divisions of modernity, the botanic garden remains as a shrine to a hierarchical, technocratic spirit. The explanation for the survival of the botanic garden alongside the government's changing conception of the nature of urban space lies in the continued significance, both within Singapore and on the wider global stage, of those ideals of governance. It suggests that, during the history of botanic gardens in the region, local environmental priorities have often conflicted with the agenda of promoting the image of enlightened government both locally and beyond. It is the influence of local groups interested in these ideas, and the strength of communications links and politicoeconomic ties to such groups abroad (notably scientists), that have determined which set of priorities government pursues. Yet the Singapore government, postcolonial and colonial, has always attempted to reconcile the two agendas, to share the garden between the two rather than to waste valuable urban space on one of them alone.

The continuities in the history of the Singapore botanic garden can be contrasted with the discontinuities in the histories of botanic gardens in Malaysia. Both regions came under British colonial rule and had intermingled administrative histories between the foundation of British Singapore in 1819 and the island's departure from Malaysia in 1965. Yet in Singapore the Botanic Gardens has remained large, well-funded, and internationally regarded from 1859 to the present, while in West Malaysia no such botanic garden existed between the downgrading of Penang in 1910 and the opening of Rimba Ilmu in 1974. (A fuller treatment of the history of Malaysian botanic gardens would have been desirable had space permitted, and remains necessary.) The comparison emphasizes how the much more limited and extractive ambitions of colonial government in Malaysia than in Singapore constricted and retarded the creation of a natural-scientific establishment devoted to the encyclopedic universalism of the Enlightenment. Instead, colonial science in Malaysia was technological rather than philosophical in intent; it aimed to understand how to achieve particular functions (botanists worked to improve agriculture) rather than to acquire complete knowledge of the world. At the very end of its colonial history and in the postcolonial period this changed, but the historical vogue for the grand botanic garden had passed. As this article will show, in the absence of pressure from either an established botanic garden tradition, or from a shortage of space, there was little incentive to force a combination of the urban and the scientific agendas, and two sets of institution have in Malaysia been allowed to develop separately.

GARDENS OF THE MIND

Through the prevalence throughout its history of literary and visual representation, Singapore's Botanic Gardens has acquired a role as an ambassador for the island-city. To a global conservation community, the garden is evidence of Singapore's commitment to conservation, at a time when the very last "wild" spaces of the island are increasingly experiencing threats to their biodiversity.[13] The garden's herbarium (dried specimens), living plant collection, and team of experts signal to morphological botanists that Singapore wishes to participate in global morphological botanical research. The superabundance of the flora and the existence of the garden at all in the crowded space of the city signal to tourists that Singapore enjoys, or wishes to claim to enjoy, luxury without greed; luxury in Singapore, the garden suggests, sprouts from the earth, can be harnessed with diligence, and is potentially available to all. There is an obvious postcolonial continuity here, as demonstrated by historiography considering imperial botanic gardens as symbols of the European "cult of measurement" and domestication of nature.[14] They can be seen as icons of broader colonial mastery, proclaiming imperial power in the metropolis and colonial capitals alike.[15] What all these messages have in common is the notion of conspicuous but sophisticated consumption. The city is rich but uses its riches wisely and harmoniously. The oversized garden provides a site where the Aristotelian objective of using money and leisure to fund wisdom is given a physical form.

This process of representing the city, of creating a model of what a city should be (what Anthony King has called the "citying of the city"), has occurred throughout Singapore's history as a major settlement.[16] Singapore was always intended to be, and within a hundred years became, a world city. This is meant not simply in the sense that it was to be a city of global significance (though it was) but rather that it was intended and expected to be a city of a certain distinct type. Broadly speaking, these categories are similar to those identified by modern urban theorists speaking of the "world city": dependence on global trade flows, global-scale market for goods and/or services, professional and intellectual services, international capital accumulation, and large-scale migration.[17] Hence, I use the term despite its anachronism. The Botanic Gardens participated in the creation of Singapore's reputation in a number of these areas. However, it is as a symbol of a city's commitment to the production of global-scale intellectual services that the garden has had a particular grip on the imaginations of those outside Singapore.

The production of scientific knowledge represents a particularly powerful signal, above all to other scientists, that the body funding its production is devoted to research and learning. It is also a peculiarly reproducible signal; academic knowledge has always enjoyed a privileged relationship with information collection and distribution technologies, because of its claim to universality and the rarity and wide geographical distribution of specialists. Scientists are experienced in compressing their ideas so as to take up as little space on the page (or bandwidth) as possible.[18] While many of the garden's other messages had little currency until the twentieth century, its scientific message was spread beyond Singapore from its earliest days, though sometimes only with difficulty. Consequently, some of the features of the "information society" are novel not in their existence but rather in their intensity, wider distribution, and democratization.[19] It illustrates that stereoscopy, in which individuals are concerned simultaneously with both an immediate physical world and a remote world of communication technology, finds echoes in the mentalities of past generations, though confined to a wealthy elite.[20] Scientists and those formulating science policy throughout the period examined here operated in two environments simultaneously, much as do modern citizens. This observation suggests that theoretical reliance on a mythical past of local autonomy from global networks is both historically inaccurate and theoretically constricting, as an analysis of the processes articulating global networks in the eighteenth and nineteenth centuries can provide clues to what is truly new about the postcolonial city.[21]

So strong are the links between scientists that one theorist has referred to "invisible colleges" linking physically disparate colleagues.[22] As this article shows, the Singapore Botanic Gardens has formed a stable part of an "invisible college" of international morphological botany since the later nineteenth century, located in the conceptual space of scientific community as surely as it has been located in its immediate tangible environment. Such a strong statement is justified by the solidarity between colleagues, which in the history of the Singapore Botanic Gardens has sometimes proved stronger than governmental decision-making and even proved stronger than the divisiveness of the World War II. Initially sustained by fragile epistolary connections, from the later nineteenth century the sense of botanical community was supported by a continuous exchange of periodicals and reports between different scientific institutions across the world, ensuring awareness of each other's research program and discoveries.[23] Like many other groups, scientists were able to employ the structures of empire, from postal services to training opportunities, to promote their own ends, in return for services directly rendered to empire itself and the vaguer imperial loyalty engendered by their own entanglement with it.[24] In the postcolonial world, science has rapidly adopted international communication technologies, from television to the Internet, to expand both its internal connections and its links to democratized political power.

For most of their history, governments have been the dominant force in botanic gardens: by understanding how governments wished to project themselves and their concerns, a government's conception, whether philosophical or pragmatic, of the purpose of governance becomes acutely apparent. The contrasting but overlapping political, colonial, and natural history of Singapore and Malaysia make them ideal comparative case studies, where botanic gardens are a mirror held up to the wider intentions of the colonial and postcolonial states constructed there. I will concentrate primarily on the pre-Independence period, attempting to identify and describe those multiple imperial discursive traditions, and then draw them briefly into the postcolonial period. The language of governance, which will be familiar to many readers, is discussed extensively elsewhere in this volume.

"LAUDABLE ESTABLISHMENTS": COMPANY GARDENS AND PLANTATIONS, 1786–1834

Early British government gardens in Southeast Asia pursued a simple agenda, as the East India Company's interest in botany stemmed from looking with one eye to influential scientists in London and with the other to the wealth of the spice trade.[25] Cultural schemes such as botanic gardens boosted the Company's self-portrayal in the metropolis as a benevolent government.[26] These gardens had urban features even before the settlements around them could properly be called cities. They were designed to serve widely spread intellectual and economic networks, which traced Company trade routes across Asia to India and on to London, where they fed into other networks connecting Britain with continental Europe and the Americas. When the Company acquired Penang in 1786, a garden was founded at Ayer Hitam to function as a plant clearinghouse and later to serve as an experimental spice nursery.[27] However, without scientific direction the garden failed to deliver agricultural benefits. A private planter was the first to get nutmeg to fruit on Penang, and the Company relied on his plants for evidence that investment in nutmeg was worthwhile—precisely the reverse of the intended relationship between a private planter and a government experimental plantation.[28]

Influential scientists in London and India took an interest in the fate of Penang's garden, insofar as they were aware of it. Joseph Banks, a leading London botanist, claimed that research and nursery work at the Penang garden would strengthen the spice trade on the island and so consolidate the Company's control over the Straits of Malacca, a key aim in securing Company access to the sea lanes of Southeast Asia and beyond.[29] In the hope of realizing the potential financial and publicity benefits of a successful botanic garden, the Company decided to risk the expense of appointing a super-intendent. However, the Company garden at Sibpur near Calcutta came to see its Penang affiliate as a competitor for scarce resources.[30] At the start of the nineteenth century Southeast Asia, and even British India, were too weakly connected to each other and to London for the notion of a pan-imperial scientific community to operate. Sibpur doubted how much influence it exerted over the distant Penang garden. Besides, Sibpur itself felt vulnerable to potential Company retrenchment, unsure that London opinion would be able to prevent (or would even be aware of) any such plans from the government in Calcutta—fears that were borne out by the collapse of the Penang garden. The Penang garden had failed to make itself "stereo-real"; it had not become part of a network of invisible colleges, and the garden was liquidated in 1805.[31]

Fifteen years later, Thomas Stamford Raffles attracted London attention to Southeast Asia with his insistence that only knowledge of its lands and peoples would bring order and hence prosperity to the Company and its subjects alike.[32] Raffles wanted British imperial rule to be thought of "as the gale of spring reviving the slumbering seeds of mind and calling them to life from the winter of ignorance."[33] In 1819, Raffles contacted Nathaniel Wallich, Company botanist at Sibpur, about establishing a botanic garden on Government Hill in the new colony of Singapore and reestablishing a garden in Penang.[34] Both gardens were intended to serve as branch establishments to Calcutta, the continued existence of which was now comparatively entrenched in Company policy.[35] Although Raffles and Wallich believed that knowledge was the foundation of beneficent government, they also emphasized the possibility of taming the perceived brutality of the tropical landscape and making it more familiar to British eyes, a popular theme in the early nineteenth century.[36]

Raffles wanted Singapore to be the "emporium and pride of the East," with scientific services to match its urban ambitions, including a "botanical establishment of much greater magnitude [than smaller Penang] and promising the most splendid fruits."[37] From the start, however, the government refused to sanction the permanent appropriation of the Singapore land, because "reasons of a public nature might possibly require its alienation"; or in other words, the Company retained the right to close the garden if it ran short of funds or thought of something better to do with the land.[38] The possibility of combining agricultural development and scientific cachet, both valuable commodities when establishing a new settlement, was again too much for the Company to resist; but the Company could not guarantee that it would be able to afford to buy scientific goodwill in the future. Governor-General Lord Bentinck (nicknamed "the Clipping Dutchman") visited the Straits in 1829 and cut covenanted personnel by 60 percent as part of a general retrenchment to fund the Anglo-Burmese Wars. With Raffles dead and Wallich sick in London, the Singapore garden lacked prominent supporters and was allowed to fade away.[39] Penang's garden had never been given the kind of resources that Singapore had briefly enjoyed in the mid-1820s, and decay was rapid after its superintendent returned to Sibpur; it closed in 1834.[40]

The short-lived gardens established by the Company had been spaces rooted in misunderstanding. With the Company's actions a source of great interest in London, the Indian government was frequently prepared to pay for gardens as expensive symbols of the European rationality it claimed to be propounding, which with luck might also yield useful results.[41] However after the 1790s, the Company often doubted that government investment was actually necessary to promote agriculture (and hence revenue) in Southeast Asia, and both European and Chinese planters generally shared this view. The gardens were little more than window-dressing for a Company that saw its real commitment to Southeast Asia located in the establishment of lucrative entrepôts rather than in understanding nature. The emphasis of Raffles, Banks, and others on the necessity of an intimate knowledge of Southeast Asia for efficient governance had not persuaded the Company establishment that this view was correct, but merely that it was sometimes necessary to appear to think the aim "laudable." When the regional scientific networks that Raffles and Wallich had hoped would secure the gardens' position proved both to be more weakly connected to Calcutta than they had imagined, the gardens ceased to hold a position in the imagination of those remote observers either, and obscurity and closure were the inevitable result.

PRIVATE BOTANIC GARDENS AND STATE ASSISTANCE, 1836–1866

If the first European planters had felt themselves to be confident pioneers who did not need the assistance of horticulturists ignorant of agriculture, the next generation of merchants began to organize, lobby, and research. They wanted to extract concessions from local governments over land, trade duties, and other issues. As part of flexing their muscle, however, Europeans were keen to be seen as an engine for growth and development in the empire. Like the Company in a previous generation, local notables wanted to combine self-interest with an explicit commitment to the learning and research that would allow them to pursue their self-interest rationally, and so to claim to be contributing to economic efficiency and the good of all. Across the British empire, agricultural societies were being formed at this time, with a similar combination of political and technological concerns.[42] Unlike the Company, however, these traders and others were aiming to impress a local rather than a pan-imperial audience, because it was local rather than metropolitan government that concerned itself with details of economic development.

The Agri-Horticultural Society established in Singapore in May 1836 boasted among its leading lights two gutta-percha pioneers, and a number of other merchants and administrators. The Society hoped to survive without large government grants, and charged its members a subscription.[43] It reestablished spice plantations on a few unallotted hectares of the abandoned botanic garden land, expecting that these spice plantations would provide revenue for further agricultural research. However, the Agri-Horticultural Society suffered badly from the collapse of nutmeg prices in the 1840s.[44] The society had focused on researching spices that planters already understood well; rather than an urban garden, this was almost a town garden, contributing exclusively to local agricultural and social structure. Because it was simply losing money in a fashion that its members could have managed on their own, there was no reason for its continued existence. In 1846 the Society collapsed and the land reverted to the government. A similar association founded by planters in Penang apparently failed to establish significant plantations and was also abandoned in 1846.[45]

Still locally focused but broader in ambition, another botanic garden was launched by a second Agri-Horticultural Society formed a decade later in November 1859, with a committee of fourteen prominent Singapore citizens, including Hoo Ah Kay and J. E. Macdonald, 77 subscribers, and funds of $1,925.[46] The Society's chairman, Colonel Cavanagh, concluded that there was insufficient remaining unallotted land on Government Hill for a third successive garden to be established on that site.[47] Instead the government arranged a land swap with Hoo, giving him a smaller plot of land conveniently close to the river in return for a substantial plot in the fashionable and largely European northwestern suburb of Tanglin.[48] This site was less convenient than Government Hill for small entrepreneur-farmers (generally Chinese), who would for other purposes regularly come from the countryside into the city center but who had little cause to visit the suburbs. However, Tanglin was accessible to wealthy Europeans and to the Chinese like Hoo and Tan Kim Seng who moved in similar circles. The garden was not to be racially exclusive; as was so often the case in this early period of European involvement in Singapore, shared possession of wealth bridged many gaps created by a perception of racial difference. Indeed at a meeting on August 28, 1860, Hoo and Tan were urged to "afford the Society their valuable assistance in inducing their countrymen in Singapore to join the Society."[49]

Unlike its 1836 predecessor, this garden aimed to provide a leisure space for the elite, fitting scientific, agricultural, and horticultural research activities around that social function—a shared-space botanic garden, but aimed only at those with sufficient cash to support its upkeep. This was the first attempt to create a large urban park or equivalent in the Straits Settlements, reflecting the rapid growth of the town of Singapore and the concomitant need for leisure spaces. Partially developed Tanglin offered sufficient room to create pleasing vistas and pleasant strolls, and the first project undertaken by the Society in the garden was the construction of a bandstand and the organization of fortnightly regimental concerts, "a source of attraction to a considerable number of the community."[50] Secure public support was necessary because the Society had wider ambitions; in 1861 the Society decided to hire several Chinese gardeners to "stimulate men of their nation" to cultivate European vegetables. The Society also promoted crops grown by Malays; on July 27, 1861, the Society held its first agricultural show:

> and although the products shown were not numerous, they were certainly as many as could reasonably have been expected. As a first attempt, and seeing

the interest taken by the natives on this occasion, your committee are sanguine that much good will result from it.[51]

Botanical activities began to link the garden to wider networks, gardens in Calcutta and Mauritius, from regional planters in Penang, to gardens from other empires, notably at Bogor on Java.[52] However, the Society lacked the scientific skills to capitalize on its links; much of its correspondence was inadequately answered, due to its "utter ignorance."[53] The Society was trying to fund a large and ambitious inter-national garden through a socially narrow and localized body of members. Although the European community in Singapore "subscribed very liberally to the Gardens," they numbered only around one hundred, and apart from the very richest, the Chinese felt unrepresented and uninterested in the gardens and declined to support it.[54] By 1863 the garden was subsisting only through *ex gratia* donations.

After two disastrous attempts, it was clear that mixed-use botanic gardens in the ethnically fractured community of Singapore could not secure sufficient private funding. For the first time, however, a garden in the region was offering services that interested not only imperial elites in London but also colonial elites locally. As Singapore became a more sizeable settlement, the Singapore administration had more resources with which to engage in publicizing itself and the island, particularly if in doing so it could also impress and please leading locals. It supported the Society as a surrogate for an official agricultural research policy.[55] However, the Indian government, whose local opinion formers mostly had no interest in Singapore, refused to support Singapore's position; from their point of view, the situation had changed little since 1829, with the garden serving a publicity purpose but doing India no practical good.[56] The urban space of Singapore no longer fitted neatly into the Indian empire; its inhabitants wanted to pursue their own fiscal agenda, and the city was forming international connections on its own. The potential usefulness of botanic gardens to government was becoming apparent, but interest arose from and emphasized the fact that Singapore's growth had created political tensions that could not be contained within the existing structure of governance.

GOVERNMENT GARDENS FOR EMPIRE, 1867–1912

In 1867 the importance of the Straits Settlements was recognized with Crown Colony status and financial independence from India, and the Straits government was able to make its own funding decisions. Rapid waves of Chinese immigration and the expansion of European business interests throughout the mid-nineteenth century had made Singapore a substantial imperial port, and with Crown Colony status European institutions in Singapore now looked first to London rather than to Calcutta, and found

considerably more enthusiasm there for colonial science.[57] Communications, and hence imperial botanical cooperation, improved rapidly as the
Suez Canal opened in 1869, as steam was introduced on more local routes,
and later as the telegraph spread.[58] After 1869, Singapore's position as a
gateway from the Pacific Rim to the Indian Ocean made it a direct gateway
all the way to Europe. Over the following decades, the city-colony became
a world city, with rapidly increasing global prominence. Colonial gardens
were gaining unprecedented favor in British imperial policy in this period,
and became an indispensable feature of any city with major imperial pretensions. Joseph Hooker, Kew's director, emphasized local and imperial agendas operating in parallel in botanic gardens. He echoed Banks and Raffles
in stressing the value of botanical knowledge to Britain's ambitions to run
the empire as cheaply and efficiently as possible, and found a political climate
ripe for the idea of imperial development.[59] Located at the seat of a new government with access to funds, Singapore's Botanic Gardens secured increasing government subsidy, and in 1869 the Straits agreed to double the grant
in exchange for a much greater level of government interference.[60] By August
1874 the government had acquired the debt of the Agri-Horticultural Society and established a new committee to control the Society.[61]

Rather than waste resources through duplication, the government
hoped the garden could provide leisure for all of Singapore's diverse population.[62] The garden became effectively free, gained a zoological collection
("for the native mind they possess an interest and attraction" was the predictably patronizing observation of one European visitor), and improved its
landscaping.[63] The government was attempting to create a unique urban
space based on cultural values that would be acceptable to all groups.[64] Yet
although the government had no enthusiasm for much explicit acculturation, the botanic garden in this period was codifying acceptable behavior
among its visitors.[65] Garden bylaws were designed to create a space that was
clearly urban, social, and serious, rather than wild, isolated, or frivolous.
Visitors had to place the well-being of the garden's plants first; chaotic
behavior of all kinds, whether swimming, shooting, or driving a carriage
on the lawns, was forbidden.[66] Moreover, whatever the intention, urban
planning plundered British visual culture, and specifically imperial visual culture, more than anything else. For Britons, the Singapore garden represented
the reassuring familiarity of imperial rule balanced against a seductive ori-
ental landscape, the imperial set against the local. As a government-approved
Singapore guidebook of 1905 told potential visitors:

> subtle elegancies . . . transport the observer from one hemisphere to the
> other as he strolls across [the garden's] broad and smiling acres; at one
> moment you can imagine yourself in some old English demesne . . . the next

step opens up a glorious tropical vista, and you stand enchanted with the view, looking over the jungle undergrowth away into the heart of the island and its sloping uplands crested with the giants of the forest primeval. . . .[67]

The first test for the garden's prominent position in the new logic of governmental priorities came when the funds of the Straits Settlements government ran seriously short for the first time, in 1894. Pressure had been increasing in London and in the garden itself for the Singapore garden to begin to play its part in the wider imperial project. Branch gardens were established at Penang in 1884 and in Malacca in 1886.[68] In 1888, a well-regarded botanist, Henry Ridley, was selected as director of the Singapore garden.[69] The agricultural research conducted by "Mad Rubber" Ridley, which also covered coffee and palm oil, laid the foundations for the prosperity of colonial Malaya. Ridley put the Singapore garden onto the world scientific map, compiling the first catalogue of the flora of the Malay peninsula, publishing endless journal articles and contributions, and maintaining a considerable correspondence with botanists across the British empire and beyond. However, in 1894 the government attempted to abolish Ridley's job but to keep the garden. The government wanted to keep the garden as a pleasant and tangible representation of a commitment to scientific management of the natural world without having to pay for the actual science, a suggestion that was accepted happily enough by planters and traders who remained to be convinced of the value of Ridley's agricultural ideas.

The Singapore government discovered that they could not have it both ways. To project an image as a government committed to science, Singapore had established a garden that was by this time a full member of the international scientific community, the representatives of which in London reacted with horror to the proposal. The director of Kew speculated that the governor had become "possessed by the devil." The Colonial Office concluded that it should be "rather afraid of what the Scientists can do to us, if this proposal is once made public" and Singapore was instructed to change its plans.[70] Singapore's government could not simply turn its international profile on and off as it chose; its botanical institution was as much a part of the immediate world of botanists in London, though only in conceptual form, as it was part of that of Singaporeans. As a subject colony in an empire, impressing London worthies was a financially and politically useful exercise; but antagonizing them was at this point politically impossible. Singapore had been so successful in persuading London that it should be treated as a major imperial city, with world-renowned institutions like the botanic garden, that it would not be permitted to reinvent itself on a less culturally ambitious scale.

Equally significantly, Ridley's retention reflected a new policy on agricultural research in mainland Malaya, as a proportion of the funds was to come from the Federation of Malay States, an umbrella structure formed in 1896 to consolidate British territory in Malaya under a central administration, subject to the Straits's governor but not to its government.[71] The aims of the F.M.S. government were simply the generation of political stability and the stimulation of British trade in the peninsula; it was even less inclined to the pretension that the empire in Malaya was intended to further science than the Company had been in the Straits in Raffles's day. Purely intellectual botanical endeavors, including cataloging Malay flora, was left to the Straits. For its first few years the F.M.S. was keen to encourage agricultural research so long as the money did not come from its central funds. When the Planters' Association wrote in 1898 suggesting that British planters establish private botanic gardens, the F.M.S. was enthusiastic until Ridley pointed out that, as the period of private gardens in Singapore had demonstrated, government funding would eventually be required.[72] Agriculture was developing into an increasingly sophisticated science, with its own equipment, procedures, and trained professionals, diminishing the overlap with systematic botany and reducing correspondingly the case for sharing facilities between agricultural and botanical science in the form of a botanic garden.[73] Reflecting the colonial government's locally focused scientific ambitions, in 1906 the F.M.S. used its increasing wealth not to expand botanic gardens but instead to put all the gardens and agricultural research stations of the peninsula mainland under an agricultural department.

Leisure and agriculture were subsequently pursued separately, as the colonial government had no interest in demonstrating a commitment to the idea of a common philosophical root to both, in the form of the scientific environmental manipulation displayed in a botanic garden. Just as agriculture squeezed botany out of the research station, leisure squeezed botany out of the public garden. Kuala Lumpur's Lake Gardens was established with some botanical aims by the Selangor state treasurer, Alfred Reid Venning, in 1888, supported by prominent locals including the Cantonese trader Chow Ah Yeok and a small public grant.[74] However, while Singapore's garden had matured from its socially exclusive origins into a space reflecting the complex balance of power between Singapore's racial groups, Kuala Lumpur's garden reflected that city's more ethnically segregated colonial character. Venning's other ambition for the garden, to establish a European-only social club by the lake, came to fruition in 1890 and the Lake Club dominated Kuala Lumpur European society for half a century, while his botanical intensions for the garden were allowed to lapse.[75] In 1906, the botanical post of Superintendent of the Gardens in Kuala Lumpur was abolished.[76] No enduring British botanic garden was ever established on the mainland of the peninsula.

GOVERNMENT GARDENS FOR THE REGION: 1912–1946

Over the next thirty years, Singapore's continued economic expansion ensured that its institutions and government were no longer so dependent on
London. So for the Singapore garden, the horizon moved from the empire
to region, from London to Bogor and Taiwan. After Ridley's retirement
in 1912, the disparate scientific functions his garden had fulfilled were
divided between Singapore and the F.M.S. Agricultural Department. Kuala
Lumpur acquired agriculture, while systematic botany remained in Singapore. In 1928 the director of Kew, Arthur Hill, noticed that while Kuala
Lumpur was energetically conducting agricultural research to support its
plantation industries and food supply, the Straits government's enthusiasm
for botany was declining. Hill suggested that the Singapore herbarium be
moved up to Kuala Lumpur, and Singapore and Penang would then
become branch gardens, part of a new Botanical Department to be shared
between the budgets of both colonies.[77] Hill had not grasped that in the
imperial scheme, Malaya was not supposed to fund science unless it generated revenue. Nor was the governor prepared to spend more money on
botany in Singapore; unlike his predecessor in 1894, he had secured sufficient independence from London not to be overruled on such a matter. The
Colonial Office in London was left to "deplore their [the Straits government's] attitude."[78] Singapore's success had won it an international position
that meant that, although still subject to London, it no longer required
imperial goodwill to flourish.

The transformation of the scale of the city meant that the Singapore
garden no longer needed the support of international botanists to survive,
but even if the government had still cared much for London scientific opinion, botanic gardens generally could no longer rely on the unquestioning
support of all scientific colleagues, as gardens' scientific usefulness came
increasingly under attack from the powerful lobby of laboratory-based
botanists.[79] Without the agricultural functions that had made it popular
under Ridley, the garden maintained support among locals by providing a
model of how to manage the physical environment, and using its expertise
in other parts of the city. The Singapore garden concentrated on improving
the urban environment to make itself indispensable. Hill commented that
"the general lay-out and the landscape effects are admirable" and he felt that
the garden's leisure function was winning out at the expense of its duty
to educate the public through scientifically illustrative planting arrangements.[80] The garden also continued Ridley's work in orchid breeding,
always popular with the public. Both the Singapore and Penang gardens
continued to influence the wider space of the city, receiving $1,200 per
annum by the 1930s from their respective municipalities for the provision
of advice on greening roadsides and the maintenance of trees, and in 1937

Singapore doubled this for advice on horticulture in public parks. When in 1936 the Straits decided to permit greater private forest utilization, the areas that remained protected, notably Bukit Timah, came under closer control from the Botanic Gardens.[81]

Even when remodeling the environment and attempting to serve the whole population of Singapore, the garden was still in the late 1930s an overwhelmingly European-controlled colonial institution, laid out in British-influenced designs familiar to visitors to the other major botanic gardens of the empire. The senior non-British botanist was a Goan, Dr. C. X. Furtado; Chinese Singaporeans became significant in the garden only after the war. Malays like Encik Kiah bin Haji Mohamed Salleh and Ridley's friend Ahmad bin Hassan were employed as plant collectors; but however skilled they might be, they found it hard to progress up the organization.[82] A typically quaint role given to several Malays was to train the berok monkeys that the Singapore garden began to use to collect botanical specimens from treetops in 1937—"the first apes to enter government service," as Corner referred to the beroks.[83]

Yet during the 1920s and 1930s the Singapore garden began to shift the geographical basis of its virtual community, if not its personnel, away from the empire and toward Asia. Its new environmental focus gave the garden a role that the government found boosted Singapore's international image as much as botany had done in a previous generation, as well as being useful to Singaporeans. The Singapore garden was able to stretch the value of its environmental work beyond the island, through books and societies that carried the garden's ideas across physical space. In 1940, E. J. H. Corner produced his *Wayside Trees of Malaya,* and also in 1940 he and R. Eric Holttum acted as founding members of the Malayan Nature Society.[84] In both cases, the attempt was to promote an interest among literate laypeople in enhancing the natural environment, with the Singapore garden identified as the nucleus of local environmentalism.[85] The Japanese emperor was said to keep *Wayside Trees* on his bedside table.[86] Under the eminent botanists who acted as director between Ridley's resignation and World War II, Isaac H. Burkill, and then Holttum, the garden had developed its links to other botanists in Southeast Asia, particularly Japanese scholars based at Taihoku in Taiwan.[87] Economic links between Japan and Singapore were developing rapidly, but few other British institutions were so quick to adapt.[88] The garden's links to Japan proved crucial to its remarkable treatment during the war. It was not unscathed; the garden was slightly damaged in fighting, and became rundown during the occupation due to a lack of funding. Many staff died on the Siam-Burma railway. However, the senior botanists, Holttum and Corner, were allowed to continue their research work. Holttum more or less ran the garden for much of the war. By contrast, the overwhelming majority of the civilian British administrative staff in Singapore were interned in Changi.[89]

This was stereoscopy at its starkest; in the physical world, the garden was a governmental institution of a British colony, staffed by government servants, but at a conceptual level the senior botanists shared an interest in nature so strong as to constitute a bond transcending nationality, which even war could not shatter. This anomalous position created a gulf between Holttum and Corner and their fellow British citizens in Singapore. Corner recorded that he was considered "pro-Japanese . . . and a person to be avoided."[90] Just as in 1895, during the Japanese Occupation the Singapore garden was saved from harm by the mystique of control of the natural world when the local government could not protect it. The war reiterated that Singapore was, behind all of its cultural and economic functions, still a military base for a British state aiming at supremacy in the Eastern hemisphere. However, in the botanic garden, the imperial connection was already dissolving before the war. Singapore had turned away from the old imperial project of systematic botany and toward an emphasis on environmental management in a fast-growing city, which held a predictable appeal in Japan and took on wider relevance beyond in the following fifty years. Singapore was still using the garden to publicize its commitment to order and rationality, but where the city had once presented its expertise in pure science as evidence, the cityscape itself was now becoming the message.

POSTCOLONIAL GARDENS AND ECONOMIC DEVELOPMENT, 1947–2000

Freed of the impositions of colonial status, the postcolonial government of Singapore inherited a space on which could be, and had been, projected a number of different images of the island as an ordering spirit in the world: as agricultural research center, as botanical classifier, as environmental improver. The Botanic Gardens was also a space in which formal colonial politics had exercised little influence. The population of Singapore had voted with their feet, visiting the gardens when they found the space congenial and ignoring it when they did not. They found a space that was at once elitist in its approach to nature and in the priorities of its administration, and democratic in its accessibility. Although the traditions of racial exclusivity in European scientific institutions generated the classic postcolonial difficulties, including a need for a rapid change in personnel, the more lingering issue was only partly postcolonial. The anodyne appearance of the gardens had perhaps stifled a political debate that postcoloniality reawakened: Was it actually appropriate that so much space should be devoted to something of so little benefit to the majority of the population?

By contrast, postcolonial Malaysia inherited an absence—its lack of a botanic garden tradition emphasized what it had not been under colonial rule, but gave it the opportunity to invent new significations for botanical research almost, though not completely, from scratch. Malaysia inherited no botanical research gardens, though it did get what was left of the Penang garden. Still convinced that Malaya could never support botany, some British administrators proposed a bizarre arrangement after the war, whereby Penang's garden would have been attached to Singapore though the island itself became part of Malaya.[91] Although similar arrangements were made for other bits of land, the survival of the Penang garden was far too trivial an issue for an exception to be made, and the Penang garden took the same nationality as the island. The garden lost its herbarium in the divorce from Singapore, and thus lost its vestigial role in taxonomic botany. Consequently, Malaysia inherited a pleasant tourist attraction with a sideline in municipal tree-planting.

The Singapore Botanic Gardens was able to adapt to the new localized political priorities to retain its high status. It was staffed with a new generation of Singapore-Chinese botanists trained at the Singapore campus of the new University of Malaya, who were able to mobilize it in the service of an explicitly local policy program. The garden's old colonial function of promoting urban arboriculture fitted neatly into the program of regeneration that preoccupied Lee Kuan Yew and his colleagues.[92] Tree-planting campaigns began in 1963; by 1965 they had developed into the Garden City concept; and in 1971 the Tree Planting Day became an annual event. The enthusiasm for planting ornamental trees in the city center, and promoting Singapore as a garden city, disguised the fact that Singapore's rapid expansion was bringing about the destruction of its few remaining wild habitats. For Lee, the physical space of Singapore was, like a garden, almost infinitely malleable to human designs, and the resulting environment was intended to promote virtue and efficiency. But where colonial governments had conceived botanic gardens in this way as an antidote to the excesses of the city, for Lee the garden should symbolize the city as a whole.[93] The garden slotted itself into this vision, and in 1972 it opened a School of Ornamental Horticulture.[94]

To concentrate on local priorities, the garden minimized work on basic science in the 1970s. Government policy argued that luxuries had to be foregone to strengthen Singapore through difficult political times.[95] Reflecting the restriction of its role to leisure and environmental improvement, in 1973 the garden was merged with the Parks and Trees branch, and devoted increasing resources to rearing plants and trees to be planted out in the city as a whole. From its traditional dual environmental role, promoting forest conservation and ornamenting city streets, political priorities pushed the garden from the 1960s into concentrating on the latter alone. The effective head of the botanic garden, Ng Siew Yin, herself a botanist, remarked to one interviewer that taxonomic study had to give way to applied botany and horticulture to meet the Republic's goals of a better environment.[96] The political success of the garden's display of self-sacrifice was confirmed by Lee Kuan Yew celebrating the tenth Singapore Tree Planting Day in the botanic garden and planting a tree there himself. Not for the first time, scientific research seemed to be a dispensable additional cost at the garden, though the release of resources was thought to be necessary not to fund war, as the Company had done, but to create the prosperity that would prevent it.

By the 1980s, Singapore's rapidly increasing standard of living was creating a more confident atmosphere in which nonessential services had a better chance of funding, and in which the importance to the economy of seemingly irrelevant scientific research was recognized. In 1988 the research and horticultural functions of the Botanic Gardens were recombined under a director, Dr. Tan Wee Kiat, who confirmed that

> The Singapore Botanic Gardens will endeavour to become a research and resource centre of international repute, while meeting the educational and recreational needs of an increasingly better educated and affluent society.[97]

The botanic garden placed a renewed emphasis on taxonomy and also re-emphasized public education, introducing more informative exhibitions and displays of economic plants.[98] After a twenty-year interval, it suited government social and economic purposes that the botanic garden should rejoin the global scientific community, and attempt to link that to the social space of the city.[99] These connections were becoming more politically useful, because across the world in the 1980s the status of botanic gardens was improving rapidly. In 1987 the Botanic Gardens Conservation Secretariat was founded to encourage concerted responses to species and habitat loss.[100] The Singapore garden's role in international conservation efforts helped to assuage mounting environmentalist anxiousness.[101] The government was able to stress its commitment to the idea of global habitat conservation and species diversity through the garden's research, but presented Singapore's transformation into a fully urbanized space (albeit a new, greener kind of city) as the inevitable outcome of economic necessity. As a largely urban island, the government argued that Singapore should concentrate on being a garden city, committing itself to token wilderness preservation for leisure and tourism purposes.[102] Thus, in the 1990s the Singapore government resolved effectively to subcontract habitat retention to other countries in the region, paying for research but requiring other states to provide what Singapore could afford least—space.

Meanwhile in Malaysia, with less pressure on space, botany developed distinct from leisure. After many years during which botanical research was focused on agriculture and arboriculture, from the late 1970s horticulture and conservation (for ecological tourism) gained economic importance.[103] Malaysia's only true botanic garden in the late twentieth century, combining the various functions in one institution, was not run directly by government. The Rimba Ilmu ("Forest of Science") garden at the Universiti Malaya opened in 1974. Located on campus, its physical community is approximately contiguous with its virtual community. The Rimba Ilmu garden, as its name implies, did not need to rely on satisfying the needs of urban residents, and needed simply to facilitate the pursuit of knowledge. At its opening, speakers emphasized links to medieval Arab botanical traditions; and indeed it echoed the oldest traditions of scholarly gardens, being intended for research and teaching, and with a good herbarium.[104] Its emphasis on teaching made it quite unlike its colonial predecessors in British Southeast Asia, as colonial governments generally had little interest in higher education and the Singapore garden had taken on a botanical teaching role only very late in its history. Rimba Ilmu symbolized Malaysia's commitment to participate in international scientific exchange but to prioritize the expansion of higher education alongside, or above, conducting the most original research.

A secondary aim has been environmental conservation in the midst of Malaysia's rapid economic growth, and the consequent strain on the environment. Those factors make conservation a concern for Malaysian botanists, but they also create a governmental desire to be seen to be attempting to do something about the situation, particularly given the concerns regularly raised by environmentalists about forestry practices in Sarawak and elsewhere. From its opening, the garden stressed conservation, and established a gene bank of plant specimens.[105] Rimba Ilmu also reflected a new determination to challenge Singapore for intellectual laurels; among the motivations for its establishment was the perception of the Singapore garden's scientific weakness in the early seventies.[106] Malaysia's leading university took this opportunity to compete for international prestige, the glow of scientific success reflecting back warmly on the state as a whole. No less than in Singapore, the ambitions of the state have been reflected in the space of the garden, reacting against the colonial past, but encouraged by political logic and cultural continuities to employ many familiar discursive tactics.

CONCLUSION

Throughout their history, botanic gardens have occupied a vulnerable position in Singapore and Malaysian government finances, making them a weathervane of prevailing cultures of governance. Government support for both nonessential services such as science and leisure has generally been highly instrumentalist, aiding the pursuit of other aims. This has made botanic gardens intriguing political spaces. Poor governments have focused expenditure on producing tangible local economic or social results, whereas richer ones have used botanic gardens as spaces on which to project the state's intellectual pretensions into a wider regional, imperial, or global sphere.

Thus, botanic gardens are a microcosm of the state's Janus-like nature, looking both inward and outward. In Singapore and Malaysia, harmonizing the two has been difficult and sometimes impossible. Under colonial rule, colonial governments often found the weight of metropolitan imperial priorities constricting, and often disagreed with imperial authorities over the appropriate policies for the botanic garden. However, local colonial decision-making privileged the interests of a few and distorted the concerns of the masses. After independence, the emphasis on the domestic agenda detached Singapore and Malaysia's botanic gardens from the international mainstream, partly as a response to the imperially focused vision of the colonial period. However, toward the end of the twentieth century, as both countries reconsidered both their international image and their science policies, botanic gardens were pushed back onto the international stage to advertise national development. The shared-use garden model survived in Singapore, still relevant to Singapore's quintessentially crowded urban space. In independent Malaysia there was no shared-use garden to revive, and the institution that came closest, Rimba Ilmu, did so not in the politically and economically valuable space of Kuala Lumpur, but in the intellectualized and less competitive space of a suburban campus.

Gardens' dual situation within local and global networks has been a source of tension, as the priorities of the two environments may differ, but also of strength, as when one source of support falters, the other may endure. In the colonial period, scientific and political networks across the empire enjoyed a symbiotic relationship; though the politicians had more power, they relied on international botanists to promote governmental scientific credentials. In the postcolonial period, the political fate of Malaysia or Singapore is no longer decided abroad, though it may be heavily influenced by external events and connections; but faster media and communications and the "death of distance" give international scientific networks their influence. Scientists no longer require dispatches from London but simply televisions and computers to carry their message into the local centers of power, and so to help shape local space.[107] The financial necessity for gardens to share their space, and to gather support for a scientific understanding of the natural world from as wide a variety of people as possible, has bound together scientists and the public, colonizers and colonized, and the local and the global, revealing not a fractured patchwork of space but a web of intersecting networks and interests.

NOTES

1. Naturally there are exceptions to this, particularly about Singapore, for example, S. H. K. Yeh, "The Idea of the Garden City," in *The Management of Success: The Moulding of Modern Singapore,* ed. S. Sandhu and P. Wheatley (Singapore: ISEAS, 1989).
2. Adrian Franklin, *Nature and Social Theory* (London: Sage, 2002), 136–7, 139; Keith Thomas, *Man and the Natural World: Changing Attitudes in England, 1500–1800* (London: Allen Lane, 1983).
3. M. J. Daunton, *House and Home in the Victorian City* (London: Edward Arnold, 1983).
4. Rem Koolhaas, "Singapore: Portrait of a Potemkin Metropolis; Songlines . . . or Thirty Years of Tabula Rasa," in *S, M, L, X-L,* by Rem Koolhaas and Bruce Mau, Office for Metropolitan Architecture, ed. J. Sigler (Rotterdam: O10 Publishers, 1995), 1026–7.
5. Dr. Ahmad Mattar, Minister for the Environment, Republic of Singapore, at the Osaka International Forum on "Global Environment and the City," 2 July 1990.
6. R. Tan C. G., "Quasi-Public Good and the Allocation of Provision Burden: the Case of Singapore Botanic Gardens," unpublished B.Soc.Sci thesis, National University of Singapore (2000). This contains some of the only quantitative data on the social makeup of Botanic Garden visitors.
7. Susan M. Pearce, *Museums Objects and Collections: A Cultural Study* (Leicester University Press, 1992), 116–7.
8. See Jacques Derrida, *La vérité en peinture* (Paris: Flammarion, 1978), 10.
9. *Annual Report of the Botanic Gardens, Singapore, 1884* (Singapore, 1885), 1; B. E. D'Aranjo, *The Stranger's Guide to Singapore, with Maps* (Singapore: Sirangoon Press, 1890), 6.
10. *Singapore Historical Postcards from the National Archives Collection,* ed. Gretchen Liu (Singapore: Times Editions, 1986), 44–5; *Singapore Retrospect through Postcards: 1900–1930,* Archives and Oral History Department, Singapore (Singapore: Sin Chew Jit Poh, 1982), 74. See also the garden website at http://www.sbg.org.sg/.
11. Paul Virilio, *The Information Bomb,* trans. Chris Turner (London: Verso, 2000), 15, 65–6.
12. James M. Blaut, *The Colonizer's Model of the World: Geographical Diffusionism and Eurocentric History* (New York: Guilford Press, 1993); Bruno Latour, *We Have Never Been Modern,* trans. Catherine Porter (New York: Harvester Wheatsheaf, 1993).
13. Larry Pardue, "The Changing Role of Tropical Botanic Gardens," in *Proceedings of the Botanic Gardens' 130th Anniversary Seminar* (Singapore, 1989), 26.
14. For example, see M. Adas, *Machines as the Measure of Men: Science, Technology and Ideologies of Western Dominance* (New York: Cornell University Press, 1989); Harriet Ritvo, "Zoological Nomenclature and the Empire of Victorian Science," in *Victorian Science in Context,* ed. B. Lightman (Chicago: Chicago University Press, 1997), 337.
15. Michel Foucault provided an expansive discussion of his thought on the relationship between space and power in an interview with Paul Rabinow, published as "Space Knowledge and Power," in *The Foucault Reader,* ed. P. Rabinow (Harmondsworth: Penguin, 1984). On cities and empire, see the discussion in Anthony R. Pagden, *Peoples and Empires: Europeans and the Rest of the World, from Antiquity to the Present* (London: Weidenfeld & Nicolson, 2001), chapter 1.
16. Anthony D. King, "Re-presenting World Cities: Cultural Theory/Social Practice," in *World Cities in a World-System,* ed. Paul L. Knox and Peter J. Taylor (Cambridge: Cambridge University Press, 1995), 216. King links his observation to a comment by Gayatri Chakravorty Spivak about the "worlding of the world."
17. John Friedmann, "The World City Hypothesis," in *Development and Change,* 17 no. 1 (1986): 69–83. Friedmann also mentions acute social stratification and concentrated poverty, which certainly occurred in Singapore but were not pursued as ends in themselves. On Singapore's economy, see W. G. Huff, *The Economic Growth of Singapore: Trade and Development in the Twentieth Century* (Cambridge University Press, 1994).
18. On privileged information, note the important ambiguity between information as quality and information as quantity. F. Webster, *Theories of the Information Society,* 2nd ed. (London: Routledge, 2002), 23–4.
19. See T. Standage, *The Victorian Internet: The Remarkable Story of the Telegraph and the Nineteenth Century's Online Pioneers* (London: Phoenix, 1998).
20. Virilio, *Information Bomb,* 15, 65–6.
21. See Robert A. Beauregard, "Theorising the Global-Local Connection," in *World Cities in a World-System,* ed. Paul L. Knox and Peter J. Taylor (Cambridge: Cambridge University Press, 1995), 240–1.

22. D. Crane, *Invisible Colleges: Diffusion of Knowledge in Scientific Communities* (Chicago: University of Chicago Press, 1972). University of Chicago Press.

23. Richard Drayton, *Nature's Government: Science, Imperial Britain, and the "Improvement" of the World* (New Haven: Yale University Press, 2000), 253–4.

24. On other networks parasitic on the structures of empire, see T. N. Harper, "Empire, Diaspora, and the Languages of Globalism, 1850–1914," in *Globalization in World History*, ed. A. G. Hopkins (London: Pimlico, 2002).

25. On early civil society in the Straits Settlements, see Elizabeth K. Gillis, "The Rise and Fall of Civil Society in Singapore," unpublished Ph.D. thesis, Murdoch University, Perth, Australia (2001).

26. On this view of Company rule, see Thomas R. Metcalf, *Ideologies of the Raj*, vol. 3 of *The New Cambridge History of India* (Cambridge: Cambridge University Press, 1995), 10, 17.

27. India Office Records, Board's Collections (1803–4) F/4/142, no. 2485, "State of the Spice Plantations on Prince of Wales Island," George Leith (Lt. Govnr. PWI) to C. R. Crommelin (Sec. Pub. Dept. Bengal), 15 March 1802, 8–9.

28. India Office Records, F/4/142, no. 2485: George Leith (Lt. Govnr. PWI) to C. R. Crommelin (Sec. Pub. Dept. Bengal), 15 March 1802, 8, 10–11. The source of Caunter's nutmeg is unclear, as Light's 1884 plants were thought by Leith to have died (see note 26). Caunter's nutmeg appears to have been privately imported.

29. "On the Importance of the Prince of Wales's Island for the culture of spice &c.," *Annals of Botany* 1 (1804–5), 570–2, transmitted by Joseph Banks.

30. Straits Settlements Records E1 Penang; "Letters from India": John Lumsden to R. T. Farquhar, 18 April 1805, 50–51; Mr. Roxburgh Jnr. to Lumsden, 15 April 1805, 51–55. Mr. William Roxburgh was acting as superintendent while his father Dr. William Roxburgh was on leave.

31. IOR Factory Records G/34/9, "Penang Miscellaneous Papers and Reports, 1805–1810": Report by Farquhar on his departure, 30 September 1905, 13–14ff. The Lieutenant-Governor, Robert T. Farquhar, had strong reservations about the sale.

32. See Raffles to Thomas Murdoch, 9 October 1820, cited in Sophia Raffles, *Memoir of the Life and Public Services of Sir Thomas Stamford Raffles*, vol. 2 (London: John Duncan, 1835), 160–1; but see Syed Hussein Alatas's pamphlet, *Thomas Stamford Raffles: Schemer or Reformer?* (Sydney: Angus and Robertson, 1971) for a critique of Raffles's benign self-image.

33. Raffles on the opening of the Singapore Institution, 1823, quoted in *Souvenir of Singapore: A Descriptive and Illustrated Guide Book of Singapore* (Singapore: Straits Times Press, 1905), 16.

34. "Letters of Nathaniel Wallich Relating to the Establishment of Botanical Gardens in Singapore," ed. R. Hanitsch, *Journal of the Malayan Branch of the Royal Asiatic Society* 42, no. 1 (December 1969): 145–54; J. Bastin, "The Letters of Sir Stamford Raffles to Nathaniel Wallich 1819–1824," *Journal of the Malaysian Branch of the Royal Asiatic Society* 54 (December 1981): 1–73.

35. India Office Records, F/4/760, no. 20668: Wallich to Raffles, 2 November 1822, 95–6. Wallich had been expanding the numbers of botanical establishments in India and centralizing control of them in his own hands since 1820—see in the same file Lushington to Wallich, 16 June 1820, 63–4, 65.

36. Wallich to Raffles, 2 November 1822, 87–89. That passage includes a discussion of the need to identify and examine the trees of the "primeval forest" in the center of Singapore. See Sophia McAlpin, *The Landscape Palimpsest: Reading Early Nineteenth-Century British Representations of Malaya* (Clayton, Australia: Monash Asia Institute, 1997). The garden at Peradeniya near Kandy in Sri Lanka was established in 1822, with one of its most important purposes being to "acclimatize" European vegetables for the delectation and reassurance of British expatriate planters. Sri Lanka National Archives 6/283 (Colonial Secretary's Letters: Botanic Gardens Superintendent, 1820–2): A. Moon, Supt. BG, to John Rodney, Chief Secretary to the Governor, 26 September 1821.

37. India Office Records, F/4/760, no. 20668: Wallich to Lushington [Government at Fort William] 7 January 1823, 129–30.

38. India Office Records, F/4/760, no. 20668: Wallich to Lushington, 7 January 1822, 128–30; Public Letter from Bengal, 1 Apr 1823, 8 (para. 69).

39. Straits Settlements Records N6 Singapore Resident's Diary 1827–1829: May 1828–July 1829: E. Presgrave to James Caswell, June 30 1829, 159–60.

40. Straits Settlements Records U3, "Sale of Botanic Gardens (Penang)," 1834, 312. The sale raised 1,250 rupees; H. N. Ridley "The Abolition of the Botanic Gardens of Penang," *Agricultural Bulletin of the Straits and Federated Malay States* 9, no. 3 (March 1910): 101.

41. Deepak Kumar, "Evolution of Colonial Science in India: Natural History and the East India Company," in *Imperialism and the Natural World*, ed. John M. MacKenzie (Manchester: Manchester University Press, 1990), 51.

42. The Royal Agricultural Society was founded in England in 1838, and a similar society in Ceylon in 1842. E. J. Russell, *A History of Agricultural Science in Great Britain, 1620–1954* (London: Allen & Unwin, 1966); W. M. Tilakaratna, *Agricultural Credit in a Developing Economy—Ceylon* (Colombo: Central Bank of Ceylon, 1963), 124.

43. This was of between $2 and $8. C. B. Buckley, *An Anecdotal History of Old Times in Singapore* (Kuala Lumpur: Oxford University Press, 1965), 305–6.

44. This was due to increasing production in Singapore and Malaya. T. Oxley, "Some Account of the Nutmeg and Its Cultivation," *Journal of the Indian Archipelago and Eastern Asia* (Series 1) 2 (1848): 657, 660. The rapid increase in production in the Netherlands East Indies was even more important. J. C. Jackson, *Planters and Speculators: Chinese and European Agricultural Enterprise in Malaya, 1786–1921* (Kuala Lumpur: Malaya University Press, 1968), 112; J. T. Thomson, "General Report on the Residency of Singapore Drawn up Principally with a View to Illustrating Its Agricultural Statistics," *Journal of the Indian Archipelago and East Asia* 4 (1850): 41–77, 102–6, 134–43, 206–19.

45. H. N. Ridley "The Abolition of the Botanic Gardens of Penang," *Agricultural Bulletin of the Straits and Federated Malay States* 9, no. 3 (March 1910): 103.

46. *Straits Times,* 12 November 1859; I. H. Burkill, "The Establishment of the Botanic Gardens, Singapore," *Gardens Bulletin of the Straits Settlements* 2 (August 1918): 55. Various silver dollars were interchangeable at this point; the Straits dollar was not minted until a little later. The dollar sign here denotes the Mexican dollar, the preferred dollar over the Spanish and U.S. dollar, and the British minted silver coinage to name a few.

47. Straits Settlements Records W32, Governor's Miscellaneous Letter In September–December 1859, no. 116 Captain G. C. Collyer, Secretary of the Agri-Horticultural Society, 15 November 1859, 619f.

48. Straits Settlements Records V29 Governor Miscellaneous Letters Out November 1859–March 1860, Captain James Burn to Captain G. C. Collyer, 30 November 1859, 36–7.

49. *Singapore Free Press,* 13 September 1860.

50. *Singapore Free Press,* 15 August 1861.

51. Ibid.

52. *Singapore Free Press,* 13 September 1860; *Singapore Free Press,* 15 August 1861.

53. Archives of the Royal Botanic Gardens, Kew, Miscellaneous Reports 6.21 Singapore Botanic Gardens etc., 1874–1917, 400f, Dr. Robert Little [Committee Chairman] to Professor Balfour, April 1874.

54. *Singapore Free Press,* 17 November 1864.

55. Straits Settlements Records X24 Governor's Diary General, September 1864–November 1866: Agri-Horticultural Society to Government, 9 August 1865, no. 20.

56. Straits Settlements Records S34 Governor's Letters from Bengal, January 1865–December 1866, Lieut. M. Protheroe to Agri-Horticultural Society, no. 96, 13 July 1866, 95; and no. 102, 19 July 1866, 96.

57. By contrast, many Singaporean Chinese and Chinese institutions looked first to China; see C. M. Turnbull, *A History of Singapore, 1819–1988,* 2nd ed. (Singapore: Oxford University Press, 1989), 105.

58. On the importance of telegraphy to other branches of science, see Bruce J. Hunt, "Doing Science in a Global Empire: Cable Telegraphy and Electrical Physics in Victorian Britain," in *Victorian Science in Context,* ed. B. Lightman (Chicago: University of Chicago Press, 1997), 325.

59. See *Annual Report of the Gardens at Kew, 1867;* D. Kumar, *Science and the Raj 1857–1905* (Delhi: Oxford University Press, 1997), 81; R. H. Drayton, *Nature's Government: Science, Imperial Britain, and the "Improvement" of the World* (New Haven: Yale University Press, 2000), 248–255.

60. Straits Settlements Records R43 Governor's Letters to Bengal, January 1862–April 1867, no. 30, 25 August 1866, 307; Straits Settlements Records S35 Governor's Letters from Bengal 1866, 19 September 1866, 207f; Draft "Report to be Presented to the Society at a Meeting of Feb. 24th 1870," in I. H. Burkill, "Establishment of the Botanic Gardens, Singapore," 71.

61. Burkill, "Establishment of the Botanic Gardens, Singapore," 61. The government took formal ownership of the garden in 1877.

62. For the British idea of the urban park, see Belinda Yuen, "Creating the Garden City: The Singapore Experience," *Urban Studies* 33, no. 6 (1996): 955.

63. *Singapore Daily Times,* 19 December 1874 (advertisement). On garden beauty, see for example H. J. Murton, "Singapore Botanical Gardens," in *Gardeners' Chronicle,* 22 October 1881. On the gifts of live animals, see I. H. Burkill, "The Second Phase in the History of the Botanic Gardens, Singapore," *Gardens Bulletin of the Straits Settlements* 2, no. 3 (November 1918):

93–108. *Souvenir of Singapore: A Descriptive and Illustrated Guide Book of Singapore* (Singapore: Straits Times Press, 1905), 62.

64. T. N. Harper, "Globalism and the Pursuit of Authenticity: The Making of the Diasporic Public Sphere in Singapore," *Sojourn* 12 (1997): 285–86.

65. See M. L. Herskovits, *Acculturation: The Study of Culture Contact* (New York: J. J. Augustin, 1938).

66. *Guide to the Botanical Gardens* (Singapore: Government Printing Office, 1889), i.

67. *Souvenir of Singapore: A Descriptive and Illustrated Guide Book of Singapore* (Singapore: Straits Times Press, 1905), 61.

68. See *Annual Progress Report of the Assistant Superintendent of Forests, Penang, for the Year 1885* (Singapore Botanic Gardens, 1886).

69. Archives of the Royal Botanic Gardens, Kew: Ridley Collection "Letters Vol. 6," Thiselton-Dyer to Ridley, 9 February 1886, 151–53.

70. Public Record Office, U.K., CO 273/200, no. 15326, Thiselton-Dyer to CO, 29 August 1894, 701r; Minutes on no. 17938, 725v (Edward Fairfield, 27 October 1894).

71. Straits Settlements Records COD/102 No. 381, CO to SS, 16 November 1894.

72. Arkib Negara Malaysia: High Commissioner's Office (Resident General letters) no. 83/1898, "Proposed Experimental Gardens in the Native States," 25 January 1898.

73. G. B. Masefield, *A History of the Colonial Agricultural Service* (Oxford: Clarendon Press, 1972); Worboys, "Science and British Colonial Imperialism, 1895–1940," D.Phil. thesis at the University of Sussex (1980), 36.

74. J. M. Gullick, "Kuala Lumpur, 1880–1895," *Journal of the Malayan Branch of the Royal Asiatic Society* 28, no. 4 (1955): 7.

75. D. J. M. Tate, *The Lake Club 1890–1990: The Pursuit of Excellence* (Singapore: Oxford University Press, 1990), 10; J. G. Butcher, *The British in Malaya 1880–1941: The Social History of a European Community in Colonial Southeast Asia* (Kuala Lumpur: Oxford University Press, 1979), 64.

76. Public Record Office, U.K., CO 273/319: FMS despatch to the Colonial Office no. 418 of 1906, 22 October 1906.

77. Public Record Office CO 323/1007/2 (Colonial Office: General Department: Miscellaneous, 1928), "Botanic Gardens, Kew": A. W. Hill to H. Clifford, 24 March 1928.

78. Public Record Office CO 273/553/25 (Colonial Office, Straits Settlements, 1928 Correspondence), "Botanical Matters: Observations of Dr A. W. Hill On [Singapore Herbarium]" Minutes, 4 January 1929.

79. David E. Allen "Natural History and Social Research," *Journal of the Society for Bibliography of Natural History* 7, no. 4 (1976): 509.

80. Public Record Office CO 323/1007/2: A. W. Hill to H. Clifford, 24 March 1928.

81. *Annual Report of the Botanic Gardens, Singapore, 1937* (Singapore, 1938), 2, 8.

82. R. Eric Holttum, "In Memoriam: Encik Kiah bin Haji Mohamed Salleh (1902–1982)," *Gardens Bulletin of Singapore* 35, no. 2 (1983): 227–9. Ahmad shared his friend Ridley's remarkable longevity; both lived to a hundred, and Ahmad was still working in the garden in 1940. Ahmad, a "walking dictionary" on Malayan flora, was honored with several medals. See B. Tinsley, *Singapore Green: A History and Guide to the Botanic Gardens* (Singapore: Times Books International, 1983), 48.

83. *Annual Report of the Botanic Gardens, Singapore, 1937* (Singapore, 1938), 5. It had been Corner's "intention to breed and train a whole school of botanical monkeys," but he liberated his five simian assistants two days before the outbreak of war, and apparently the idea was not taken up again. E. J. H. Corner, *The Marquis: A Tale of Syonan To* (Singapore: Heinemann Asia, 1981), 97–98.

84. E. J. H. Corner, *Wayside Trees of Malaya* (Singapore: Government Printing Office, 1940).

85. B. Tinsley, *Vision of Delight: the Singapore Botanic Garden Through the Ages* (Singapore: Singapore Botanic Gardens, 1989), 37.

86. Corner, *The Marquis*.

87. See the annual reports, such as *Annual Report of the Botanic Gardens, Singapore, 1936* (Singapore, 1937), 6.

88. Hiroshi Shimizu and Hitoshi Hirakawa, *Japan and Singapore in the World Economy: Japan's Economic Advance into Singapore, 1870–1965* (New York: Routledge, 1999), 53. The director of fisheries, William Birtwhistle, also enjoyed good relations with Japanese scientists prior to the war (Corner, *The Marquis*, 162) and shared the comparatively mild treatment Corner and Holttum received after 1942 (see note 89 below).

89. Joseph Kennedy, *British Civilians and the Japanese War in Malaya and Singapore, 1941–45* (Basingstoke: Macmillan, 1987), 84, 100; Robert Heussler, *Completing a Stewardship:*

The Malayan Civil Service, 1942–1957 (Westport: Greenwood Press, 1983), 42. As a Goanese, Furtado was not considered an enemy alien. Although some British medical, engineering, and administrative personnel were employed temporarily by the Japanese at the beginning of the occupation, only Corner, Holttum, and Birtwhistle (see note 88) were retained in government service throughout. Turnbull, *A History of Singapore, 1819–1988,* 192.

90. Corner, *The Marquis,* 88, 90. Suspicion that Corner was a Japanese spy has endured ever since, though a note from Governor Shenton Thomas urging the importance of preserving the collections has been recently located; see David Mabberley, "A Tropical Botanist Finally Vindicated," *Gardens Bulletin, Singapore* (2001) and Lea Wee, "Botanist Dogged by Spy Rumours Vindicated?" *Straits Times,* 10 June 2001. I am grateful to Chang Yueh Siang for drawing my attention to this.

91. Public Record Office CO 927/104/3, no. 13, 37.

92. On Lee and urban greening, see *Lee Kuan Yew: The Man and His Ideas,* ed. Han Fook Kwang, Warren Fernandez, and Sumiko Tan (Singapore: Times, 1998), 12.

93. Victor R. Savage, "Human-Environment Relations: Singapore's Environmental Ideology," in *Imagining Singapore,* ed. Ban Kah Choon, Anne Pakir, and Tong Chee Kiong (Singapore: Times Academic Press, 1992); Rem Koolhaas, "Singapore: Portrait of a Potemkin Metropolis," 1031.

94. National Archives of Singapore, Speech by Lee Yiok Seng at the School of Ornamental Horticulture, 5 May 1979.

95. See Chua Beng Huat, "Not Depoliticized but Ideologically Successful: The Public Housing Programme in Singapore," *International Journal of Urban and Regional Research* 15, no. 1 (1991): 27.

96. B. Tinsley, *Singapore Green: A History and Guide to the Botanic Gardens* (Singapore: Times Books International, 1983), 53. It is also the case that botanic gardens all over the world were declining in the wake of rapid developments in molecular botany, a trend that R. E. Holttum tried to forestall in his "The Historical Significance of Botanic Gardens in S.E. Asia" *Taxon* 19 (October 1970): 707–14.

97. Tan Wee Kiat, "The Role of Botanic Gardens in the 21st Century," in *Proceedings of the Botanic Gardens' 130th Anniversary Seminar* (Singapore, 1989), 5.

98. On the perceived importance to the Singapore government of promoting public education for environmental improvement, see Victor R. Savage, "Sustainable Development: Government Intervention and Environmental Education," in *Environmental Stakes: Myanmar and Agenda 21,* ed. Victor R. Savage and L. Kang (Singapore: National University of Singapore, 1997).

99. C. J. Wee Wan Ling, "Contending with Primordialism: The 'Modern' Construction of Post-colonial Singapore," *Positions* 1 (1993): 715–44.

100. *The Botanic Gardens Conservation Strategy,* IUCN-BGCS and WWF (1989).

101. Victor Savage, "Human-Environment Relations," 187, 206–7. See C. Briffett, *Master Plan for the Conservation of Nature in Singapore* (Singapore: Malayan Nature Society [Singapore Branch], 1990).

102. National Archives of Singapore, speech by Dr. Ahmad Mattar to the Osaka International Forum on "Global Environment and the City," 2 July 1990; see also Concept Plan 2, 1991: "Singapore will be cloaked in greenery, both manicured by man and protected tracts of natural growth." Savage has emphasized the importance of pragmatic environmental possibilism (the view that the environment is infinitely malleable by humans) in postcolonial Singapore government thinking (Savage, "Human-Environment Relations," 189, 201–5).

103. J. Cochrane, "Tourism and Conservation in Indonesia and Malaysia," in *Tourism in South-East Asia,* ed. M. Hitchcock, V. I. King, and M. J. G. Parnwell (London: Routledge, 1993).

104. Speech by Prof. Ahmad Ibrahim, in *The Role and Goals of Tropical Botanic Gardens, Proceedings of the Symposium at the Ceremonial Opening of the Rimba Ilmu University of Malaya Botanic Garden, August 1974,* ed. B. C. Stone (Kuala Lumpur: Penerbit Universiti Malaya, 1977), 1.

105. See speech by Dato Haji Taib Mahmud, in *Role and Goals of Tropical Botanic Gardens,* 11.

106. P. F. Cockburn, "Tropical Botanic Gardens: Science or Public Amenity?" in *Role and Goals of Tropical Botanic Gardens,* 173.

107. Frances Cairncross, *The Death of Distance 2.0: How the Communications Revolution Will Change Our Lives,* 2nd ed. (London: Texere, 2001).

The position of Bangkok as a "gay capital," both within Thailand and internationally, serves as a productive *topos* for the examination of global processes that affect sites and the people in them in unique and complex ways. Finding the simplistic application of Foucauldian theories on the history of sexuality unproductive, Jackson generates a nuanced reading of the interaction between the world's homoerotic cultures and radically different local discourses surrounding them, without falling into a reductive global–local binaristic scheme. Central to his analysis is the role that capital has played in transforming both familial structures and ways of being in traditional societies, not the least of these being the commercial power of gay purchasers. Jackson, therefore, explores two sets of issues fundamental to this volume: how the region forces a reconsideration of global flows as unidirectional, and the use of alternative networks to question the hegemony of globalization practices while revealing the specific and contradictory ways global cities relate to each other and the systems that link them. In this way, Jackson's article complements those by Marcus, Pile, Armitage and Roberts, Bishop and Clancey, King, and Patke. At the same time, Jackson opens the very productive space of enunciation that explores how a phenomenon such as a "gay capital" comes into being in a site such as Bangkok, but in so doing changes the parameters by which a "gay capital" can be understood and articulated elsewhere. It is the specific attention to the various ways in which material and empirical data intersect with discursive formations in revealing possibilities for actions and modes of existence that places Jackson's site of enunciation within the central concerns of this volume.

7

Gay Capitals in Global Gay History: Cities, Local Markets, and the Origins of Bangkok's Same-Sex Cultures

PETER A. JACKSON

As a cultural historian interested in the sources of patterns of cultural complexity and hybridity in Thailand, I have been studying the origins of contemporary forms of transgender and homosexual identity in Thailand. Until the 1960s, local discourses in Thailand possessed only three categories to mark distinctive forms of gendered or erotic being. These three categories were *chai,* a word denoting manhood or masculinity; *ying,* a term denoting femaleness and femininity; and a third term, *kathoey,* which referred variously to a man who was too effeminate, a woman who was too masculine, or to an intersexed person born with indeterminate male or female genitals. *Kathoey* was a catchall label for anyone who failed to match local expectations of normative sexual physiology or culturally appropriate gender behavior. Same-sex erotic behaviors per se did not mark a person as being a *kathoey.* Homosexually active masculine men and feminine women were not distinguished from their heterosexually active counterparts. The *kathoey* therefore marked a physiological or gender category, not a homosexual status or identity.

However, by the 1980s the Thai language had come to possess eight or nine categories to mark diverse eroticized forms of masculinity and femininity.[1] In the two decades from the 1960s to the 1980s, new gender/sex cultures also emerged around these categories. People living in Bangkok and other Thai cities identified themselves in terms of new categories such as "gay," *tom,* and *dee,* and built their sexual and social lives around these emerging identities. In a relatively brief two decade period, a society that previously had had a quite limited range of explicitly differentiated forms of gender and eroticism became much more highly differentiated, not only in terms of discourses, but also in terms of gender and sexual cultures. I have been trying to understand the historical forces behind this dramatic explosion in the number of categories and cultural forms for types of gender and / or erotic preference.

Part of this exploration has involved tracing the discourses that mark the explosion of categories. For example, I have studied Thai language discourses to understand when and how new categories such as "gay" came into being as identities distinct from the transgender and/or intersex *kathoey*.[2] I have sought to locate the origins of new female homosexual identities—the masculine *tom* (from "*tom* boy") and the feminine *dee* (from "la*dy*")—as well as determine how contemporary notions of transgenderism and transsexualism have altered as forms of gender normative male and female homoeroticism (i.e., masculine gay men and feminine homosexual women) came to be marked as something different from the historical *kathoey*.

However, theoretical models that have been used to try and explain similar phenomena in Western societies, drawing on Michel Foucault's *History of Sexuality,* are not particularly helpful in Thailand. This is because the forces that Foucault identified as leading to discursive transformations and the emergence of homosexual and heterosexual identities in nineteenth century France—new, highly intrusive forms of religious, legal, and biomedical power over human sexuality—were not present in Thailand in the years that saw the explosion of new categories. I have argued that the absence in Thailand of the forces that produced contemporary Western discourses and understandings of sexuality means that, despite apparent similarities between contemporary Thai and Western homoerotic and transgender cultures, local Asian understandings of the meaning of identity categories such as "gay" differ considerably from Western cultures.[3] Similar global gay fashion styles and the internationalization of the originally English identity label "gay" mask the persistence of different worlds of homosexual meaning in culturally distinct societies. In Thailand, gender distinctions of masculine versus feminine are much more important than sexuality distinctions of homosexual versus heterosexual, even for categories such as "gay," *tom,* or *dee.* Despite the proliferation of these new homoerotic gender identity categories, Western-style discourses of sexuality have not been established unequivocally in Thailand.

This means that we need a different type of explanation from current formulations of the Foucauldian history of sexuality to understand the comparatively recent explosion of Thai identities. The explanatory limitations of current theories of the history of sexuality have forced me to look at other forms of intervention and different processes from those identified by Foucault that may have led to the proliferation of categories and cultures of gender and sexuality in Thailand. I will consider distinctive local forms of power in Thailand that have produced what, at least superficially, look like a gay male community, a lesbian community, and a transgender community such as one might find in a large Western cities, but whose historical emergence must be imagined within a totally different frame of reference.[4] What is required is a nuanced analysis that explains the emergence of certain similarities between the world's homoerotic cultures even as radically different local discourses—that is, distinctive worlds of meaning within which ostensibly similar sexual cultures are understood in markedly different ways—continue to persist. The explanatory task for students of the comparative history of sexuality is to understand the simultaneous emergence of some forms of similarity (e.g., homosexual lifestyles) and of some forms of difference (e.g., diverse meanings of "gay identity") between homosexual cultures at the global level.

Dennis Altman has written about a phenomenon he labels "global queering," that is, the emergence of "gay" as a global homosexual category.[5] Details of his ideas have been contested,[6] but in broad terms he has put his finger on a significant phenomenon: In the second half of the twentieth century something similar to what I have just described for Bangkok took place in a wide range of societies. Globally we have seen a proliferation of new forms of gendered and erotic being, which in turn have formed the basis of new gender/sex identities, cultures, and communities. What we need is a frame of reference to enable us to understand this both as a transnational phenomenon and yet also as something with distinctive local features.

In considering the way that the Thai case fits into the broader pattern, something that has struck me is that historical research on the phenomenon of "global queering" has tended to concentrate on cities that, in popular gay parlance in English-speaking countries, are called "gay capitals." A gay capital is a large city commonly regarded to be the first site of the emergence of new homosexual identities and cultures in a particular region. Gay capitals are often sites of in-migration from rural areas, which seem to be morally conservative and sexually oppressive. They are sites of commercial gay culture: gay bars, gay magazines, gay service industries, and, of late, national and international gay tourism. Some of the cities that are most often called gay capitals include Amsterdam, London, Paris, New York, San Francisco, Rio de Janeiro, Sydney, Bangkok, and Tokyo.

In Southeast Asia, Bangkok is the most important gay capital. A key criterion that marks a contemporary gay capital is that it is a site of international gay tourism, quite often (but not necessarily) from societies that have sexually more repressive legal systems or cultures. Bangkok functions in this way in Southeast Asia. Many gay Malaysians, Singaporeans, Taiwanese, Japanese, and Chinese visit Bangkok for vacations. Despite stereotypes, Bangkok is not only a site for Western gay tourism; rather, it is the most important site for informal international gay networking in the Southeast Asian region.

As Dennis Altman has pointed out, there is an international network of connections between those cities imagined as gay capitals. However, from an urban studies perspective, what is interesting about gay capitals is that, apart from Paris, they are all ocean ports in countries with a long historical involvement in capitalist trading networks. Significantly, no gay capital emerged in any Eastern European country during the communist era. Since the fall of communism, Eastern European cities such as Budapest, Prague, and Moscow have begun to develop visible gay scenes and gay cultures; however, this is only a post-communist phenomenon. There are then a number of similarities among the cities popularly labeled as gay capitals. What I have been considering in terms of these similarities is the importance of urban spaces as sites for the emergence of new forms of gendered and erotic being, and the formative role that market economies have played in the history of global queering.

It cannot be emphasized too strongly that it is only cities in market-based economies that were also major nodes of trade, commerce, communications, transport, immigration, and tourism that first emerged as gay capitals in Europe, North America, Asia, and Australia. Within English-speaking gay cultures, "gay scene" is the name given to the urban space within which gay culture is imagined as existing. In Thailand, this idea is rendered by the notion of *sangkhom gay* or "gay society." In fact, Thailand's *sangkhom gay* and all Western gay scenes are commercial spaces. The notion of a gay scene as a space or stage on which an autonomous homosexual identity can be performed requires a commercial base. Indeed, what permits a gay scene or *sangkhom gay,* and hence a gay culture, to come into being in any gay capital is the existence of commercial enterprises—bars, discos, bookshops, and restaurants—that cater to a gay market. In different cities, in different cultures, commercial gay scenes have emerged at different points in history. We are now seeing the emergence of commercial gay scenes in formerly communist Eastern European cities.

I am not suggesting that capitalism works to channel preexisting forms of transgenderism or same-sex sexuality into urban spaces to form new homoerotic cultures. On the contrary, it is the capitalist city itself that provides the site for the coming into being of new homosexual possibilities. Indeed, it appears that it is only in capitalist urban spaces that the contemporary forms of same-sex cultures that we call gay, lesbian, transgender, and transsexual can come into being. In pre-urban, rural Thailand, same-sex locales such as Buddhist monasteries may well have been sites of underground, semitolerated homoerotic cultures. However, it is only amid the anonymity of large cities whose market economies provide opportunities for independent living that public gay-type homoerotic cultures can form. The market is absolutely central to this historical process. As historian John D'Emilio has argued, in late nineteenth and early twentieth century America the transformation of heteronormative family networks brought about by a move away from subsistence farm labor to marketized urban labor permitted individuals to live independently, thus building the collective forms now called homosexual cultures in large American cities.[7] The modern forms of homosexual cultures can only come into being where individuals can build sexual and social lives independently of heterosexual relationships, which is extremely difficult in subsistence rural communities based economically on family labor. That is, there is a crucial economic dimension to a person's ability to maintain a non-heterosexual relationship.

Another reason to emphasize the market in the narrative of global queering, as well as in the history of Thailand's new sexual cultures, is that two themes relating to the market recur in the sources that I have been studying from twentieth century Thailand. The first theme is of a general population movement from the subsistence village to market-based employment in the city, as D'Emilio has already noted. However, a second theme in the Thai case is of homosexual people already living in the city moving out of employment within the government bureaucracy to private sector jobs to evade the gender/sex conservatism of state policies. Within Thai gay, lesbian, and transgender cultures there is a widespread imagining of self-employment and work in the private sector as constituting a zone of homosexual autonomy. That is, one part of the story of the emergence of modern homoerotic cultures involves broad processes of capitalist industrial urbanization and the autonomy that comes of moving away from a subsistence, rural lifestyle. However, a second part of this story—not dealt with in Western-oriented homosexual urban history research based on D'Emilio's work—is that additional personal autonomy derives from self-employment in the private sector.

There is a commonly expressed desire by Thai homosexual people— *gay, tom, dee,* and *kathoey*—to either avoid or move out of employment within the Thai state sector because of the bureaucracy's extremely conservative gender norms. In Thailand, the market—in particular, self-employment—has become a key site for imaginings of a life lived outside heteronormative constraints of both rural villages and the conservative state bureaucracy. Arguably, the ideal of self-employment rates much higher as a marker of personal autonomy for Thai homosexual and transgender peoples than does "coming out," which within Western gay and lesbian communities is commonly seen as marking an individual's transition from heterosexual oppression to full membership in a homosexual community. For Thai gay men, lesbians, and transgenders being one's own boss is far more important than the Western homosexual cultural practice of very publicly announcing to the world that one is queer.

A common critique of Bangkok gay culture expressed by many Western gay visitors and tourists is that the Thai gay scene is overcommercialized, lacks a sense of gay and lesbian community, and is apolitical. Early politicized homosexual movements in the West tended to emerge from 1970s and 1980s left-aligned organizations that were intensely critical of capitalism and commercial gay scenes. Even with the decline of the organized Marxist left in the West, many Western homosexual men and women continue to regard "commercial gay culture" negatively. However, today "commodified gay culture" is more likely to be regarded as an inauthentic or nongenuine form of homosexual culture than viewed as antirevolutionary.

In the West, Bangkok is widely perceived to be a site of overly commodified sexualities, both heterosexual and homosexual. I am trying to think beyond this common Western narrative of Thailand as a society of the excesses of the market, and also to move beyond analyses that see the market as only ever constituting a site of sexual exploitation. The local cultural valorization of self-employment as a marker of homosexual autonomy, together with the relative unimportance of coming out and becoming a politically engaged homosexual activist, appear to contribute to negative Western homosexual stereotypes of gay Thailand. That is, the culturally distinctive ways by which one becomes an autonomous gay man or lesbian in Thai and Western queer cultures—via self-employment or marketized labor in Thailand versus via coming out and/or political engagement in gay issues in the West—impact the ways that members of Asian and Western homosexual cultures perceive, or more often misperceive, each other. What, from a Western gay perspective, may be seen negatively as the commodification or commercialization of homosexual identity, is, from a Thai perspective, seen as the very condition for the coming into being of that autonomous homosexual identity.

The differential valuing of the market in Thai and Western queer imaginations demonstrates the significant differences that continue to mark gay cultures around the planet, despite the intensification of intercultural contact brought about by 1990s globalization. In Western queer cultures, gay and lesbian identity is seen as emerging from a personal public statement, or "confession," of homosexual preference, and at least verbal commitment to advancing homosexual rights issues. That is, Western gay identity is imagined to emerge from an assertion of personal autonomy and self-definition independent of the market, which if anything is seen as a source of polluting "commercializing" and "commodifying" inauthenticity. In the popular ideology dominant in Western gay and lesbian cultures, "real" homosexual identity is presumed to be able to exist outside of marketized networks of commercial relations. Tremendous inequalities and disruptions are indeed produced by the commodification of labor. However, as D'Emilio has pointed out, it is only because of the disruptions of traditional family structures wrought by capitalism that contemporary forms of homosexual desire, identity, and culture have been able to emerge. Furthermore, given the conservative gender constraints that the Thai state imposes on those who work within the bureaucracy, the marketplace and work in the private sector are often the only possible sites of autonomy for people who transgress dominant gender and sexual norms. The fact that in Thailand involvement in the market is a much more central marker of achieved homosexual status requires us to think through Western homosexual preconceptions on the role of capitalism in the formation of "legitimate" homosexual identities and cultures.

Following Foucault, quite a lot of research has been conducted on the emergence of new discourses and understandings of sexuality; however, much less work been done on the role of urban spaces and of the economy in the formation of new sexual identities and cultures. D'Emilio's and Altman's emphasis on the importance of capitalism in modern homosexual cultures has tended to be overlooked in much of the research conducted over the last fifteen or so years, as the Foucauldian discourse–centered history of sexuality has become more popular, even hegemonic. In this context, returning to D'Emilio's arguments to help us understand processes of global queering proves quite productive.

In particular, I am interested in drawing on historical evidence from Bangkok to test a hypothesis put forward by Peter Drucker,[8] who has drawn on D'Emilio in attempting to develop a Marxist-inspired urban economic approach to understanding the proliferation of gay and lesbian cultures internationally. Drucker suggests that processes of urbanization in market economies may produce similar cultural forms independent of direct contact or cultural borrowing. Rather than seeing global queering as a process of Western gay cultures diffusing to the rest of the world, as Altman appears to argue, Drucker suggests that capitalism and urbanization may together incite the emergence of ostensibly similar homosexual cultures in different societies. My current project is to look for evidence of the ways in which urban space and commercial processes may intersect to provide opportunities for the emergence of similar homosexual cultural forms internationally. I am especially interested in the ways that urbanization and commodified forms of culture provide opportunities for new types of sexual autonomy and individuality.

In the case of Bangkok, evidence indeed suggests that some aspects of contemporary Thai gay culture emerged independently of any direct contact with similar cultural forms in Western societies. I am talking here about the establishment in the early 1980s of Thai language gay magazines oriented toward a local gay market. Internationally, gay lifestyle magazines oriented toward a local gay market are now extremely common. By the late 1990s, fifteen or sixteen bimonthly Thai language lifestyle magazines were published in Bangkok for the local gay market, a very extensive gay publication network indeed for a developing country of sixty million people. However, it was only after this type of commercial publishing activity had been established for the local Thai market that its publishers came in contact with homosexual communities in other parts of the world. In fact, it was the establishment of this type of commercial enterprise that provided the publishers and editors of Thai gay magazines with the wherewithal to contact gay men in other societies. Rather than emerging by a process of cultural borrowing or diffusion from the West, Thai gay magazines emerged independently, only subsequently becoming linked in international gay publishing and communications networks. Almost as soon as these local commercial cultural forms came into existence, they established contact with similar Western forms. However, originally they emerged independently.

The first Thai gay lifestyle magazines appeared in the early 1980s, into a context in which an imagined Thai gay community had already formed and reached a sufficient size and degree of organization that it could form a potentially lucrative new market. One needs a certain critical mass and a degree of organization or consistency in a market of consumers for a product or service to be saleable. In the case of gay services, one needs a sufficiently large number of potential consumers who identify themselves as gay for the provision of "gay services" to constitute a commercially viable enterprise. I have interviewed the editor of the first gay magazine set up in Bangkok in the early 1980s. Before conducting this interview I had imagined that this Thai gay man must have had significant international gay connections before starting his local Thai language gay magazine and that he had probably copied examples of similar publications from America, Australia, or Europe. However, the story of how the first Thai gay magazine was set up confounded my expectations. The young man in question began the magazine in 1983 at the tender age of twenty-one as a recent graduate from a Bangkok university. He was, in fact, quite closeted at the time. While he knew that he was gay, he had had no direct experience of the then already well-established Thai gay scene and he saw the establishment of a gay lifestyle magazine as a way to explore and develop an imagined gay lifestyle that, until that time, he had not known how to realize. He saw the setting up of a small business publishing a gay magazine as providing him with an independent income with which he would then have sufficient personal autonomy to live a gay lifestyle. It was only after the magazine had gone through several issues that he came in contact with Western homosexual men. Indeed, he used the pretext of being an editor of the magazine to interview Thai and Western gay men—such as the owners of Bangkok gay bars and other enterprises. Putting on the hat of a magazine editor gave him both the finances and the justification to become part of Bangkok's gay culture, a world that he had previously found too intimidating to enter.

This is a pattern that I have found repeated in Bangkok. A range of other gay-oriented enterprises have been set up in Bangkok by young gay men as a way to try to establish the means *and the justification* to live an imagined gay lifestyle. At the time, they did not realize that they were following patterns that gay men in many other countries had traced before them. They were merely using the resources at hand—the anonymity of the metropolis of Bangkok and the possibilities that the Thai labor market provides for financial independence—to create a space for leading a gay lifestyle. It was only in the process of establishing and conducting their commercial activity oriented toward a local gay market that these (typically young) gay men came into contact with preexisting gay communities, both in Thailand and internationally.

There is a distinctive history here, somewhat different from a stereotypical narrative of homogenizing globalization that pictures contemporary gay cultures emerging first in the West and then being disseminated to the non-West. Rather, homosexual people in different capitalist metropolises appear to have independently taken advantage of local opportunities to mould an autonomous gay lifestyle. Rather than a unilinear model of gay history by which gay identity and culture radiates from a single "originary" site in the West, the story behind the global explosion of categories of gender and sexuality in the second half of the twentieth century is more likely to be one of multiple, independent or semi-independent origins. Looking at the history of commercial activities developed by and for homosexual people, we get a picture of the semi-independent origination of contemporary gay cultures in widely scattered gay capitals, which only subsequently came to be linked with each other into the global queer network that Altman takes as the object of his study. What this tells us about processes of capitalist urbanization is that at least some of the apparent international cultural similarities taken to be emblematic of globalization may emerge locally before they become connected with similar cultural forms in other societies. Urbanized capitalist societies may provide opportunities for the semi-independent emergence of apparently similar cultural phenomena that only subsequently come into contact with each other through international trade, travel, and communications networks.

This more complex model of how new homosexual cultures emerge under globalizing capitalism provides a picture of gay capitals developing from the changing *local* conditions brought about within cultural and geographical regions by the impact of intensifying international trade, finance, communications, and travel movements. It is the simultaneous location of urban homoerotic cultures within rapidly changing local and global conditions that permits us to begin to understand the continuing differences between gay capitals, despite their similarities. In particular, it is the fact that commercial gay scenes in gay capitals such as Bangkok first emerged to provide services to their respective *local* gay markets that confers a degree of difference and cultural specificity to these cultures.

Following this model, one could formulate a rather basic and simplistic thesis that a body of capital precedes the emergence of queer bodies. But, of course, a series of quite different relationships of queer bodies to the market take place over a relatively brief period. First, a market-based economy is the necessary prerequisite for imaginings of gay autonomy to come into being. However, once gay identities and cultures do emerge and are realized in marketized urban spaces, they are very readily commodified as sites of investment and easily become gay niche markets. At an earlier stage in the 1960s in Bangkok, a commodified urban cultural space provided the basis for the initial emergence of zones of homosexual autonomy, and this period marked the beginning of the rapid explosion in the number of Thai gender/sex categories. However, twenty years later in the early 1980s, that autonomous gay culture subsequently became a site of investment for entrepreneurs. The notion of the "pink dollar" in the United States and Australia, or the "lavender baht" in Thailand, then becomes relevant.

Furthermore, gay politics can also become linked to marketization. Commodified gay lifestyles are now celebrated in regular cultural events such as Sydney's annual Gay and Lesbian Mardi Gras. The organizers of events such as Sydney's Mardi Gras, and more recent annual gay festivals in Bangkok, Phuket, and Pattaya in Thailand, often seek to legitimate these public expressions of homosexual culture by emphasizing the volume of gay tourism dollars that such festivals bring into their city. That is, dollar values of the size of the gay market can be used as a strategy to legitimate gay culture within a sexually intolerant but materialist, wealth-fixated, market-oriented culture. The implicit argument in such strategies is something like, "I'm gay, I shop, and so I'm worth taking seriously," which adds a political edge to gay purchasing power. In a sense, one's demonstrable capacity to become a member of a lucrative niche market can serve to justify one's right to claim a recognized space in modern capitalist societies. The market has not only helped give birth to modern homosexual identities, but subsequently permitted the commercial exploitation of those new identities as convenient niche markets.

The discourse of the market is also drawn upon to legitimate the transgressive sexual identities that it has spawned within morally conservative societies. One sees, therefore, a range of processes that relate homosexuality and capitalism. While capitalism can be a source of new homosexual imaginings, once in existence those new identities become sites of commercial exploitation, and the rhetoric of the market may be appropriated to legitimate those sexualities. In Thailand, the Bangkok, Phuket, and Pattaya gay festivals—first staged in 1999, 2000, and 2001, respectively—were all initiated by Thai and Western homosexual men with financial interests in local gay enterprises.

Yet the market is as much a site of exclusion as it is of inclusion in the making of new homoerotic cultures. In the interviews I have conducted with Thai gay men, perhaps the most poignant comment was made by a poor man from a remote province working as a day laborer in Bangkok. While aspiring to the ideal of an autonomous gay lifestyle represented in Thailand's many gay magazines, this man remarked bitterly, "I'm too poor to be gay." His statement indicated that in his mind "gay'" was identified with a well-off lifestyle that required a significant amount of money to purchase—money he did not have. The intense marketization of gay identity—in its origins, in its constant reproduction in urban sites, and also in justifications of homosexuality that refer to gay purchasing power—exclude those homosexual men who have insufficient money to purchase such a highly commodified model of autonomous sexual individuality.

Despite the liberating potentials of homosexual autonomy that are made possible by the city and the market, modern gay identity is only achieved at considerable cost, financial and moral. This cost can be quantified as the income required to sustain an aspirational middle-class consumerist lifestyle. In many Asian societies—not only Thailand but also the Philippines, Indonesia, and elsewhere—there is often an intensely middle-class bourgeois cachet associated with being gay. A class status factor is as closely linked with the label "gay" as it is with fashion labels such as Gucci, Dior, Adidas, or Levi. Many working-class and poorer homosexually oriented men in Thailand and other Asian societies aspire to gay identity not simply for the pleasures and comforts of autonomous homosexual relationships, but also as a marker of class advancement. There is a very strong aspirational middle-class element to Thai imaginings of gay identity, and with this there is a marked exclusion of poorer homosexual men from the "gay dream" in this society divided by gaping income differentials.

The above narratives of the intersection of the city, the market, and the queer body—that is, the formation of queer gender possibilities—complicates Altman's image of a global gay scene, especially when we add to this mix the cultural demands articulated by religion. The market and processes of urbanization are moderated and at times dominated by strong cultural influences. Islam, for example, is an exceptionally powerful global and regional force, and offers many more complications to an already dense network of relations impacting on the historical emergence of queer cultures and identities. The relative strength of religious cultural opposition to non-normative sexualities is an important factor in the conditions that underpin the emergence of gay cultures, whose origins lie in more than merely the rise of industrial trading cities under capitalism. If the law or local religious culture is intensely prohibitive, then it may not be possible for a commercial gay scene to emerge even in a highly urbanized market-based society. No Middle Eastern Muslim country currently has an extensive commercial gay scene of the type found in many Western and East Asian societies. A certain cultural openness is required to become a gay consumer performing one's purchased sexual identity on a commercial gay scene.

Thus, it is important to reemphasize the role of local cultures in shaping the persistent differences between commercial gay scenes. It is the fact that most commercial gay scenes respond to the culturally specific needs of local homosexual markets that continues to imbue them with their often distinctive qualities. Gay scenes are not identical spaces in all the gay capital cities in which they exist. For example, the geographical layout of a gay scene reflects the sexual and gender culture of the city in which it is located. The urban geography of some gay scenes minimizes the sense of shame that some customers may feel if they are seen entering a venue labeled as a gay bar or gay restaurant. In Bangkok, there are two major gay scenes or commercial centers of gay cultural activity. One is located downtown and is internationally oriented. It is a place where gay tourists from Western and Asian countries congregate with openly gay Thai men. The other gay scene is in Bangkok's northern suburbs. The structure of these two gay scenes is very different. In the downtown gay scene one finds several small streets that are tightly packed with gay bars, discos, restaurants, and boutiques catering quite openly to both a local Thai and an international clientele. In contrast, the northern suburban gay scene is formed around a street about a mile long that has a series of many small *sois* or side streets. One, and only one, gay venue is located in each of these side streets, often inconspicuously situated next door to a print shop, grocery shop, or other non-gay small business. This type of layout caters to a market of gay men who do not want to be seen entering these venues. Because the venues are not congregated together, if one enters a particular bar one is not immediately identified as having a particular sexuality. The urban geography of the suburban gay scene responds to the shame that many Thai gay men still feel about being publicly identified as gay. In contrast, the layout of the downtown gay scene corresponds to that sector of the gay market for which shame in being identified as gay is not a hindering factor. Bangkok's downtown and suburban gay scenes are both commercial spaces and are equally important sites of Thai gay culture, but they operate in distinctive ways that reflect the diversity of local cultural norms that are found even within this single gay capital.

NOTES

1. Peter Jackson, "An Explosion of Thai Identities: Global Queering and Reimagining Queer Theory," *Culture, Health and Sexuality* 2, no. 4, (2000): 405–24.
2. See Peter Jackson, *Dear Uncle Go: Male Homosexuality in Thailand* (Bangkok: Bua Luang Books, 1995); Jackson, "*Kathoey* < > Gay < > Man, the Historical Emergence of Gay Male Identity in Thailand," in *Sites of Desire/Economies of Pleasure, Sexualities in Asia and the Pacific,* ed. L. Manderson and M. Jolly (Chicago: University of Chicago Press, 1997), 166–90; Jackson, "Thai Research on Male Homosexuality and Transgenderism and the Cultural Limits of Foucaultian Analysis," *Journal of the History of Sexuality* 8, no. 1 (1997): 52–85; Jackson, "An American Death in Bangkok: The Murder of Darrell Berrigan and the Hybrid Origins of Gay Identity in 1960s Bangkok," *GLQ: A Journal of Lesbian and Gay Studies* 5, no. 3 (1999): 361–411; Jackson, "Tolerant but Unaccepting: Correcting Misperceptions of a Thai 'Gay Paradise,' " in *Genders and Sexualities in Modern Thailand,* (Chiang Mai: Silkworm Books, 1991), 226–42.
3. See Jackson, "*Kathoey* < > Gay," "Thai Research," and "Explosion of Thai Identities."
4. See Jackson, "Thai Research" and "American Death."
5. Dennis Altman, "Rupture or Continuity? The Internationalisation of Gay Identities," *Social Text* 14, no. 3 (1996): 77–94; Altman, "Global Gaze/Global Gays," *GLQ: A Journal of Gay and Lesbian Studies* 3, no. 4 (1997): 417–36; Altman, "The Emergence of Gay Identities in Southeast Asia," in *Different Rainbows,* ed. Peter Drucker (London: Gay Men's Press, 2000): 137–56.
6. See Donald Morton, "Global (Sexual) Politics, Class Struggle, and the Queer Left," *Critical InQueeries* 1, no. 3 (1997): 1–30; and Michael Connors, "Prefacing Research on the 'Global Gay,' " *Melbourne Journal of Politics* 24 (1997): 44–48.
7. John D'Emilio, "Capitalism and Gay Identity," in *The Lesbian and Gay Studies Reader,* ed. Henry Abelove, Michèle Aina Barale, and David M. Halperin (New York & London: Routledge, 1993): 467–76.
8. Peter Drucker, "Introduction: Remapping Sexualities," in *Different Rainbows,* 9–42.

King's groundbreaking work on globalization, postcolonialism, and urban space has been justifiably influential in setting out terms for scholarship and debate, and this issue brings a characteristically wide frame of reference to bear on questions of postcolonialism and postcolonial scholarship. One crucial and significant phenomenon is the division between postcolonialism as it is practiced by scholars in the humanities—many of whom focus "overwhelmingly on textual and literary studies"—and as it actually occurs in different geographical and political situations in different parts of the globe. King's focus is on work that, in the context of recent calls to engage with "material practices, actual spaces and real politics," largely ignores the theorizing of postcolonial critics and turns instead to more descriptive accounts of actual situations. As we analyzed at length in our introductory essay, the apparent institutional division between theoretical and empirical approaches to postcolonialism manifests one of the most tenacious difficulties for scholars working in the field, and King's impressive handling of the problem does not fail to acknowledge both the strengths and weaknesses of both sides. His main focus nonetheless remains with "the scholar of the one-time colonized society," whose position allows her "to contest the metanarratives that emerge from the west and offer alternatives on the basis of a more intimate local knowledge." While careful to note the risk in attempting to ground knowledge in a kind of cultural relativity of authentic experiences, King's argument concedes that postcolonial criticism often "understates the materiality of colonialism and aestheticizes oppression." His overview of scholars working on the political dimensions of specific postcolonial spaces reveals a wide range of effective engagements.

8

Actually Existing Postcolonialisms: Colonial Urbanism and Architecture after the Postcolonial Turn

ANTHONY D. KING

The internal mental structures of colonial power outlive their epoch. Habits of thought, from the most inconsequential practices of everyday life through to the most highly formalized systems of philosophical abstraction, still reproduce inherited and often unseen colonial mentalities. —*Bill Schwarz*[1]

In his intriguing essay on "actually existing postcolonialism" (from which both my title and epigraph are taken), cultural historian Bill Schwarz writes, "To think about divergent historical forms of postcoloniality means working through the political configurations of specific conjunctures."[2] The specific conjuncture he addresses is the early to middle twentieth century origins of the racist ideologies of British Conservative politician Enoch Powell, and their sinister popular political effects, generally referred to in Britain as Powellism. As a dyed-in-the-wool imperialist, Powell's recognition in the 1960s that Britain's empire had come to an end was also a recognition that, with black immigration into the United Kingdom, "'Race' [was] billed to play a major . . . part in the battle of Britain."[3] In Schwarz's careful argument, it was in this context that "postcolonialism" in the metropolis was first popularly experienced as "Powellism," with its connotations of racism, in the 1970s.

Why begin with this story? First, because in a collection of essays on Southeast Asia, including Singapore, 1970s Britain is neither the expected period nor site that we associate with postcolonialism. Second, because in the Singapore of the new millennium, this particular understanding of "postcolonialism" is not one uppermost in our minds. And finally, because the story not only helps to confirm that "postcolonialism" no longer has any fixed meaning (if, indeed, it ever had), but also because it has apparently nothing to do with Singapore.

Or has it? In fact, in one of the most notorious of Powell's speeches, delivered in 1970, he opened his address not with Birmingham (where he was speaking), but with Singapore. Having served in the army during the war, Powell compared the Japanese sinking of two British warships in the Gulf of Siam and the subsequent fall of Singapore in 1942 to the moment in 1970 when Britain was once more "under attack," according to Powell, from "the enemy within" (the phrase, incidentally, by which this speech became known).[4] In this context, as Brenda Yeoh has reminded us, "Not only are the 'colonial city' and the 'imperial city' umbilically connected in terms of economic linkages as well as cultural hybridization, but their 'post-equivalents' . . . need to be analyzed within a single 'postcolonial' framework of intertwining histories and relations."[5]

In stark contrast to the racist connotations invested by Powell in the idea (if not the actual term) of postcolonialism in 1970, we can see from a more positive—indeed, celebratory—viewpoint what sociologist Phil Cohen says about the "postcolonial city" (implicitly, London) in 2000:

> A new kind of hybridized intellectual culture has emerged in which the invention of tradition, the profession of modernity, the cultivation of roots, and the embrace of liminality are no longer specialized strategies but can be combined in various permutations to compose a vibrant "postcolonial" intellectual mix. . . . The invention of the "postcolonial city" not only anchored these terms [i.e., new ethnicities, hybridity, diaspora] but gave Black and Asian cultural politics its own distinctive local/global habitation and a name, its own invented traditions, its own imagined history and geography, its own permeable . . . boundaries of belonging.[6]

If these varied political and cultural connotations of "postcolonial"—first negative, second positive—are to be found in relation to what I have referred to as the "post*imperial* city,"[7] more recent ideas about the term "postcolonial" may disturb our settled understandings even more.

Thus, James Sidaway,[8] in his suggestive "exploratory essay" on postcolonial geographies, sets out a whole new agenda for productively introducing the concept across a range of historical and geographical situations. Starting from the premise that, until comparatively recently, "postcolonial has usually been used to describe a condition referring to peoples, states and societies that have been through a process of formal decolonization," he then addresses more recent political, cultural, and critical inflections that have come to be invested in the term (in cases, drawing on poststructuralist, feminist, and psychoanalytic interpretations, among others). In these senses, "postcolonial approaches are committed to critique, expose, deconstruct, counter and (in some claims) to transcend, the cultural and broader ideological legacies and presences of imperialism." In the realm of literary criticism, postcolonial consciousness is also about "the possibility and methods of hearing or recovering the experiences of the colonized"; it has the aim to "invert, expose, transcend or deconstruct knowledge and practices associated with colonialism, of which objectification, classification and the impulse to chart or map have been prominent."[9] For the editors of the journal *Postcolonial Studies,* launched in 1998, "postcolonialism has directed its own critical antagonism towards the universalising knowledge claims of 'western civilization' . . . its desire to trouble the seemingly impassive face of western rationality has found expression in its will to, in Dipesh Chakrabarty's phrase, 'provincialise Europe.'"[10]

I shall not reproduce here Sidaway's (own) classification of some of the different types of colonialism though it is in the spirit of his essay that he draws attention to the fact that much of Europe has, at various times, been subject to imperial rule (Hapsburg, Ottoman, English, French, and, for a brief time, Italian Fascism and German Nazism). Can these situations, as also those of the post-Soviet and post-Yugoslav republics, be considered as "postcolonial"? As the possibilities and pitfalls of the term have been frequently discussed,[11] I shall not pursue this question. Instead, I shall adopt Sidaway's two interpretations, as and where appropriate. I take the second to include recognition of the voices of the one-time colonized, acknowledging the power of their agency and the identities that implicitly go with them.

There are also, of course, the negative dimensions of the paradigm. One, if not the most common, charge leveled against postcolonial criticism is that it both understates the materiality of imperialism and aestheticizes oppression; historical, economic, and material dimensions have persistently been excluded.[12] Many postcolonial studies have focused overwhelmingly on textual and literary studies, being only weakly concerned with "what happened."[13] In the context of these criticisms, calls to engage with "material practices, actual spaces and real politics"[14] have increasingly, if belatedly, brought into the debate recent as well as earlier studies of colonial urbanism and architecture, largely ignored in the literary discourses on the postcolonial.

In this essay, therefore, I want to focus quite narrowly on some recent writings on what is represented by their authors as "actually existing postcolonial" urbanism and architecture as well as "actually existing postcolonial" writing on this topic. In both cases, of course, these are essentially textual representations—but representations do not exist independently of the material conditions and realities they aim to represent.[15]

WRITING "COLONIAL CITIES"

At what was possibly the first conference to be held on "Colonial Cities" over twenty years ago, my paper concluded with the following statement: "What my unilateral view [on the colonial city] has underplayed is the contribution of the indigenous society and culture. The next book on 'colonial' or 'ex-colonial' cities might come from representatives of those cities themselves."[16] I did not imply at that time, nor do I here, that "location" alone should be treated as an essentialism that, irrespective of other factors, would give indigenous inhabitants of the one-time colonial city a privileged insight. As Robert Young writes, "Nowadays, no one really knows where an author 'is' when they read a book, apart from guarded information about institutional affiliation on the dust jacket, and nor should it matter. The difference is less a matter of geography than where individuals locate themselves as speaking from, epistemologically, politically, culturally and politically, who they are speaking to and how they define their own enunciative space."[17] While I would agree with this in principle, it is also the case that, generally speaking, it is statistically more likely that members of the one-time colonized society (rather than that of the colonizer) are not only fluent in the colonial as well as the national language, but possibly also in local and regional languages of the one-time colonized state. They may also have better knowledge of (if not always access to) local sources. Exactly *where* scholars do their research, where they write it up, and the intellectual, social, political, cultural, and other environments that influence their subjective identities may be more or less important. Hence, while generally accepting Young's statement, I have in the following overview nevertheless aimed to identify interpretations that are not only recent but also produced primarily by indigenous scholars from the one-time colonized society.

The works I address fall into one or both of two categories. First are the postcolonial studies of contemporary or recent developments in postcolonial cities that have a particular focus on urban space and form, sociospatial structure, and aspects of building design. The second category, what I shall call "postcolonial writings," is accounts by scholars who, in giving agency and voice to the (historically) once-colonized, are both contesting and rewriting the history, geography, and architecture of the one-time colonial city or of colonial urbanism broadly conceived. In either case, scholars might be located, permanently or temporarily, in the postcolony, postmetropolis, any other part of the anglophonic postcolonial empire (e.g., the United States, Australia, Canada, or Singapore) or elsewhere. Though the accounts refer mainly to South and Southeast Asia, my essay by no means attempts to be comprehensive. Its purpose is rather to foreground the issues raised in these accounts but also to ask about the conditions that give rise to their production.

POSTCOLONIAL URBANISM: KOLKATA, DELHI, MUMBAI

If one pressing analytical question is "to see what the colonial and the post-colonial have done to each other,"[18] the next is to ask what the global is doing to the postcolonial, and vice versa. This is addressed by Sanjoy Chakravorty in "From Colonial City to Globalizing City? The Far-from-Complete Spatial Transformation of Calcutta."[19]

As with other studies, urban geographer Chakravorty nests his analysis of the spatial structure of Calcutta in a three-phase frame of political economic development: colonial economy during the first global period, postcolonial (or command) economy during a nationalist period, and reform economy during the second global period. He makes a number of assertions. While the colonial city was "deeply divided" between colonizers and natives, he says that "would be wrong to assume that this spatial division was strictly enforced."[20] Nonetheless, the thrust of his argument is to show that "this basic structure, created in the eighteenth century, still dominates the spatial pattern of work and home in the city."[21] With Independence in 1947, "the spatial divisions of the colonial city (demarcated by class and race barriers) were largely retained, with the native upper class (capital and land owners, political leaders and top government officials) now occupying the privileged space once occupied by the colonizers."[22] The new (postcolonial) space retained much of this inheritance with the race divisions being replaced by class divisions; some residential segregation by occupation, religion, caste, and ethnicity continued into the postcolonial period.

With the coming of the "new" economy and the postreform city, a more significant change has taken place in Indian society, where there is "increasing (and more acceptable) social, cultural, and technological polarization."[23] These include new town projects, and an expanded international airport, though with these new towns, "colonies" are named after specific corporations (e.g., AVB colony, MAMC colony), apparently following well-worn (colonial) public works department practices.

Chakravorty concludes that Calcutta's spatial structure "cannot be separated from its political economic history," but he adds that it is quite different from its "more colonial counterparts . . . the more segregated, hierarchical, monolingual Chennai (Madras) or the dynamic, polyglot, recently chauvinistic Mumbai." Unlike Mumbai and Delhi, Calcutta has not been plagued by communal riots and "the bourgeois planning apparatus has worked and continues for the benefit of the upper classes."[24]

Chakravorty's analysis might be fairly characterized as a straightforward political economic narrative. Another essay on a similar topic, though in this case referring to Delhi, demonstrates that postcolonial analysis can be more focused on cultural politics. Cultural geographers Chatterjee and Kenny[25] argue that, despite five decades of independence, attempts to bridge the vast spatial, social, economic, and infrastructural inequities, as well as religious, cultural, and lifestyle differences between old and new Delhi, to overcome the legacy of hegemonic colonial planning, and to create a single capital symbolizing the unity and identity of the nation have yet to be resolved. In offering reasons for this, the authors point to the essential ambiguities of the postcolonial: "the replacement of previous hierarchies of space, power and knowledge has not been complete," and "Muslim, Hindu and western socio-cultural norms co-exist, albeit uneasily, in Delhi's built environment."[26] Multiple identities produce a multiplicity of spatialities.

The book *Bombay: The Cities Within* (1995), by architect Rahul Mehrotra and writer Sharada Dwivedi,[27] is clearly about colonial and postcolonial Bombay (since 1996, officially known as Mumbai); however, the narrative does *not* adopt an explicitly postcolonial position, as implied in Sidaway's second interpretation of that term. The historical evolution of Bombay's built environment is addressed apolitically, without any particular reference to power hegemonies, treating urban form as "the text of the city."[28] As "Bombay was not an indigenous city but was built by the British expressly for maintaining trade links with India,"[29] the colonial presence is taken for granted, a *fait accompli* not worth contesting. Whether writing of the many ancient as well as recent Hindu shrines, sacred tanks, Buddhist temples, Muslim mosques, Moghul palaces, or British colonial commercial or government buildings, the authors treat all as cultural resources or heritage and not as material objects on which to exercise a cultural or sociopolitical critique. No ideological divide or difference is read into the policies of city planners before or after 1947. As their primary commitment is to urban design and conservation, the authors regard every building, every space, as a neutral historical and aesthetic resource. In "One Space, Two Worlds," their social and urban design critique is reserved for the single major force that they see as having impacted the city in the last four decades—"distress migration." Only here is there a passing reference to the potential of colonial power:

> Undoubtedly, the urban poor as well as rural migrants have always formed an identifiable element among urban developments in Bombay. However, formerly under colonial rule their direct contact with, and influence on the city was very limited, both worlds lived in different spaces. Today, the city is clearly comprised of different worlds [and in the proposals by city authorities,] there's a sense of induced dualism . . . which relegates the homeless poor to the periphery.[30]

Finally, we can consider Nihal Perera's *Decolonising Ceylon: Colonialism, Nationalism and the Politics of Space in Sri Lanka* (1998).[31] Combining approaches from political economy, world-systems, and cultural studies of colonial urbanism, Perera deals at length with both postcolonial nationalist as well as socialist responses to the colonial system, examining ways in which new spatial, urban, and architectural forms have been produced as outcomes of the transfer of political power. Compared with the urban cases reviewed above, Perera maintains that governments in postcolonial Sri Lanka have made major efforts to reduce and correct the social and spatial inequities of the colonial system, modifying or replacing its symbolic signifiers. New spatial and architectural manifestations of a postcolonial national identity are evident in that the capital city has been moved from its old site at Colombo and the new parliamentary complex at Sri Jayawardhanapura speaks through a new critical vernacular architecture. New settlement schemes, massive housing programs, and economic and social development plans have largely transformed the earlier colonial spatial system and the economy on which it was based. Although the ethnic conflict, a legacy of colonial policies, has not been resolved, Perera does draw attention to significant realignments in the regional economic and political orientation of Sri Lanka.

POSTCOLONIAL SUBURBS: THE METAMORPHOSIS OF THE BUNGALOW

Where the previous articles address the spatial and social forms embodied in the postcolonial city, the following two speak, at least initially, to the architectural and social form of the building, including the bungalow-compound complex as a distinctively colonial product[32] and the suburban social and spatial forms it helps to construct. In over half a century following independence, how do Indian (and other) scholars see what has happened to both the idea and reality of the postcolonial sprawling bungalow, its space-consuming suburban setting, its role as status symbol for old and new elites, and, not least, its significance as subject of scholarly investigation?

Anita Sinha's "The Bungalows of Lucknow"[33] traces "continuities and changes in the Lucknow cantonment from the colonial to the postcolonial era." She concludes that "the landscape retains its colonial image in large part because it is governed by the zoning regulations and bylaws of a century ago." Despite alterations to the bungalows to meet the needs of the extended Indian families who live in some of them, she suggests that "the continuity of colonial imagery in the post-colonial era implies the internalization of colonial values by planners and residents of the cantonment."[34] Like other cantonments in India, that at Lucknow was a major constituent part of the "colonial landscape of power," physically manifest in its spatial separation from the indigenous city and segregation according to racial group and military rank. However, because the cantonment depended heavily on Indian manpower (for servants) and financial resources, "the separation was never complete." The continuity of colonial values is largely attributed to the fact that Lucknow cantonment today forms the headquarters of the central command of the Indian army with almost a third of its population consisting of army personnel. Though the names of Indian (rather than British) politicians and generals label the streets, and a dozen Hindu temples (also a gurdwara and mosque) have been constructed, Lucknow cantonment "has not seen any drastic changes in the half century since independence."[35] Despite the persistence of the typical colonial social maldistribution of space, with 90 percent of the cantonment population living on 7 percent of the land, the two bodies responsible for the area manage it according to the (colonial) Cantonment Act of 1924, their "conceptual framework . . . shaped by colonial ideas."[36] Sinha quotes a senior military official: "bungalow area is seen as sacrosanct . . . land cannot be carved out of it to accommodate the civilian population of the bazaars."[37] Sinha's interviews with residents, undertaken in the 1990s, reveal interesting differences between civilian owners and army officers. While the Cantonment Board forbids modifications exceeding 10 percent of the structure, civilian owners had adapted the bungalow's internal space to accommodate extended family needs (in one case, with rooms divided up among seven siblings). Owing to the escalating costs of servants, maintaining the bungalows and compounds (from one to five acres in area) was a major problem. On the other hand, senior army officers and wealthy civilians kept their bungalows in good colonial style: lawns to the front, orchards at the rear, occasionally with a bar for evening parties at the back and the occasional badminton court.

Sinha maintains that the colonial bungalow "has had a profound impact on Indian residential architecture." Adopted by the Indian elite in the last century, "new housing in the post-Independence era shows its influence . . . [even though] the adoption of its form has never been total."[38] She cites a mid 1990s study of a new residential enclave in south Delhi inhabited by retired officers of the ICS and the military as "a representation of colonialism in a decolonized space." The colony's by-laws do not permit parking and vending on its tree-lined streets. Similar middle-class and upper-income developments have occurred in other Indian cities.[39]

Significantly, Sinha states that, in Lucknow, half a century after Independence, "there are no signs of a post-colonial sensibility with regard to planning the physical environment." Though no longer "overtly a symbol of the Other," the cantonment's image "speaks of the past." It "sustains colonial traditions of social inequalities" previously between Europeans and Indians, but now between the wealthy and lower income Indians," and its future is "dependent on the military's ability to support its resource-intensive infrastructure."[40]

Sinha, as landscape historian, highlights the larger structural, institutional, and locational factors that keep (even modified) colonial environments in place and the structural economic, social, and spatial inequities they help sustain. American social anthropologist Thomas Rosin, on the other hand, provides both a methodologically different study and one with an unexpected outcome.

Rosin charts the social biography of a single bungalow where he stayed, intermittently, over three decades, in one of the colonies of garden suburbs built in Jaipur in the 1950s. These new colonies were "modeled on the civil lines and cantonments that once housed the British colonial elite"; after Independence they "embodied Nehru's vision for a modern India," one where "the educated middle class would lead the nation in uniting science and technology into the very construction of their daily lives."[41] Many such colonies, favored by middle-class professionals, government servants, and entrepreneurs, grew up around administrative cities. The idea was to replace the fortress-like courtyard houses (*havelis*) that existed in the old walled cities such as Jaipur.

The original two-story bungalow that Rosin studied, its design much influenced by colonial PWD concepts and 1940s modernistic codes of design, was located in one such colony. Rosin shows how the individual bungalows, originally on their own plots, have been totally transformed outward and upward through incremental building over three or four decades. To accommodate additional family members, provide facilities for servants and renters, create working space at home, and, especially, provide for the inheritance of offspring, the enlarged, extended bungalows have produced a space "similar to an old city ward with towering courtyard houses (*haveli*) abutting the property lines."[42] This, of course, has been achieved only by violating the building code, including linking up walls to the houses next door, removing trees and shrubs, and excluding access to sunlight.

Rosin positions his study in the context of statements by Indian and other commentators from the 1970s to the 1990s predicting that "the older havelis are no longer being built," having ceded their place in the culture to suburban house-types derived from the villa—that is, a house "whose external space is outside its walls." According to Rosin, this view that the suburban villa or bungalow would replace the courtyard house, a view that "echoes throughout the literature on vernacular architecture in India"[43] (including Sinha above), is based on an insufficiently observed, long-term perspective.

Rosin's anthropological interpretation suggests that the values of public interest and community-wide planning underpinning the original concept of the garden village have been subordinated to the "primacy of the family and its sovereignty in relationship to its neighbors."[44] The transformation of the bungalow suggests that the questions of lifestyle, class identity, and taste that prompted middle-class emulation of the bungalow lifestyle fifty years ago have, in practice, proven less important than deep-seated dispositions about the family, descendants, and the transmission of heritage.

I move now from accounts of what these various authors see as actually existing postcolonial spatial conditions in the late 1990s to actually existing postcolonial scholarship and writing. This research brings back into the "sometimes unilateral"[45] accounts of colonial urbanism and architecture the voices of scholars from the one-time colonized society, who contest and transform the one-time colonial accounts.

POSTCOLONIAL WRITING

Exemplary of the transformative approach is the opening paragraph of Siddhartha Raychaudhuri's essay, "Colonialism, Indigenous Elites and the Transformation of Cities in the Non-Western World: Ahmedabad, 1890–1947."

> Processes of transformation in cities in the non-western world during the colonial period have often been described as one-way processes through which European colonial regimes restructured the physical and social environments of the cities and established their dominance there. . . . [and] the ordinary residents of the city had hardly any voice in those developments.[46]

Raychaudhuri's study of the "non-western" city of Ahmedabad in the first half of the twentieth century sets out to remedy this perspective. She writes a history in which a section of Indian elites contested the restructuring attempted by the government in order to effect their own reorganization of the city center. By the 1940s, the Indian business elites had become the major players in this process. The resultant changes not only reflected but also facilitated the rise of new social and political classes who, with control over municipal bodies, exercised both coercive power and moral hegemony among large sections of the city's population, particularly the emergent working class and the increasingly self-conscious Muslim population. Neighborhoods that had been organized according to differences in caste, religion, and regional identities were brought together to form new working-class localities, bestowing new identities. What distinguished Ahmedabad, therefore, making it different from other Indian cities such as Bombay and Calcutta, was that it was the indigenous elites with their concern to preserve local traditions and practices, rather than the colonial government, that played the major role in restructuring the city. In the process, they constructed their own versions of modernity. The new social, cultural, and spatial order promoted new national ideas and linguistic and literary forms; though all were essentially "modern," they were also not "Western."

Raychaudhuri suggests that the Ahmedabad experience could also have implications for understanding the transformation, under colonialism, of other cities in the non-Western world. In cities such as Cairo, Rabat, Kuala Lumpur, and Jakarta, late nineteenth and twentieth century changes were also marked by attempts on the part of the government "to foster colonial difference." However, in smaller, inland cities—as opposed to colonial port towns where colonial military, economic, and political power was strong— the Ahmedabad experience could have been more typical. Raychaudhuri hypothesizes that the "substantial number of elites who assumed power in post-colonial states hailed from urban areas," that their power at the national level was first established in the inland, intermediate cities.[47]

There are parallels here, though at a local rather than national scale, with Jyoti Hosagrahar's innovative study of what she calls "indigenous modernities." Based on the assumption that the many studies on imperial Delhi have uncritically adopted a set of binary classifications where colonial/ indigenous, new/old, European/Native are unquestionably taken to represent "modernity" and "tradition," and where the scholarly lens has focused disproportionately on "imperial" New Delhi, Hosagrahar instead shines her investigative light on the "old" city.[48] Here, both social and spatial forms of the merchants' space of the old city of Shahjehanabad—never historically static, never unchanging—continued to be transformed throughout the nineteenth and early twentieth century, partly influenced by the colonial building program, but more by the ongoing social, economic, and cultural agendas of the merchant occupiers. Hosagrahar's sophisticated architec- tural history, based on interviews with long-term residents, oral histories, Urdu novels, and analysis of existing structures, deemphasizes the divide between the "*haveli* city" and the bungalow landscape of early colonial set- tlement. "Beneath the apparent opposition," she writes, "was a charged interconnection between the two spaces. The new residents of Delhi re- sponded to the new model of urban life in a variety of ways: by disdaining and rejecting, mocking and mimicking, participating and conniving, and learning and accepting."[49] From the sources she cites, the new "colonial" environment evidently offered opportunities for some Indian residents to construct new identities, a way of identifying with the new by rejecting the old, or when occasion demanded, of moving between the two. "The pene- tration of indigenous residents into the landscape of bungalows implied a dilution in the identity of the area as an exclusive European enclave."[50] In the old city, the new changing space provided "a battleground for contesting and negotiating identities," and the *havelis,* "not a timeless or changeless house form, gradually became home to a new petite bourgeoisie." In Delhi, Hosagrahar concludes, "monolithic and oppositional categories such as traditional and modern, ruler and subject, Orient and Occident, masked a dynamism of identities that were composite, nuanced, and, at times, contradictory."[51]

As with Rosin's study, Hosagrahar's essay carries an important note of caution for any attempts to construct "snapshot" categories, frozen in one point of time. This theme is also central to Meera Kosambi's review essay on colonial urbanism. Any attempt to create typologies and categories conceals changes over time as well as space, not just in relation to notions about the colonial city but to the vaguer concepts of colonial urbanism that, dependent on global location, might extend between fifty to three or four hundred years.[52]

Brenda Yeoh's book *Contesting Space: Power Relations and the Urban Built Environment in Colonial Singapore* was published a few years prior to the studies already discussed. Yeoh's detailed narrative, showing how the built environment of colonial Singapore was shaped "by conflict and negotiation between colonial institutions of control . . . and Asian communities who lived and worked in the city" is probably the first, and most carefully documented, account that challenged the notion of the colonial city as being simply a product of "dominant forces" without attending to the "underside . . . the conflict and collision, negotiation and dialogue" with the colonized population. Looking especially at everyday life in the city, and the "contested space" of modifications to streets, public areas, and housing, and the installation of utilities or naming of spaces, Yeoh views the colonial urban landscape as "a terrain of discipline and resistance" where the colonized "must be seen as knowledgable and skilled agents with some awareness of the struggle for control, not just passive recipients of colonial rule."[53]

CONCLUSION

This recent scholarship prompts far more thoughts than space permits to be discussed. First, while all authors address what I've called "actually existing postcolonialisms" and are, *ipso facto,* written with a postcolonial consciousness, none actually cite or draw on the theoretical literature informing the more literary genre of "postcolonial studies." This is neither criticism nor commendation—but does it deserve a comment? I have argued elsewhere[54] that much of the early development of that particular discourse developed in association with a postcolonial diasporic community of scholars and, for various reasons, was primarily directed to an audience in the one-time metropolitan society, rather than the postcolonial society itself. Moreover, few, if any, of these studies focused on issues of colonial urbanism. The obvious exception is the edited collection *Postcolonial Space(s)*, where the editors write, "Postcolonial space is a space of intervention into those architectural constructions that parade under a universalist guise and either exclude or repress different spatialities of often disadvantaged ethnicities, communities or peoples."[55] The chapters on South and Southeast Asian topics (on the traditional Javanese house, on "recovering what we never had" in the context of "Identity Production in Postcolonial Indian Architecture," and on "cacophony" as the dominant tone of contemporary East Asian architecture) successfully contest the boundaries of what "architecture" is usually taken to be; however, the commitment of contributors to exploring poststructuralist, psychoanalytic, feminist, and other approaches characteristic of postcolonial theory in literature needs to be read alongside other accounts that acknowledge the persistent and powerful material factors of uneven development worldwide[56] and the corporate *knowledge* influences of global capitalism.

A second comment returns me to Young's thoughts on the earlier question of "location"[57] and the respective insights into issues of colonialism and postcolonialism offered by scholars "who inhabit the postcolonial world" and others from the one-time "metropolitan" societies.[58] One is tempted to suggest that it is the "grand theories" and metanarratives that have, in the past (and perhaps still continue to), come from one-time metropolitan locations. Most recently, these include the "modeling" of Southeast Asian cities within larger trajectories of urban development where postcolonial cities are projected to develop into one or the other of "four unique forms of postcolonial (urban) space."[59] Alternatively, other one-time metropolitan scholars argue that "postcolonial urban futures" will converge with metropolitan urban forms "as a result of the inexorable logic of globalization": "[T]he postcolonial city as a distinct type is an 'unusual and transitory experience' . . . which will soon be eclipsed by the globalizing city."[60] In these grand scenarios, the task of the scholar of the one-time colonized society is to contest these metanarratives, and offer alternatives on the basis of her or his "local knowledge."

This seemingly adversarial position aside, the obvious problem in writing on issues of colonial contact (and not only these) is that of speaking on behalf of, and "representing the other." My own position here is that scholarship in this field emerges best as a result of dialogue and collaboration. There is an inherent contradiction here. The logic of globalization is, constantly, to produce cultural difference, even if the processes by which this happens may well be similar. In this sense, as can be seen today in many postcolonial (and other) cities worldwide including Singapore, the colonial is no longer erased but rather rebuilt, refurbished, commodified, and celebrated. Complete with museum, the Raffles Hotel becomes a destination for local and global tourist elites.

At one level, therefore, these different scholarly accounts raise myriad questions about the *difference* of both colonial and postcolonial experiences, about the different histories, geographies, politics, and cultures of different cities, and the extent to which their populations were indeed "colonized," whatever is understood by this impossibly monolithic term. What we have in these accounts is a range of representations: that an indigenous class hierarchy simply replaced the colonial hierarchy, of racial divisions replaced by those of class; that the reason for the persistence of colonial space and form is to be found in colonial regulations and bylaws and the internalization of colonial values by planners, among others; that for some writers, colonialism is more an absence than a presence, or, alternatively, that the postcolonial state has erased its historic social, spatial, and architectural effects; that for some the deep-seated dispositions and "traditional" cultural values about family and heritage have transformed colonial space; that operating with monolithic categories in historical social and spatial situations that are always dynamic is dangerous. Yet more than this, these accounts raise questions about the cultural and political positions, life experiences, social agendas, memories, and intellectual perspectives of the authors themselves, and the way they are represented—including here, in this essay.

In her recent essay on "Postcolonial Cities," Brenda Yeoh asks, "To what extent can the 'postcolonial' endure as a meaningful category [of urban analysis] amid other competing adjectives and approaches? . . . How essential is the influence of empire for understanding the contemporary city?" A better understanding and "clearer assessment of postcolonial impacts can only come about through a wider range of works on urban space which give greater credence to diverse voices, different mediums of representation and therefore different perspectives on the city including a whole variety of different analytical frames."[61]

One of the more recent frames seems to be the concept of the hybrid. Hybridity, "a palpable material outcome of the primary subversion of the colonial divide,"[62] is the one central idea emerging from Bhabha's notion of the "third space." This is the logic of Nezar AlSayyad's recent collection on *Hybrid Urbanism,* where he offers seventeenth century Mombasa and nineteenth century Ismir as "multicultural" cities before the term was invented, cities that embodied "the spatial reconciliation of incommensurable constructions of subcultures." But he also cites sociologist Jan Pieterse to add a caution that "cultures have been hybrid *all along;* hybridization is, in effect, a tautology."[63] Other analytical frames might be developed through what might be called the "dialectics of dual development," in this particular case, prompted by the problem of considering a variety of different historical conditions (of which colonialism is merely one) where the social and spatial form of a city develops not in the "usual" way in relation to one society, but rather in relation to two or more, a condition increasingly typical of our global times.[64]

Another problem of the postcolonial paradigm is raised by Abidin Kusno, who suggests that there has been a tendency to undertake a critique of colonial discourse around a broad, often undifferentiated critique of "the

West," without acknowledging that colonialisms come in many forms. Recognizing historical differences between various colonial states, Kusno argues that, until the demise of Suharto's "New Order" regime in 1998, Indonesia in fact continued as a colonial regime in all but name. Arguing against a key theme in much postcolonial criticism, he maintains that colonialism in Indonesia did not bring about a displacement of indigenous culture. As Indonesians were encouraged by Dutch orientalist discourse to remain "Indonesian," they never thought of themselves as part of a colonial legacy.[65]

Thus, rather than asking whether the concept of the postcolonial "can endure," we might want to ask, once more, about the history and sociology of the concept of the colonial city itself. In 1990, Indian sociologist Meera Kosambi wrote, "the search for the intellectual antecedents of the current debate about the 'colonial city' becomes an interesting exercise in the sociology of knowledge, spanning the social science literature of the last four decades. Among the shifting perspectives and underneath ideological camouflages, the concept has remained, for a long time, both elusive and chameleonic."[66]

What these various accounts show is that, on one hand, for their writers (and doubtless many others), half a century after Independence, issues apparently prompted by colonial urbanism are alive and well—in this case primarily in people's heads, but also on the ground. On the other hand, just *why* these different authors should address these issues (and others not), and what social, cultural, and especially political significance they should ascribe to them are questions that need to be asked—questions that are central to the construction of our own consciousness and subjectivity. Ultimately, such questions are at the heart of the politics of writing itself. In regard to issues of racism, multiculturalism, disputed heritage, or social equity, apart from addressing the *conscious* elimination, preservation, or restructuring of colonial space in its material sense, it is equally if not more important to address the *unconscious* persistence of colonial space, not only out there in the real world, but as expressed in Schwarz's incisive words, in the colonial space in our heads. This is a matter of our own knowledge and subjectivity, informed as it is by historical knowledge and the understanding we have of the contemporary world. How or what we *write*, for whom, and with what political agenda, to bring about what political and policy transformations, clearly depends on what we believe to be important. But that is a topic for another essay.

NOTES

Many thanks to Abidin Kusno for his incisive comments and suggestions on this essay.

1. Bill Schwarz, "Actually Existing Postcolonialism," *Radical Philosophy Review* 104 (2000): 16–24.
2. Ibid., 16.
3. Ibid., 20.

4. Ibid.
5. Brenda S. A. Yeoh, "Postcolonial Cities," *Progress in Human Geography* 25, no. 3 (2001): 456–68.
6. Phil Cohen, "From the Other Side of the Tracks: Dual Cities, Third Spaces, and the Urban Uncanny in Contemporary Discources of 'Race' and 'Class,'" in *Companion to the City,* ed. Gary Bridge and Sophie Watson (Oxford: Blackwell, 2000), 324–25.
7. Anthony D. King, *Global Cities: Postimperialism and the Internationalisation of London* (London and New York: Routledge, 1990).
8. James Sidaway, "Postcolonial Geographies: An Exploratory Essay," *Progress in Human Geography* 24, no. 4 (2000): 591–612.
9. Ibid., 592, 594.
10. Sanjay Seth, Leela Gandhi, and Michael Dutton, "Postcolonial Studies: A Beginning," *Postcolonial Studies* 1 (1998): 7–11.
11. For example, see Anne McClintock, "The Angel of Progress: Pitfalls of the Term 'Postcolonialism,'" *Social Text* 31/32 (1992): 1–15; Ella Shohat and Robert Stam, *Unthinking Eurocentricism: Multiculturalism and the New World Order* (London and New York: Routledge, 1994); Ania Loomba, *Colonialism/Postcolonialism* (London and New York: Routledge, 1998); Robert Young, *Postcolonialism: An Introduction* (London: Blackwell, 2001).
12. Patrick Wolfe, "History and Imperialism: A Century of Theory, from Marx to Postcolonialism," *American Historical Review* 102 (April 1997): 388–420.
13. Schwarz, "Actually Existing," 16.
14. Yeoh, "Postcolonial Cities," 457.
15. Anthony D. King, "Writing Colonial Space: A Review Essay," *Comparative Studies in Society and History* 37 (1995): 541–54.
16. Anthony D. King, "Colonial Cities: Global Pivots of Change," in *Colonial Cities: Essays on Urbanism in a Colonial Context,* ed. Robert Ross and Gerard Telkamp (Leiden University Press, 1985), The Hague: 7–32. The conference was held in spring 1980 at the Centre for Studies of European Expansion, University of Leiden, the Netherlands. In the context of my later comments, it is worth noting that all contributors to the volume were Europeans, with experience of colonial cities outside Europe.
17. Robert Young, *Postcolonialism,* 62.
18. Abidin Kusno, *Beyond the Postcolonial: Architecture, Urban Space, and Political Cultures in Indonesia* (London and New York: Routledge, 2000), 14.
19. Sanjoy Chakravorty, "From Colonial City to Globalizing City? The Far-From Complete Spatial Transformation of Calcutta," in *Globalizing Cities: A New Spatial Order,* ed. Peter Marcuse and Ronald van Kempen (Oxford, U.K./Malden, Mass.: Blackwell, 2000), 56–77.
20. Ibid., 65.
21. Ibid., 66.
22. Ibid., 67.
23. Ibid., 70.
24. Ibid., 74.
25. Suparna Chatterjee and Judith Kenny, "Creating a New Capital: Colonial Discourse and the Decolonization of Delhi," *Historical Geography* 27 (1999): 73–98.
26. Ibid., 96.
27. Rahul Mehrotra and Sharada Diwedi, *Bombay: The Cities Within* (Bombay: Indian Bookhouse, 1995).
28. Ibid., 6.
29. Ibid., 8.
30. Ibid., 309.
31. Nihal Perera, *Decolonising Ceylon: Colonialism, Nationalism, and the Politics of Space in Sri Lanka* (New Delhi: Oxford University Press, 1998).
32. Anthony D. King, *Colonial Urban Development* (London and Boston: Routledge and Kegan Paul, 1976), chapter 6; King, *The Bungalow: The Production of a Global Culture,* 2nd ed. (Oxford: Oxford University Press, 1995).
33. Anita Sinha, "The Bungalows of Lucknow," *Open House International* 24, no. 2 (1999): 56–63.
34. Ibid., 57.
35. Ibid.
36. Ibid., 58.
37. Ibid.
38. Ibid., 61.
39. Ibid., 62.

40. Ibid.
41. Thomas Rosin, "From Garden Suburb to Olde City Ward: A Longitudinal Study of Social Process and Incremental Architecture in Jaipur, India," *Journal of Material Culture* 6, no. 2 (2001): 165–92. As is common in India and elsewhere in Southeast Asia, "bungalow" refers to a free-standing, detached house of one or, in this case, two stories, developed as a hybrid outcome of socially interactive European–Indian influences under the conditions of colonialism.
42. Ibid., 169.
43. Ibid., 183.
44. Ibid., 171.
45. See also "From Garden Suburb," 186, 189.
46. Siddhartha Raychaudhuri, "Colonialism, Indigenous Elites, and the Transformation of Cities in the Non-Western World: Ahmedabad (Western India), 1890–1947," *Modern Asian Studies* 35, no. 3 (2001): 677. The four accounts referred to are King, *Colonial Urban Development;* Narayani Gupta, *Delhi between Two Empires, 1803–1931* (Delhi: Oxford University Press, 1981); Veena Oldenburg, *The Making of Colonial Lucknow* (Princeton University Press, 1984); and Mariam Dossal, *Imperial Designs and Indian Realities: The Planning of Bombay City, 1845–75* (Delhi: Oxford University Press, 1991).
47. Raychaudhuri, "Colonialism," 720–26.
48. Jyoti Hosagrahar, "Mansions to Margins: Modernity and the Domestic Landscapes of Historic Delhi, 1847–1910," *Journal of the Society of Architectural Historians* 60, no. 1 (March 2001): 24–45.
49. Ibid., 36.
50. Ibid., 38.
51. Ibid., 43.
52. Meera Kosambi, "The Colonial City in Its Global Niche," *Economic and Political Weekly,* 22 December 1990, 2775–81.
53. Brenda S. A. Yeoh, *Contesting Space: Power Relations and the Urban Built Environment in Colonial Singapore* (Kuala Lumpur: Oxford University Press, 1996), 9–14.
54. Anthony D. King, "Cultures and Spaces of Postcolonial Knowledges," in *Handbook of Cultural Geography,* eds. Kay Anderson, Mona Domosh, Steve Pile, and Nigel Thrift (London: Sage, 2002).
55. Gulsum Nalbantoglu and W. B. T. Wong, eds. *Postcolonial Space(s)* (Princeton, N.J.: Princeton University Press, 1997).
56. Neil Smith, *Uneven Development: Nature, Capital, and the Production of Space* (Oxford: Blackwell, 1984).
57. See note 17.
58. Yeoh, "Postcolonial Cities," 462.
59. Ibid. Yeoh is citing D. Forbes, "Metropolis and Megaurban Regions in Pacific Asia," *Economische en Sociale Geografie* 88 (1997): 457–68.
60. Ibid. Yeoh here cites H. W. Dick and P. Rimmer, "Beyond the Third World City: The New Urban Geography of Southeast Asia," *Urban Studies* 35 (1996): 100–9.
61. Yeoh, "Postcolonial Cities," 463, citing Forbes (see note 59). The frames may, of course, include not simply as implied here the indigenous city and the colonial settlement, but the indigenous city compared to other indigenous cities (as in Raychaudhury, "Colonialism"), the colonial settlement in relation to metropolitan cities and other colonial settlements (as in King, *Colonial Urban Development*), or, on a larger scale, other "colonial cities" in comparable contexts of space, time, and culture, not to exclude other possible frames.
62. Wolfe, "History and Imperialism," 416.
63. Nezar AlSayyad, *Hybrid Urbanism: On the Identity Discourse and the Built Environment* (Westport, Conn.: Praeger, 2001), 8, 16.
64. See the special issue of *City and Society* 12, no. 1 (2000) on the theme, "Urbanism: Imported/Exported," in which six authors consider this situation in relation to Calcutta, Izmir, Algiers, Singapore, and Qatar.
65. Abidin Kusno, *Behind the Postcolonial.*
66. Kosambi, "The Colonial City," 2775.

Wildsmith and Rosenau examine the postcolonial urbanism of Jakarta to find the factors of strife and division of its life as a "mega-city" in the city's environment and architecture. The city's built environment embodies the energies of "fragmegration," generated by interests centered variously on the distinction from or embrace of global influences. The city is designated as a site of "fragmegration," containing twelve possible orientations, each reflecting the stakes of separate interest groups in Jakarta in political, cultural, and social terms. The writers contend that globalization is not simply the effect of a homogenizing technological revolution from the First World. In a heterogeneous, postcolonial city such as Jakarta, cultural specificities and unresolved economic problems make it a place of multilayered interaction and conflict between local and global bodies, each with its own agenda and internal fissures. This article explores the limits of describing Jakarta via binary configurations by setting all possible oppositions in play within an all-encompassing structure that is built conceptually and revealed architecturally. In its rethinking of binaries within the locale of Jakarta, it provides a contrast to Lim's article where the binary opposition of the global and the local is destabilized through consideration of the regional. In Wildsmith and Rosenau's analyses, the multifarious, densely historical, and deeply conflicted city itself provides this destabilization. Perhaps no other city in the region bears the many marks of colonialism, postcolonialism, nationalism, Cold War ideology and post–Cold War globalization as blatantly as does Jakarta. Wildsmith and Rosenau provide a productive and subtle schematic for reading this city.

9

Jakarta as a Site of Fragmegrative Tensions

JAMES N. ROSENAU AND DIANE WILDSMITH

Just as it is erroneous to posit global urbanism as solely the result of technological homogeneity, so is it a mistake to ascribe the abrupt and violence-ridden halt of growth and progress in Jakarta to the globalizing processes underlying the collapse of the baht in Thailand and the onset of the Asian financial crisis in 1997. Such responses are excessively facile because they neglect the inherent cultural diversity of the postcolonial city and ignore the internal and unique circumstances that set Jakarta apart as a complex urban community. They ignore the conflicting forces that have marked postcolonial Jakarta. They fail to differentiate between those forces that support the integration of Indonesia into the global economy and those that prefer to minimize or even avoid globalization, not to mention the conflicts generated by the forces that are accepting of a truncated Indonesia versus those that aspire to maintaining the coherence of the archipelago. Nor, perhaps most notably, does globalization allow for the tensions among the parties competing for the reins of power subsequent to the collapse of the Suharto regime. But to account for the internal conflicts is not to deny that Jakarta and Indonesia are also subject to a host of economic and other pressures that originate abroad and are sustained by one or another globalizing process.

How, then, to capture these dynamic, complex, and endlessly interactive forces in a short compass that facilitates comprehension of Jakarta as a global city? How to trace the larger meaning of the minutiae that sustain everyday life in the 9.4+ million mega-city that reaches up with a skyline of international offices and out with spreading pockets of low-lying urban sprawl? How do we frame the morphology of Jakarta in a context that

187

highlights urbanizing or integrating forces as well as counterurbanizing or fragmenting energies, that portrays the replacement of the "empirial" imperialism of the colonial city with the empirical diversity of the postcolonial mega-city[1] under the auspices of the New Urbanism?

CONES OF FRAGMEGRATION

Our response to such questions focuses on the fit between Jakarta's historical and present-day circumstances and a conceptual scheme that conceives of globalization as shaped and sustained by two primary forces at work throughout the world. One involves all those dynamics that are promoting integration, centralization, and globalization at every level of community and organization. The other, no less powerful or pervasive, consists of the diverse dynamics whereby communities and organizations at every level are undergoing fragmentation, decentralization, and localization. Not only do these two sets of polarities endlessly interact, but they also frequently clash in ways that are causally linked, as if each increment of integration fosters an increment of fragmentation and vice versa. To capture and highlight these links, we conceive of them as occurring in cones of "fragmegration," a label that is grating but nonetheless serves to arrest attention to the close and interactive foundations of fragmenting and integrating processes by intertwining them together in a single phrase that evokes the dynamics underlying both globalization and localization.[2] The key is the dynamic interaction, rather than a static binary relationship, between the two forces.

The cones of fragmegration are phenomenological spaces through which people and organizations interact and establish connections between close-at-hand, local practices and remote, global institutions or issues. In effect, the cones are intermediary arenas wherein what we call "distant proximities"[3] link the fragmenting and integrating dynamics as they unfold between and among any of twelve worlds (outlined below) in which the people of Jakarta are conceived to reside. The twelve worlds are distinguished by the orientations and practices of their residents, with four of the worlds being in a global domain, while four are in a local domain and four in a private domain.[4] Fragmegration occurs when people or practices in a global, local, or private world converge or collide with persons or practices in one of the other two domains. Figure 9-1 locates the cones of fragmegration and suggests the interaction among the worlds that may occur within them. The rioting that occurred in the streets of Jakarta following the Asian financial crisis is illustrative in this respect: While international financial institutions were seeking to alleviate the untoward consequences of the crisis, people took to the streets to protest the measures undertaken by the IMF and World Bank.

The advent of massive attacks by terrorists offers another dramatic example of fragmegrative processes and the ways in which their repercus-

Figure 9-1

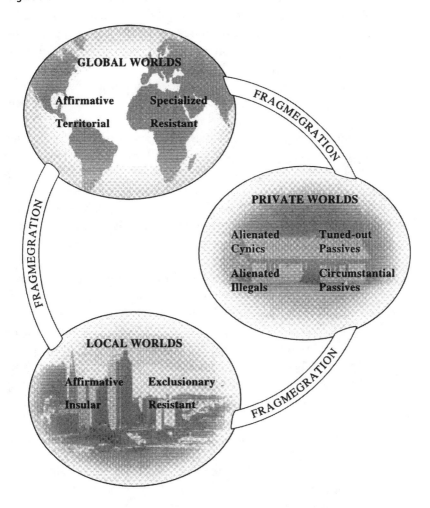

sions can be worldwide in scope. Just as the United States immediately sought to form a global coalition against terrorism, so did local groups resort to the streets to protest the American reaction. No less conspicuous are the worldwide repercussions of fragmegrative dynamics. Within hours of the World Trade Center's destruction in New York City, for example, a bomb scare resulted in the evacuation of the Petronas Towers in Kuala Lumpur. Likewise, in Jakarta anti-American riots occurred near the U.S. embassy to protest the U.S. counterattack on Afghanistan. Globalizing forces are represented by the U.S.-led coalition against terrorism even as localizing forces in Jakarta used the coalition in an effort to consolidate the political status of Islamic parties. Thus does the war on terrorism illustrate the fragmegration inherent in distant proximities, with the plight of the Afghan people being at once globalized through the mass media and the Internet and localized as riots from Islamabad to Jakarta. In short, it is in Jakarta, or in any global city, that the cones of fragmegration join the core and periphery, the global and local, and states and markets.

Of course, most fragmegrative dynamics are not nearly so dramatic as those that followed from the events of September 11, 2001. While geographically Jakarta is a local entity, functionally its scope as a mega-city is global. A multiplicity of global repercussions flows from its daily routines and, in turn, the mega-city is the recipient of innumerable stimuli, both good and bad, from abroad. The tensions that mega-cities experience between their global mercantilism—the integration of investment, production, trade, and consumption into a global network—and their local efforts at urban planning exemplify the fragmegrative challenges they must endlessly confront. It is likely, for example, that the obstacles to urban infrastructure, health, and transport development get caught up in the dynamic interplay between global and local forces, just as demographic flows on a global scale, such as urbanization and transmigration, lead to infrastructure and development problems at local levels.

It should be noted, moreover, that the cones of fragmegration are not the site for every instance of fragmegration that unfolds within the mega-city. Some tensions between the integrative and fragmenting forces at work in Jakarta are confined to the local domain and thus do not get caught up in the flows between domains. To be sure, the cones of fragmegration are normally overflowing with tensions that link the domains in this epoch of ever-greater global interdependence, but some of the conflicts among and within the worlds that comprise each domain may not spill over into the other domains. After all, the fragmegration model is just a model and, as such, does not purport to serve as an explanatory scheme for every development that may occur in Jakarta or any mega-city.

TWELVE WORLDS

To delineate the tensions through which fragmegrative dynamics are played out, the model posits twelve worlds (listed in Figure 9-1), any one of which is presumed to be the orientational home of all the residents of Jakarta. As the lives of people periodically or continuously lead them into the cones of fragmegration, they bring with them orientations toward the tensions inherent in fragmegrative dynamics that result in their occupancy of one of twelve worlds. Depending on a variety of personal or situational factors, the orientations of one or another of the twelve worlds are evoked when people experience firsthand the tensions generated by the clash of local and global dynamics. If their stay in a cone of fragmegration is continuous, they may occasionally undergo an alteration of their orientations, but normally the orientations are so fundamental to their personalities, attitudes, and prior experiences that they remain fixed and serve to shape reactions to the tensions that pervade the cones of fragmegration. Migrant workers are conspicuous exceptions inasmuch as they may pass through the local-to-global cone of fragmegration in the process of transferring their skills from one place to another. The boundaries of mega-cities are porous, expressing their vulnerability or indicating the dynamic quality of networking between global and local worlds, whereas the private worlds are composed of people who are passive, cynical, or apathetic about their participation in public affairs.

Jakarta's indigenous inhabitants, the *orang betawi,* comprise the city's *Insular Locals.* They live in closed communities, have familial ties with the land, and their horizons do not extend beyond their neighborhood or the city. Others with limited territorial horizons are the *Exclusionary Locals;* they live in enclaves and share a tendency to retain their ethnic ties and a reluctance to engage in business with newcomers or expatriates. While *Resistant Locals* are also oriented toward the territory they regard as home, at the same time they are aware of global developments and opposed to them. Indonesian architects, for example, are concerned about the 2004 Asia Pacific Economic Cooperation (APEC) and World Trade Organization (WTO) free trade agreements, which open the local market to competition from foreign architects. Jakarta's middle classes accept rather than resist the localizing influence of McDonald's with ethnic variations in the standard hamburger fare, and, in so doing, they live in open communities and express the orientations of *Affirmative Locals.* The latter also confine their orientations to local horizons but are nonetheless accepting of the global dynamics that intrude on their space.

The nomenclature of the four global worlds roughly parallels that used for the local worlds, but their occupants are distinguished by a sharing of orientations that are not confined by spatial boundaries and may even be worldwide in scale. *Affirmative Globals* consist of those individuals in Jakarta who lead conglomerates and multinational companies and thus believe in and profit from the benefits of globalization. In terms of urban development, they recognize the need for connectivity and interaction on urban planning problems such as water quality control. In contrast, Jakarta's *Resistant Globals* are categorically opposed to global capitalism and its economic, cultural, and ecological consequences. According to their logic, the loans of the World Bank and the International Monetary Fund (IMF) increase the indebtedness of Indonesia and perpetuate a cycle of poverty based on the exploitation of natural resources and low wages. *Specialized Globals* include the financiers, architects, and engineers who provide the support, both in the form of capital and expertise, that enables the multinational corporations to conduct their affairs. *Territorial Globals* are those in diplomatic and foreign policy circles tasked with advancing Indonesia's interests.

Those in Jakarta who are the chronically poor such as the *orang kecil,* and live in squatter housing on unclaimed or public land tracts with marginal facilities and substandard sanitation conditions, have neither the time nor energy to be concerned about local or global affairs. They occupy one of the four private worlds, that of the *Circumstantial Passives.* In contrast, for diverse reasons the *Tuned-out Passives* are disinclined to be concerned about public affairs. Like the university students who prefer to concentrate on their studies, they devote their time and energies to pursuing personal goals. However, in the overthrow of the Suharto government, the students set aside their apathy and joined the ranks of the Resistant Globals and Locals to protest in front of the parliamentary (MPR) building in Jakarta. *Alienated Cynics* comprise the third private world, which is populated by persons such as the Chinese-Indonesian businessmen who are apathetic, not because they lack concern about the course of events, but because they are deeply disillusioned by political processes and their potential for changing the system of government. The fourth private world consists of the *Alienated Illegals* such as Islamic militants like the *Laksar Jihad,* who are so antagonistic to the local and global worlds that they are ready to resort to violent means to "sweep" Americans from Indonesia, to arrange for paid demonstrators to riot in front of the U.S. embassy, and to enlist recruits to fight in a holy war or *jihad* in Afghanistan. It can persuasively be argued that the war on terrorism has enabled Alienated Illegals to propel some global cities into the cones of fragmegration; in Jakarta, they encourage the clash of localizing and globalizing forces to play out in the streets, with the city as a target for arson and destruction.

MEGA-CITIES IN THE CONES OF FRAGMEGRATION

According to UN projections, more than three-fifths of the world's population will live in urban areas by 2025.[5] There will be more than thirty-five mega-cities with more than five million inhabitants by 2010. Seven out of twenty of the world's largest cities will be located in Southeast Asia, with Jakarta projected as the ninth largest city in the region. Similarly, the Asian Development Bank anticipates that there will be twenty-seven mega-cities with ten million or more people by 2015; seventeen of these mega-cities will be in Asia.[6] These figures highlight the utility of probing the dynamics of mega-cities in a fragmegrative context. The planning problems of Jakarta are perhaps especially suitable for exploration through the fragmegration paradigm.

Given their size and the diversity of their populations, mega-cities can readily be regarded as sustaining cones of fragmegration through which persons in all twelve of the foregoing worlds may interact at all times, often conflictually, sometimes cooperatively. Space does not permit further elaboration of how Jakartans in each of the worlds are likely to conduct themselves with respect to the various issues that presently crowd high on the global agenda. Rather, we have identified the several worlds to stress not only the tensions that pervade mega-cities, but also to emphasize the numerous complexities that sustain politics and economics in the emergent fragmegrative epoch. In addition, the notion of people adhering to one or another of twelve basic orientations evoked by the convergence of global and local dynamics serves to indicate our deep conviction that both the benefits and detriments of globalization rest as much on agency as on structure. Neither globalization nor fragmegration involve hidden hands shaping the course of history.

Put differently, fragmegrative cones are sites where city boundaries are transfigured into mega-city regions as globalization impels rural folk to migrate into them, or they otherwise intrude ever more fully upon local practices and orientations. Two astute observers capture these dynamics by noting that "globalization fragments the urban–regional territory into areas or groups that are 'in' or 'out,' while at the same time 'universalizing' the products and messages of the metropolitan city."[7] What differentiates mega-cities from each other is their cultural identity, which counterbalances the homogenizing tendencies of globalization with branded stores and international architecture. Urbanization involves a spatial articulation for inhabitants and activities that presuppose a local identity established by geographical, sociological, economic, and architectural attributes. Whether via the BNI building in Jakarta, the Petronas Towers in Kuala Lumpur, the Jin Mao Tower in Shanghai, or Sun Tec City in Singapore, each city aspires to an individual identity as a global icon. Architecture and space thus become integral features of fragmegrative cones and, as such, are central to the processes of economic development and modernity.

Likewise, immigration flows into the city from the countryside expand the spread of urban influence to articulate the amorphous borders of mega-cities. The fragmegrative disconnect between rural and urban activities occurs partially because of the digital divide between the two areas, with the middle class in the cities connected to the Internet and the poor in rural areas of Indonesia barely serviced by solar-powered *wartels* (telephone shops).

Ideally, mega-city development involves responses to global market demand as well as to local demographic growth. To achieve this equilibrium, mega-cities "have to overcome not only major political, economic, and structural barriers (including the international flow of capital and labour, the debt crisis and structural adjustment and elite-dominated political systems), but also internal mind-set obstacles that block any creative leap towards urban transformation."[8] For example, global currency flows triggered the 1997 currency crisis in Asia and halted Jakarta's mass transit program and numerous buildings projects. However, local factors and the territorial mind-set of Resistant Locals impeded the sale of bankrupt companies and the restoration of foreign investor confidence. On a global scale, the financial markets need to be convinced that improvements in the rule of law and transparency in the banking system are sufficient to develop bond markets for infrastructure development, the resolution of corporate debt, and the resumption of multinational construction projects in Jakarta.

The process of globalization ignites both homogenous and heterogeneous forces to modify urban culture as well as diversify its form. In a comparative analysis of South Asian cities, one analyst notes that the driving force for a modern city is "based on specific energy sources, an advanced transport and communications technology, a complex system of urban government and administration, and a 'high technology' built environment."[9] Furthermore, he observes that the variables of colonial development including culture, technology, and the colonial power structure resulted in urban diversity in British India. Indeed, in colonial capitals from Calcutta to Batavia, the monopoly of British or Dutch power over the indigenous community controlled the development of the city's infrastructure. Roads, railroads, canals, warehouses, and administrative buildings were built to impose empirial power and to support the mercantile economy at the expense and exclusion of indigenous culture, thus suggesting that present-day global urbanism can be regarded as a homogenous outgrowth from Europe or America and has served as a unifying factor whereby the colonial landscape has given way to industrialization.

Much the same can be said about the ways in which colonial culture yielded to industrialization. In colonial society, the metropolitan culture was reinforced by the predictability of urban activities, the ubiquitous church, library, club, theatre, and museum. As an island of globalization in a vast archipelago of local cultures, the colonial functions of the garrison, the warehouses, and the town hall manifest the distribution of social and political power within the city walls. Reinforcing the symbolism of empirial forms, the colonial City Hall (1710) in Batavia features a classical portico and cupola in the grand Fatahillah Square. Its functions combined the hall of justice and the prisons. Executions and markets were held on the square.

Moving rapidly from a colonial to a postmodern time frame, the main traffic circles of Jakarta, rather than focusing on a statue of Lieutenant Governor Thomas Stamford Raffles, have giant electronic video screens that link Jakartans with simultaneous advertising broadcasts. The pervasive spread of technology adds to the homogeneity of postcolonial societies and accounts for the stereoscopy or the simultaneity of virtual and real environments. It also provides glimpses into the conflicting tensions that sustain fragmegrative dynamics. The impact of the CNN electromagnetic realm shapes world opinion and determines in part an individual politician's ability to communicate national policy. The instantaneous broadcasts of the Indonesian parliament voting for Megawati Sukarnoputri provided legitimacy and validation on a global scale for the new government. Instead of verification by an independent election commission, the world witnessed flag-waving supporters and protestors as well as the democratic and peaceful transition from one administration to another. Within hours world financial markets registered their approval of the transparent political processes with an increase in the value of the rupiah from Rp 10,500 to Rp 8,500 to the U.S. dollar. Just as the urban *agora* in Greek and Roman times functioned as a place for public discourse, the Internet expands the possibility for communications and argumentation. With the assimilation of local concerns into a wider social movement linked to humanitarian concerns for adequate housing, the Internet also opens up dialogue between the different members of urban communities.

The dynamics of fragmegration do not necessarily lead mega-cities in negative directions. The power of such conurbations to generate wealth is considerable: "The global and the local complement each other, jointly creating social and economic synergy, as they did back at the beginnings of the world economy in the fourteenth to sixteenth centuries, at a time when the city states became centres for innovation and commerce on a worldwide scale."[10] Thus did the colonial period of trade between the Dutch, English, and French establish the foundations for Jakarta as a city in a global network. As in the past with the Dutch East India Company, the connection between private companies (as individual agents) and local governments perpetuate the fundamental institutional and organizational foundations for commerce and manufacturing, thereby marginalizing the authority of the nation-state. Accordingly, "globalization enhances the role of local governments (the principle of proximity), and large, complex action programmes that are also highly localized require precisely institutions and political bodies that keep very close to their territories."[11] The power of local governments has been further enhanced by the recent autonomy legislation in Indonesia to devolve authority away from the nation-state and the central government to local provincial governments as well as to grant Jakarta separate autonomy as the capital city. However, the policies have mixed results and are currently being rewritten by Megawati's administration under the banner of national unity with empowerment of the regional governments.

On the other hand, fragmegrative processes may derive from the fact that local governments lack the resources to fund and administer regional development across the Indonesian archipelago. Furthermore, the central government is discouraging the ability of local governments to fund their expansion from multinational loan sources, thereby impeding the need for financing urban development projects. The role of local governments thus assumes paramount importance as a vehicle to attract investors, to encourage public/private partnerships, to raise civic pride, to stimulate employment, and to provide urban services that support security and public spaces. In sum, "just as democracy is in our times a universal value, the decentralization of national political systems strikes us as an indispensable corollary of economic globalization, of the creation of supra-state structures, of economic-social complexity and of the need to increase the mechanisms of public–private cooperation."[12]

JAKARTA IN THE CONES OF FRAGMEGRATION

With high-rise buildings funded by global capitalism jostling side by side with village neighborhoods (*kampungs*), Jakarta's urban environment is expressive of the fragmegration paradigm. The stereoscopy of the postcolonial city reflects the urban continuum linked by artifacts and the simultaneity of interactive technology. The polarities between the opposing forces of globalization, between capital flows generating development in Jakarta's Golden Triangle and the fractures of Asian economic crises, are readily apparent in the skeletons of rebar and concrete, which aspire toward realization as towers of a mega-city suspended in cones of *fragmegration*.

Like other postindustrial, postcolonial cities, Jakarta functions as a node in a global hypergrid, exchanging not only physical goods, but also bytes of information technology. Centrifugal forces renovate the historic city as a magnet for cultural tourism. At the same time, counterurbanizing forces drive production and consumption to the edge of the city. Industrial parks, shopping malls, and hypermarkets mushroom along the periphery. Kota Wisata is an example of a satellite city outside of Jakarta, which combines suburbanization along with globalization as a marketing theme. Individual neighborhoods are identified as world cities with entry gates, guardhouses, and town squares designed as "Amsterdam," "Napoleon," "California," or "Kyoto." Classical motifs include an Egyptian entry portico and a replica of the Roman Coliseum, which functions as the community center and town hall. One shudders to think of the iconography planned for Cyber City on the western side of Jakarta. Such examples of light-hearted kitsch express the symbols of globalization and the connectivity between local and global citizens. In the same manner can a contemporary Jakartan live in an "Amsterdam" neighborhood and enjoy all the benefits of modern-day technology and consumption without ever leaving Indonesia. However, in the case of Kota Wisata, the implied urbanism is only symbolic, as the housing development was built in advance of the shops and cultural buildings that give life to any city.

JAKARTA'S FRAGMEGRATIVE ROUTE FROM COLONIALISM TO MODERNITY TO GLOBALIZATION

Originating in the historic town of Batavia (1619) with its Dutch-styled canals and town houses, Indonesia's capital city evolved from a Sundanese port called Jayakarta to a colonial entrepôt named Batavia to a European-styled city in the tropics renamed Jakarta. From its inception, Jakarta's development was steered by mercantile forces, affirming the contention that "[t]he imperialism in each case serves the interest of the centralized power, its military supremacy, and the maintenance of an economic monopoly."[13] Pecuniary rewards were the primary motivation for colonial governments. The master plan of the colonial city favored by the Dutch East India Company (VOC, *Vereenigde Oost-Indische Compagnie*) was a mercantile entrepôt laid alongside canals:

> The Dutch, unmindful of a difference of some 45 degrees of latitude, [were] determined on having a town after the model of those of the Netherlands, within six degrees of the equator and on the level of the sea. The river [Ciliwung] spread over the town in many handsome canals, lost its current, deposited its copious sediment, and generated pestilential malaria, which was transported by the land-wind even to the roads. Fatal remittent fevers followed.[14]

Colonial governance imposed an autocratic style on urban planning principles in Batavia from the 1600s onward. With the impetus of mercantilism, European powers negotiated trading agreements and treaties for their colonial outposts. European and American city planning principles and architectural styles were shipped literally and figuratively around the world and interpreted in response to local cultural and geographic conditions. Although mercantilism in the seventeenth century offered a glimpse of globalization, the trading network was the precursor for future political and economic ties between Western centers of production and consumption with Eastern markets for raw materials and commodities.

However, to argue that global urbanism is a uniform or homogenous growth pattern is to concentrate on integration and to neglect the inherent diversity of globalization and the myriad of cultural interpretations. The similarity between Amsterdam and Batavia is deeper than the morphological pattern of canals and town houses. A comparison between the city map of Amsterdam and Batavia reveals a similar urban pattern. However, Batavia's development spread in a rectilinear rather than a radial pattern. It is not necessary to delve into the sociological relations between the Dutch and local inhabitants to appreciate that the authoritarian governor-generals of the Dutch East India Company set the precedent for autocratic governance based on commerce and conquest.[15]

In addition to the ideals of European commerce and governance, Indonesian architects were exposed to European architectural and urban planning principles. Most notably, the twentieth century buildings in Jakarta started to change character with the advent of international and Art Deco styling. Thus, geometric streamlining was transposed to Jakarta and Bandung in the form of post offices, hotels, and commercial buildings. Indonesian architects blended indigenous styles with modern forms. The University of Bandung (1920) is an example of localization, where sloping Javanese roof shapes express the indigenous cultural values for the technical university.

During the Japanese occupation from 1942–1945, the Dutch were imprisoned in war camps and Batavia was renamed Jakarta in honor of its precolonial days. After liberation from the Japanese occupation at the end of World War II and following Indonesia's independence from the Dutch in 1949, the new nation expressed its sovereignty and adopted modern architecture even as "[the] internal markers of identity that arose under colonialism were adapted by Indonesian nationalists for their own purposes."[16] Relative to the idea of hidden historicity, Indonesia's national boundaries are coincident with the former Dutch colonial territory, with the exception of East Timor, which was a Portuguese colony. As a result of localization, globalization, and decolonization, Indonesia, Malaysia, and Singapore were acknowledged as independent nation-states.

The process of nation building in Indonesia and demolishing the memory of Dutch colonialism was as important as the symbolic building of arterials, monuments, and government buildings during the Sukarno era. "The national monuments in Jakarta have quite specific secular objectives: they represent a quest for international recognition as well as a means to build national pride and express Indonesian independence and modernity."[17] The National Monument, Monas Tower, designed by President Sukarno, an engineer by profession, is Indonesia's beacon of nationalism, its Eiffel Tower in the global urban panoply.[18] Another early example of the modernism and the multinational corporate linkage is the Hotel Indonesia, designed by a Danish architect Sorenson (1960) and operated by the Sheraton hotel chain. To underscore the influence of politics on architectural forms, Indonesia's Communist party grew in the early sixties, with Soviet funding providing infrastructure development for highways in the provinces and super-scale cultural monuments in Jakarta as well as the Senayan Sports Stadium. The Parliament building (1965) features a hyperbolic shaped roof reminiscent of German rationalist and Corbusian design concepts.

After a military coup in 1965, Suharto took over the Indonesian presidency from Sukarno. Like its predecessors during the independence movement, the New Order government under President Suharto launched a massive building program. Funded by oil revenues, the New Order's development program symbolizes the fragmegrative interplay between global and local forces. In that sense, fragmegration is expressed as the mixture of local architectural styles at Taman Mini contrasted with modernist and postmodern architecture in the city center. A shift occurred from an empirial order based on colonial rule to an empirical and administrative order based on autocratic authority combined with modernist and indigenous styles.

Jakarta's growth was spurred by the processes of globalization that gave rise to the need for connections between modern office buildings as well as telecommunications and transportation links. Multinational corporations such as banks and oil companies provided the incentive for the construction of tall buildings with larger floor plates. Clad in modern glass curtain walling, serviced by elevators and cooled by air conditioning, the multistory buildings represented a radical departure from the 1960s precast concrete brutalism. The late 1990s BNI building soars to a height of forty-six stories and its nib-shaped top celebrates technology and symbolizes stereoscopy— the simultaneity of virtual and real environments. Additionally, the multinationals in the telecommunications sector provided the installation of cabling to improve telephone and Internet access. Height restrictions were lifted, which fostered the urban problems of congestion and parking. Nonetheless, the modern edifices represented symbols of material progress. Prior to the 1997 economic crisis, poverty levels decreased by 30 percent and the annual disposable per-capita income in Jakarta averaged U.S.$1,300. A growing middle-class population manages the business and the office buildings in the city center. Yet regional disparities exist that generate fragmegrative tensions between the rich globals and poor locals. In comparison with Singapore's income levels of U.S.$24,337.59, the average annual income in Indonesia was U.S.$3,468.57 in 1999.[19]

This is not to imply, however, that the growth of Jakarta's office sector and the urban environment was solely the result of the postcolonial efforts of multinational companies. To draw such an inference is to lack a degree of sensibility to the national efforts of the Indonesian people. The current issues of corporate debt restructuring under the Indonesian Bank Restructuring Agency arouse nationalistic sentiments from Resistant Locals. As a manifestation of the negative aspects of global capitalism, many Indonesian business people are against the sale of Indonesian assets to foreign parties. Perhaps it is a moot point to quibble whether postcolonialism or globalization led to the modernity and expansion of Jakarta and other postcolonial Asian cities. It is less culturally offensive to think in terms of globalization as a process and a phenomenon common to all countries and cities in the world rather than the localized exploitation of developing countries.

POSTCOLONIAL URBANISM—MEGA-CITIES

Jakarta's route from colonialism to modernity to globalization was sharply disrupted in the later 1990s.[20] At that time the mega-city's issues were a rapidly growing population, unemployment, poverty, congestion, and transportation problems as well as environmental degradation. In the wake of the region's financial crises, Jakarta's boom in private sector development was curtailed by the paucity of bank financing. These problems in the urban-built environment persist.

While the development of the central business district and the construction of the Jakarta Stock Exchange herald the success of government and private sector efforts to create the Golden Triangle for commerce, other urban projects are on hold due to the aftermath of the Asian financial crisis. Erasing the Dutch colonial past resulted in the neglect of historic districts and urban policies for demolition in lieu of historic preservation of old houses and warehouses. An exception is the UNESCO 2001 Asia-Pacific Heritage award to the National Archives Building (ARSIP) for the architectural and cultural restoration of Governor-General Reynier de Klerk's former residence, built in 1760. Since the economic recovery in Jakarta hinges in part on culture and tourism, the valorization of historic districts occurs for economic rather than historic reasons. Therefore, the resurrection of the postcolonial city occurs simultaneously with the futurist projections of the global city. Synonymous with the fabric of the city are its colonial street patterns and infrastructure. The value of mixed-use neighborhoods is implicit in future planning for integrated urban districts. The fallacy of the modern city with an isolated central business district is revitalized with the infusion of electronic global networks and financial capital.

PERPETUATING THE NEW URBANISM

The New Urbanism in the United States advocates performance-based planning standards, which allow for flexibility in zoning, housing types, and circulation standards.[21] Planning policies include mixed-use developments clustered around bus and light rail stations. Where financing is concerned, public/private partnerships are proposed. Municipal governments provide tax relief and commercial banks offer low interest loans to diversify the housing stock and restore old neighborhoods. By revitalizing brown-field or disused sites, municipal governments and developers recapture urban land use for commercial and residential purposes, yielding a productive tax base for infrastructure development.

However, a fallacy of the New Urbanism is its reliance on the concentration of pedestrianized neighborhoods with medium-density housing ratios, which inevitably results in sprawling mega-cities with higher transport and infrastructure costs. Despite the momentum of globalization, there is space for localizing interpretations that allow for the combination of high technology workplaces and living spaces. These issues are salient for American and European city planning as well as for Asian mega-cities. The difference between the empirial city and the empirical city is that the New Urbanism for Asian cities involves globalization with an exchange of ideas and capital alongside the reality of localization with culturally diverse solutions.

Perpetuating the city in Southeast Asia involves inventing new pattern types and urban forms in response to both globalizing and localizing forces. The dynamic of the cones of fragmegration implies its perpetuity. Just as the impact of technology as a globalizing force increases communications and decreases the localizing impact of geographical distance, the New Urbanism demands integrating technological and sociological factors and alleviating fragmegrative tensions. If modernity means commuting for two hours in Jakarta, then postmodernity involves questioning the quality of life and the relationship between working and living conditions. Technology is merely the catalyst for these new mega-cities with livable neighborhoods composed of schools, workplaces, and entertainment facilities.

Theoretically, rapid expansion of globalizing and urbanizing forces will result in different living patterns in Southeast Asian cities. This is not to imply an imposition of suburban-style New Urbanism on the dense populations of Singapore, Jakarta, or Hong Kong. In the postmodern city, the impact of an international hotel like the Grand Hyatt next to a traditional neighborhood in Tanah Abang clearly illustrates the fragmegrative tensions that can coexist between global and local interests in Jakarta. However, the binary relationship alludes only to the complexity of multilayered negotiations and the empowerment of the local community, developers, politicians, international hotel operators, and financiers as well as those outsiders alienated from the processes of urbanization and globalization. Sociological concerns regarding gentrification and relocation of indigenous populations outweigh notions of eradicating urban blight with new building types. Theories of integrated urban communities, which combine work or living places and perpetuate the discourse of globalizing and localizing forces within the cones of fragmegration, are future models for Jakarta and the network of global cities. The New Urbanism in Southeast Asia will depend on the vitality and compounded density needed to accommodate the mega-cities of tomorrow.

NOTES

1. See John Phillips on "empiricialism" in "Singapore Soil: A Completely Different Organization of Soil," in *Urban Space and Representation,* ed. Maria Balshaw and Liam Kennedy (London: Pluto, 2000), 181–82, 192.
2. For an elaboration of the concept of fragmegration, see James N. Rosenau, *Along the Domestic-Foreign Frontier: Exploring Governance in a Turbulent World* (Cambridge: Cambridge University Press, 1997), especially chapter 6.
3. This concept is elaborated in James N. Rosenau, *Distant Proximities: Dynamics beyond Globalization* (Princeton: Princeton University Press, forthcoming).
4. This twelve-world formulation is amplified at length in Rosenau, *Distant Proximities,* chapters 4–7.
5. Akhtar A. Badshah, *Our Urban Future: New Paradigms for Equity and Sustainability* (London and New Jersey: Zed Books, 1996), 2.
6. "Mega-solutions for Asia's Future Cities," *Asia Week,* 25 October 1996, 50.
7. Jordi Borja and Manuel Castells, in collaboration with Mireia Belil and Chris Benner, *Local and Global: Management of Cities in the Information Age* (London: Earthscan Publications, 1997), 159.
8. Badshah, *Our Urban Future,* 5.
9. A. D. King, "Colonialism and the Development of the Modern South Asian City: Some Theoretical Considerations," in *The City in South Asia: Premodern and Modern,* ed. Kenneth Ballhatchet and John Harrison (London and Dublin: Curzon Press/New Jersey: Humanities Press, 1980), 3.
10. Borja and Castells, *Local and Global,* 3.
11. Ibid., 174.
12. Ibid., 226.
13. See Ryan Bishop, John Phillips, and Wei-Wei Yeo, "Perpetuating Cities: Excepting Globalization and the Southeast Asia Supplement," in *Post-Colonial Urbanism: Southeast Asian Cities and Global Processes* (New York: Routledge, 2002).
14. John Crawfurd, *Descriptive Dictionary of the Indian Islands and Adjacent Countries,* 2nd ed. (London, 1856), cited in Adolf Heuken SJ, *Historical Sights of Jakarta* (Kuala Lumpur: Times Books International Singapore, 1989), 153. First published in 1982.
15. The VOC directors complained of their loss in profits due to the expense of weapons and defense for territorial conquest. David S. Landes, *The Wealth and Poverty of Nations: Why Some Are So Rich and Some Are So Poor* (New York: W. W. Norton, 1998), 137–49.
16. Michael Hitchcock and Victor T. King, eds., *Images of Malay-Indonesian Identity* (Kuala Lumpur: Oxford University Press, 1997), 4.
17. Ibid., 14.
18. Abidin Kusno, *Behind the Postcolonial: Architecture, Urban Space, and Political Cultures in Indonesia* (London: Routledge, 2000), 63–65.
19. "The Asia Week Quality of Life Index," *Asiaweek,* 17 December 1999, 46 and "Asiaweek Standard of Living Index," *Asiaweek,* 25 October 1996, 46. In an annual quality of life index for 40 Asian cities, Jakarta ranked 37 out of 40 in 1996, 35 out of 40 in 1998, and 29 out of 40 in 1999, an indication of improvement following democratization reform and the change of government. According to these average figures, Jakarta's standard of living has improved from U.S.$1,236 per capita average disposable income in 1996 to U.S.$3,468 in 1999. The middle class is stabilizing its position; however, an estimated seven to ten percent rate of inflation in 2000 will dilute the projected four percent gain in the GDP. Since the recovery is in progress, it is doubtful that the living conditions for the poor have improved measurably in the past three years. Relevant benchmarks include an increase in state expenditure for education to U.S.$173.12 per capita. However, in relation to Tokyo (U.S.$559.43), Jakarta lags behind in expenditures for education and health. Jakarta has only 0.7 hospital beds per thousand in comparison to 13.2 in Tokyo. Although Jakarta's living conditions are improving, once the recovery occurs in the macro-economy, additional public expenditures are desirable in the education and health sector.
20. From its historical roots, Jakarta's growth was inspired by mercantilism, which led to suburban sprawl and the concept of mega-cities. In what Badshah describes as a "mega-urban region" ("The Future of Asia's Cities," An International Conference on Urban Culture in Asia sponsored by The Asia Society and CIDES, Center for Information and Development Studies, 2–5 December 1996, Jakarta, Indonesia), Jabotabek, Jakarta's metropolitan area, spreads from Jakarta's northern waterfront to Bogor on the south, to Tangerang on the east and to Bekasi on the west. Due to outward migration to the suburbs, Jakarta is growing at a slower rate.
21. Andrea Oppenheimer Dean, "The Principles of Smart Growth," *Architectural Record,* June 2000, 76–82. See also "Congress for the New Urbanism," in *Charter of the New Urbanism,* ed. Michael Leccese and Kathleen McCormick (New York: McGraw-Hill, 2000).

Singapore regards itself as part of Southeast Asia in disparate ways—through membership in the Association of Southeast Asian Nations (ASEAN) and representations of the region in Singaporean English narrative. The pragmatic objectives of political solidarity and mutual economic support convey the most commonly known aspect of Singapore's identification with the region, but they tell an incomplete story. Through a range of readings from contemporary Singaporean writers, Lim shows that the Singaporean English narrative betrays Singapore's detachment, or rather its sense of apartness from its neighbors. The region seems to evoke a mixed sense of association and incompatibility. Lim also draws attention to this ambivalence as having appeared only after the 1970s, becoming most prominent in the 1990s. One might surmise, particularly in Singapore's regional identity with Malaysia, that this development testifies to the gap between the generations before and after Singapore's separation from the Federation of Malaysia in 1965. In fact, it is only recently that "the region" featured in Singaporean English literature has included countries other than Malaysia. The literary evidence suggests that there are elisions or misrecognitions in Singapore's self-reflection as a Southeast Asian nation. Lim draws on Deleuze and Guattari's paradigm of the rhizome to offer an approach in which the missing or puzzling angles on the region can be apprehended and taken into consideration in the context of Singapore's global self-definition. This contention is interesting, not least in its extension of a wider discourse on regionalism as an increasingly important perspective in positionings of the local against the global.

10

Regionalism, English Narrative, and Singapore as Home and Global City

SHIRLEY GEOK-LIN LIM

How do English-language writers in Singapore "conceive" of their city-state in relation to "elsewhere," the rest of the world? How does the desired status of the "global" operate in the imagined national selves represented in Singaporean novels, and what emerges from the dominance of the global in Singapore imaginative literature? I will examine examples of Singapore's English narratives to illustrate the asymmetrical relationship between the dominance of the desire for a Westernized global city and the lack of purchase on the power of regionalism as a component of the Singaporean city imaginary. The state-driven discourse of global and local, based on the oxymoron of appeal to a global culture that is simultaneously uniquely local, leads to the "forgetting" of the region as an important signature in Singapore's city identity. Instead of the tree binary of local/global that appears to have ruled state paradigms for the city-state, the rhizome provides a different productive structure that admits multiple presences into the imagined community of Singapore, including the presence of regional signifiers in its historical and cultural formation.

Ever since the Western empires began breaking apart in the first half of the twentieth century, decolonizing and independence discourses have placed in the foreground the creation of national literatures that reflect, express, consolidate, and participate in the establishment of the nation-state. A national literature was and is expected to achieve multiple, varied goals. It would overcome the humiliation of a colonial history, further the process of unifying recently subjugated, even disparate, communities, constitute the legitimacy of the new nation, and rescue or enlarge a minor or vernacular language.[1] This call to found a national literature is often complicated by postcolonial language controversies, by social conflicts, and cultural contra-dictions rising from the state's increasing imbrication in late capitalist global economies. For authors who identify themselves with newly independent states and who reflexively position themselves as writing against world metropolitan cultures, the use of English narrative as the language and genre of choice poses a number of internal and external stresses. Internal stresses take the form of tensions between overt national ideology and covert English-language metropolitan aesthetics; external stresses create a gap between non-English-language national communities that form the apparent addressee and English-language metropolitan and Western audi-ences that emerge as the indirect addressee in the economy of world pub-lishing and markets. Taking the English narrative as the genre dominating the post-Independence era, it is important to note the contradictions in the genre's deployment by post-Independence authors; anticolonial and nation-building narratives—imaginaries of nation identity that construct a post-colonial national canon—have only served to contribute to the dominance of the English narrative globally. These contradictions wearily repeat the polarized phantasms of nation and empire, local and global, that thematize many of these national narratives.

What happens when we attempt to problematize the term "global" and displace it from the binary of the global/local nexus? When we shift the parameters of Anglophone writing from the community of newly indepen-dent nation-states that non-metropolitan literatures allegedly address, to the broader parameters of a "regional" community? Arguably, to a greater extent than was acknowledged in the twentieth century—the century of empire's end and of nation-states—regionalism is reemerging as a significant force in twenty-first century political and international relations.[2] "Regionalism" in the form of security, military, and economic alliances has been histori-cally part of realpolitik. But incorporating regional cultural entities into a national curriculum is a fairly recent phenomenon. This examination of the Singapore English narrative moves the discussion from twentieth century polarities of national and metropolitan identities, markets, resources, and audiences, to the region (both in the sense of territorial regionalism and epis-temological and other affiliative proximities) as a third space of imagination.

My remapping of what conventionally is viewed as Singapore national literature is a response to the already emergent regional entities operating today, entities emerging almost in parallel with the nation-state, particularly in the economic sphere. Such regionally identified territories form what Kenichi Ohmae in 1995 had termed "region-states." Region-states include the North Atlantic Treaty Organization countries (NATO), the European Union (EU) nations, the North American Free Trade Alliance (NAFTA), the Organization of Petroleum Exporting Countries (OPEC), and closer to home the Asia Pacific Economic Consortium (APEC), the Asian Regional Forum, and the Association of Southeast Asian Nations (ASEAN). Regional formations spin off perhaps even more acronyms, at a faster pace than they are used in Singapore society. Any casual reading of the daily papers should persuade us that the present evolution of human political economy is down the path of regionalism.

On a contrary trajectory, UN agencies appear to point us toward a twentieth century vision of internationalism, as in the operations of the UN Human Rights Commission. A vision of internationalism verging on globalism can be seen in the dizzying numbers of acronyms that appeared during the Sydney Olympics in 2000: IOC, IAAF, WBC, IABA, and so forth. Still, suspicions that national interests drive the discourse of globalism prevailed even during the Olympics. Is the existence of the World Anti-Doping Agency, for example, evidence of the movement toward global regulatory apparatuses? Or do these global regulatory apparatuses mask separate nationalist ambitions, as was claimed in the controversy over the U.S. authorities' mild response to allegations of drug-use among American athletes?

Many economists, political scientists, and politicians have argued for a different valence to the national-global structuration of world power, a valence instantiated by the ever-increasing formation of regional bodies. For one thing, multinational corporations, multilateral security alliances, and multi-interest trade agreements form other trajectories, flows, and deterritorial flights (to use a term from the theorists Gilles Deleuze and Felix Guattari that will be discussed later). These flows or flights compete with the complex negotiating powers of global agencies such as the United Nations, World Trade Organization (WTO), International Monetary Fund (IMF), and World Bank.

This remapping of the tradition of the Singapore English narrative does not bring political science disciplinary perspectives to its revised literary cartography. Rather, its interest in regionalism is related chiefly to the study of literary disciplines and activities. Over the last thirty years, it has become evident to me as an editor, anthologist, scholar, and author that many of the cultural and social identities imagined in contemporary literary texts possess "regional" attributes as well as, or even rather than, national cores. I use the term "imagined" here in a similar fashion as Benedict Anderson had deployed the term in his seminal book, *Imagined Communities: Reflections on the Origin and Spread of Nationalism.*[3] Anderson's concept of the nation as an imagined community, emerging out of print culture, has been gratefully seized on by a generation of graduate students and scholars to explain the complex relationships between representations and cultural products and politics, between text and the world. The process of nation-building continues today, as evidenced in state subvention of books and newspapers, state cultural agencies aimed at producing publications that assert and legitimate state-sponsored nationalism, as well as awards and support of writers for these projects. The Dewan Bahasa in Malaysia is one example of a state-sponsored intervention in the construction of the imagined community of the nation.

Literary critics ask what kinds of literary considerations give rise to unities that are provisional, flexible, curricular, and textual rather than permanent, rigid, canonical, and political, that address regional instead of national concerns. Arguably, cultural workers reflect and contribute to evolving and changeful social identities. Those who work with the English-language narrative genre may be said to be constricted by the genre's history as a product of English culture; but it can also be said that they may be liberated by the transnational postcolonial condition of the genre. Like capital, the English narrative has proven itself borderless, slipping across national boundaries to establish modalities in territories that fall outside the traditional West. As early as the post–World War II era, Western presses have published anthologies that draw together narratives based on geographical proximity and that imagine looser, contingent, and provisional affiliations. E. D. Edwards's *Bamboo, Lotus, and Palm: An Anthology of the Far East, Southeast Asia and the Pacific,*[4] for example, appeared in 1948; its title alone suggests an amazing mobilization of many kinds of differences into a flexible semiotic chain. Even when anthologies evoked more particular regional entities, they subsumed local differences under some classificatory unity. Albert Wendt's *Lali: A Pacific Anthology*[5] focused on the cultural expressions of the Maoris—an indigenous although migrant Pacific people—across multiple island territories and states.

Scholars, like editors, are drawn toward frameworks that elicit a critical mass. Thus, it appears entirely rational to publish a collection of essays that look at varieties of English in Southeast Asia, the premise being that there are more commonalities to be illuminated than differences to be lost through the construction of this regional matrix. In the early 1990s, a new Malaysian-based, London-distributed venture, Skoob Pacifica, took on a similar ideal of regional cultural formation and brought out two edited volumes, *Southeast Asia Writes Back!* and *Southeast Asian Writing.*[6] During that same period, Skoob Pacifica also published a collection of my essays under the classificatory rubric, *Writing South/East Asia in English.*[7] Indeed, research centers such as the Institute of Southeast Asian Studies (ISEAS) appear to be devoted to the promulgation of a Southeast Asian identity formation. K. S. Sandhu's 1992 *The ASEAN Reader*[8] is very much a collection of discourses that focuses on this regional formation.

Significantly, however, the economic, strategic, and financial discursive formations included in Sandhu's reader excluded a study of the semiotic production of the English narrative in Southeast Asia. This exclusion reflects the tendency among Singapore intelligentsia to separate literary and cultural studies from, and thence to ignore them as, a contributory and crucial component of economic and political culture. Second, despite the overt and unambiguous imbrication of Singapore's material and economic foundations in regional formations, the exclusion of its literary culture in this formation suggests that, aside from critical studies assembled under a regional collective rubric, Singapore imaginative literature, and its English narrative in particular, lacks a purchase on the power of regionalism as a component of its imaginary. A recent newspaper analysis of the 1997 Asian currency crisis wryly observes, "Let's remember that the lesson of 1997 was that today's Asia is, for better and for worse, an increasingly integrated economic neighborhood: Half of its trade takes place within the region. Its recent climb out of the tank was due more to increased trade within the region than outside of it. In 1997, when the currency infections began to drag down the Thai economy, a lot of people said, who cares? But as Thailand went, so went the neighborhood."[9] Contrast the relative absence of a regional identity in Singapore writing and publishing with this economic realpolitik; or contrast it with the recent development of journals and anthologies of English prose narratives devoted to the mapping of regional literary forces and voices. *Manoa,* from the University of Hawaii, for example, offers an interesting instance of the determination of one journal to make itself the vehicle for a regional Pacific imagination.

To elaborate on the argument, by the English narrative I mean the genres of the novel and the short story as they have been practiced in English. English narrative deploys the strategies and stylistics associated with the great English fiction writers, ranging from Jane Austen, William Makepeace Thackeray, Charles Dickens, and Mark Twain all the way to modern and postmodern practitioners such as Doris Lessing, Saul Bellow, and Thomas Pynchon. In the Philippines, India, Malaysia, Singapore, Samoa, Trinidad, St. Lucia, Nigeria, Ghana, South Africa, Kenya, Somali, not to mention the settler nations of Canada, Australia, and New Zealand, the English narrative has not merely survived but has strengthened its hold on elite and popular cultural production in the face of overt policies to displace it with seemingly more indigenous forms. An explanation lies in the increasing globalization of cultural production; according to Armand Mattelart, it is not just that certain cultural media have become more international; they have become globalized.[10] These media-culture flows are inextricably related to capital, labor, finance, and idea flows, as Arjun Appadurai's seminal concepts on global disjunctures convincingly suggests.[11]

The English narrative, like the English language from which it takes its source and vitality, has arguably emerged as the genre best suited to the operations of global flow. It is not only the chief literary currency in all major airports, a non-national, extraterritorial space, but also in international and multinational corporate book industries, from publishing to retailing. The English narrative dominates the cultural life of literary elites in national capitals and global cities, from London to New York, from San Francisco to Los Angeles. English narratives dominate the bestseller lists also in Sydney, Auckland, Toronto, Vancouver, Cape Town, Singapore, Manila, and Kuala Lumpur, in contrast, for example, to other possible genres, such as the epic, *pantun,* or Cantonese opera.

The dominance of the English narrative has been noted and promoted by editors and anthologists, for whom the English language has served as a vector for penetration into a global cultural market. The difference in structural relation between twentieth and twentieth-first century manifestations of the English narrative is evidenced in the shift in paradigms from center and periphery to rhizome. A metropolitan culture like Rome that embraced the provinces in an imperializing unidirectional flow is different from the model of the rhizome or net like the Internet, in which provisional and relational matrixes connect flows of ideas, products, capital, and so forth. Deleuze and Guattari posited this shift in their seminal essay, "Rhizome versus Trees," in their appeal for a more organic trope of development and relationship: "in nature, roots are taproots with a more multiple, lateral, and circular system of ramifications, rather than a dichotomous one."[12] A dichotomous system of thought, they argued, "has never reached an understanding of multiplicity." Modernity's affinity for proliferation and fragmentation, based on a fascicular system, reproduces a mystification of unity in which the world "accedes to a higher unity, of ambivalence or overdetermination."[13]

Deleuze and Guattari's paradigm of the rhizome begins not with the one, the unique, but with the multiple, from which the one or unique must be subtracted. The rhizome is characterized therefore by principles of connection and heterogeneity: "any point of a rhizome can be connected to anything other, and must be." Also, "not every trait in a rhizome is necessarily linked to a linguistic feature: semiotic chains of every nature are connected to very diverse modes of coding (biological, political, economic, etc.) that bring into play not only different regimes of signs but also states of being of differing status."[14] The model of rhizome taken to understand (rather than explain) Singapore cultural production, for example, will frame analysis of the Singapore English narrative not as a unique or single entity but as a multiplicity from which is to be subtracted its unique features.

When Singapore literature, for example, is taken not as a unity identified in dichotomous relation to Malay, Chinese, Western, or any other literature but as a rhizomatic formation, it will be read in subtraction from any other or all of these multiples. The multiplicity of regional and global identities is an assemblage that "has neither subject nor object, only determinations, magnitudes, and dimensions that cannot increase in number without the multiplicity changing in nature."[15] That is, in theorizing the canon of a Singapore national literature, we should subtract it from the multiplicity of regional and global literatures, without any "points or positions such as those found in a structure, tree, or root."[16] We cannot, therefore, with any determination claim a piece of Singapore writing as related to a single root that is linearly Chinese or British or Malay; rather, it is related to multiplicity, to any number of semiotic chains with regional and global determinations, magnitudes, and dimensions. Especially in the Singapore case, with its marked plurality of immigrant peoples, histories, languages, religions, and social practices, the rhizomatic structure of the English narrative in relation to region and world should be intensely visible. As described by Deleuze and Guattari, "a rhizome ceaselessly establishes connections between semiotic chains, organizations of power, and circumstances relative to the arts, sciences, and social struggles."[17] In such a structure, there are no "linguistic universals, only a throng of dialects, patois, slangs, and specialized languages. There is no ideal speaker-listener, any more than there is a homogenous linguistic community. . . . There is no mother tongue, only a power takeover by a dominant language within a political multiplicity."[18] Rather than examining the power takeover of English in the political multiplicity of the Singapore state, bring attention to Deleuze and Guattari's observation that "language stabilizes around a parish, a bishopric, a capital . . . the rhizome . . . can analyze language only by decentering it upon other dimensions and other registers."[19]

The rhizome structure is also evident in the production of the contemporary English narrative. An Arundhati Roy, author of *The God of Small Things,* may emerge from an Indian subcontinental metropolis to contest not the aging master of American fiction, Saul Bellow, but Salman Rushdie, an author identified with a pre-Partition Moslem India. At such a particular cultural moment, the English narrative appears to emanate not from the tree of Western literature but from a South Asian regional matrix that includes writers such as Romesh Gunesekera, Anita Desai, Ruth Jabvala, Vikram Seth, and Pico Iyer. The 1997 *New Yorker* special issue on "Indian literature" accommodates this regional dominance of the English narrative without registering a single U.S. national-based reservation, as if in the domain of the English narrative national competition has no existence.

The late twentieth century's expanded notion of U.S. culture, encouraged by the achievements of African American and other ethnic writers, explains in part this contemporary receptivity in the United States to English narratives produced by non-Western authors. A poll of the most significant twentieth century books of fiction in English, for example, carried out among the readers of the *Heath Newsletter* (as a supplement to the Modern Library's notorious poll of the top 100, which produced almost all books by canonical white males), placed four African American novels among the top ten. (Toni Morrison's *Beloved* and Ralph Ellison's *Invisible Man* appeared as first and second choice.) The second top ten included Leslie Marmon Silko's *Ceremony,* Maxine Hong Kingston's *The Woman Warrior,* and Alice Walker's *The Color Purple.*[20] Moreover, Western critics and readers find it easier to accept non-European-based English narratives because these narratives are received as part of a regional rather than national canon. Successful Anglophone narratives are often not identified with a particular (alien) nation-state nor with an undifferentiated globality—like microchips, which can be manufactured in any economically competitive export-producing zone. With 189 nation-states now entered into the United Nations, and with the shifting fragmentations of postcolonial territories whose sovereignty may often not be a matter of distinct linguistic, folk, and even ethnic identity, the aura of competitive national identity has dimmed even as the necessity for regional coalition and cooperation has become more urgent. In short, one may say that intellectuals as well as capitalist forces are suffering from nationalism fatigue, as inner and outer circles dissolve in the digitalized circuits of transnational exchanges. If modernity has been theorized by Marshall Berman as a melting into thin air of social bounds and identities,[21] twenty first century post–Cold War global capitalism has unglued the structures that nation-states had deployed to regulate and contain their populations as citizens.

National citizenship will not quickly lose its preeminence in the regulatory apparatus of the nation-state. But in the domain of cultural reproduction, the matter of the politics of representation is not synonymous with the politics of intervention. Representation is motivated by presence—including phantasmal presence—in a specified location; that motivation includes contiguity, context, comparison, contrast, juxtaposition, and postmodern strategies of collage and bricolage. Representation, therefore, restlessly seeks new materials for assembling identity; and the novel, particularly, as M. M. Bakhtin had argued, is the preeminent genre of the new most adapted to these heteroglossic, carnivalesque, polysemous impulses.[22] The global dominance of the English language has placed the English narrative as a dominant global genre for social expression, despite the clearly contradictory position it occupies vis-à-vis localizing and particularizing forces.

The rise of the English novel as a globally identified phenomenon should be set beside its paradoxical critical identity as a regional and national product. Thus, we seldom read V. S. Naipaul as a Trinidadian author but as a West Indian; nor do we read Chinua Achebe strictly as Nigerian, rather as West African. Similarly, Romesh Gunesekera is viewed as South Asian, less frequently as Sri Lankan. At the same time, the early twentieth century reading of English narrative writers from the provinces of the empire as undifferentiated "English" authors has convincingly been interrogated and undermined, if not overthrown, by the insertion of nation-specific cultural formations. Katherine Mansfield's reputation as a New Zealand national author has recently been asserted, and Doris Lessing's early novels that came out of her life in Rhodesia are now recognized as part of a Zimbabwan literature. More complexly, it is not only the nation-identities of such authors that are emerging from the dismantling of imperializing canons. Rather, Mansfield and Lessing's works placed in a rhizomatic net may be seen to emerge from a multiplicity of regional points (Pacific and African, for example) and global dimensions (a history of women intelligentsia from settler societies, or globalized feminist movements, seen in the politics of gendered representation in their works). Neither single nation identities nor the unity of empire can contain the heterogeneous materials covered in their productions.

What does it signify therefore for Singapore literary studies when we put a model of the nation as a uniqueness subtracted from a multiplicity of determinations, magnitudes, and dimensions together with the evolution of the English narrative within a rhizome structure? We would correctly expect the Singapore English narrative to reflect, express, constitute, and imagine such multiplicity, in language that is "an essentially heterogeneous reality."[23] But the model of the rhizome in relating the nation to region and globality appears not to have challenged the conventional binary or tree-structure of taproot that still pervades the Singapore imaginary, seen in the literature and criticism being published today.

Ironically, the narrow focus on Singapore as a self-contained or even as a binary society (Asian or Western) is fairly new. Until the 1970s, generally there was little distinction between Malaysian and Singapore English language writing. Singapore Anglophone novelists were and still are often approached as joined at the hip, with the historical linking of Singapore and Malaysia as British administered territories throughout much of the nineteenth century, concluding only with the ejection of Singapore from the Malaysian union in 1965. Malaysian authors such as Lloyd Fernando, K. S. Maniam, and Lee Kok Liang continue to be studied by Singapore-based critics. National novelists such as Catherine Lim, after all, were born and raised in Malaysia prior to separation. Regional affinities and affiliations cannot be ignored in the face of originary commonality.

Such regional identity, however, appears to be fading, although historical and contemporary exceptions may be cited. Goh Poh Seng's 1970s novel *The Immolation,* for example, is a powerful narration of the Buddhist struggle in Vietnam against American militaristic intervention in the nation-alistic civil war. Goh, however, left Singapore in the 1980s and is now a Canadian citizen. Indeed, a new generation of Singapore English narratives has appeared that seems to have aroused little interest in Malaysia, partly because regional affiliation itself is completely erased in these texts. Philip Jeyaratnam's *Abraham's Promise* (1994) and Claire Tham's *Skimming* (1999), for example, focus exclusively on Singapore-bounded social and political issues and characters, as if the territory's relation to Malaysia were insignificant—that is, not within the domain of symbolic action and without any links in their semiotic chain. Even more, many young adult novels, such as those by Aaron Kwok, offer little clue that Singapore exists in relation to regional and global matrixes. These texts or semiotic systems appear self-enclosing, approaching creative and generative isolation.

To a greater degree, the Philippines, Indonesia, Thailand, and all the other eight states encompassed by ASEAN have even less imaginative reso-nance and semiotic connections in the Singapore English narrative. Much contemporary Singapore writing imagines an insular world enclosed within the borders of the island state, in ironic contrast to the material, political discourses of regionalism from which Singapore draws its economic vital-ity. The near absence of the Southeast Asian region from younger Singa-porean imagination goes together with the construction of a globalized other, an other than is often strictly Western. Compare two Singapore novels on homosexual experiences that were published in the early 1990s and that seemed to have vanished from literary memory. In Johann S. Lee's *Peculiar Chris* (1992), the protagonist's first love is Kenneth, an Indonesian from Jakarta who is studying in Singapore. Kenneth's Indonesian cultural identity remains unexplored in the text, in contrast to Jack, Chris's sec-ond lover, an Australian he meets in Sydney. At the novel's conclusion, after the death of his lover Samuel from AIDS, Chris leaves Singapore for Lon-don, to visit his gay friend Nicholas, who had earlier escaped Singapore for this great metropolitan center, for the nation from whence E. M. Forster's gay novel *Maurice* had emerged. In Lee's novel, Sydney and later London offer two different visions of possibilities for life as a gay Singa-porean in the world.

Andrew Koh's *Glass Cathedral* (1995) also privileges Forster's *Maurice* as a cultural forerunner for his text. But, in this later novel, despite the ref-erence to Chieng Mai, to which the secondary character, the Catholic priest Norbert, is sent to repent of his homosexual tendencies, the novel's entire action is contained within a Singapore social context. At the novel's con-clusion, Colin, as narrator and point-of-view, drawn by James's overtures, has come out of the closet, as has Norbert, his childhood friend. But James, the object of Colin's desire, unable to disengage himself from his parents' heterosexual expectations, ironically chooses to retreat into sexual denial, and is finally seen squiring a "slender lady" around Centrepoint.

The two different concluding locations, London and Centrepoint, for protagonists whose dilemmas on how to live as a gay male in homophobic Singapore remain unresolved, illustrate the two trajectories taken in Singapore English narratives. Lee's *Peculiar Chris* begins with the closed world of Singapore prejudices and is able to break out of it only through deterritorialized flights to a Western global space, first to Sydney and finally to London. Similarly, in other Singapore English narratives only two poles emerge, the local and the global; these are always manifested as a Western space, so the narrative texture assumes the hybrid contours of what has been called "glocalization," the presence of global markers on the local scene, or the presence of local elements on a Western scene associated with a global culture.[24]

Simon Tay's short story, "My Cousin, Tim," in his collection *Stand Alone* (1990) treats the theme of the conflict of values between Singapore and the West. The narrator expects to study in England, just like his three sisters.[25] His cousin Tim, who was sent by his family in Malaysia to study in Singapore and who becomes Ek Teng's brother-figure, also goes off to study in London, but turns out to be huge disappointment to his family. He fails academically, lives a seemingly dissolute life, and rejects the familial values that bind Ek Teng to the island. Ek Teng's father, abhorring the corrupt influence of the West on Tim, keeps his son home in Singapore. Ek Teng completes studies at the local university, marries, and ends up as "a manager in an accounting firm."[26] The story centers on Tim's return to Malaysia for his father's funeral. Despite the different trajectories of their lives, Ek Teng still finds a sympathetic bonding with Tim, who serves as the alter ego for the frustrated, home-bound if filial son. However, while Tim is figured as the transformed Westernized Asian, Ek Teng is never unambiguously the untransformed native son. When he visits Tim in the West, he takes on the Anglicized name, Eddie, that Tim confers on him. His local station is one that was reluctantly adopted, in submission to a patriarchal decision to save him from the deleterious influences of Westernization, as seen in Tim's fall away from his family's expectations. Ek Teng, as Eddie, also yearns for the liberatory culture associated with living in the West.

The story comes to a climax in a male-bonding scene when the two cousins strip for a late-night swim. The discovery lies in the surprise ending; instead of being the failure that had lead to his father's violent rejection, Tim has become a successful real estate agent, a sterling millionaire.[27] The story thematizes the threat of Western (corrupt) values and shows them as harmless and finally even materially positive. The story concludes with Ek Teng and Tim in a moment of shared merriment, united against a disapproving, conventional, and domestic collectivity.

> I don't know which of us started first or what everyone in the house of mourning must have thought of the laughter that burst from our lungs, escaping the quiet and dark. My cousin Tim and me, we didn't care.[28]

This happy "resolution" elides the narrative action that sets out, in his removal to the West, Tim's alienation from his family and his abandonment of traditional Asian values. The narrative also critiques the social expectations that regulate Ek Teng's life; Ek Teng's obedience to his father's choice of local education for him results in his absorption into a completely conventional and restricted life in Singapore. The final vision of Ek Teng in harmonious partnership with his Westernized cousin Tim is not wholly convincing. Indeed, if we understand global cities to be open to migrant populations and mobility as one of the features of globalization, the story's construction of Ek Teng's sacrifice of mobility and the extended family's disapproval of Tim's social, professional, and geographical mobility suggests that it is still the in situ identity of the city community that is to be defended from the dissolving powers of global mobility.

The Other (whether feared or admired) to the insular imagination is the imaginary of the West, as seen in Tay's story. The Southeast Asian region, Singapore's neighbors, and its mediate and immediate contexts appear less frequently in Singapore English narratives. Instead, the fictions are dominated by an imaginary of the local, sometimes approaching island stasis. For all the strum und drang, the agoniste of failed or tragic relationships, many novels cannot imagine forces and actions outside of what is already present in the local. Claire Tham's *Skimming* begins with the bohemianism of student life in Britain, but closes with the claustrophobic, circular, almost incestuous, and dyadic-constructed bonds of Singapore heterosexual society. Koh's *Glass Cathedral* never really leaves the shores of the island. Indeed, perhaps even more tellingly, Colin, who arrives at a kind of acknowledgment if not liberation of his gay identity, must be ironically located at a juncture of unself-reflexive, uncritical stasis in the heart of materialist Singapore: "I met Norbert outside Emerald Orchard and we proceeded to Centrepoint. I was distracted by the display windows along the way. . . . At the last one, after I had my fill of a set of silverware in Robinson's I turned around to join Norbert."[29] The hero remains "distracted" by the window displays of Centrepoint; caught at the center of Singapore's material lavishness and exhibitionism, local to the very end. This scene stages the ironic theme that Singapore, symbolized by its one widely recognized avenue of emporia, can be viewed as global only in the way in which it has become a marketplace and consumer of global goods. The narrow Confucianist mores than keep James closeted within his homophobic family and Colin compulsively consuming characterize the very local pressures that mock the notion of the city as having a purchase on a wider, global, consciousness.

The absence of the imagination of regionalism in Singapore English narratives and the enormous presence of the local in the imagination of state discourse may be counterpointed with the discourse on Singapore as a "global city." Singapore's identity as a global or world city, however, must always be complicated by its difference from all other world cities, for, unlike any other city, Singapore is also a city-state. The pressures of nation-building and protection apply in Singapore in a unique measure that set up disabling forces to its development as a global city. That is, the kinds of free mobility and migration between urban center and rural feeders or between a city that gives global cities their excess masses from which to draw talent, bodies, consumers, and workers are not salient in the Singapore context, Singapore being a nation historically formed through the coercive enforcement of restrictive borders in 1967.

As it is a city-state without hinterland resources, the discourse of Singapore city identity in the 1970s to the present moment continues to be valorized as local difference. Because identity can only be understood and constructed through perceptions of difference and division, Singapore's physical identity was imagined as a series of differences between "kampongs" or distinctive villages. The trope of Singapore as a "global village," popular in the 1980s, served as an oxymoron to defuse the contradictions inherent in the problematic political status of a "city-state." The image of global village, however, is radically dissimilar from that of global city. The kampong, with its associations to a past, memorialized, rural, and communal locus, continues to be circulated by a number of Singapore politicians as a major mythos of nostalgia for unity among their constituents, and the persistence of its usage manifests the appeal of a superior provincialism that pervades and legitimates everyday life in the city. In comparison, Hong Kong, less burdened by pressures of nation-building and the necessity of establishing regimes to regulate and stabilize citizenship identities, may attempt with fewer constraints to deregulate and stimulate the flows of capital, information, media, goods, ideas, and particularly people, in which speed serves as the fuel of global growth. In much Singaporean discourse of the home, the world or outside the home continues to be figured as the *Unheimlich*—the unhomely or uncanny—and therefore the feared Other to be avoided. The home is not imagined as resident within the global city but as its radical Other, the local. Thus, William Lim's remarks[30] on home in Singapore as local anchorage and the global as mobility are useful distinctions in the understanding of the Singapore double-bind.

Moreover, as a political and social work in process even prior to 1967 when it was asked to leave Malaysia, Singapore continues to be a site of multiple contradictions—a city where the majority of citizens are secular, English speaking, and of Chinese descent in a geographical territory where the majority are Muslim and Malay speaking. The popularity of ghost stories in Singapore writing, offering one evidence of the city's fascination with the *Unheimlich,* is a version of the oxymoronic discourse of a global city that is at the same time the best home for Singaporeans. In such Singaporean discourses, the global city has to be contained within the discourse of home, this despite the commonsensical understanding that cities are not about homes; homes are local, while global cities are about the world and the metropolis.

In such a contradictory fusion of home and global city, Singapore continues to be presented as a local space that has global ambitions. One easy mode for displaying such ambition is through the consumption of globalism. Western—that is, U.S., British, and European—musicals, orchestras, operas, films, CDs, and designers are imported, invited, recruited to Singapore. If you are what you eat, if patterns of consumption identify a habitus, then Singapore may be said to have achieved globalism. The city's cultural productions, however, do not circulate as global productions. The success in the West of *Crouching Tiger, Hidden Dragon,* a film associated with Hong Kong production and that won the 2001 Oscar for the best foreign film, signals Hong Kong's circulation in global cultural production. The semiotic significance of the Oscar awards is greater than the nominal recognition. The Oscar signals that Hong Kong as a global city is consumed by world cities, including cities such as New York and Los Angeles. Singapore has no such global production status; the relationship between consuming and producing globalism remains asymmetrical in Singapore, denoting an unequal relationship of subordination to other metropolitan centers.

In other matters, the process toward achieving global status may well be under way. For example, the policy to increase the presence of green in the overwhelming press of urbanization follows upon historical developments of eighteenth and nineteenth century imperial cities that mark their power over nature and space as well as over populations by grafting to imperial stones immense boulevards full of trees. New York's Central Park and London's Hyde Park both manifest the impulse of the imperial city, now developed into a global center of capital, to display urban power and wealth through massive architectural grids of greenery.

Global cities, insofar as they are imbricated in global capitalist flows and dominate world banking, investment, corporations, and other industries of capital, are collaborators and creations also of late twentieth century Fordism. Intellectual property rights, for example, are sited through the legal networks established in these global cities. The rest of the world is ideologically pressed to incorporate and implement rules of corporate law including those pertaining to intellectual property rights, notions of transparency and of bank credit that were articulated first in systems of marketing that came from the West. The un-negotiated, uncritical, and wholesale adoption of Western systems of marketing as the law that rules all global transactions may be viewed as a triumph of Western regulatory systems. Cities that succeed in achieving the status of global cities must be cautious to avoid the position of operating as outposts for a Western-dominated notion of global capital.

In the twenty-first century, geographical space or physical territory does not signify the way it did in earlier centuries. Although the vision of a borderless world remains merely a utopian thought, at the same time, capital no longer has to be carried in your pocket. While humans physically need passports to cross from one border to another, capital is passport-less, as are pollution and information. Singapore has moved aggressively into an intensely information-driven form of the new economy that also nets it into the global circuit of capital-information flows. Singapore writers are only beginning to catch up with these economic and physical realities, to imagine a city no longer territory-bound to Singapore island, whose enormous currency reserves have found a home in Thailand, Vietnam, China, and elsewhere in the world.

This lag arguably may be related to the choice of literary language itself. Singapore's neighbors being in the main non-English readers, English narrative reaches toward a Western rather than Southeast Asian addressee. In contrast, in the domain of performance and drama, where English and even language itself serves a secondary rather than primary role, Singapore theater has been able to absorb the Malay *wayang,* the Indonesian *silat,* and Balinese *gamelan,* Thai costumes, and other regional cultural characteristics to generate a regional cultural identity. Such diverse regional cultural elements enriched many of the performances presented by Singapore's directors and theater groups such as Kuo Pao Kun, K. K. Seet, Ong Keng Sen, Haresh Sharma, Asian Theatre Research Circus, and TheatreWorks.[31] Similarly, Singapore painting, architecture, and foodways exhibit strong influences from its ASEAN neighbors.

But a closer analysis may undermine this linguistically determined explanation for the absence of regional imagination in Singapore English narrative. It can be argued that a particular ideology of state-identity formation, in defense against a West viewed as hegemonizing and all-too-attractive to citizens contemplating emigrating, may have resulted in the narrow confinement of a singular Singapore character in its English narrative. Beginning in the 1990s, the Goh Chok Tong regime introduced the discourse of home ("Singapore my home") to balance the discourse of glob-ality that arrived with the economic and cultural flows that also transformed Singapore materially and in its self-representation to a global village. Alarm over the out-migration of Singaporeans to Western territories (Australia, Canada, the United Kingdom, and the United States) was raised in news-paper reports and parliament, and letters to the editors and editorials in the *Straits Times* engaged in a debate on how best to retain the nation's bright-est. The Singapore International Foundation was established to maintain contact with emigrants and citizens living abroad to develop new relation-ships between the nation and Singaporeans who have or may decide to leave the country permanently. In 1992, the foundation estimated that 100,000 Singaporeans were living and working overseas.[32] Prime Minister Goh Chok Tong's National Day Rally speech in 1996 worried that many young Sin-gaporeans were thinking of migrating.[33] Commentators often expressed strong disapproval of citizens looking outside the borders of the nation-state; they were seen as selfish: "those who took on foreign permanent resi-dence without renouncing their Singapore citizenship merely wanted the most at the least cost."[34] Emigrating for the good of one's children was com-pared to the Chinese tradition of foot-binding for females.[35] The United Press International picked up this alarm; reporting that "most of those moving . . . are young and highly educated," and it noted the prime minis-ter's chastising tone: "To opt out is to cop-out."[36] Such disapproval went together with scare stories of the evils in Western societies: "multicultural-ism, meritocracy and mutual respect are largely empty and grudging tokens to political correctness in many Western societies."[37]

Similar concerns with emigration were raised in 1997 after a Master-Card International survey reported that 1 in 5 Singaporeans wanted to emigrate,[38] and concerns continued to be raised right up to the new mil-lennium. Koh Buck Song, in an article titled innocuously "S'pore a Dream Home?", used alarmist language to urge more state action on the issue of emigration: "the government will have to do more, much more, to cushion the impact [of economic and social stresses]. Otherwise, it may add to its cost—and that of social cohesion and national survival itself."[39] As recently as October 13, 1999, during a visit to Japan, Prime Minister Goh again voiced his anxiety with Singapore's shrinking population and the related issue of emigration, noting the "worrying trend" of some 2,000 Singapore-ans emigrating each year.[40]

But the punitive attitudes of the early 1990s and coercive language of loyalty to the state went together with and have been followed by a differ-ent language of persuasion, as well as by state actions to increase the qual-ity of life on the island. In 1997 the Chief Statistician Paul Cheung sought to allay anxiety by comparing the rate of emigration to that of Hong Kong.

"After 32 years, psychological roots have sunk in and there is a high degree of bonding," he said, using the language of emotional attachment in contrast to the statistics he was supposed to convey.[41] Tan Sai Siong's article a few days later took a different tone from her 1996 piece. Instead of berating Singaporeans who were considering leaving, she elaborated on Minister of State Matthias Yao's statement, "To consider emigrating is a good thing."[42] The mental exercise of considering the advantages and disadvantages of emigration, she now argued, was "a good way of focusing one's mind on what one holds dear in this country."[43] By October of 1997, Koh Buck Song reported that there was a new red carpet treatment for Singaporeans living overseas, in sharp contrast to "the old system" when "anyone who left Singapore was regarded almost as a traitor."[44]

At the same time, the government convened a new Singapore 21 Committee, "to develop a consensus among Singaporeans about the sort of society they want in the 21st century."[45] The goal of the committee was to study what citizens wanted in order to make "Singapore a global city and the best home for its people"—that is, to reconcile the two apparent urban cultural contradictions, globalism and localism. The creation of the subcommittee "Internationalism/regionalism versus S'pore as Home" indicated that for Singapore policy makers, internationalism and regionalism were perceived as synonymous phenomena, structured in opposition to localism. "Regionalism" was conflated with "internationalism" rather than distinguished as a possible enlargement of the Singapore home. Clearly the concept of a vitalizing relationship between the local and regional set in productive tension with globalism was not then circulating in policy discourse, and the symbolic acts represented in Singapore narratives support this persistent erasure of the regional in the discourse of Singapore identity formation.

Instead, increasingly, together with material progress, quality of life issues particular to the island are seen to include cultural products, approached as cultural consumer items—musicals and orchestras from the West, for example—and as opportunities for creative cultural expression within the island. By 1999, the state was deploying a different rhetoric for the nation: a "New Singapore" of "people power," as "a nation of ideas."[46] A *Straits Times* report notes a study that suggests that "the state toning down its influence—which it is trying to do by creating more space for the people, can become a competitive asset."[47] This evolving state rhetoric of "Singapore 21 vision . . . a 'house to home' agenda," focuses on "heartware" rather than hardware.[48] But this late 1990s discourse of home and roots versus the allegedly rootless mobility of globalism is itself as much a symptom of insular nation-building as was the 1970s discourse of survival and state loyalty. Indeed, such intensifying island-absorption may be seen to parallel and produce similar semiotic enclosures in the English narrative.

Exceptions are to be found that counter the contemporary tendency toward the double frame of a state-insular, Western-oriented imaginary, but usually with Singapore authors who have chosen to live elsewhere. Ho Min-fong's *Sing to the Dawn* (1985), a young adult novel about a Thai peasant girl, is one of the few narratives manifesting an imaginary that looks outward to the Southeast Asian landmass for its materials. Colin Cheong's prize-winning novel *Tangerine* (1997) follows photojounalist Nick, the Singaporean protagonist, as he travels across Vietnam before meeting with his Singapore friends for a reunion at Ha Long Bay. Nick is guided by the liberal Western observations contained in the Lonely Planet guidebook to Vietnam. Much of the novel reads like a travelogue, a genre usually associated with the West's consumption of an exotic Other, and with colonial and capitalist apparatuses of control of relationships and exchange value. *Tangerine* offers a postcolonial variation of the travel book. The Singaporean, taking the place of the Western traveler, may be viewed as merely reproducing those unequal systems of relationships that characterized colonial East–West encounters, a danger that the narrative, even as it acknowledges the difference between Hollywood representations and the reality of present-day Vietnam, takes into account.

> But this was not *The Green Berets* or *Apocalypse Now* or *Deer Hunter.* This was Vietnam, and even the colour of his skin and his Chinese face could not hide the fact that he was as much an alien as a teenaged American boy from the Bible Belt would have been.[49]

The language here is oddly ambiguous, for even as the sentence denies the Hollywood representations of Vietnam engaged in a violent American war, it reaffirms a vision of Vietnam as seen through the eyes of a raw American recruit. Nick, imagining himself as alien in Vietnam as the white G.I., shows us a Westernized imagination already and inevitably steeped in U.S. myths of Vietnam.

Like earlier travel books, *Tangerine* moves between the external travel of discovery to an internal voyage of self-discovery. Observing the ordinary lives of Vietnamese, Nick discovers the necessity to "only connect" (a dictum I take from E. M. Forster's expressed humanism), an ethics of empathy that has atrophied in the insular self-absorption of Singapore life. Nick "had grown up ruthlessly efficient, organised and prepared for most things."[50] The epiphany emerges at the end of the narrative: "it had taken a journey alone to find this sense of pity again."[51] One may critique the novel for the ways in which the Vietnamese fall away at the novel's conclusion once the hero's moral victory has been attained. That is, like so many colonial texts, it is the bourgeois subject that dominates the action.[52] Still, Nick's moral growth, the novel suggests, is no solipsistic triumph; rather it connotes an enlargement of his imagination to admit the significance of a larger community than self to whom something is owed:

> But something had been suppressed, kept dormant and he knew it was pity. Not a condescending pity, but a pity that sought to do something so that another's pain could be eased. . . . that sense of pity that let him connect with other people. And maybe that was why he had been lonely after all—a free flowing organism disconnected from the empathy that made one human.[53]

Tangerine indicts the reproduction of the nation discourse of home and the West, the local and the global, that leaves out the bonds of neighborliness, bonds that are capable of constituting a rhizomatic vitality for Singapore in its Southeast Asian and Asian matrix.[54]

NOTES

1. See Bruce King's *New National and Post-colonial Literatures: An Introduction* (Oxford: Clarendon Press, 1996) and Rumina Sethi's *Myths of the Nation: National Identity and Literary Representations* (Oxford: Clarendon Press, 1999) for a discussion of these issues.
2. This includes, for example, the newest initiative from the United States to create looser but more inclusive multilateral security arrangements for the post–Cold War era, which would include ASEAN, APEC, and China as well (Barnes 8). This initiative comes from the commander-in-chief of U.S. forces in the Pacific, Admiral Dennis Blair, to encourage multilateral rather than bilateral military exercises in the region.
3. Benedict Anderson, *Imagined Communities: Reflections on the Origin and Spread of Nationalism* (London: Verso, 1983).
4. E. D. Edward; *Bamboo, Lotus, and Palm: An Anthology of the Far East, Southeast Asia and the Pacific* (London: W. Hodge, 1948).
5. Albert Wendt, *Lali: A Pacific Anthology* (Auckland: Longman Paul, 1980).
6. *Southeast Asia Writes Back!* (London: Skoob Books, 1993) and *Southeast Asian Writing,* (London: Skoob Books).
7. Shirley Lim, *Writing Southeast Asia in English: Against the Grain, Focus on Asian English Language Literature* (London: Skoob Books, 1994).
8. K. S. Sandhu, ed. *The ASEAN Reader* (Singapore: Institute of Southeast Asian Studies, 1992).
9. Tom Plate, "A Miracle with New Correctives," *The Los Angeles Times,* 30 August. 2000: B9.
10. See Armano Mattelart, Networking the World, 1974–2001 (Minneapolis: University of Minnesota Press, 2001).
11. See Arjun Appadurai, "Disjuncture and Difference in the Global Cultural Economy," in *The Global Transformations Reader: An Introduction to the Globalization Debate,* ed. David Meid and Anthony McGrew (Malden, Mass.: Polity Press, 2000), 23–33.
12. Felix Deleuze and Giles Guattari, "Rhizome versus Tree," *The Deleuze Reader,* ed. Constantine V. Boundas (New York: Columbia University Press, 1993), 27.
13. Ibid., 29.
14. Ibid.
15. Ibid., 30.
16. Ibid., 31.
17. Ibid., 30.
18. Ibid.
19. Ibid.
20. Paul Lauter, "The Heath Top 100," *The Heath Anthology of American Literature Newsletter* 10 (1999): 1.
21. Marshall Berman, *All That Is Solid Meets into Air: The Experience of Modernity* (New York: Penguin Books, 1982).

22. See *The Bakhtin Reader*, ed. Pam Morris (London/New York: E. Arnold, 1994).

23. Deleuze and Guattari, "Rhizome," 30.

24. Fiona Cheong's second novel, which is in progress (an excerpt appears in *Tilting the Continent: Southeast Asian American Writing*, eds. Shirley Geok-lin Lim and Cheng Lok Chua [Minneapolis: New Rivers Press, 2000]), looks at Singaporeans living in the United States. In this excerpt, the apparition of local images and motifs is felt in the space of the West—Florida in this case.

25. Simon Tay, *Stand Alone* (Singapore: Landmark Books, 1990), 14.

26. Ibid., 15.

27. Ibid., 41.

28. Ibid.

29. Andrew Koh, *Glass Cathedral* (Singapore: EBP, 1995), 114.

30. Remarks made at the international experts' workshop, "Perpetuating Cities: Postcolonial Global Urbanism in Southeast Asia" held at the National University of Singapore, May 2002.

31. See Krishen Jit's introduction to *Kuo Pao Kun's The Coffin Is Too Big for the Hole . . . and Other Plays* (Singapore: Time Books International, 1990) for a brief history of Singapore theater.

32. Claudette Peralta, "More Singapore Migrants Returning," *The Straits Times* nd:1.

33. "What the Prime Minister Said," *The Straits Times,* 22 August 1996: 32.

34. Tan Sai Siong, "Are Parents Really Emigrating for the Good of Their Children?" *The Straits Times,* 25 August 1996: 3.

35. Ibid.

36. "More Singaporeans Emigrating," *United Press International,* 11 September 1996.

37. Sharon Lim Su-Ting, "Grass Is Not Greener Elsewhere," *The Straits Times,* 14 September 1996: 38.

38. "1 in 5 S'poreans Want to Emigrate: Survey," *The Straits Times,* 17 April 1997: 43; Leong Ching Ching, "The Who, Where, and Why of Emigration," *The Straits Times,* 15 August 1997: 40.

39. Koh Buck Song, "S'pore a Dream Home? Let Me Count the Ways," *The Straits Times,* 10 August 1997: 3.

40. Hayashida Hioaki, "Successful Singapore Stops to Think," *Yomiuri Shimbuum,* 19 May 1999: 7.

41. Leong, "Who, Where, and Why."

42. Tan Sai Siong, "Try a Mental Exercise in Emigration," *The Straits Times,* 25 August 1997.

43. Ibid.

44. Koh Buck Song, "Come Home Call? Try Overseas Voting and Dual Citizenship," *The Straits Times,* 9 November 1997.

45. Warren Fernandez, "Giving Singaporeans a Sense That They Own This Place," *The Straits Times,* 5 July 1997: 45.

46. Prime Minister Goh Chok Tong, quoted in Chua Mui Hoong, "We're Not Quite There Yet," *The Straits Times,* 16 October 1999: 4.

47. Ibid., 3.

48. Fernandez, "Giving Singaporeans," 45.

49. Colin Cheong, *Tangerine* (Singapore: SNP Publishing, 1997), 7.

50. Ibid., 154.

51. Ibid., 155.

52. Gopal Baratham's stories, collected in *In the City of Forgetting: The Collected Stories of Gopal Baratham,* ed. Ban kah Choon (Singapore: Times Books International, 2001), often foreground a bourgeois male protagonist who travels regionally—to Bali, Thailand, Malaysia, and so forth— but whose regional adventures are restricted to a sexual Other who serves to gratify the protagonist's physical and emotional needs. The protagonist is sometimes satirized, sometimes valorized, but in every instance, he is the central and dominant figure.

53. Cheong, *Tangerine,* 155.

54. That the absence of regionalism as a signifying force in the calculations of the Singapore state may serve to disadvantage its social, political, and military security may perhaps be glimpsed in the Indonesian president's outburst against Singapore's senior leaders after the recent ASEAN summit meeting on November 26, 2000. As reported in the *Hong Kong Mail,* "In a surprise verbal attack, Indonesia has accused Singapore of pursuing foreign policies only for profit and of underestimating the indigenous people of its neighbours." See "Wahid Lashed Singapore over Policies for Profit," *Hong Kong Mail,* 27 November 2000: A12.

Many cities have colonial pasts and global futures, but the ways in which they engage either of these larger sets of processes is often very specific to the city itself. The problems of governance that result from these histories and potential futures have been exacerbated by the teletechnologies essential to globalization. The result has been a direct challenge to civic authority insofar as it must mediate between the intricacies of local pasts and the contending hegemonic demands by global forces. Marcus and Rivas Gamboa use a "global" city that is only peripherally a global city, like many in Southeast Asia, to explore the effects on public discourse, authority, governance, and the relations between rulers and the ruled in such a setting. Calling the need "to specify the difference at the experiential level in the 'same' " the essence of the "anthropological stake in globalization studies," Marcus and Rivas Gamboa wish to reinsert the notion of the public sphere, especially a critical inquiry into the bourgeois public sphere, into the analyses of globalization precisely because the public sphere has been decentered by the loss of the nation-state in the hegemony of globalization processes. In so doing, they add to this volume's attempts to provide frames for sustained, sensitive descriptions and analyses of these processes. They do so through an examination of the lives of the subjects these processes supposedly effect. Rather than necessarily looking at the point of enunciation then, the article examines the addressee: in this case, the bourgeois subject upon whom governance depends and to whom public discourse is directed. As with Lim's and Yeo's articles, this one is interested in evoking issues of national identity formation from an ethnographically based description that is aware of regional influence, U.S. influence, and the problems exerted on civic consciousness by stereoscopy.

11

Contemporary Cities with Colonial Pasts and Global Futures: Some Aspects of the Relations between Governance, Order, and Decent, Secure Life

GEORGE E. MARCUS AND ANGELA RIVAS GAMBOA

Certain key issues in the study of major cities with colonial pasts and global presents (and futures) define national identity and urban life simultaneously. Hence our ongoing interest in the challenges that the unruly conditions of Bogotá, Colombia, present to those charged with its rule. These issues are given specific shape as distinctive contemporary forces and processes that are labeled "global" or "globalizing" in the work of Paul Virilio, the motivating frame in this volume. We present Bogotá as a striking contrast to the very orderly conditions of the ruling and the ruled in the city-state of Singapore, a primary focus of contemplation in this volume. The central issues for the successful regimen of city governance in Singapore are the same for Bogotá, yet the latter struggles to impose them. This suggests that comparisons outside of the Southeast and East Asia area frame can provide a useful dimension to this discussion; that is, for the issues in which we are interested, conditions in Singapore are just as relevant to conditions in Bangkok, Hong Kong, or Djakarta—or even Bogotá.

Everyone who lives in the environment of large cities today—either cities that have cosmopolitan ambitions or those that have these ambitions thrust upon them by powerful globalizing models—is abundantly aware of the existential consequences defined by the condition of stereoscopy—Virilio's concept of living simultaneously in virtual and real worlds of different quality and dimension. However, while residents and citizens of such cities are free (differentially, of course, according to their means) to indulge this condition in their imaginations, in their self-fashionings, in their aspirations and hopes, and in daily predicaments of living in such huge organized masses of humanity, those who govern such cities are not so free. They know what citizens know, but they are wedded to the fictions of the primacy of place and power, to the rhetorics of traditions of the greatness of cities as realized through focused, settled, and manageable human community. Stereoscopy is the "public secret" (after Taussig[1]) between governors and governed in large cities that forms the basis of the unwritten, acted out compact of their relationship. Most importantly, especially for the propertied middle classes, this compact is what defines the conditions of personal security and the enjoyment of wealth and consumption, defined increasingly by global, transnational standards.[2]

My own (Marcus's) superficial experience of Singapore is as a long-time resident of Houston, Texas, a city known for its lack of character ("no there there") but one that actually works quite well under the fiction of community with a minimum of civic concern or virtue required of its residents. (Houston is famous for its lack of zoning laws, and for its money-making ways, originally associated with the oil business and real estate—why else would anyone have chosen to settle this humid floodplain?) My attention focused on Bogotá, through my own time there and the fieldwork of Angela Rivas Gamboa. My sketchy knowledge of Singapore has been shaped by the epic story of its fall to the Japanese in World War II, and by stories of its more recent conversion into a consumer mecca, one of the most prosperous and most orderly of the Southeast and East Asian cities. (Interestingly, several academic friends warned me that they found Singapore the least interesting of cities, with its lack of easy access to a visitor's sense of disorder, adventure, and "local color.") Indeed, Singapore proved to be such a place for me on my first brief visit—a clean, orderly, luxurious shopping bazaar. It took the articles in this volume to give me another view via their tellings of local stories and counterstories—of hauntings and inhabitings of places that do not define themselves in total conformity with the popular and outsider's image of Singapore.[3]

Still, I have no knowledge of the particular "public secret" or tacit, unspeakable understandings that bind rulers and ruled in Singapore. Getting at these strongly felt, but hardly articulated, senses of things is what anthropology and cultural studies scholarship generally could contribute to the study of the layered histories of colonialism and globalizing capitalism in defining the present of cities like Singapore, among others. The predicament of governance of such cities is a useful vantage point from which to gauge the challenge that stereoscopy poses to civic authority. The politicians and mayors are the ones who must still speak explicitly in terms of the historically embedded local, and thus they must be in partial denial of the globalizing forces of stereoscopy that distract the attention and weaken the commitment of citizens to life in the urban polity, as traditionally understood, to guarantee the performance of authority that governance requires. In the environment of urban politics, this can breed mutual cynicism and suspicion as the mode of relationship between the governors and those among the governed who can most vocally and effectively demand services. This uneasy atmosphere is what defines the civility of the public sphere in many major cities today.

Angela Rivas Gamboa has made more general reflections on such issues, based on her fieldwork in Bogotá, Colombia. A lifelong resident of Bogotá, Rivas Gamboa is concerned generally with how the struggling attempts to achieve security and order distinctively create a sense of everydayness in a city that bears the marks and traces of Colombia's peculiar and defining modern history of violence—criminal and civil—and has been, at certain moments, enclaved from it as well. Rivas Gamboa's focus specifically is the question of governance: the relations of political authority to images and experiences of daily life in the city. Her major site of ethnography was the office of the mayor, in its literal and symbolic senses; in particular, she focused on the career and practices of Mayor Antanas Mockus, a Menippean figure, to elude to the tropological category revived by Mikhail Bakhtin, who reveals through satire and absurdity a position generally critical of the prevailing social and intellectual assumptions. Mockus's career as a politician illustrates how humor, satire, and play with the absurd can in certain contexts define the effective bases of both civic and political culture, and therefore support the exercise of power and authority in governance. Eccentric, surreal performances of leadership address in complex ways such contradictory mass orientations as hope, cynicism, the desire for control and order, and the desire for reassurances in acts of civic disorder. Yet they also promote the sense that forces of change are exceeding the capacities of given institutional regimes of management and administration.

Given that Rivas Gamboa's, Bogotá seems so far removed geographically and categorically, how does her study apply to global (yet postcolonial) cities in Southeast Asia? Indeed, the "feel" of Latin American cities is quite different from Southeast Asian ones. While fitting well into the context of broad themes that have defined postcolonial experience, Bogotá is by no means on the path to becoming one of the global cities that somehow have transcended the context of identifications, issues, and commitments limited to the category of the nation-state. Bogotá, as will be seen, is very much held to its national and postcolonial history and present. Yet it is also very much defined by globalizing trends, especially in its governance (also in its economic base, which is not of concern here), an issue that is very relevant if only to differentiate globalizing tendencies that are felt everywhere in cities and the making of what is a different sort of city—or global city—out of a postcolonial past. In considering this difference, it is probably wise to avoid the self-generated, booster-ish hype of global cities themselves, whose discourses sometimes overlap with those of the social sciences discovering an emergent new phenomenon, in a hyped-up theoretical/conceptual language of marveling and fear. This means we must talk about differences between the globalizing and the definitively global in terms of the ethnography of specific institutions and relations, not in terms of the overall frame of structure or system. We can regard Bogotá as an example of a training ground for politics in the cities, despite the palimpsest of a long postcolonial tradition of political families and styles. So in Colombia the contemporary shaping of governance is thoroughly in a globalizing regime of practices—selected in particular ways that reflect specific colonial pasts. In the following discussions, globalizing processes can be seen in the power of the media to shape successful political careers and leadership, and in the full submission of local politics to this change. They are also evident in the importation and spread in Colombia of the public health epidemiological program for controlling violence as a social problem (a remarkable example of Foucault's biopower that is disseminated as good government practice in many countries now). Here we see very particular relationships between a postcolonial history of the nation-state and the form that globalizing tendencies take. They mutually reinforce one another.

The globalization of governance in Bogotá follows the channels of an instantiated set of postcolonial relationships to the United States. In places like Colombia, globalization is, at least politically, very much Americanization; and of course this question about how controlled (or not) globalization is in various places, and by what forces, is perhaps the key issue of debate in the current academic interest in globalization generally. In a global city like Singapore or others, would these globalizing tendencies in the institutions of governance of a still thoroughly postcolonial city take a different form? Or are they the same form but shaped by different controlling forces? These forces might not be direct Americanization, but they might be indirect through the operation of international finance, Americanized in its own way. Are these layers and nonlinear histories of domination what are at stake in accounts of globalization?

The other area in which the political/civic cultures of cities everywhere are being globalized is the spread of involvement in the communities and regimes of virtual space made possible by the Internet. We do not have sufficient material on how the mayor's office in Bogotá is registering this "distraction" in its relations of governance to its citizenry, either directly or on the periphery of its performances of authority. Clearly, this worldwide customized involvement of individuals in diffuse electronic networks is something that every city leader feels, senses, and registers, but for which they have no explicit discourse, program, or policy. One of the most pressing jobs of ethnography is to capture the "traces" of this sense of the loss of power in the powerful and those in office. How viabile are older political arrangements in informal cultures of rule, and what are the literal effects of these changes on governance in global and globalizing cities?

As a stimulus question for wider comparison, in the specific case of Bogotá an interesting question might be what structural and historic contexts would account for the success of a political style as unconventional, if not bizarre, as that of Antanas Mockus. The contemplation of Mockus's career tells one much about the contemporary situation of Colombia, but such political styles are not limited to Colombia or Latin America. The Manippean is an integral part of successful political performance in many places now and probably has much to do with the social and cultural insight and emotional power that are located in the humorous, the satirical, and the cynical. One interesting suggestion has been that Mockus represents the playing out of a political style of activism common to leadership in European social movements of the 1960s and 1970s that spread through various parts of the world and eventually adapted itself to standard political careers. This in itself might then be an example of transnational cultural diffusion that is (or is not?) a part of de facto globalization, as opposed to the hyped story of globalization that is told nowadays by its agents and critics, both academic and otherwise.

What this consideration of globalization and its relation to changing or possible political styles of urban governance further suggests is that what defines a particularly anthropological project or stake in globalization studies is indeed this capacity to specify difference at an experiential level in the "same." This is the very traditional goal and contribution of anthropological studies of modernity. The challenge is posed precisely by the extraordinary weight placed on the homogenizing aspects of conceptions of globalization even though the tenor of much theoretical discussion of it is to caution against this weight and to assert the importance of countertendencies toward variation and difference. The "grail" for anthropology in this is, of course, to find frames and contexts in which to provide discussions of difference that nonetheless do not fall prey to the older "culture area" essentialisms on which the framing of diverse ethnographic traditions depend in one way or another. (This old regime of representation—not at all dead—is what the 1980s "writing culture" critiques[4] and colonial discourse critiques firmly addressed and exploded.)

In this regard, a weakness that we perceive in much of the discussion of global cities and globalization is that it clearly argues for difference, but tends not to develop the frames for sustained or sensitive description and analysis of it. Based on Rivas Gamboa's Bogotá writings, we want to propose the following ideas for such a necessary frame. Every situated discourse about globalization, anxious about globalizing forces or enacting them, addresses an implied subject. In many cities, the "subject" of governance discourses, tinged by concerns with globalizing transformation, is not some generic citizenry, that includes the poor, the underclasses, or the newly arrived. Rather, it is the latter-day bourgeoisie, the professional middle classes, upon whom the governance of cities depends. The political discourses in global or globalizing cities are thus not different in this regard from the past: The poor and underclasses as social referents have always tended not to count. They are overlooked even in periods of so-called reform politics (often in response to literal urban rebellions and mass violence from below). In the midst of arrays of globalizing changes now more than ever contemporary political discourses in cities address and respond only to the most privileged segments of its citizenry and those who can presume or imagine themselves to be within this circle. Even though more and more people see themselves within the middle-class referent of political discourse, it makes this referent no less exclusionary and privileged in character. In many cities, postcolonial and/or global, it is the fear, frustration, and cynicism—an imaginary created and articulated by media, entertainment, and word of mouth (the circulation of "good stories" of the kind Rivas Gamboa finds, which create a certain sense of community)—to which political discourse of governance must orient itself.

So understanding the special character of postcolonial and global cities anywhere depends on the kind of "native" account that Rivas Gamboa offers. In her descriptions are the elements that will come to define the specific situation of Bogotá as a globalizing/postcolonial city. To understand the predicament of governance, one has to understand the privileged subject of governance—the people governance discourse addresses. These subjects are defined in the first instance by the reflexive and broadly class-specific account that Rivas Gamboa offers in a preliminary way. It is a very necessary step in her work to satisfy the kind of knowledge of places that anthropology desires. However, the same could be said for any other condition of globalizing change in cities, whether they be in Latin America, Africa, Asia, Europe, or North America.

The referential discourse about bourgeois citizenship in cities is more arrogant and plutocratic than it has ever been in the high period of industrial capitalism. It is now veiled less by a liberal discussion of welfare provision because of the vast increase in "public goods" brought about by globalizing forces that are supposedly and evidently available to all. The problems (security and otherwise) exacerbated by local and globalizing trends are seen as generic, as universally shared; in reality they are not shared or at least they are not shared in the same ways. The exclusions are just a lot less visible, even in the moralizing discourses that oppose or look at the "dark side" of globalizing forces. In a sense, perhaps what is called for analytically, is a return of the discussions of the public sphere that were so current in the 1980s but are now considered outmoded because globalization has decentered the nation-state on which the idea of the public sphere depended for its coherence.

Also, the Habermasian notion of the bourgeois public sphere was revived in the 1980s only to be transcended by complicating it with the then-current discussions of multiculturalism, diaspora, and ethnically fragmented national and urban spaces. However, while there are new technologies and boundaries that shape the bourgeois public sphere, we think it could be a useful device once again for constructing a frame for ethnographically describing the de facto exclusive "subject" on whom much of the discourse of urban governance in postcolonial cities, undergoing globalizing tendencies or reaching global status, orients itself. The mood of the citizenry that matters in Bogotá is undoubtedly not the same as in Singapore or other cities of Southeast Asia, but the sort of account that Rivas Gamboa offers is essential also to understanding what the parameters of globalization are institutionally in these other cityscapes. Less self-consciously, the considerable autobiographical content found in this volume also begins to provide the narrative raw material on which understandings of the compact of governance in Singapore specifically, and other cities in Southeast Asia generally, could be clearly defined.

Finally, another way that our account of contemporary Bogotá might be relevant to the themes of this volume is in the prevalence of the trope of disorder in Rivas Gamboa's writing. In fact, much of the critical writing on globalization and cities depends on the use of this trope in negative or positive ways. The assessment of urban disorder—its forms, types, and quantities—seems to be an integral part of making arguments about the nature and consequences of globalizing processes. But the construction of such a discourse depends on an informed sense of long-standing, culturally normative modes of experiencing the city among its bourgeois subjects. In the case of Bogotá, little or none of the disorder—the object of endless satire and comedic, cynical commentary by its middle classes—seems to be attributable to the irony of globalizing impacts (save, of course, for "narco-culture"). Insecurity and disorder have long been the problems of civic culture in Colombia, and any sense of present conditions as different from other periods of the country's and city's modern history has to be carefully generated by a cultural history of the informal conditions of bourgeois citizenship. Resignation to the eternal problems and frustrations of chaotic and often violent public spaces is deeply constitutive of what it is to be a public-minded and responsible (perhaps fearful) bourgeois citizen of Bogotá. Expectations of coping with conditions of urban disorder—what is normative, what is not, what appears new, what seems to be wholly continuous with the past—depend on a sensitive cultural history of bourgeois citizenship in this city or any other. Although this might seem obvious, and even bordering on the essentialist sins of past cultural analysis, still it is surprising how rare such specificity (which is not at all to be associated with the "local" in contrast to the global—in this sense Colombians or Singaporeans have always been global) is in discussions of globalization. Deep histories have disappeared or are no longer as relevant as they once were; instead new principles are applied by which urban landscapes are being transformed according to unprecedented, world-defining processes. No doubt such processes are relevant to some degree. But such an assessment can only proceed by critically assessing in turn the tropes on which visions of globalization—academic or otherwise—depend. Disorder is one of the most important of these tropes, and it is more at home in the articulation of urban experience by privileged subjects in some cities (as in Bogotá) than in others.

This discussion of the importance of the trope of disorder to the composition of globalization discourse as it applies to cities also summons up the most visceral and most currently relevant example version of it, at least since September 11, 2001, the disruption and massive destruction of cities through acts of terrorism. There is no more powerful example of contemporary globalization as a pervasive structure of feeling, distinct from its usual reference to a specific post–Cold War triumphant regime of neoliberal capitalism. Terror has long been an integral and unrelieved component of the urban public spheres that are produced by consumer-oriented bourgeois subjects in many places including Colombia. Nothing is more exemplary of a cultural globalization effect than the fear, empathy, and partial identification inspired in the world's urban middle classes by the terrorist attack in New York City, experienced through the visceral apprehension of a universally disseminated media event. Since that time, it has been frequently associated in after-commentary with the images already familiar from the popular genre of disaster movies.

In their ability to create spectacle and instill fear, the complex clandestine organizations that produce terror are as global in reach as the regime of corporations and the neoliberal market organization of national economies. The effect of such terror in its unity and diversity defines an opportunity to crystallize an object of study of anthropological interest that captures a sense of the internally diverse community of bourgeois subjects to whom globalization discourse conventionally speaks. It disrupts at its core the often implicit ideological promise of wealth, prosperity, progress, and a new civilization or world order. Here, the key subject of terror—the urban bourgeois beneficiary of new forms of global capitalism—is the same as the subject of governance in contemporary large cities. Symbolically the power of massively destructive terror in one of the most prominent global cities has an effect of psychological saturation at least as powerful as the ideologies of progress linked to spreading markets and neoliberal polities for their intended beneficiaries.

Whatever the long-term fates of the extremist organizations that produce them, a single unprecedented act of spectacular terror creates a snapshot-like event when the implicit urban subjects of globalization are for a moment unified in a structure of feeling. The power of the images of disaster and the stories of the suffering of the multitude of families of the dead create a fear and trembling that perpetuates in cities and their bourgeois subjects in the most globalizing sense. In the material that follows on the political styles of governing Bogotá, terror has long been a major component of the milieu in which its bourgeois citizens have had to define normalcy—the same sense of normalcy in work, consumption, and plans for the future links them to their counterparts elsewhere. Bogotá is prescient of a structure of feeling that has only very recently become a globalization effect of the most pervasive sort. Its governance exhibits a global style of politics for cities fully participating within but not yet part of the networks generating the regime of structural and institutional globalization of this era.

THE SCORPIO CITY AND ITS MENIPPEAN MAYOR

Bogotá is a city that belongs to everybody, but nobody seems to belong to it. The people of Bogotá have seldom been committed to the city. And the city never seems to be committed to anybody. In the last decade it witnessed more than 29,018 homicides.[5] For the last few years it has been a hostile refuge for uncounted internally displaced Colombians who arrive in the capital city every day. It is an aggressive host for all of those who come to the capital city from other parts of the country. It is also a heartless space for growing numbers of both local and newcomer unemployed. Thus, as in Diego Mendoza's stories, the Colombian capital city may be aptly called "Scorpio City."

ABOUT DAUPHINS AND OTHER CREATURES

Chaotically organized, untamed, cruel, eccentric, and satirically joyful, the Bogotá of the late twentieth and early twenty-first century stands at the heart of a wounded state that furiously fights to survive. Through a long series of battles the weak and centralist Colombian state has sought to modernize itself, legitimize its governmental apparatuses, and come to terms with an unmanageable national territory. In these processes, the capital city has historically been the epicenter of political activities and the practice of politics. It has been an important staging ground in the making of national politicians. This is particularly the case with the post of mayor of Bogotá, a position often described as the second most important public position in the country. An important post in the career of any politician, it is often seen as an important step in running for president.

In the 1980s, local rulers were elected by popular vote for the first time in Colombia. In 1988, Andres Pastrana, a 34-year-old lawyer known as the director and anchorman of a daily nationwide news program *TV Hoy*, was the first publicly elected mayor in Bogotá's history. During the campaign for mayor, Pastrana was kidnapped by the Medellin cartel; after a dramatic rescue, he was lucky to escape with his life. In politicians' argot, the lucky mayor of the capital city was the perfect incarnation of a *delfin*, a word used in Spanish to refer to either a dolphin or a dauphin, depending on the context. The concept of *delfin* as it is used by Colombian politicians is equivalent to "dauphin." As such it is commonly used to refer to young male politicians whose fathers are well-known politicians who have occupied important positions; like actual princes, the sons' core credentials are based not on their performances as individuals, but on their kinship. As the son of former Colombian president Misael Pastrana Borrero, and the graduate of one of the country's most prestigious and traditional schools as well as Harvard, Pastrana worked in mass media journalism for a long time. He initiated his political career when, in the early 1980s, he was elected twice to the Bogotá City Council.

By contrast, in 1994, Antanas Mockus, a 43-year-old polemical and eccentric academic, was elected mayor in a landslide victory. Unlike Pastrana, Mockus was not a dauphin but the incarnation of an "anti-dauphin." Born in Bogotá as the son of Lithuanian immigrants, he was trained in mathematics in France and received a master's degree in philosophy at the *Universidad Nacional* in Bogotá. He was the former rector of the *Universidad Nacional* and one of the many scholars who had participated in the *Movimiento Pedagogico* (Pedagogical Movement) promoted in the last decades in Colombia.

The election of Mockus occurred in a moment often described by scholars as transitional. It was a moment marked by official efforts to legitimize and modernize state institutions, as well as by legislative attempts to democratize the society. This moment also was marked by initiatives that sought to change political practices that supported a system of governance often described as bipartisan, presidential, and authoritarian; 1994 was the first electoral year in which constitutional tools that allowed a more active civilian participation were promoted. The Colombian constitution of 1991 anticipated most of these tools and sought to create a new institutional regime. In particular, it sought to promote civilian participation and to "renew" political practices, and in the so-called postconstitutional era, the style of local politics did indeed change. In Bogotá this change was expressed though the emergence of numerous nonbipartisan groups and candidates who ran for public positions. This might have been also the case in other parts of the country; however, as Gutierrez states, in 1994 the capital city was "the epicenter of the telluric 'revolution of the anti-politicians.' "[6] This veritable revolution was related to Mockus's campaign for mayor of Bogotá, as well as his subsequent administration. It represented a shift in the ways in which political campaigns had been traditionally run, as well as in the ways authority had been traditionally constructed and maintained.

In the political arena Mockus appeared at once as an eccentric and mockingly clever person, but also as a newcomer and a totally inexperienced player. He was a "nobody" among politicians. He was not a member of a family that had traditionally participated in politics, nor was he a member of a political party. He was a recognized scholar, but his formation in philosophy and mathematics was antithetical to the educational background expected of Colombian politicians. He did not present any credentials in terms of previous public activities except for his service as rector of the *Universidad Nacional*. In fact, his name was publically known only through an event that had made him controversial as rector, he responded to a confrontion with a group of obstreperous students during a lecture by dropping his pants.

After the "dropping pants" incident and his resignation from the *Universidad Nacional,* Mockus became the media and public's idea of a desirable figure to run for public office in the atmosphere of the constitutional reforms. For instance, an article written by Maria Isabel Rueda, a well-known national journalist, and published in *Semana* in November 1993, was typical:

> The University was doing better than ever before but Mockus, its rector, fell down because of his own gravity. He fell down and, at the same time, the country has been divided in two sides. On one hand, there are those for whom his buttocks are unacceptable. On the other hand, there are those who have taken Mockus's buttocks in a humorous and symbolic way. Between these two positions, some others—like me—think a little bit like the first ones and a little bit like the second ones. For us, a man with the capabilities he has shouldn't fail. We would like to see him in politics. We would be glad to vote for him for a public position that demands bright and honest people such as the Congress of the Republic.[7]

In February 1994, local news shows announced Mockus's aspirations to the mayorial office. From the first moment he was welcomed by public opinion. His name was the first among the favored candidates.

Months later, the candidacy of Mockus was officially registered. His campaign focused on the construction of symbols and the introduction of different forms of acting within politics, as well as uncommon forms to refer to it. It addressed new conceptions of political activity and unconventional political styles. It also exhibited novel behaviors toward electors, as well as the development and use of original ways of communication. The Mockus campaign included not only topics that have often been addressed by politicians, but also both new and seldom addressed topics. The newness of this campaign, however, was not in the topics it was addressing, but rather the ways in which they were addressed. Thus, for better or worse, as some analysts have pointed out, the "debut" of Mockus in the political arena "disorganized the traditional forms of political language that were instituted among the Colombian people."[8]

The uncommon nature in the ways of addressing particular topics displayed by Mockus can be exemplified in the metaphorical use of the notion of game and in the use of expressions distinctly outside the traditional language of politics in Colombia. The metaphor of game was often used by Mockus with regard to regulating the behaviors of his collaborators, electors, and citizens in general. Through this metaphor, issues such as participation and collectivity were emphasized, along with the definition of and respect for common values. These elements were presented and reinforced through references to actual games, couched in pedagogical, playful, and affective language. This rhetorical strategy also included the use of well-known slang and street language expressions, as well as "common people's language."

THE TWIRLING DANCE OF *LA PIRINOLA*

The connection that Mockus's campaign sought to create with the Bogotá people in general was antithetical to the widespread and often criticized models of politics, especially those in which relations among politicians and between them and their potential electors are traditionally established in terms of personal favors. Through his campaign, Mockus criticized those same relationships, but he did this in unexpected ways. For instance, as a candidate he explicitly denied the use of any kind of promise of future personal favors as core elements in building relationships between himself and supporters. This critique formed one of the core elements in Mockus's campaign. It addressed not only the practice of politics outside traditional roles and relationships among politicians and electors, but also the creation of citizenship beyond voting, by looking into how citizens relate one to each other and to the city. To this end, the campaign made reference to slogans and well-known games. This was the case with the metaphorical use of the *pirinola* and one of the main mottoes in Mockus's campaign: "Everybody put and everybody take."[9] This was also the case with slogans such as "Let's educate the Mayor."

Among the games and slogans employed by Mockus and his campaign, the metaphor of the *pirinola* is perhaps the one that synthesizes best the relationships that were promoted by his campaign. As in the actual game of the *pirinola,* in which sooner or later everybody will put and will be allowed to take, Mockus sought to promote the understanding and practice of politics as a collective enterprise that depends upon everybody's participation and that produces achievements that could benefit everybody.

ABOUT AMPHIBIANS, CHAMELEONS, AND OTHER CREATURES

In 1995, Mockus took over a city with one of the highest murder rates in the world. In addition, chaotic car traffic, numerous accidents during holidays and festive events, a prevalence of aggressive interactions, and a generalized mood both distrustful and apathetic were characteristic of the capital city. In such a context, Mockus was determined to reduce murder rates and eliminate the diverse expressions of violence by teaching "civilian manners" to the people of Bogotá. To achieve these aims, Mockus's administration designed several pedagogical campaigns that came to be related to the notion of a "cultural amphibian." Such a notion was used in the early 1990s by several Colombian scholars to describe the ideal role of teachers and educators, as well as to address current problems and future goals in education. A few years later, Mockus applied this notion of cultural amphibian to the problem of the divorce between law, morality, and culture. He moved the application of this trope from the educational arena to the current situation of the country.

COUNTING MOCK/MUCUS/MOCKUS

Mockus's governmental program focused on pedagogical campaigns and sought to enforce preventive legal measures. At the same time, one of the core issues in his governmental program was the respect for life and the reduction of violent murders in the city. To this end, the mayor's office worked on campaigns and programs that in diverse ways addressed expressions of urban violence. These initiatives were informed not only by pedagogical practices and the uses of symbolic devices, but also by epidemiological principles. This was in particular the case with programs and policies concerning civilian security and *convivencia.*[10]

Through these policies the mayor's office sought to address crime and urban violence. A healthy policy in security and *convivencia* is defined as any policy that not only prosecutes delinquency and gives attention to the victims, but also seeks to prevent the development and occurrence of events that predispose or generate violent situations. The mayor's office sought to achieve these preventive goals through the creation and promotion of civilian culture. Such a culture was defined as a frame that regulates the behavior of the citizens by establishing minimum common rules that make possible relationships among citizens and between them and their environment. To this end, the mayor's office favored the participation of scholars and experts familiar through their research with expressions of urban violence. Pedagogical practices and epidemiological principles were translated into a set of campaigns and programs that sought to efface urban violence and criminality as well as to create and promote *convivencia* among the people of Bogotá.

"LA REVOLUCION CACHACA" (BOGOTÁ'S REVOLUTION)

Bogotá not only has "grown up," but also has gone through important changes in terms of both practices of governance and daily constraints. Today, the capital city is not only bigger, but also a much more—for better and worse—experienced city. As a recent report in *Semana* states, in the last six years Bogotá has initiated a revolution that surprises not only those who left the city years ago, but also those who have witnessed the changes. The access to education has been increased by more than 30 percent. The rates of violent murders have been reduced to almost half. The city's credit rating has moved from A to AA+. It has doubled the taxes it has collected. At the end of 2001, all the families of the city had access to running drinking water. In addition, public leasing, years ago recognized as one of the biggest areas of corruption in the country, has been cleaned up. Similarly, the relationships between the mayor's office and the council have been clarified. Bogotá looks neater, but at the same time it is living through a dramatic economic stagnation. The city, like other parts of the country, has experienced increasing expressions of violence. The capital city is witnessing a devastating emigration of its inhabitants, who are leaving the country because of fear of crime, lack of opportunities, and economic slump. Those who remain have been compelled to face growing rates of unemployment and increasing expressions of criminal violence.

In spite of the initial aversion and controversies generated by the mayor and his initiatives, Mockus ended his first administration with a high level of popularity. In this context, the metaphoric use of games and symbolic campaigns had to address not only the older issues, but also new ones as well. Several initiatives proposed by the mayor were highly controversial—this was the case with economic measures suggested by him involving tax increases, as well as campaigns inspired by epidemiological principles and idiosyncratic experiments. The conjunction of current urban situations and highly controversial measures promoted by Mockus did affect his image, but the people of Bogotá elected Mockus for a second time as their mayor, and his initiatives will again encounter controversy, social protests, and oppositions. As the new mayor of the capital city, Mockus faces not only the issues he sought to address during his last administration, but also a city that has become both more learned and yet more exhausted.

CONCLUDING NOTE

Our study heeded the spirit of the following caution, well articulated by Anna Tsing:

> Globalization draws our enthusiasm because it helps us imagine inter-connection, travel, and sudden transformation. Yet it also draws us inside its rhetoric until we take its claims for true descriptions . . . national and regional units are mapped as the baseline of change without attention to their shifting and contested ability to define the landscape. We lose sight of the coalitions and claimants as well as their partial and shifting claims. We lose touch with the material and institutional components through which powerful and central sites are constructed, from which convincing claims about units and scales can be made. We describe the landscape imagined within these claims rather than the culture and politics of scalemaking. This essay suggests approaches to the study of the global that seem to me to hold onto the excitement of this endorsement of planetary interconnection without trading our critical stance for globalist wishes and fantasies.[11]

The same suggestion goes for the study of cities and urban spaces, as some of the most impressive scholarship on globalization has been focused on the conditions that have transformed some of the world's major cities into so-called global cities. The danger in such scholarship is that it can overly identify with the very explicit ideologies of globalization that are in play in study and in theory within the academy that sets scholars on the path of inquiry. Here, we have sought to identify the play of global forces in the transformation of cities that qualify for the explicitly globalizing urban project but are not commonly thought of in this light. Acts of translation, familiar to anthropology, are required. The flows and networks of global force are specific and variable; the effects are very local. Actors on the scene understand viscerally what globalization is in their own idioms, and the effects of global forces are best understood as enacted—as performed in social conflicts and tensions—rather as explained in terms shared with the scholar or field-worker. The latter accounts are regrettably not to be trusted. Globalization discourse is so fluid that it is available virtually anywhere as "native accounts" of local predicaments so valued by anthropologists.

In the spectacle of the career of Antanus Mockus, successful politician and two-term mayor of Bogotá, Colombia, we have a figure whose style evokes and plays to urban middle classes who increasingly define their standards of living in global terms. The urban middle class looks to how its counterparts live in the Untied States, Europe, and in other places that experience similar stresses. For Bogotá, comparisons are made not only to other parts of Latin America, but to Asia as well. As a result of a history of colonialism and related moderization, Bogotá's middle class is caught in a despairing national project. Mockus's projects are double-edged: They appeal to logics that just might work, but they are also based on a fantasy sense of community on which their success depends. Bizarre and absurd as they may seem, they are indeed alternatives to failed long-established political styles. As a performed statement of critique, their appeal to a desperate middle class—ill at ease at home, but able to go with global flows through innovations in forms of transnational travel and communication—cannot be underestimated.

And in Mockus's performance as politician we can see the opportunities made possible by certain global effects. The conduct of politics with an eye to media exposure and entertainment value is something that can be observed on urban and national scenes worldwide. Politicians like Mockus are not that rare—and the success of such a style, where it occurs, is interesting to contemplate. When research is not defined and encompassed by globalizing ambition and ideology, then what constitutes the global can only be apprehended in a certain structure of feeling that requires the sorts of ethnographic readings and interpretations of the performances found in fieldwork with which anthropologists, among others, have long been familiar. And most of the world's cities qualify for such studies.

NOTES

1. Michael Taussig, *Defacement: Public Secrecy and the Labor of the Negative* (Stanford: Stanford University Press, 1999).
2. See Teresa Caldeira, *City of Walls: Crime, Segregation, and Citizenship in Sao Paulo* (Berkeley: University of California Press, 2001).
3. See the articles in this volume and its companion volume, *Beyond Description: Space Historicity Singapore*, ed. Ryan Bishop, John Phillips, and Wei-Wei Yeo (London: Routledge, 2003).
4. See James Clifford and George E. Marcus, eds., *Writing Culture: the Poetics and Politics of Ethnography* (Berkeley: University of California Press, 1986).
5. This data has been taken from *Medicina Legal* (the official institution that is in charge of these issues in the capital city).
6. F. Gutierrez Sanin, "Tendencias de cambio en el sistema de partidos: el caso de Bogota," *Analisis Politico* 24 (January–April 1995): 73–82.
7. Maria Rueda, "Esconda las con 'raiting'," *Semana*, 9 November 1993: 58.
8. See S. L. Peña, "Rito y simbolo en la Campaña electoral para la alacaldia de Bogota," *Analisis Politico* 24 (January–April 1995): 22–35.
9. The *pirinola* is a traditional game in Colombia and elsewhere in Latin America. The *pirinola* is a kind of top that is twirled not by means of a cord, but by taking its superior part with one's fingers. Unlike tops, *pirinolas* are not round but have flat sides. Each of the sides has written commands: take everything, put everything, everybody puts, everybody takes, put one, take one, put two, take two . . . and so on. Players use bent coins of low value or tokens such as beans. They take turns to *hacer bailar la pirinola* (to make the *pirinola* to dance) by twirling it, and then follow the written command that is shown in the flat side that is shown at the top of the *pirinola*.
10. We haven't found an English term for *convivencia*. This expression is now used to refer to all those activities that seek to promote nonviolent behaviors, pacific solution in daily conflicts, and so on.
11. Anna Tsing, "The Global Situation," *Cultural Anthropology* 15, no. 3 (2000): 330.

Yeo's article begins by noting two characteristics that seem to be defining for contemporary experience in the postcolonial city of Singapore. The first concerns how questions of national identity become pressing both in government policy and in cultural production. The second locates phenomena of speed that dominate even the most quotidian experiences of city dwellers generally. In the former case she argues that the question of identity has generally been thematized anachronistically, implanting a kind of fictional nostalgia and an inappropriate set of expectations, while simultaneously producing an amnesia for actual historical conditions. So in the context of the phenomena of speed, and the apparent demand on city dwellers for an increasing intensity of the repeatable present tense, Yeo suggests a term, *distraction,* that would help account for the perpetuation of inappropriate and unproductive modes of self-identification. By focusing on some recent experiments in Singaporean theatre, which attempt to provoke states of distraction in their audiences, Yeo develops a thesis about the theatricality of the city, according to which a constructive distraction emerges as a kind of condition for surviving the overload of stimulation that a modern city typically imposes on its dwellers. By bringing issues connected with postcolonialism into contact with those of urbanism, Yeo is able to focus on the kinds of constitutive historicity that underlie urban processes. History need no longer be thematized in the nostalgic or utopian mode but rather as theatricality—the performance or the coming-to-be of the historical—of processes that help to determine urban life, specifically, the "reign of speed over history" *as* history.

12

City as Theatre: Singapore, State of Distraction

This society is based on the spectacle in the most fundamental way. —Guy Debord[1]

A city built for speed is built for success.   *—Le Corbusier*[2]

At the limits of the body considered as a perceptual apparatus, distraction produces the modern artwork.   *—Tim Armstrong*[3]

That which lies at the root of the perennial questioning of Singapore's national identity is the fundamental shift in our sense of collective being that has been brought about by the orientation of society and culture around speed. Such questioning persists because the characteristics of national identity are sought through the fulfillment of anachronistic expectations. *Under the Last Dust* and *Invisibility*, two Singaporean theatre productions, show that theatricality can provide some suggestions as to how the fleeting, surface-oriented present might be weighted in the national identity question.

In her novel *Playing Madam Mao*, Lau Siew Mei evokes the hyper-reality of Singapore through the interweaving of historical, mythical, oneiric, hallucinatory, apocryphal, and theatrical materials. Most prominent among these is the part played by theatre. The author's critique of Singapore's society of the spectacle, a society governed by appearance over truth, is implicit in her portrayal of the city in terms that conjure its theatricality. The novel depicts Singapore in perfect fitting with Debord's description of the society of the spectacle:

> Understood on its own terms, the spectacle proclaims the predominance of appearances and asserts that all human life, which is to say all social life, is

mere appearance. But any critique capable of apprehending the spectacle's essential character must expose it as a visible negation of life—and as a negation of life that has *invented a visual form for itself*.[4]

The city in *Playing Madam Mao* is a place of shimmering, shiny surfaces, reflective but also unyielding: "Glassy shop fronts. Neon lights. . . . Under rain, the city lies glistening . . . like a luminous pearl. . . . White light bounces from it into the clouds, as though from a giant mirror."[5] Life in the city moves in fixed cycles like the endless repeat performances of the play in the novel. The city manifests the negation of life within it, not negation in the sense of death but forgetfulness. A collective amnesia seems to hold the city under its spell: Lives within it press on with an ever-increasing sense of urgency about the present, not having time or space for thinking about the past. The novel illustrates Debord's point that "what the spectacle expresses is the total practice of one particular economic and social formation," the "agenda" that "is also the historical moment by which we happen to be governed."[6] The power of the spectacle makes it seem irresistible, as if it were the ideal when it is simply ideological. In Debord's words, it is an "objective force," "an enormous positivity, out of reach and beyond dispute." It compels "passive acceptance" through "its seeming incontrovertibility" and "its monopolization of the realm of appearances," asserting full control as it insists on its irreplaceability.[7] In the novel, this power is embodied by the city's architecture. The modernity of the city is apparent from its modern facades, but so is its anonymity. "It could be anyone's city. It has no past, no roots," writes Lau, who also sees it as a likeness of America, a "mini-America" with its "lighted towers, shopping complexes, neon advertisements, and traffic lights."[8] Unreality is the city's identity, it seems. The city's skyline and the impressive facades of buildings are markers of its success, but the novelist's attention to the glassy, polished surfaces of the city's buildings suggests that the city is memorable only as a place of visible surfaces. The interiors behind them, the space beyond the front, seem bereft of depth and alterity. Surfaces define and perpetuate the city, just as its people are recognized and motivated by their consumerism—the pursuit of "life on the surface."[9] Lau laments:

> There comes a time when you begin to realize that [people] prefer nothing more than to experience life on the surface. All their loves, hates and passions go no further . . . they don't desire a life lived intensely, the superficial is what counts.[10]
>
> It could be anyone's city. It has no past, no roots, so that one can say, "This is mine, it belongs to me."[11]

The quest for national identity and the centrality of the superficial in Singaporean life have an important relation. The question of national identity concerns the Singaporean's sense of belonging to the country. Unsurprisingly, the novel raises the question but is unable to provide any solution, for the question is impossible by dint of its terms. How does one articulate what it means to belong to a place, or to have a claim to it, when the way of thought on which such a question finds its basis in the first place is daily undermined or treated as obsolete? Economic pragmatism dominates Singaporean life on macro and micro levels. Change to the environment is nearly always implemented for economic reasons. Planning aims to achieve an ever more efficient use of the limited land resource. The pragmatic approach discourages emotional attachment to the city as a lived place. Permanence becomes irrelevant next to the cause of further urban redevelopment of the land. Apart from the intolerance of history seen in the demolition of historic buildings, there is the commercialization of history seen in the makeover of old shophouses and go-downs into shops, pubs, and restaurants for tourists and white-collar workers in the business district. Memories are constantly under the threat of displacement: Coffeeshops, historic buildings, and old thoroughfares have been cleared, made to disappear, when seen as economically unviable obstructions to the way of the future.

The city becomes less a place where history is physically inscribed and architecturally intact than the site of an endless cycle of erasure and reconstruction. As Rem Koolhaas put it, the city is "a (former) theatre of the tabula rasa . . . on its way to yet another configuration. . . . perpetually morphed to the next state. . . . [which] makes Architecture impossible." The city is cursed as such, as Koolhaas explains:

> The curse of the tabula rasa is that, once applied, it proves not only previous occupancies expendable, but also each *future* occupancy provisional too, ultimately temporary.[12]

In place of history one finds facades of the next model. The city is a blueprint that has never left the drawing board. What are the implications for collective memory? The speed of change in the city ensures the loss of places, in themselves and in the people's remembrance of them. The novel underlines the loss of memory that comes with the constancy of accelerated change:

> My city has sprung up almost magically. Nothing has remained the same.
> I have known the transience of what appears solid. Some things are better forgotten, they tell me.
>> It is like this with those who have lived through the world war. "Nothing much happened," they say.
>> "Nothing?"
>> "Only grandma died."

I have often wondered at the amnesiac state of my city's people. Do they forget? Or does the past cease to exist, once it is past?[13]

In this city, you can't walk away and return to find things the same as they were. What then of the city's inhabitants who have to live with so much inconstancy in their landscape? Is there a foundation for a stable identity?[14]

The city's fixation with speed counters the claims of permanence, rendering the past in terms that show and reinforce the message of its obsolescence. In a place where life on the surface prevails, the significance of theatricality is not incidental. In Lau's novel, Singapore is a city of shadows and doubles; most of its inhabitants play the roles they have been assigned, knowingly or otherwise. The protagonist Ching is an actress who is at home both in herself and in the role she plays, as Madam Mao. The blurring of self and role is also an effect of the sharing of the same name by the actress and Madam Mao, both called Chiang Ching. When the actress says that she has betrayed her husband by having an affair with a political leader known not by name, only by his title of Chairman, it is not clear whether her confession comes as part of her role in the play or if she has indeed been unfaithful to her husband in real life, Tang Na Juan. The life of the actress, her role onstage, and the historical woman that the role is based on seem to collapse into the one and same image of self at various points in the novel.

The novel projects through the story of Ching the idea that citizenship alone makes every person an actor of sorts in the city. Just as history is seemingly paradoxically displaced and found in a landscape made up of changing surfaces, the city's people situate and identify themselves through a flux of appearances, slipping in and out of roles. The novel and the two theatrical productions, to be dealt with later, show that theatricality is a fundamental element of social life in Singapore but they do so in different ways. The novel carries a political agenda, showing that with a culture of self-censorship and strict government control over all media agencies, information and opinions in the city are regulated, making their appearance like lines in a script. Thus the city *is* a stage, not simply *like* one, and the search for national identity is one of its most popular dramas. The plays also reveal the city as theatre but the insight they avail, in comparison to the novel, is not so much political as cultural-anthropological.

A recent newspaper article about young Singaporeans' views on national identity wrote that the question exists at "the very *heart* of being Singaporean" (emphasis mine).[15] The question is part of the condition it seeks to describe. As the following will demonstrate, this self-repetition simply perpetuates the questioning, turning the city into an endlessly repeated echo of its people's impossible expectations concerning history, not realizing that its hollowness as nonaccumulative life-on-the-surface generates the same echoes, the hollowness that is essence.

Frederick Wong is an undergraduate student who supports English football clubs, eats steak and sushi, watches weekly Taiwanese television dramas, and chats online with friends in Hong Kong. He was singled out as a typical young Singaporean who finds "little in [his] life that is intrinsically Singaporean." This article is not the first to ask how one sets about "defining the Singapore essence." The ways in which the issue is articulated suggest not only the degree of anxiety that surrounds the question but also the expectation of its resolution in certain terms. National identity is a matter of the "heart," part of "the Singapore essence," "intrinsic" to every Singaporean. The phrasing implies that the space of description for national identity is predetermined. There is a privileging of depth over surface. Like a heart inside a body, the definition of national identity is buried deep within the Singaporean psyche; it cannot be seen on the surface; it is encased in the depths of the country's body politic.

The newspaper article quotes a widely held and often expressed sentiment among the Singaporean young: the search for national identity bespeaks a "yearning for something that's deeper, something that's more noble in spirit." It is as if "intrinsically Singaporean" qualities and the "essence" of the country and her people cannot be found in instances of "life on the surface." This valorization of depth in a society of the spectacle is curious. It suggests that some areas of common knowledge about the city are rejected in any configurations of Singaporean identity because they are unacceptable. "Singapore's economic success was the one major source of pride cited by four out of five youths polled in a recent survey"—but the same survey also showed that the affluence of the city and the short time it took to achieve this are seen as either irrelevant to or insufficient for the characterization of national identity:

> Here, we enjoy a good standard of living, a low crime rate and good job opportunities. But for many, there is a nagging feeling that there has to be something more.   —Aloysius Cheong, age 23

> Cold, hard GDP growth rates, even if in double digits, are hardly the stuff to stoke patriotic flames.   —Noel Tan, age 23

> I can't tell a foreign friend that I'm proud of Singapore for our ten percent growth.   —Frederick Wong, age 23

> I'm proud of Singapore's growth from a tiny dot on the map to a truly global player in the world, but I can't think of much else that I would be proud of as a Singaporean.   —Boo Koh Chin Chai, age 22

The article mentions that feelings of national belonging are commonly defined as "shared feelings which spring from national crises" such as the crash of Singapore Airlines flight SQ006 in Taipei in October 2000 and the burning of the Singapore flag in the Philippines over the death penalty of Flor Contemplacion, a Filipino maid, convicted of murder, in 1997. The emotional responses of Singaporeans to these experiences are acceptable as registers of national feeling because they arise out of causes that are seen to bear deeper import than the economic well being of the city. They fulfill the "yearning for something that's deeper, something that's more noble in spirit." The rarity of such experience in the everyday is widely taken as further indication of the city's lack of distinctiveness or, more crushingly, its want of integrity.

In actual fact, the city's constant perpetuation of change makes the prospect of attaining a settled sense of identity over time unrealistic and quite beside the point. The treatment of certain historic areas and buildings in the city makes this clear. The forms of change undergone by the city testify to its uniqueness as "a *city without qualities*"[16]; they add up as a "sum . . . of a series of systematic transubstantiations," making the city "one of the most ideological of all urban conditions."[17] When considering Singapore's identity, the city's inexhaustible changefulness must not be neglected. The narrative of its citizens' struggle with the question of identity suggests a failure at self-recognition. Changefulness is manifest in the city's anchorage of self on models rather than history. Entire cemeteries have been exhumed so that the land can be used more profitably (the latest instance is the Bidadari cemetery where graves are being exhumed to provide land for a new public housing estate and about 40,000 residents);[18] since December 2001 hawker stalls have been returned to Smith Street in Chinatown to re-create the ambience of street dining, deemed unhygienic and banned by the authorities in the 1970s. Time and again the city has endured dispossession of its past: its river cleaned up and emptied of boats; its graves exhumed; its roads reorganized; its history painted over, torn down, rebuilt, landscaped. This process made the city first a Garden City, then a Tropical City of Excellence. The next phase lined up to happen: Renaissance City.

What role might theatre perform in the quest for national identity? The question of national identity persists due to a failure in self-description. Inappropriate terms and ways of evaluation can be circumvented through theatre where the showing of *what is* reflects the unrecognized aspects of identity to the consciousness of those who inhabit it. Theatre can bring about consideration of our everyday as spectacular and hyperreal; as such it provides a sense of the city's liveliness, vitality, and danger, qualities that orthodox searches for national identity seek in vain to arrest and make known through a slogan or a campaign.[19] Further, there is potentiality for theatre to function as theory, a critical commonplace drawn from theatre's

Greek root: *thea* designates a place from which to observe or to see, implying analysis. Two productions in Singapore in 2000 performed such a role:
Invisibility, a Mandarin play written by Quah Sy Ren and directed by Sim
Pern Yiau for Drama Box (September 2000) and *Under the Last Dust,*
devised and directed by Jean Ng for The Necessary Stage (October 2000).

The failure of self-recognition for which the survey provided examples
is repeated in the reviews of *Under the Last Dust.* The comments of one
reviewer are representative: The production is as memorable in its "disturbing portrait of contemporary society" as it is flawed "in being unable to
push beyond some of the boundaries it set for itself."[20] What is considered
the chief flaw of the work is also recognized as a factor of its success. Actions
found in everyday life are presented through several short mime pieces.
These collide or pass by one another throughout the play. The moments of
contact between the different narratives are outnumbered by those of non-
interaction. The play is fragmentary not only in the sense of its structure of
episodes but in its fundamental insistence on showing up the irrelevance of
some of its narratives to each other so that when the production is considered as a whole these pieces seem most resonant as instants of self-contained,
incidental action. The critic also writes that "[*Under the Last Dust*] is a piece
that haunts you both because of the poetry that it achieved on stage. And
what it did not." What bears thinking about here is that while the critic is
alert to the ways in which the production daringly reconfigures the manner
by which its action fills the space onstage, she remains constrained in her
response—or in her critical judgment at least—by an expectation that the
work should at the end of the day deliver its message in a form that is, by
her own admission, fundamentally contrary to its experimentalism. If there
is an expectation of the play to gather up all its layers in a forceful gesture
of affirmative statement, this strikes me as something that the very power of
the play renders futile. The moments when the dynamism of the action
onstage is most magnetic are also times when the audience becomes not so
much absorbed by what is being *said* by the action as it is absorbed into the
acting of the *saying.*

In *Playing Madam Mao* theatricality evokes the hyperreality of the city.
Insight comes from theatre's simulation of the nation in the very banality—
or to use the language of the young people in the survey, the un-uniqueness—
of Singaporean life. In the productions of *Invisibility* and *Under the Last
Dust* hyperreality is simulated inside the theatre by the actors and the audience. There is a distinct sense of an almost constant effort being directed
toward diffusion of the audience's concentration, done in such a way that
the audience's attention is not only not lost but becomes sustained in what
is at once a state of heightened percipience and distractedness. The suspension of the audience in such a state effects simulation of everyday processes

of perception, feeling, and thought in the hyperreality of city life. Theatre enacts theory about everyday experience of the hyperreal by drawing upon the ordinary in its sphere, summoning the most common scenarios and energies through simulation. The inversion and the smoothness of its operation bring recognition of theatricality's place outside of the physical space of theatre, that is, the relevance of theatricality to an understanding of modern urban experience—an experience oriented by technology. Johannes Birringer's comments on Laurie Anderson's performance of *America* come to mind:

> All the visual information in Anderson's performance, including the signs and the words of her body outlined and mirrored on the screen, moves around us as if we could not perceive anything, any place, except in passing, as we try to keep up with the transitional ready-made images from the postmodern media that "work us over completely," as Marshall McLuhan predicted . . . we are kept from knowing that this completeness would also be frighteningly banal, an environment of a luminescent emptiness.[21]

Theatre provides a self-reflexive medium for life-on-the-surface, experience made sense of in passing: Theatricality draws attention to itself as a process that narrative is based on rather than that which represents narrative. In the context of Singapore's national identity question, such foregrounding of process through narrative is significant. For the city-state the most crucial narrative consists of the search for national identity, a search peculiar to Singapore and peculiar in that it exists and becomes increasingly vocal as an anxiety. In narratives about being in the city, such as that found in the two theatrical productions, this anxiety informs narrative through the foregrounding of process and its incompleteness.

Under the Last Dust explores the bare essentials of human life via going through the motions of "very ordinary everyday activities." As Jean Ng, the director of the devised play, has said:

> We look at three of the most basic things that all human beings do from time immemorial—shitting, eating and sleeping—so they do a lot of that throughout the play. . . . [But the] play isn't about shitting, eating and sleeping; it's using some of these basic activities to explore human lives, human fears and relationships. . . . Through the everyday life activities, we try to see how human beings have departed from something very basic and yet there's a need to return to the basics—to be direct, honest and truthful.[22]

Inquiry into the essence of life is played out through actions found in the ephemeral and familiar Singaporean everyday. In the play, fragments of narrative are in constant flux, episodes kinetic inside themselves and suspended alongside each other with moments of intersection or none at all. Narrative does not form from accumulated layers of related knowledge and experience; nor is significance created for the fleeting moment through a naming as history.[23] Narrative is pieced in passing, reflecting the way that urban city-life makes sense as *erlebnis* rather than *erfahrung*. The terms come from Walter Benjamin, who was concerned with the ways in which technological modernity has radically transformed the everyday processes by which we make sense of things. When he speaks of "experience" Benjamin could be referring to two different things. On the one hand, there is *erfahrung*, life-experience, an integrated stock of experience built up through the individual's assimilation of sensations, information, and events. On the other, there is *erlebnis*: immediate, living experience consisting of sensations, or in a more basic sense, a series of atomized, disconnected moments that need not be related to each other in any way and do not become integrated into the corpus of *erfahrung*.[24] The atrophy of experience in modernity can be understood as the prevalence of *erlebnis* over *erfahrung*: life on the surface over life as "a matter of tradition."[25] Experience becomes "less the product of facts firmly anchored in memory [*erfahrung*] than of a convergence in memory of accumulated and frequently unconscious data [*erlebnis*]."[26] *Erlebnis* entails coping with fleeting, superficial impressions whereas *erfahrung* involves "gradual initiation into tradition."[27] *Erlebnis* can only be registered in passing, and the remembrance of experience as such takes the form of fragmentary, unanchored moments. The process that relates *erfahrung* and memory moves at a slower pace and with greater coherence, integrating new experiences organically, deepening and enriching the space of memory.[28] The primacy of *erlebnis* guarantees the demise of tradition and likewise the obsolescence of traditional configurations of history. In Singapore the question of identity through history persists because the primacy of *erlebnis*, though irrevocable, remains undiscovered, unacknowledged.

A framework for identifying the impact of the theatrical productions *Invisibility* and *Under the Last Dust* can be found through Benjamin's reflections on the aptness of Bertolt Brecht's epic theatre for the mass audience of industrial and postindustrial times. For Benjamin, concern with everyday perception in the technological age was part of a greater inquiry into the fate of art. Benjamin's study of Brecht shows that he considered the relation between everyday perception and response to art in the sphere of theatre. He was interested in how Brecht harnessed the energies of *erlebnis* in the audience, making theatre effectively sociopolitical.[29] Brecht's works on the stage relate effectively to their audience because the dramatist possessed a suitable understanding of their capacity for engagement:

> Epic theatre appeals to an interest group who "do not think without reason." Brecht does not lose sight of the masses, whose limited practice of thinking is probably described by this phrase.[30]

Brecht makes his audience "relaxed" by presenting drama in ways that will not alienate the audience. Epic theatre takes the conditioning of *erlebnis* into serious consideration. Significantly, Benjamin likens the appeal of its most distinctive feature to the effect of seeing images projected from reels of strips joined together in film:

> Epic theatre proceeds by fits and starts, in a manner comparable to the images on a film strip. Its basic form is that of the forceful impact on one another of separate, sharply distinct situations in the play [known as *verfremdung*, "interruptions"].[31]

Shock effects in film and theatre assault the senses of the spectator such that he or she is compelled to engage with what is shown before him or her through distraction. Benjamin observes that in the modern city "technology has subjected the human sensorium to a complex kind of training," recognizing that there has been an unprecedented transformation of the human frame in the face of all that it has to handle as part of its everyday urban existence.[32] From the use of the telephone and the camera Benjamin infers that in modern everyday life there are countless occurrences of shock that are initiated, sustained, and absorbed by the human subject whose "one abrupt movement of the hand triggers a process of many steps."[33] Mechanization brings convenience but it also produces a conditioning to shock. Benjamin gives the example of traffic on the street. Motor vehicles and crowds move, sometimes in opposite directions, at the command of electric traffic signals; man and machine are regulated by currents of electricity. Benjamin writes:

> Moving through this traffic involves the individual in a series of shocks and collisions. At dangerous intersections, nervous impulses flow through him in rapid succession, like the energy from a battery.[34]

The human body is powered with adrenalin likened to electric energy from a battery. This analogy is significant for it implies the body's simulation of motorized electronic operations. A field of inquiry that emerged in the late nineteenth century, the body's "fragmentation and augmentation . . . in relation to technology," continues to fascinate scientists and writers alike.[35] Benjamin is singular however in the direction he takes with his insight about the training of machine-like reflexes in city people. Noting the readiness of the consciousness to register shocks for everyday survival in the modern city, Benjamin highlights the concomitant emergence of an appetite for shock in areas of recreation and art; this "new and urgent need for stimuli," he contends, is satisfied by film where "perception in the form of shocks was established as a formal principle."[36]

The satisfaction of audience appetite for shock is witnessed in *Under the Last Dust* and *Invisibility*. A different understanding of absorption underpins the productions. This is most conspicuous in the way the focusing of the audience's attention is not sought after so much as its diffusion. The presentation of material onstage is devised such that the audience's sense of how it all comes together as a narrative or a web of interrelated narratives can be likened to a constantly interrupted conversation with discrete items of information entering into the frame almost every moment, items that do not so much integrate into the material already present as tag onto these without any sense of their relevance or relation being necessarily clear or present. Customary features and habitual actions of everyday life such as eating, dressing, and waking up to alarm clocks are explored through several short mime pieces in *Under the Last Dust*. The production calls on the audience to follow its journey with their own everyday modes of perception, but it does so in a way that suggests that it has not only such modes as they have been conditioned by city-life in the streets in mind; there is also consideration of the daily influence of media like television and film. The production requires its audience to make sense of where it is headed in a way that is somewhat similar to the viewing of several short films edited and spliced. It may also be compared to the watching of television in the sense that its structure evokes what is familiar and, for those who watch television regularly, habitual in that kind of viewing experience. *Under the Last Dust* is a non–text based work, and its action is played out through a sequence of short narrative pieces and choreographed passages in between these involving either one character or the entire cast. There is a discernible resemblance to the presentation of material on television: first in the aspect of programs broken up by segments of commercials; second in the absence of pauses between images.

In *Under the Last Dust* and *Invisibility*, the transience of *erlebnis*—its effect of shock and the sense that it makes in passing—is arrested as parts of fragments of dramatic action. Theatre seems charged by the hyperactivity of the city as it makes the city's energies—in streets, in shopping malls, in homes with telephone lines, television sets, and Internet access, and in classrooms with multimedia facilities—visible and felt within its domain. The city's "life on the surface" is reflected through intervals connected as surfaces rather than as links in a random series. By attendance alone the audience would have been present in the theatre in much the same way as they carry on their lives of "hurried contemporaneity."[37]

The primacy of *erlebnis* in Singaporean life is not only represented onstage but also evoked through audience energies. The Drama Box production of *Invisibility* was situated on the rooftop of the Chang Clan Association building in Geylang, Singapore's red-light district. A cast of four actors played out vignettes of city life in all the available spaces on that rooftop where the audience was also seated. Their movements made it necessary for the audience, positioned on straw mats and makeshift seats of bricks, to change their sitting positions constantly. Audience attention was also deflected sporadically by the flashing of photographic and advertising images from an overhead projector onto a wall. What resulted from all this was the suspension of the audience in a state of constant restlessness and distraction. There was a sense of connection and disconnection from all that was going on around oneself. When the play refers to the many distractions of modern city life, there is a certain irony in that the audience on the exposed rooftop was itself subjected to the distraction of typical street noise and sounds of Chinese opera from the neighbouring temple during the entire production. In scene 4, the Woman complains to the Man:

> Woman: . . . Everyday if not Orchard Road, then Marina Square. Too many people, too crowded. Not in the mood to go there and squeeze with the crowds.
>
> Man: Ya, it's very crowded, very noisy. Everywhere also got music.
>
> Woman: Then you forget everything—people's clothes, faces, smells. . . .[38]

As theatre, the Drama Box production constantly disrupted the concentration of its audience; as drama, the play *Invisibility* presents various exchanges between individuals through fragments that do not fit together as a coherent narrative. In the Drama Box production, the audience's sense of connection and disconnection from all that was going on around them seems particularly in tune with the play's concern with the loneliness of urbanites.[39] The play features a cast of eight characters whose names reflect their anonymity: A, B, C, D (the last three letters form an ensemble playing various roles), Man, Woman, Hermit Master, Pugilist. Aside from the Prologue and the Epilogue, there are eleven scenes. These do not form a linear plot or narrative. The scenes show encounters between the characters, always presented as random, chance occurrences. The anonymity of the characters suggests the faceless familiarity of individuals who know each other by literary stereotype or professional relation, such as the Hermit Master and the Pugilist in scene 7, recognizable figures from popular twentieth century Chinese serial fiction, and the exchange between B, C, and D (who rotate playing a barber) and A (who plays the customer who has come for his regular haircut). The characters could be strangers to each other, like the Man and the Woman in scene 4 or the two men in a public toilet in scene 6. All the scenes are not linked to each other in any way; in fact, they seem deliberately disconnected. There is also inconsistency in the reappearance of characters throughout the play.

In the year the play was first performed, Kuo Pao Kun, one of Singapore's most respected theatre practitioners, was asked in an interview if it is possible for theatre to become popular again in spite of the competition from other forms of mass media and if theatre can become a dynamic force of social expression. In his reply he alluded to a particular role that theatre can play as a place for the gathering of people. He noted that in a capitalist economy there is an ever-increasing sense of apartness between persons as "collective groupings and identities," which are broken down for the same reason "the breaking up of the large family becomes a necessity": "because you want to maximize the mobility of labour agents as individuals" for the well being of "this capitalist economy."[40] In a society with a significant proportion of highly educated people who lead lives dominated by the needs of production above all else, there are rising levels of "frustration" and "loneliness," problems of "management of personal relationships with people."[41] The situation is also characterized by a new and evolving sense of what is entailed in being part of a collective—to date the most significant factor is surely the emergence of new possibilities for exposure and the making of connections with other persons whom one may not have met in person through the Internet.

What has been quoted so far hardly paints a new picture. That which is radical in Kuo Pao Kun's response resides in his thoughts on theatre's role given the new social reality:

> [W]ith the fall of religion, the removal of religion from the realms of state and cultural activities, what do you have? Mainly the arts. As an expression of frustration. As a device for communication with others. . . . The more crowded the cities are, the more lonely they become. People need to have physical contact with other people. And I see the performing arts, the *live* arts, as a growing need rather than a falling need, because of this modern mode of existence. This is even more true in the information age when people can work away from each other. . . . It's just that the only kind of performing arts that fulfills this function are the big musicals—they appeal to the masses, thereby serving as a medium for a huge interpersonal, physically interpersonal congregation. I call them aesthetic congregations. . . . If you see this as an innate need, then theatre cannot die, it can only get bigger. [emphasis mine][42]

In a sense, the new social reality is one where not only are the coordinates of collective identities changed, gone also are the "old" ways of conducting oneself as part of a community, the "old" ways of relating to others, of being interested in and being available for them.[43] The role theatre needs to play must show that it is not only alert to such change but that it is able to incorporate that recognition in its relationship with the audience. Kuo Pao Kun paints a particular picture: The space inside a theatre is envisaged as a place where people's "need to have physical contact with other people" can be satisfied. Seeing theatre as a way of satisfying such a need suggests that the audience is being perceived as persons who come together in anticipation of a certain good that can be attained through attendance and participation. The need for communication with others and the need for their companionship are met through the watching of a play with them, the sharing of an experience that is free from the pressures and strains of ordinary interpersonal relationships. Theatre performs a role as an actual space where people are physically placed together for something other than work; nor is this a place where they have to socialize with the other people around them in the ways they are obliged to with family, friends, colleagues, and acquaintances. Going to the theatre provides the audience with a sense of being part of a collective as a "huge interpersonal, physically interpersonal congregation" without exacting costs other than that of buying the ticket.

This makes a curious image: theatre as a sanctuary of sorts, functioning in a similar way to church or temple. The audience is a predominantly silent gathering of people who find a certain comfort in the very event of being gathered in such a fashion. To see theatre now as a place of "action" requires consideration of the dynamics of the audience as occupiers of this space in addition to the dramatic action onstage. Kuo Pao Kun's rhetoric casts relationships between people in an audience in the light of relationships between people in a congregation, and this seems to implicitly foreground the relationship between the people and that which awaits them inside a theatre.

Kuo Pao Kun's thoughts are shaped by the recognition that on the part of the arts community, there is the need "to re-adapt . . . to a different mode of social activity."[44] This comment is based on a view of postcolonial Singapore's transformation into a modern capitalist economy, a transformation that has wrought dramatic changes in the structure and ways of community on all levels. The mode of social activity that is most readily associated with Singaporeans is shopping, and speaking of shopping in Singapore brings Orchard Road to mind. In a study by Henry C. Yeung and Victor Savage, it is noted that "apart from the home, Orchard Road is the second place in Singapore that most of the respondents to a survey of Singaporeans have the most vivid impressions of."[45] The implication, in an interesting parallel to the case at home where the family gives the individual his or her first sense of relation to a collective, is that something similar may result from the individual's experiences of being part of a crowd in the Orchard Road area. Incidentally, Kuo Pao Kun's term for the audience, "aesthetic congregations," appears in Yeung and Savage's description of Orchard Road as a place for "the congregation of the trendy, evident in Singaporeans who dress up in their most fashionable clothes, speak English, smoke American-branded cigarettes, listen to the latest pop music, and follow the latest dance crazes on the streets."[46] The crowd is a collective, on the streets and in the stalls of a theatre, but in both guises it is energized by the vibe and the will to survive of city life. The rhythm of people in the streets can be said to flow "naturally" in the sense that it comes from their instinctively honed responses to the urban environment. To detect a similar kind of rhythm in the space of communication between a play and its audience suggests that the dynamism of the collective in the shopping zone or street has been generated inside the theatre.

Looking at the question of how the way one moves as part of a collective in the streets might be simulated in the totally different physical environment of a theatre, it seems pertinent to begin with some observations on the crowd seen as a collective in both general and Singaporean contexts. Since the nineteenth century such collectives have come under scrutiny. Benjamin was not the first to be fascinated by the peculiar dynamism of a crowd on the streets. Here he speaks of its movements as if they were made by one whole living thing:

> Streets are the dwelling place of the collective. The collective is an eternally wakeful, eternally agitated being that—in the space between the building fronts—lives, experiences, understands, and invents as much as individuals do within the privacy of their own four walls.[47]

The above description bears a certain resonance in the Singaporean context of the Orchard Road area. Apart from days when festivals and activities that invite participation from people are staged in the area, there is generally a latent sense of excitement about the place that distinguishes it as the " 'main street' of the nation."[48] The following description suggests that the energies of an Orchard Road crowd are perceptible as a rhythm of their persons as a collective. It is also important to see the connection between this rhythm and a buzz about the place and its seemingly endless offerings and outlets of things to do and see, something that seems to emanate from the shops and streets themselves:

> Rhythm, defined here as the movement and pattern of people and traffic in the landscape, is another integral part in the character of Orchardscape . . . a landscape of perpetual movement, liveliness, and dynamism, both day and night. This rhythm is further facilitated by the lively diversity of activities and shops that allow people a wide variety of choices to shop, eat, window-shop, walk, browse, or just hang-around.[49]

How is the pace at which one moves and that at which one sees new things related? It can be said that a certain habit develops from walking, and seeing and hearing new things all the time without pause, and being at once acutely aware of the surroundings while not actually registering anything. There is absorption, but it needs to be distinguished from the kind that comes from concentration, because here I am thinking of absorption as an outcome of a primary state of distraction. The condition is described by Benjamin:

> A man who concentrates before a work of art is absorbed by it. . . . In contrast, the distracted mass absorbs the work of art. This is most obvious with regard to buildings. . . . Buildings are appropriated in a twofold manner: by use and by perception—or rather, by touch and sight. Such appropriation cannot be understood in terms of the attentive concentration of a tourist before a famous building.[50]

The parallel drawn between people's absorption of a work of art (as opposed to their absorption by it) and their everyday familiarity with a building is significant, because it foregrounds the fact that experience of a work of art has in modern times become as available and, in certain ways, as fundamental to everyday life as the experience of living and being in buildings. The recognition that such a leveling has taken place is still uncommon. It underlies Kuo Pao Kun's claim that the "live arts" can perform a vitally important social role in modern Singapore, for his thoughts revolve around a conception of the space inside a theatre as a place of transient inhabitation. It's transient because the relationship between audience and space inside the theatre lasts only as long as the show they have come to see; it's inhabitation because he draws attention to the aspect of the theatre as a space that holds and keeps the audience physically together, housing them as it were. *Under the Last Dust* and *Invisibility* are accommodated by their audiences in the sense that their audiences absorbed them through being at home with the mode of distraction.

Ruptured dramatic narratives and a multimedia apparatus can produce theatrical works that relate to the spectator through distraction. The appetite for shock is manifest in the new ways of presenting narrative, the new ways of telling something. It is also apparent in the way the audience is called upon to respond to the uneven textures in the form and content of the production through their habitual alertness and reflexes to shock effects. More importantly, there is the recognition that making sense of things through distraction is the norm in everyday perception. Inside a theatre, within a space clearly set apart from concrete reality, the recognition comes—the sense that for the audience the distracted mode of perception is at once unexpected and familiar. The distraction of the audience is generated by its purposefulness as it seeks to arrive at a whole picture by assembling as best as it can the seemingly discrete and unrelated parts of a play. Distraction is spread furthermore by the production's juxtaposition of video or transparency projected images that bear little or no apparent relation to the acting that goes on concurrently onstage. Constructive distraction is crucial to the audience's capacity for making sense of what they see before them, just as it is essential in the keeping of one's balance in everyday city life where one has to cope with the incessant and potentially overwhelming supply of external stimuli. This is the narrative of everyday life in the city, a narrative of *erlebnis*. It is also diachronically present in the reign of speed over history as historical presences in the city are reworked or removed to maintain the pace of change and to adapt the city to its latest self-portrait on the drawing board. It perpetuates the search for identity in Singapore that will not cease, at least not until its self-reflections—as city-state, nation, postcolonial, postmodern, prototype—register its essence of *erlebnis*. Recognizing the theatricality of the city is a beginning.

NOTES

1. Guy Debord, *The Society of the Spectacle,* trans. Donald Nicholson-Smith (New York: Zone Books, 1994), §14. First published as *Société du spectacle* in 1967.
2. Le Corbusier, *Urbanisme* (1925), cited in Geoffrey Broadbent, *Emerging Concepts in Urban Space Design* (London: E&FN Spon, 1990), 131.
3. Tim Armstrong, *Modernism, Technology and the Body: A Cultural Study* (Cambridge: Cambridge University Press, 1998), 187.
4. Debord, *Society,* §10.
5. Lau Siew Mei, *Playing Madam Mao* (Australia: Brandl & Schlesinger, 2000), 153.
6. Debord, *Society,* §11.
7. Ibid., §12.
8. Lau, *Playing Madam Mao,* 23.
9. See Rem Koolhaas, "Singapore Songlines: Portrait of a Potemkin Metropolis . . . or Thirty Years of Tabula Rasa," in *The City Cultures Reader,* ed. Malcolm Miles, Tim Hall, and Iain Borden (London and New York: Rouledge, 2000), 22–25: "As a manifesto of the quantitative, Singapore reveals a cruel contradiction: huge increases in matter, the overall effect increasingly unreal. The sinister quality of the windows—black glass, sometimes purple—creates, as in a model-railroad landscape, an additional degree of abstraction that makes it impossible to guess whether the buildings are empty or teeming with transplanted Confucian life" (22).
10. Lau, *Playing Madam Mao,* 189.
11 Ibid., 153.
12. Koolhaas, "Singapore Songlines," 22.
13. Lau, *Playing Madam Mao,* 110–11.
14. Ibid., 197.
15. *The Straits Times,* 20 February 2000.
16. Koolhaas, "Singapore Songlines," 23.
17. Ibid., 24.
18. *The Straits Times,* 31 March 2001.
19. An example of the unconventional approach can be found in Goh Chee Seng, *Bleeps, Tones, and Frequencies: Electronic Music, Identity and Postmodernity* (Honours Thesis, Sociology, National University of Singapore, 1998–1999) where postmodernity in Singaporean national identity is addressed through a study of youth culture in clubbing and techno music.
20. *Business Times,* 21 October 2000.
21. Johannes Birringer, *Theatre, Theory, Postmodernism* (Bloomington: Indiana University Press, 1991), 30.
22. Parvathi Nayar "A Tantalising Journey that Stops Short," *Business Times Singapore,* 21 October 2000.
23. See Goh Chee Seng, *Bleeps, Tones,* 29. Referring to club music, Goh makes a similar observation: "The song is dead, replaced by 'the decentred, unresolved and infinite house track', any attempt at narrative is superceded and a replacement of 'characterization, motivation by sensational effects.' "

24. Walter Benjamin, "Some Motifs in Baudelaire," in *Charles Baudelaire: A Lyric Poet in the Era of High Capitalism,* trans. by Harry Zohn (London and New York: Verso, 1992), 117. First published as *Charles Baudelaire, Ein Lyriker im Zeitalter des Hochkapitalismus* in 1969.
25. Ibid., 110.
26. Ibid.
27. See Hilde Heynen, *Architecture and Modernity: A Critique* (Cambridge, Mass.: MIT Press, 1999), 98.
28. Ibid., 98–99.
29. Walter Benjamin, "What is Epic Theatre?" in *Illuminations,* ed. Hannah Arendt, trans. Harry Zohn (London: Fontana/Collins, 1982). Selection of essays taken from the German *Schriften,* first published in 1955. See page 150.
30. Ibid., 152.
31. Ibid., 21.
32. Benjamin, "Some Motifs," 132.
33. Ibid., 131.
34. Ibid., 132
35. Armstrong, *Modernism,* 3.
36. Benjamin, "Some Motifs," 132.
37. Walter Benjamin, *The Arcades Project,* trans. Howard Eiland and Kevin McLaughlin (Cambridge, Mass. and London: The Belknap Press of Harvard University Press, 1999), 221.
38. For the original Chinese text, see *Invisibility by Quah Sy Ren,* trans. Sim Pern Yiau (Singapore: Ethos Books, 2000), 37. The translation used here is my own.
39. See my review of the production in *The Straits Times,* 15 September 2000.
40. See "Between Two Worlds: A Conversation with Kuo Pao Kun," in *Nine Lives: 10 Years of Singapore Theatre 1987–1997* (Singapore: The Necessary Stage, n.d.), 136.
41. Ibid.
42. Ibid., 136–37.
43. "Collective idling" is an example. See Chua Beng Huat, *Political Legitimacy and Housing: Stakeholding in Singapore* (London and New York: Routledge, 1997), 157–60.
44. *Between Two Worlds,* 137.
45. See Henry W. C. Yeung and Victor Savage, "The Singaporean Image of Orchardscape," in *Portraits of Places: History, Community and Identity in Singapore,* ed. Brenda S. A. Yeoh and Lily Kong (Singapore: Times Editions, 1995), 85.
46. Ibid., 74.
47. *The Benjamin Arcades Project,* 879.
48. Yeung and Savage, "Singaporean Image," 85.
49. Ibid., 74.
50. Walter Benjamin, "The Work of Art in the Age of Mechanical Reproduction," in *Illuminations,* ed. Hannah Arendt, trans. Harry Zohn (London: Fontana/Collins, 1982), 232–33.

The corporeal costs enabling globally mobile labor and investment cannot be underestimated—a point registered by Pile, who takes a unique direction by counting up the costs and profits in empire and business by attending to the alienness and familiarity of vampires in a range of different tales and relations to empires. Physical dislocations and the desire of acquisition are common enough features in the interrelations within a world solidly aimed at better economic ends; but in the light of the vampiric emigrant's search for new blood, a strangeness emerges from these familiar things. The global city's cosmopolitanism grants acceptance to the vampire as one of the many strangers who become citizens through their common distinction of otherness. The vampire's body fleshes out the empirial: Its circulation of blood from myriad nationalities provides something of an analogy for global circulations of "bodies, information, goods, money, and ideas," availing unexpected dimensions in issues raised by the Derderian and Jackson articles. Through their ambiguous existence as "the living dead," vampires also reveal temporal disjunctions that the city embodies but elides. The vampire provides specific links between colonialism and globalization: Both involve the flow of peoples from one end of the world to another, giving rise to greater interactions and, in some cases, suppression of otherness. Pile draws attention to the often elided aspect of the physiological in academic discourse, using it to convey the bodily realities of transnational exchange behind representations and analyses. The global city's drive for gratification of insatiable appetites suggests another vampiric resemblance. The desire for blood that drives the vampire to kill and "turn" more bodies into the same kind of deformity as itself presents an analogy for the allure and potency of the global city, converting new arrivals, new seekers of opportunity and experience, to its own will.

13

Perpetual Returns: Vampires and the Ever-Colonized City

STEVE PILE

W hat does the vampire have to tell us about cities? In many ways, the vampire might appear to belong to no particular place—except perhaps a castle deep in Transylvania! However, I believe the vampire gives us a way to track the global and the colonial in city life. Vampires themselves, of course, require very little introduction—the blood-sucking fiends have been close to our hearts for a very long time, maybe as long as time itself. Myths surrounding vampires have taken many different forms, in many different places, in many different periods. I don't intend to review—or even synthesize—these myths into any coherent image of the vampire. It is probably the case that variations in the form of the vampire are more interesting. The figure of the vampire is shadowy, intangible; and the powers of the vampire are various. But we all know that they have sharp teeth and drink blood, and that they are immortal, if only to the extent that they are very hard to kill. In fact, vampires are very likely to return from the dead if they are not disposed of properly. For this reason, the vampire might also tell us something about "the perpetual" in city life: a figure that roams and hunts by night, but returns itself to its deathly resting place during the day, only to rise again as night falls. Our hero, the vampire, can wait and wait, letting the years fall by before it returns. Time and space are no longer linear and uniform, for the vampire defies our mortal embodied groundings.

I will approach the city through the vampire. I will follow the vampire to see where he or she goes. Tracking the vampire will allow us to see something of the city: the specificity of the global, the colonial, and the perpetual. This is not to tell all stories about vampires, nor to unfurl all stories about the globality, coloniality, and perpetuity of cities. Instead, I am searching for some strange alchemy in the lifeblood of cities, something to do with its money, its power, and its terrors. Vampires will tell us something about this. It may be that vampires have one further thing to teach us. For many, the vampire is a fiend enslaved to its hunger for (human) blood. They are all consumed and consuming. Terrifyingly, they can "turn" us all into versions of themselves by making us drink their blood. The vampire is the thing that killed us, but also the thing that gave us immortal life. There is, though, something very seductive about the vampire. They are beautiful, powerful, and they can live forever. For all their strangeness, they are also very familiar. Not simply an evil version of the human, but a super (natural) version. If there is something seductive about the vampire, some part of us that wishes to give in to the vampire—to be the vampire—then there will also have to be ways to live with the vampire.

Cities are full of strangers, familiar and unfamiliar, unknown and unremembered. In this sense, cities are the natural breeding ground of vampires. Ready to suck the life out of others, they find a ready stock of potential victims that no one will notice are missing. Maybe cities have something to teach vampires, too. Cities bring strangers into cities and mix them up. Rather than making of people a feeding ground for vampires, maybe cities can tame the vampire—and make the vampire appreciate the lives of others, or even take responsibility for its blood-sucking ways. This may not be the vampire's choice, and it will be up to cities to identify the vampire and to take the consequences of its actions seriously.

I use the figure of the vampire to speculate on the themes of this volume, to move in and out of certain ideas about cities and the ways in which various worlds—the global, the colonial, the perpetual—circulate and intermingle within cities. To do this, I will first look at the various worlds that circulate through London in Bram Stoker's well-known work *Dracula* (1897). Next, I will move the story on to New Orleans, this time using Anne Rice's *Interview with the Vampire,* both book (1976) and film (1994) versions. Finally, I will end up in Singapore, in the company of the *pontianak.* Through these stories, we will develop a sense of the different paths through which things arrive in, and leave, the city. This is an important point, as this book is concerned with thinking about the Southeast Asian city. Following the vampire shows that the linkages between cities in one place (say, the West) and another (say, Southeast Asia) are not always in broad daylight, nor do they exist in mortal times. Vampires jump times and spaces; indeed, they make vampiric times and spaces for themselves. From this perspective, colonization and globalization cease to be smooth processes, continuous in time and space, but become highly variable and particular. The vampire will tell us that colonization and globalization work through pathways and trajectories (as much as territories and periods), producing discontinuous, interrupted, delayed formations. Cities have to cope, then, with legacies and futures produced by their openness to the worlds beyond them—and the worlds within them.

Such a reading of cities leaves them with a difficult task, if they really want to rid themselves of the vampire. So we are going to follow the vampire from London, to New Orleans, to Singapore. But how did the vampire get to London?

VAMPIRES ON THE EDGE OF EMPIRE

Dracula was not the first vampire. There were vampires long before Bram Stoker wrote his classic tale. To give us some sense of context, it is worth laying out a little of the history of vampirism, because this will tell us something of blood and fear in late Victorian London, the very heart of Empire.[1] For Christopher Frayling, "the vampire is as old as the world."[2] He draws evidence for this from many myths, scattered across the ancient world, from Greece to Mongolia. Most cultures, he argues, have stories about blood draining or blood drinking, whether by gods, those in the service of gods, monsters, or humans. Frayling's interest is in tracking the vampire through literature. For this reason he begins his analysis with the relationship between Lord Byron and Dr. John Polidori, author of the seminal tale *The Vampyre* (1819). Nevertheless, Frayling's scouring of the various "authorities" on vampirism throws up evidence of the multiform geographies of vampires. This is what interests me. So let us start, instead, with Frayling's discussion of the vampire epidemics that swept across Eastern Europe in late seventeenth and eighteenth centuries. In this period, vast swathes of Eastern Europe had learnt to become terrified of vampires, not simply as a story, but as a "living" fact.

Frayling states that "these epidemics had occurred in Istria (1672), East Prussia (1710 and 1721), Hungary (1725–30), Austrian Serbia (1725–32), East Prussia (1750), Silesia, Wallachia (1756) and Russia (1771)." Cases of vampires included "Giure Grando (Khring, Istria), Peter Plogojowitz (Kisilova, Serbia), Arnold Paole (Medvegia, near Belgrade) and the vampires of Olmutz (Silesia)."[3] Laurence Rickels is equally sure that vampires (really) have been among us for centuries. He cites the notorious late seventeenth century case of the Countess Elizabeth Báthory, who would suck the blood of consenting adults whom she also killed.[4] Fears over vampirism led to legal, medical, and military investigations. Rickels found that in the fifteen years after 1728, over forty treatises on vampirism were published.[5] If, indeed, there was doubt over the existence of vampires among the intellectual elite, there was in fact good evidence that vampires existed. Thus, both Frayling and Rickels turn to the account provided by Dom Augustin Calmet of his investigation into vampire epidemics.[6] Calmet's treatise gathered together a variety of reports on vampires, including "formal reports, newspaper articles, eyewitness accounts and critical pieces."[7] According to Frayling, the book became an instant bestseller.

The vampire tales in Calmet's anthology took various forms. One story, from a village outside Olmutz, told of a spectre that attacked animals and cows. Another, from a village called Blow, near the town of Kadam in Bohemia, spoke of a shepherd who was seen some time after his death and who had failed to die some eight days later. The peasants had dug up the body of the shepherd and fixed it to the ground with a stake. The shepherd, at that point, began to deride the peasants for making him suffer in this way. The following night, the shepherd rose again, alarming several peasants, and strangling others. This time the "corpse" was delivered to an executioner. Despite his cries, the dead shepherd was staked several times through the heart and vermilion blood flowed from his body. Calmet reported that in Silesia and Moravia it was common practice to wait for six or seven weeks before burying certain "suspicious" bodies. The authorities would check to see if the limbs remained supple and pliable, whether the blood was fluid and the flesh uncorrupted. Those bodies that did not "die" would be burnt. Sometimes, even this would not work and, as a result, the villagers would be in a great deal of trouble (the nature of which Calmet does not specify, nor does he say how the vampire was ultimately dealt with).

Calmet also tells of Peter Plogojowitz who appeared to the inhabitants of the village of Kisilova in Hungary. Despite having been buried some ten weeks earlier, he managed to strangle nine people in an eight-day reign of terror. As a result of a positive identification by Plogojowitz's widow, the villagers decided that they would disinter the man's body and burn it. To do this, they needed a court order from the emperor's officer and the curé in the region. The officer and the curé decided to appease the villagers by exhuming the body. On investigation, according to Calmet, they found that Peter Plogojowitz's body

> exhaled no bad smell; that he looked as when alive, except the tip of the nose; that his hair and beard had grown, and instead of his nails which had fallen off, new ones had come; that under his cuticle, which appeared whitish, there was a new skin, which looked healthy, and of a natural colour; his feet and hands were whole as could be desired in a living man. They remarked also in his mouth some fresh blood, which these people believed that this vampire had sucked from the men whose death he had occasioned.[8]

Calmet continued with the story. The emperor's officer and the curé concurred with the villagers and they thrust a stake into the breast of the body. At this point, large quantities of crimson blood spurted from the wound and from the corpse's nose and mouth. The body was then placed on a funeral pyre and burnt.

Vampires, then, have been around for some time, at least since the time of myths and legends (in which, of course, we still live). Vampires similarly have been a popular subject for writers and poets. This list of those attracted to the figure of the vampire is impressive, both before and after Bram Stoker's classic tale.[9] The vampire might have always been with us, but Stoker's tale will show us exactly how the vampire lurks in nightmare visions of the city. More than this, we can begin to discern how an entire age—an age we now call global and, less often, postcolonial—might better be thought of as vampiric. Let us turn our attention, now, to Dracula and his geographies.

For the time being, we can be settled in the idea that vampires have occupied the edges of European geographical imaginations: They subsist and persist on the fringes of empire, at the borderlands between European and "other" empires. Vampires lie in the less controlled parts of empire: in Serbia, in Wallachia, in the spaces between Christianity and Islam. As I have indicated, vampire plagues threatened to sweep into central European areas from the edges of empire, but drastic action on behalf of seemingly hysterical villagers prevented such incursions. Peasant actions were perfectly capable of dealing with peasant vampires, who stayed close to home and killed those close to them. These premodern vampires could spread only by "turning" those close to them. If you could create a firewall, then it would be possible to stop the vampire plague leaping space (and time). However, Dracula was about to make his own leap in space and time, from feudal warlord grounded in his castle, to . . . well, we shall see.

TO LONDON: THE BEATING HEART OF EMPIRE

Much has been made of Stoker's background research into the history and geography of Transylvania and Vlad the Impaler (also known as Vlad Dracula, Voïvode of Wallachia). Bram Stoker's notes show that he used a variety of sources, including William Wilkinson's *Account of the Principalities of Wallachia and Moldavia* (1820), Charles Boner's *Transylvania: Its Products and Its People* (1865), which contained a pull-out map of Transylvania by E. A. Bielz, Baedeker's *Southern Germany and Austria, Including Hungary and Transylvania* (1880), and Emily and Dorothea Gerard's *Transylvanian Superstitions* (1885). Dracula is, thereby, set against solid research undertaken in the British Museum and Whitby Public Library. From this evidence, Stoker is able to produce seemingly authentic first-person accounts of the world. Thus, Jonathan Harker, on his journey to Dracula's castle, records the "picturesque" sights:

> All day long we seemed to dawdle through a country which was full of
> beauty of every kind. Sometimes we saw little towns or castles on the top of
> steep hills. . . . At every station there were groups of people, sometimes
> crowds, and in all sorts of attire. Some of them were just like the peasants at

home or those I saw coming through France and Germany, with short
jackets and round hats and homemade trousers; but others were very
picturesque. The women looked pretty, except when you got near them. . . .
The strangest figures we saw were the Slovaks, who are more barbarian than
the rest, with their big cowboy hats, great baggy white trousers, white linen
shirts, and enormous heavy leather belts, nearly a foot wide, all studded over
with brass nails.[10]

Stoker distils and, for his purposes, distorts the best of what we would now
call Orientalist knowledge of the region and its peoples: A colonial geographical imagination underpins *Dracula*. In many ways, we can see how
Stoker exoticizes and romanticizes Transylvania. In so doing, he makes it
different enough (from England, the self-appointed "civilized" world) to
make the existence of Dracula—the vampire—plausible enough, or at least
undeniable enough. (It is significant that Dracula's "evil" nature does not
remain uncertain for long, a point to which I will return.) Across this landscape, however, the more significant geographies refer to journeys, to geographies of communication, and to "places of rest." To begin with, the book
is structured by several long journeys: the journey Jonathan Harker makes
to Dracula, Dracula's journey to London, and the pursuit of Dracula as he
flees from London to his castle. In these journeys, however, we can see that
the "distance" between Transylvania had been collapsed in various ways:
legally, financially, physically.

The railways, as they had done elsewhere, had ensured that it was possible to travel far quicker and more reliably than before. The extension of
the railway network across Europe had effectively brought far-off places (far
off in both space and time) nearer to the heart of central European empires.
Of course, this shrinking of the world serves not only to put empire in closer
contact with its peripheries, but to bring the edges of empire in closer contact with the beating heart. It is the blood of empire that Dracula begins to
sense. He will use Jonathan Harker's legal skills to transfer himself from his
ancestral castle to the immense city of London. Dracula's time in feudal
society is nearly up: The peasants are on to the vampire and have a whole
variety of folk-weapons to use against him, from Christian symbols (holy
water, crucifixes) to "homeopathic" remedies (garlic) and precautionary measures (not going out at night). Through a variety of means, Dracula realized
that his life in London could be so much better. Harker reports Dracula as
saying that, from friends,

I have come to know your great England; and to know her is to love her.
I long to go through the crowded streets of your mighty London, to be in
the midst of the whirl and rush of humanity, to share its life, its change,
its death, and all that makes it what it is.[11]

Dracula wished to purchase a variety of properties in London. He would ship both himself and also the coffins he would require to "live" there. Harker only slowly realizes what is going on. Slowly, of course, because it is almost impossible to believe that this strange man, this stranger, is a vampire. More than this, of course, London's great crowds would act as the perfect cover for the vampire. In a city of strangers, Dracula would be just another man. Dracula himself puts it this way:

> Here I am noble; I am boyar; the common people know me, and I am master. But a stranger in a strange land, he is no one; men know him not—and to know not is to care not for. I am content if I am like the rest, so that no man stops if he sees me, or pause in his speaking if he hears my words.[12]

Despite his ability to turn himself into the form of a mist or of animals, Dracula is simply too easily recognized in his home-place. He is too easily contained in the surroundings of his castle. London, on the other hand, offers him new life . . . or, better, new death. The story, then, involves one of migration—of movement. Dracula succeeds in traveling to London (via Whitby), but he is tracked down by a band of vampire hunters, who chase him out and back to Transylvania, where they kill him. The vampire hunting gang famously include Mina Harker (née Murray), Jonathan Harker, Dr. Jack Seward, Quincey Morris, Arthur Holmwood (later Lord Godalming), and Dr. Abraham Van Helsing. In fact, these characters are continually moving around, so Dracula's is not the only journey of note. In particular, we see Van Helsing moving large distances, from Whitby to Amsterdam and back again.

Stoker's noted obsession with railway timetables and his deliberate use of dated records means that the novel is evidence of precisely the kinds of circulations that were becoming possible in late Victorian England at the height of empire. It is easy to say, of course, that this involved people, goods, money, and information.[13] It is also true that empire involved the movement of blood.[14] Clearly, Dracula already had a varied diet of blood available to him in Transylvania, but now he could feast among strangers in a very strange place, London. In the first instance, Dracula feeds on Lucy Westerna. However, in so doing he tastes the blood of five individuals, because Van Helsing uses the very modern technology of blood transfusion to put good English, American, and Dutch blood into Lucy's veins. Despite the transfusions, Lucy dies (though, on becoming vampire, she has to be killed yet again).

The transmission of information is evident in the structure of Stoker's novel: The tale is told through scraps of various kinds of evidence. These are taken from diaries, letters, newspaper cuttings, a ship's log, memoranda, phonograph recordings, and telegrams. And, presumably, if there had been the technology to do it, we might even have seen the photographs that Jonathan Harker took! Clearly, some of these bits of information travel farther than others: Telegrams cover great distances in an instant. Presumably, if Stoker were writing today, there would be glimpses of e-mail, mobile phone text messages, faxes, and the like. The circulation of legal documents, money, and messages, of course shows that empire was an open and unbounded system, in which a vast array of circuits of people, information, goods, property, money, and *blood* were possible.

It is also through these fragmentary and transitory transactions that the vampire hunters are able to track down Dracula. They follow the paper trail, they ask workers where various items were taken (for instance, Dracula's coffins), and they investigate which houses had been purchased. In the end, the vampire detectives are able to completely uncover Dracula's vast dark network of properties and coffins, and they are able to save London from the vampire plague about to break out in its crowded and unprotected streets. In this, Dracula is surely a metaphor for all plagues, but more than this, he is also a metaphor for anxieties about the vast numbers of "strangers" who were tramping London's streets. This, then, is the lesson of Dracula for understanding the imperial city: The imperial city does not simply belong to the colonizer—in a very real way it belongs to both the colonized and, further, to the world. In fact, Dracula's own colonization might even be said to resemble Bram Stoker's move from the periphery of empire (Ireland) into the heart of empire. Indeed, Bram Stoker was hardly the only, nor the first, Irishman to settle in Britain.[15] The imperial city is, in many ways, the archetypal global city: open to the world, and what the world will bring with it.

Dracula attempts to colonize the city of the colonizers. This, of course, is the terrible fear. The global, colonial city is necessarily open to a world that might bite back—at its very heart. It is not that Dracula brings with him inferior blood, but rather that he is better at making use of blood than the English. As Dracula says,

> We Szkelys have a right to be proud, for in our veins flows the blood of many brave races who fought as the lion fights, for lordship. Here, in the whirlpool of European races. . . . till the people thought that the were-wolves themselves had come.[16]

Dracula is superior not because his blood is purer than that of the English, but because he contains so many brave bloods. The imperial city is, then, an anxious place: anxious about what it brings close to its heart, but anxious too that its lifeblood will be sucked dry, that it will become vulnerable to a world more ruthless, hungrier than itself.

For me, *Dracula* lends itself to a reading of the imperial city as a place of perpetual circulation—of people, of money, of anxieties, of blood, of evil.

This circulation is perpetual in the sense that it keeps coming back, rather than describing a smooth, even process of movement through places. The vampire—like money, like ideas—can lie still, dead, for long periods of time before becoming active once again. In this sense, the perpetual in city life is not necessarily something that is always there, but something that is always threatening to return. This sense of "the return" can also evoke something of the relationship between the city and the colony, because the settlement of strangers (anywhere) can produce anxieties: anxieties about blood. It is to this idea that we turn next.

IN NEW ORLEANS: OLD BLOOD AND THE NEW WORLD

In 1803, France sold Louisiana to the United States. France, still an empire in the making, sold territory to a nation in the making. Nevertheless, Louisiana still sits awkwardly in the union of states that makes the American nation. It is still tied, by imagination at least, to its French Creole past. Its ambivalent relationship to that past, and to the present, have fostered a sense of the uniqueness and queerness of the city of New Orleans. Our next vampire story, taken from the book and film *Interview with the Vampire,* spans this period. Of course, film and book have similarities, but we will learn different things about the city and blood from these versions of the vampire's own story. I will place emphasis on Neil Jordan's 1994 film version, but it will sometimes help to refer to Anne Rice's 1976 book also.

Both book and film supposedly relate the story of the vampire Louis, who is being interviewed in the present day (whether 1976 or 1994) by an anonymous young journalist. Louis begins his story with the time before becoming a vampire and then accounts for his subsequent life (as it were) after death. Though book and film differ on exactly the nature of Louis's death wish (or "undeath" wish), they both allow full expression to Louis's doomed and melancholic heart. The film is clearest on matters of history: Louis is 24 and the year is 1791, and he is about to be "turned" into a vampire. At this time, Louis is the wealthy master of a plantation outside of New Orleans. However, he is unable to come to terms with the death of loved ones and yearns for an end to his miserable life. At this point, he is attacked by a vampire, Lestat, who drains Louis's blood to the point of death. But Louis does not die, and (perhaps surprisingly) agrees to meet Lestat. They rendezvous in a cemetery and, with his consent, Lestat "turns" Louis.

From the book, we can surmise that the vampire cemetery is St. Louis cemetery No. 1 in New Orleans (Figure 13-1). This is located just north of the French Quarter, and at the end of the eighteenth century it was located just outside the city limits.[17] In fact, the cemetery had been relocated from St. Peter's street after a fire that had destroyed four-fifths of the city in 1788.[18] Like Bram Stoker, Anne Rice did her homework. More than this,

Figure 13-1

St. Louis cemetery No. 1, New Orleans.

Rice knew New Orleans, for the cemetery has a significant presence in the city.[19] This cemetery makes of New Orleans a city of the dead: In Rice's hands, the cemetery becomes a site—and New Orleans a city—of the undead.

Indeed, the city is an ideal hunting ground for vampires, for New Orleans in this period is simply full of the dying. Every year, yellow fever would kill its citizens, and every twenty years or so the plague would take several thousands of its people. In the summer heat, this city was also prone to fires. Dracula sought refuge in a city of strangers in which he was no stranger than anyone else. The vampires in New Orleans hide themselves in the familiarity of death: perfect camouflage. Even so, New Orleans in the late eighteenth and early nineteenth century was also a bustling cosmopolitan port city, similar to London. Louis describes it this way:

> There was no city in America like New Orleans. It was filled not only with the French and Spanish of all classes who had formed in part its peculiar aristocracy, but later with immigrants of all kinds, the Irish and the German in particular. Then there were not only the black slaves, yet unhomogenized and fantastical in their different tribal garb and manners, but the great growing class of the free people of color, those marvellous people of our mixed blood and that of the islands, who produced a magnificent and unique caste of craftsmen, artists, poets and renowned feminine beauty. And then there were the Indians, who covered the levee on summer days selling herbs and crafted wares. And drifting through all, through this medley of languages and colors, were the people of the port, the sailors of the ships, who came in great waves to spend their money in the cabarets, to buy for the night the beautiful women both dark and light, to dine on the best of Spanish and French cooking and drink the imported wines of the world.[20]

Louis continues,

> This was New Orleans, a magical and magnificent place to live. In which a vampire, richly dressed and gracefully walking through the pools of light of one gas lamp after another might attract no more notice in the evening than hundreds of other exotic creatures—if he attracted any at all, if anyone stopped to whisper behind a fan, "That man . . . how pale, how he gleams . . . how he moves. It's not natural!" A city in which a vampire might be gone before the words had even passed the lips. . . .[21]

Like London, New Orleans would provide the perfect hiding place for the vampire. The vampire could hide, as it were, in plain night: visible, present, but unnoticed among the vast circulating crowd. Louis, like Jonathan Harker, is also prone to the "picturesque" quality. However, from the vampire we learn that the imperial city is exotic, a kaleidoscope of languages and peoples. Lestat will tell us something else about the city—the lifeblood of the city. In the film version, the transition from colony to purchased state is not met with unreserved pleasure by the vampires. In the interview, speaking of the period just after 1812, Louis darkly intones,

> Years flew by like minutes, the city around us grew, sailboats gave way to steamships, disgorging an endless menu of magnificent strangers. A new world had sprung up around us and we were all Americans now.

In the film, Louis recalls a conversation with Lestat at the quayside, as passengers disembarked from the steamboat Natchez (still to be seen on the river):

> Lestat: "Filthy mad tide. Lord, what I wouldn't give for a drop of good old fashioned creole blood!"
> Louis: "Yankees are not to your taste?"
> Lestat: "Huh! Their democratic flavor doesn't suit my palate, Louis."

Two ideas are caught up in this dialogue; in part, both revel in the mixed-up meanings of the word "creole." In New Orleans, creole can simply refer to Louisiana's colonial period or to someone born in that period. In this sense, creole could be of any blood, or any mix of blood. However, more generally, creole means someone who is of mixed European and African descent. In this sense, Lestat ambiguously lays claim to both pure and mixed blood. By raising the issue of blood in this way, the word "creole" actually serves to purify the blood of New Orleans of its democracy. In both London and New Orleans, it is blood that is at stake in the vampire tales. There are clearly anxieties about blood: about its transference, about its mixing, about its democracy, about its circulation, about its force of life and death. These anxieties, however, turn out to be inconsistent, pointing worried fingers in often opposite directions, waving garlic and crucifixes at the innocent and the strange alike.

In *Dracula,* it is clear that the vampire is out of place and out of time: He is sent packing, back to his time and place. Modernity conquers its foe by its superior use of the information available to its agents, and by its superior craft—its use of technology. In *Interview with the Vampire,* the vampire is similarly out of place and out of time. Louis and a child vampire, Claudia, flee to Europe having (they think) killed Lestat. They begin a quest for others of their own kind. Louis and Claudia roam all over Europe, including Eastern Europe, but find only a vampire who is almost an animal, and they are forced to kill it. After years of searching, they end up in Paris—another heart of empire. Louis finds a degree of peace in Paris, because he believes the city to be in some way the mother of New Orleans. Paris, of course, is a stage for decadence and vampirism: Blood is well known to have flowed through its streets.

From the edges of empire, the vampire is now living wherever death cannot be completely accounted for, in the crowded streets of the burgeoning metropolis. More than this, vampires reflect the anxieties and desires of the city. Of course, we have heard of the vampire thirst for blood, insatiable like a wolf. We should also remind ourselves that vampires are sexual creatures, hypnotic and beautiful, graceful and seductive. In some ways, we can begin to discern that vampires are very much like the cities they have come to see as their hunting ground. Under the influence of great cities, the vampire has become urbane, sophisticated, cultured, excited by contact with strangers, reveling in its indulgent pleasures, and capable of great sadness. The vampire has made the modern city its home. So perhaps it is not surprising that even the archetypally modern city might have its vampires. More than this, there are cautionary tales here about living in the modern city, about the relationship between the age-old and the brand new. Let us visit a modern city and see.

STOPPING IN SINGAPORE: CAUTIONARY TALES OF BLOOD AND MONEY

There are ghosts everywhere in Singapore.[22] There are vampires too—vampires that commonly go under the Malay name of *pontianak*. I will not speak to the popularity of such stories.[23] Instead, I would like to focus on one particular *pontianak* story, because this seems to be emblematic of so many others. It appears in one of the many anthologies of horror stories, this one specifically telling vampire stories. These book series have titles like *Nightmares: True Ghost Stories, There Are Ghosts Everywhere in Singapore,* and *Ghosts of Singapore.* They include authored works, but many are anonymous, and some are (seemingly) sent in by readers of such collections (ghost-written?). In most of the anthologies, the stories are short, lasting a few pages or just a few paragraphs.

In fact, what is of interest is the sheer quantity of the tales. The relentless relating of often similar horror stories furnishes them with a kind of force. By sheer weight of numbers, readers are almost cowed into submission, forced to doubt their own doubt in the existence of these fiends. More than this, stories are often told from other places in the world, so we hear of vampires in California, ghosts in London, and so on. Other stories have no distinct location and could be set almost anywhere in the world. The overall effect is to enshroud the reader in the occult, a realm only partially perceptible to the living. Stories are told from a variety of perspectives, some in the voice of the victim, others from the perspective of witnesses; many tell of close shaves with the vampire, and sometimes of the experience of seeing someone close turn into a vampire. With so many different voices, it feels as if there is a crowd of witnesses. Of course, some voices are better at telling tales than others, but the sheer artlessness of the stories also adds to their plausibility or, better, the sense that they cannot all be simply smoke and mirrors.

Vampires—or, rather, *pontianaks*—appear in almost every collection and I will turn to some of these other stories later. First, however, let us look at the tale of the "Lone Woman."[24] As in many tales, the story begins with a man driving. He is on his way home late at night after work when he spots someone by the road:

> The woman wore a long red dress and was standing by herself. Had the thought of a lone woman standing by herself at that time of the night not made him think of how dangerous it was for the women in question, he would have driven straight on. But instead, he slowed down and decided to stop for her.[25]

Unexpectedly, the woman gets into the front seat without being asked. She smiles at him and off they set. The man begins to wonder why the woman had not been able to hail a taxi, as there were many around. She smiles. And she falls asleep:

> He could not help but look at her because she was so beautiful. She smiled in her sleep.[26]

He notices her black hair, her white skin, and her red lips. He is beginning to get distracted by his desire for her. It's about to get worse. He suddenly feels her hand on his thigh, but he decides not to move her hand in case he wakes her up. But the more the man looks at the woman, the more he finds something uncanny about her. At this point, he starts to remember:

> Stories about young women who were actually monsters, and preyed on men who worked outdoors late at night, were playing back and forth in his mind. They would seduce them and then they would kill the victims to feast on their blood.[27]

Using his rearview mirror, the man takes a closer look at the woman—and is alarmed to see that the woman has two razor-sharp teeth protruding from her mouth. In his fear, he begins to drive erratically and the woman begins to stir. She smiles, and holds his thigh more firmly and lapses back into sleep. Terrified, the man stops the car and jumps out. Bemused, the woman gets out also and walks to the other side of the road. The man looks around, but she is nowhere to be seen—she has disappeared. Relieved and still afraid, the man drives off and heads back for home. He drives and drives until he eventually reaches the spot where he picked up the woman. A shudder of fear runs down the man's back as he realizes that the woman is there again, waiting to be picked up by some other unsuspecting motorist.

The "lone woman" is sometimes in a white and sometimes a red dress, but she is always young and beautiful, and becomes more and more seductive the longer the man looks at her. She often falls asleep, but her dreams are not innocent: In fact, the movement of her body and the sounds she makes are clearly—to the victim—sexual, erotic. The man has to resist severe temptation and drop the vampire off, often at a cemetery or beneath an old tree. Occasionally, the vampire shows her true form, turning into an old monstrous woman and threatening to kill the man and drink his blood.

Vampire women do not just hunt by the roadside, however. They are to be found in apartment blocks, in carparks (an Orchard Road carpark attendant, sitting innocently in his kiosk, is attacked: Figure 13-2), in hospitals, and in "old places" such as cemeteries. *Pontianak* stories often associate the women with trees, where they "live." This is the traditional home for *pontianak* in Malay stories, perhaps as a result of the root system of the tree coming into contact with the (un)dead. These vampires clearly prey on men who lay themselves open for temptation: If he gives in to her seductions, he is a dead man. In some ways, we can take these tales to be cautionary—and even a set of rules and prohibitions. The man knows the stories about dangerous women, but he fails to remember these soon enough to save himself

Figure 13-2

Careful where you park.

from a close encounter of the vampire kind. Other tales seem to offer advice, like what to do if you find a loved one craving (your) blood, or if you meet a *pontianak*. What to do? Run—and don't look back!

Of course, we know that there are vampire women who prey on men. In *Dracula,* we learn this from Jonathan Harker's diary:

> In the moonlight opposite me were three young women, ladies by their dress and manner. I thought at the time that I must be dreaming when I saw them, for, though the moonlight was behind them, they threw no shadow on the floor. They came close to me and looked at me for some time and then whispered together. Two were dark, and had high aquiline noses, like the Count's. . . . The other was fair, as fair as can be. . . . All three had brilliant white teeth, that shone like pearls against the ruby voluptuous lips. There was something about them that made me uneasy, some longing and at the same time some deadly fear. I felt in my heart a wicked, burning desire that they would kiss me with those red lips.[28]

Fortunately, or unfortunately, for Harker, Count Dracula intervenes:

> How dare you touch him, any of you? How dare you cast eyes on him when I had forbidden it? Back, I tell you all! This man belongs to me![29]

Indeed, the men seem truly to belong to the vampire. Men in the shadowless shadow of the vampire are constantly on trial, constantly tempted by the seductions of the vampire—and these are almost innumerable: beautiful, erotic, aristocratic, immortal . . . need I go on? In fact, you might well have noticed a certain similarity in the eroticism of Dracula's ladies and the vampire women of Singapore and Malaysia. This is surely no accident. I find it entirely believable when Frayling, very much in passing, states that Stoker noted the existence of vampires in Malaysia.[30] In many ways, this completes a circuit of vampires. Not only have vampires moved from the edges of empire—Eastern Europe and the United States—to its beating heart, London and Paris, they have also traveled across the empire, from Malaysia to London. These journeys through the imperial city have not simply been about sucking the lifeblood out of the living; there have been seductions, too. Sharp white teeth and red, red lips, the vampire woman is as seductive as she is deadly. It would take a man of real courage and willpower to resist. In fact, our Singaporean motorist fares somewhat better than our English lawyer, for he would have succumbed had not Dracula claimed him for himself.

So, these vampire women can tell us something about the city, Singapore. To begin with, whatever the lesson, we can tell that desire and fear have moments when they sit side by side in the driving seat. The wise will have listened to the stories and be able to respond to the possibility that there is more to "it" than first meets the eye. We can also note that being modern and being postcolonial cannot necessarily exorcize the vampire. The city can knock down cemeteries and tear up trees, but vampires are harder to expel. With their deep connection to the earth, they can learn to make use of the infrastructure that the modern city throws up: its roads, cars, carparks, hospitals, apartment blocks, and so on. Fear is never quite so easily erased as a cemetery or orchard. Then, again, neither is desire. The vampire doesn't simply tell us of the pleasures of the flesh, of the innocence of sleep and the dream of being with these beautiful women, we are also in thrall to the vampire; though we know it is a fantasy and not even remotely desirable, there is a lingering desire to be the vampire.[31] In this, we might glimpse something of the city, of its vampiric soul. Perhaps now is a good time to think back over these stories, to think about the soul of an immortal: the city.

CITIES WITHOUT END: THE COLONIAL, THE GLOBAL, THE PERPETUAL

To recap, we have heard that vampire myths are long standing and cross-cultural. Through the tales of Peter Plogojowitz, Arnold Paole, Dracula, Louis, Lestat, and the never-named lone woman, we have glimpsed the variety of forms that vampires take—both real and unreal, dead and undead. We have assiduously tracked the vampire. He has spread out from Eastern Europe and threatened the very heart of empire. She has traveled far to disturb the erotic imagination in the heart of empire. We have tracked the vampire from plantation and through French imperial connections, from New Orleans to Paris, via Transylvania. We have followed the vampire on trains and on the seas, and from mouth to mouth. And we have followed the vampire from life to death to "unlife" to resurrection. And we have found the vampire to be ruthless, soulless, damned, but also beautiful, erotic, powerful, and immortal (almost). From these various stories, we can begin to discern something of cities—for, remember, they are the focus of this story. What does the vampire have to tell us about cities? Let us address this question in three parts: the colonial, the global, and the perpetual.

In our "emperial" (imperial–empirical) stories about vampires, we have visited a city at the height of its imperial powers, another at the turn of the tide between one empire (French) and another (American), and a city that, whatever empire meant, is now definitely after empire. The vampire, of course, tells us that this neat story is not particularly a neat one. To begin with, empires do not simply occupy territory and then simply expand their control over more and more territory. There are limits to these imperial and postimperial cities. London found its limits, puzzlingly, at the border between two other empires: one Austrian, one Turkish. New Orleans was sold by the French and was occupied by an imperial power that is also a postcolonial nation (having kicked out the British only a quarter of a century previously). New Orleans is the tide-mark of a French empire in retreat and of a postcolonial colonial American nation on the turn. Singapore, of course, has its own British imperial legacies, but it is also home to what we might call a deterritorialized Chinese empire, without a state but with influence and power.[32] If Singapore was born out of its anticolonial struggles, then it also lives with the paradox of not being able to become Malaysian yet living with the Malaysian. And perhaps this is one more message the *pontianak* carries. The vampire, then, tells us that histories of empire run through cities in discontinuous ways: rising, falling, and perhaps finding new life in undead ways. More than this, the vampire shows us that empires are not simply about territories "under control," but about the circulation of people, ideas, money, information, and the like. London, New Orleans, and Singapore are not in any sense closed off from the world. It is to this point we turn next.

If we think of our three cities, we can quickly see that they are open, almost without borders. The vampire shows that the world outside the city cannot only move in, it can also feast on the city. This is not, however, to say that any of these cities are simply global.[33] In fact, the opposite is true—only specific worlds overlap within any city. These worlds arrive from particular places, they mingle or are kept apart in very specific ways once they settle within any city, and these worlds circulate and move around in very specific ways, too. Think for example of Dracula, who moves in from Eastern Europe and can move about London freely precisely because he is as strange as anyone else. Even then, London was not only an English city. But nor was it, nor is it, simply global. This is to say that cities are made up of a variety of worlds, that they have multiple histories (imperial and otherwise). More than this, these stories show that the dominant understandings of what actually underlie the global or globalization might be missing the point. Thus, the vampire can tell us about anxieties over the mixing of blood from all over the world, and this might highlight the significance of the specific (other) worldly routes through which blood arrives in cities. If blood were to become the mark of the global, then for sure we would have to think of globalization somewhat differently: We would be thinking about AIDS/HIV and viruses, rather than Coca-Cola and Sony.

So I am arguing that cities are dense nodes in wider webs of bodies, information, goods, money, and ideas. This is not a new point in itself,[34] but I am suggesting an underside—an other-worldliness—to all these arrangements. I am suggesting that, for example, the vampire shows us that the idea of mixing blood was feared and desired *in a variety of ways*. Contemporary cities live with the legacies of these blood feuds and desires. That desire and fear go hand in hand is a classic psychoanalytic point, but vampire tales give us a way to specify and situate these ambivalent emotions as they express themselves in the whirl of city life. Moreover, these ambivalences can now be seen as being part and parcel of the supposedly "real" geographies that connect cities together. That is, there is an emotional life to the seemingly abstract and cold-blooded relationships that we have come to name as "globalization," "postcolonialism," and the like. The geographies of these emotionally charged linkages between cities require some mapping, of course. There are very specific geographies to be tracked down here, and they might not be best hunted during the cold light of day, for some will barely reflect anything and others will lurk in shadows. Following the vampire, I would argue, can reveal exactly how the city becomes global by showing what exactly arrives from afar and how it arrives, and what it does when it gets there. In this way, we might gain a further appreciation of how the blood gets sucked out of the living city through wide networks of exploitation.

And what else does the vampire tell us? That the idea of perpetuating cities has sharp teeth to it. To give perpetual and never-ending life to the city—to ensure the blood of the city flows forever—might have its price, a price marked in *our* blood. For the city may be just like the vampire: It might view the worlds it sees before it simply as its life-blood. The city's hunger for people might never be satiated. So we should be wary of the idea that cities must be made perpetual and indestructible, without antidote. And maybe we should begin to gather together the tools of the vampire hunter— not garlic and crucifixes, but information, however bizarre, of those stories where cities have bitten deep into our necks.

NOTES

1. See J. M. Jacobs, *Edge of Empire: Postcolonialism and the City* (London: Routledge, 1996).
2. See Christopher Frayling, "Lord Byron to Count Dracula," in *Vampyres: Lord Byron to Count Dracula,* ed. by Christopher Frayling (London: Faber and Faber, 1991), 4.
3. Ibid., 19.
4. See L. Rickels, *The Vampire Lectures* (Minneapolis: University of Minnesota Press, 1999), 15; Frayling, "Lord Byron," 69.
5. Rickels, 15.
6. See A. Calmet, extracts from "Treatise on the Vampires of Hungary and Surrounding Regions" (1746) in *Vampyres,* 92–103.
7. See Frayling, "Lord Byron," 92.
8. Ibid., 101.
9. Ibid., 42–62.
10. See Bram Stoker, *Dracula* (Harmondsworth: Penguin, 1897/1994), 11.
11. Ibid., 31.
12. Ibid.
13. On *Dracula* as an allegory of the circulation of capital, see Franco Moretti, "Dialectics of Fear," in *Signs Taken for Wonders: Essays in the Sociology of Literary Forms* (London: Verso, 1988); K. Gelder, *Reading the Vampire* (London: Routledge, 1994), 17–20; and Karl Marx, *Capital,* vol. 1 (Harmondsworth: Penguin, 1867/1976), chapter 10.
14. See L. White, *Speaking with Vampires: Rumor and History in Colonial History* (Berkeley: University of California Press, 2000).
15. For a "contemporary" account of this "reverse colonization," see F. Engels, *The Condition of the Working Class in England* (Harmondsworth: Penguin, 1845/1987).

16. Stoker, *Dracula,* 41.
17. See R. Florence, *Cities of the Dead: A Journey through St. Louis Cemetery #1, New Orleans, Louisiana* (Layfayette, La.: University of Southern Louisiana, The Center for Louisiana Studies, 1996).
18. Ibid., 5.
19. See J. Roach, *Cities of the Dead: Circum-Atlantic Performance* (New York: Columbia University Press, 1996).
20. Anne Rice, *Interview with the Vampire: Book I of the Vampire Chronicles* (New York, Ballantine, 1977, 44–45); film version directed by Neil Jordan (1994).
21. Ibid., 45–46.
22. See articles by Ban Kah Choon and Carole Faucher in *Beyond Description: Space Historicity Singapore,* ed. Ryan Bishop, John Phillips, and Wei-Wei Yeo (London: Routledge, 2003).
23. Faucher gives us a very strong sense of this in her article. See *Beyond Description.*
24. Anonymous, "Lone Woman," in *Nightmares: True Ghost Stories. Vampires* (Singapore: ASURAS), 30–34.
25. Ibid., 30.
26. Ibid., 31.
27. Ibid., 32.
28. Stoker, *Dracula,* 51.
29. Ibid., 53.
30. Frayling, *Lord Byron,* 298.
31. See also A. Schopp, "Cruising the Alternatives: Homoeroticism and the Contemporary Vampire," in *Journal of Popular Culture* 30, no. 4 (1997): 231–44; M. Williamson, "Vampires and the Gendered Body," in *Reframing the Body,* ed. N. Watson and S. Cunningham-Burley (Basingstoke: Palgrave, 2001), 96–112.
32. See A. Ong and D. Nonini, eds., *Underground Empires: the Cultural Politics of Modern Chinese Transnationalism* (London: Routledge, 1997).
33. See J. Robinson, "Global and World Cities: A View from off the Map," in *International Journal of Urban and Regional Research* (forthcoming).
34. See D. Massey, J. Allen, and S. Pile, eds., *City Worlds* (London: Routledge, 1999).

Patke provides a subtle reading simultaneously of Walter Benjamin's *Arcades Project* and the Asian and Southeast Asian city, as a way of supporting and extending Benjamin's engagement with global modernity. Benjamin's conception of modernity implies "the industrial transformation of society by technology, as part of the Enlightenment project of progress through the application of reason to nature and society." The transformation implied here would obviously "apply" not only to the urbanization and globalization of nature and society but also crucially to thought and thus to the very horizons of our thinking. Benjamin's project, which stresses not only modernity's promise of emancipation but also its failures, opens these horizons up in all kinds of different ways. Patke suggests he would have turned to Asian postcolonialism as a way of illustrating "the twofold claim that the postcolonial experience brings out the disillusionment latent in the myth of progress, just as the postmodern brings out the phantasmal that is incipient to the myth of an evenly distributed access to capital and goods in the era of globalization." These claims are derived from a self-reflexive European critical tradition, which must be understood not simply in terms of the way that it systematically problematizes its complex inheritances (specifically here modernity's project of emancipation) but also and more crucially in the way that it affirms its unrealized possibilities. Under the heading "City Types," Patke notes that "through Benjamin, we see the city of modernity not as the habitation of the bourgeoisie, but as a threshold experience foregrounded by marginal types such as the collector, gambler, prostitute, and flâneur." If Benjamin provides a kind of vicarious experience of the threshold that unearths the hidden or forgotten grounds of modernity, then the postcolonial Southeast Asian city plays a similar role.

14

Benjamin's *Arcades Project* and the Postcolonial City

RAJEEV S. PATKE

Post-this, post-that, post-the-other, yet in the end
Not past a thing.

—Seamus Heaney[1]

Among the several Benjamins to be conjured from Walter Benjamin's *Arcades Project* is the one who invites a speculative discourse on the idea of the postcolonial city. We can imagine him first conceding, and then qualifying, three propositions about himself: He mitigates the force of the first—that he was Eurocentric—with the counterproposition that the cities he wrote about were formative of a discourse that can be transposed to other cities whose patterns of urban development was shaped by forces analogous to those he studied in the period of their inception. He then concedes that his work on the city remains problematic in several ways related to an uncertain temperament and method, but urges the recognition that his method came to resemble his object of study, and the fortuitous correspondence reinforces the self-reflexive relation between modern cities and the discourse they generate. His third concession—that his use of Marxian ideas mixes them with elements of bourgeois thought—is marginalized by the recognition that he always took his Marx with such a difference that to confine him within such a debate would be to take him in the wrong spirit. He then proceeds to reiterate, in the specific instance of the postcolonial, a more familiar general claim made by many contemporary readers of the metropolitan experience, such as Heinz Paetzold, that the set of approaches he uncovered continue to remain valid wherever the project of modernity is at work, because they help us address "the split image of modernity, modernity's promises for social and individual emancipation, as well as modernity's failures."[2]

MODERN

Benjamin would begin by reminding us that his "modern" and "modernity" refer primarily to the industrial transformation of society by technology, as part of the Enlightenment project of progress through the application of reason to nature and society. He would qualify his sense of the project of modernity through the image of "the world dominated by its phantasmagorias."[3] He would then shrug off the cloak of the Eurocentric by turning, for illustration, to the many Asian manifestations of the postcolonial. Here, he would make the twofold claim that the postcolonial experience brings out the disillusionment latent in the myth of progress, just as the postmodern brings out the phantasmal that is incipient to the myth of an evenly distributed access to capital and goods in the era of globalization. He would argue that the cities of contemporary Asia are the sites for a partial and uneven overlap between the postmodern and the postcolonial. This overlap, he would say, invites us to treat the idea of the city in a generic mode, without discounting the fact that the diversity separating the metropolitan centres in Asia makes little sense of an Asian city except as banal literalism. He would note that colonialism did not affect all of Asia, nor did it follow quite the same course from colony to colony, though the term retains some usefulness in accounting for the general factors that link different cities in Asia to what happened after colonialism. He would treat the postcolonial and the postmodern as three-tiered phenomena: Each is a historical phase of world history, a predicament affecting collectivities, and an attitude or state of mind, pointing out that, when applied to cities, the aptness of the notion of the postcolonial city increases in direct proportion to the degree to which a city acquired a distinctive identity through colonial administration or commerce, and decreases in direct proportion to the degree of discontinuity between the colonial and postcolonial phases of its history. He would add the corollary that any contemporary city in the developing world approximates to the postcolonial condition whose role in the network of power-relations negotiates a relation between the local and the global from a position of historically accumulated disadvantage.

BENJAMINIANA

If we look at the book that is now the mode of existence of the *Arcades Project,* we see that Benjamin accumulates textual details about the city but resists absorbing them into a systematic theory or model. Instead, he favors constellating ideas around thematic motifs in which ordinary features (such as street lamp or arcade) acquire allegorical significance, or apparently simple notions (such as dream or panorama) are weighted with complex associations. Like the Surrealists, he is intent on looking behind the semblance of the ordinary for the marginal, the repressed, and the potentially revolutionary. Unlike them, he found a role for the unconscious only in relation to what consciousness could retrieve from it. His practice insists that the city may contain multitudes, but in it, human experience is to be approached always at the level of the subjective.

Benjamin's city is seen more than heard, or felt, or even lived in. The image dominates and resonates. The city is approached on foot, from the perspective of a solitary individual. He encounters it as street and shop rather than map, monument, or handbook. It is traversed in space but studied in time. It historicizes space. Through that space, which is always haunted by its own history, walks a typology of marginal characters with Baudelaire at their center. They exemplify the effect of the commodity on consciousness, to which is added an interest in the effects of material technology on culture.

The city is studied for how the past looks back at us for recognition in the duration and depredation of objects, persons, and memories in time. It invites us to treat experience as stretching across time rather than simply extending in space. It accumulates metonymic objects and artifacts as a kind of involuntary memory. To elicit this memory is to arrive at a moment of recognition of how the present was—or was not—immanent in what-has-been as its future. In this sense, the city is rune and ruin, aura and trace. It is never complete, but always already debris. As an emblem in the allegory of modernity, the city stands for the failure of Enlightenment to realize Utopia, just as the postmodern—phase, predicament, attitude, state of mind—is the willingness to live in the phantasmal after having consigned the project of Utopia back to mythology.

WHO'S HECUBA?

Benjamin's direct experience of cities was peripatetic, and extended from the Berlin of his youth to the Paris of his desires and his final exile. The cities he first wrote about—Naples (1924), Moscow (1927), and Marseilles (1928)—came to represent the boundaries of a "noctambulism"[4] that was contained by Europe, with New York and Jerusalem marking a plane beyond the horizon of longing. During the last thirteen years of his life, from 1927 to his untimely death in 1940, Benjamin worked intermittently on a city project of uncertain but growing ambitions. It survives in the form of essays, revisions, and fragments scattered amid an enormous quarry of notes and extracts. The *Arcades Project*—or the *Passagen-Werk,* as it is sometimes known—symbolizes Paris as the capital of nineteenth century Europe, and its shopping arcades as the emblem of capital, whose power to transform culture extends the urban history of the Second Empire into an allegory of modernity.

COMPLICITY

Paris might appear an unpropitious starting point for approaching the discursive notion of the postcolonial city. It is twice removed from the metropolitan diversity of contemporary Asia. But "maps are of time, not place," as Henry Reed once remarked,[5] and the apparent remoteness of the nineteenth century is bridged by a dialectical relation between the politics of economic growth and the economics of cultural formations. As the first element of a twofold complicity, Europe's modernization in the nineteenth century enabled, and was aided by, its acquisition of colonies. The colonized, in their turn, were exploited by—but also made more susceptible to ideas of freedom and modernity through—the experience of colonialism. Then, during the course of the twentieth century, the asymmetries of an increasingly global capitalism in its post-Fordist phase overshadowed the belated pursuit of modernity undertaken by Europe's former colonies as part of their new histories as independent nation-states. Through this period of almost two hundred years, the city has first served as the focal point for the intersection of empire and colony, and then grown into the site for the interaction between globalism and the new nation.

DEBRIS

As a form of discourse about the city, the *Arcades Project* remains problematic in a number of ways. As process, it appears to be an interminable series of extracts interspersed with a modicum of comment. When his caustic admirer Adorno protested at so many undigested facts, Benjamin resisted the call to provide the mediation of an interpretive discourse informed by theory.[6] Instead, he invoked *montage* in order to claim—with injured pride as much as conviction—that "saying" was to be displaced by "showing,"[7] to accomplish "the art of citing without quotations."[8] As product, the *Passagen-Werk* remains frozen between the desire to generate a new type of discourse corresponding to the modern city as a new mode of experience, and the intimation that such an intention may be realized only when the experience of the city renders discourse into debris. As an "excess of intention over its object," the project "thinks in fragments," requiring faith in the belief that "reality is fragmented and gains in unity only by moving through the fissures, rather than by smoothing them over."[9]

RUINS

The image of debris scattered over Benjamin's writing equivocates between a constitutional inability to complete an undertaking and a principled resistance to closure. The project corresponds in metaphor to the city, and especially to the postcolonial city, dominated, as in Singapore, by the will to upgrade, which is the overt expression of the need for security and a repression of the fear of non-being. The postcolonial city fulfills the norm of a Benjaminian city wherever the intransitive enters into the willed aspect of production. Just as quotations do not infest his text but become the text, the cities of Asia have generally been turned inside out by their marginalia. The *barung-barongs* of Manila and the hutment colonies of Calcutta or Bombay are a series of inscriptions coagulating energies and forms into marks and shapes as central to the city as its monuments of colonial heritage. Singapore's entire housing project scheme is an antithesis, illustrating the will to minimize the play of the random in concept, theory, model, and map.[10] When Haussmann "cleaned up" Paris over 1853 to 1870, his wonderful boulevards, vistas, and strategically placed monuments and statues were accomplished by moving some 350,000 poor people out of the old quarter to make room for his model city. James Donald uses this detail to reinforce the hallucinatory element discovered by Benjamin in the idea of a planned city: "the displacements brought about by Haussmannisation lent a fantastic and elusive quality to life in the city."[11] In most cities today, the process of growth is more susceptible of subversion than planning. Each city becomes a giant kampong whose fence of rationality is open to the infiltration of design by chance.

The Benjaminian city of words, like the general trend of postcolonial urbanism, is the site for a perpetual negotiation between the providential and the unpredictable. In Benjamin's text, the euphoria that rewards the drive to betterment gets deflated. In his thought, a perspective focused on the City of God looks quizzically upon the idea that Change is always headed upward on the gradient of the Possible. In its cautionary function, his allegory of modernity treats cities and texts changing in time as the inversion of the desire for unreal places—Arcadia, Utopia—into ruins. Benjamin's cities become messianic instances of the kind of radical alterity described in the 1960s by Foucault as types of heterotopia: "counter-sites . . . in which . . . all the other real sites that can be found within the culture, are simultaneously represented, contested, and inverted. . . ."[12]

TRACES

Benjamin's texts are acutely responsive to what Ernest Bloch described in a memorable phrase as the "surrealism of lost glances."[13] They accommodate the fleeting and the fugitive with the lambent and the incendiary. They correspond to the diminution of the individual allegorized by Kafka:

> I speak of the modern citizen, who knows he is at the mercy of vast bureaucratic machinery, whose functioning is steered by authorities who remain nebulous even to the executive organs themselves, let alone the people they deal with.[14]

They also respond to how a world "dense with angels" can complement the reality of modern physics and the technology of warfare. They initiate the process of *abmontieren,*[15] which uncovers reality as the traces of what is repressed or forgotten in urban experience, while veiling our sense of the ordinary in the distance that is aura:

> The trace is appearance of nearness, however far removed the thing that left it behind may be. The aura is appearance of distance, however close the thing that calls it forth. In the trace, we gain possession of the thing; in the aura, it takes possession of us.[16]

Benjamin's city of fragments is no mere "astonished presentation of simple facts."[17] Nor does it follow the surrealist down the path of access to the unreason of the unconscious. His choice involves retrieving the traces of "what-has-been"[18] from the objects that reach out to us into the present. A city is like an archive of involuntary memory,[19] and Benjamin approaches it as a collector entering a museum of mirrors. From these he will retrieve the gazes that look back at him, soliciting recognition that a part of them survives in him. Such an approach frustrates the semblance of factuality so cherished in the urban geographer's habitual recourse to compendious numbers and statistical enumeration. Instead, Benjamin ushers in a city that is both aura and trace. As aura, it veils the fulfillment of desire in perpetual deferral and regress. As trace, it unveils the future immanent in our past as detritus.

In the city we are possessed by our own dispossession, never more so than in Asia. The traces of the colonial dominate the architecture of most Asian cities, especially in its monuments, public buildings, and in the "linguistic cosmos"[20] of street names. Wherever the nationalist impulse has prevailed, civic managements have rushed to efface such traces. Wherever the past is allowed to remain, it has provided a thread leading the traveler back into the labyrinth of historical awareness. This can be exemplified in passing through the poetics of history implicated in geography as developed in Jinnai Hidenobu's account of Tokyo, which provides a "linkage of urban sites to the people's memories laid down in poetical narratives or paintings."[21] To become aware of the past in this sense is to become aware of how it did—or did not—anticipate our present. But the will to modernity is shadowed by the gift and curse of involuntary forgetting. It opens out a carpet of blankness on which the future is invited to fly.

FETISH

Benjamin's repertoire of ideas treats the city under the constellation of several motifs familiar to the Marxist tradition. These include the transfor-

mation of use value into exchange value in the city as marketplace, the alienation of man from the products of his labor in the city as workplace, and
the reification of the commodity into fetish in the city as a culture of consumerism. Such motifs were neither unique to Benjamin, nor have they lost
all their affective or explanatory power. His treatment of urban alienation
retains a romantic aspect. Foucault remarked years later that

> the concept of the subject that was adopted by the Frankfurt School was . . .
> impregnated with humanism of a Marxist type. . . . I'm convinced that given
> these premises, the Frankfurt School cannot by any means admit that the
> problem is not to recover our "lost" identity, to free our imprisoned nature,
> our deepest truth; but instead, the problem is to move towards something
> radically Other.[22]

Despite nostalgia, there is nothing misty-eyed about Benjamin's allegorical
treatment of the commodity as broken-down matter.[23] In the writings of
Horkheimer, Adorno, and Marcuse, the project of rational Enlightenment
was treated as a modern chimera. In a related vein, Benjamin was drawn
to Marx's use of the term "phantasmagoria" to describe the delusional
aspects of the culture of commodities.[24] The peculiar heroism of Baudelaire
characterized modernity repeatedly as phantasmagoria:[25] a lantern casting
dark shadows.[26] In this ironic perspective, the city becomes the site for
mourning the ruin of what Benjamin in his *Trauerspiel* book called the
"three original satanic promises": "the illusion of freedom," "the illusion of
independence," and "the illusion of infinity."[27]

PHANTASMAGORIA

Benjamin's Europe is stitched unevenly through history to how these three
illusions constitute—and subvert—the project of postcolonial modernity,
which finds its embodiment in the metropolis. Why this should be so needs
a brief (and necessarily simplified) historical excursus. From before the
nineteenth century, colonization was always a double-edged experience. On
the one hand, it entailed sustained economic exploitation and political as well
as cultural subordination; on the other hand, it nurtured a presentiment of
rational modernity along lines already laid down by the colonizing nations
of industrial Europe. What had enabled colonization in the first place was
the gap between Europe and other regions in the application of instrumental reason to commercial, technological, and administrative enterprise. The
subordinated eventually learned to invoke the right to self-determination, and
struggled over a long period to acquire the right to independent nationhood. However, when the freedom of self-determination arrived, it did not
altogether fulfill all that it had seemed to promise.

PROGRESS

There are at least six partially overlapping explanations for the reversion of freedom to fantasy in the epoch of new nationalisms:

1. Over the period that saw the struggle for political liberation, the growth of industrial capitalism in the West grew into a global economic force. This widened the gap that had always separated the industrialized and the colonized, leaving newly independent nations with the disadvantage of having to catch up with, and accomplish insertion into, a global economy from a position of considerable disadvantage.

2. The onset of political freedom did not guarantee or ensure that new nations would also be free from colonized mindsets. Modes of dependency and imitativeness learned or inculcated in the colonial period could not, or at any rate did not, disappear.

3. The leadership in many of the new nations was not equipped to cope—through various combinations of ignorance, unpreparedness, incompetence, or corruption—with the challenges of new nationhood in an era of global capitalism. The disadvantages of asymmetrical industrialization were aggravated by aggressive-regressive forms of nationalism, which tried—unsuccessfully, and at considerable cost—to protect new nations from the effects of globalization, and to consume energies in various forms of reinventing the wheel along nationalist lines.

4. The educational base in the newly independent nations was often too small and too derivative to provide a quick maturation of the skilled labor force needed to narrow the gap between the developed and the relatively undeveloped parts of the world.

5. The enormous material prosperity, military power, high standard of living, and conspicuous consumption of the advanced capitalist societies made it inevitable for the postcolonial nation to define its goals and objectives in terms of the given notion of progress, regardless of reservations at what might be entailed in the pursuit of Utopia. Envy reinforced an imitativeness learned under colonialism.

6. The dissolution of the colony often led—despite the precariously sustained idea of nation—to various fragmenting forms of collectivity, generally based on the divisive-cohesive power of ethnicity and factionalism. Within the city, as for instance, in Bombay, "far from increasing the homogeneity of the workforce, industrialization acted to intensify its sectionalism."[28]

POSTCOLONIAL

The postcolonial is a name for the predicaments that ensued upon the combined effect of these six forces of progress; and in part, it is a name for the
attitude or state of mind preoccupied with such predicaments. For the last
half-century, the postcolonial nations of Asia have responded—as far as
nations have been able to sustain the coherence of a willed response—with
an impatient, fearful, but persistent utopianism. Its goal is progress, its means
are modernization, and the postcolonial city is the locus of its materializa-
tion. A December 2000 survey by the magazine *Asiaweek* shows how the
globalization of what began as a European project in the Enlightenment
provides the contemporary media in Asia with a set of (rather random and
provocative) categories by which modernity, and the embedding of the metropolis in that project, is measured.[29] Of the forty Asian cities ranked, the top
five are Fukuoka, Tokyo, Singapore, Osaka, and Taipei, in that order; and
the lowest five are Yangon, Chittagong, Karachi, Dhaka, and Vientiane, in
that order. Retaining all of Benjamin's scepticism about the truth-value of
statistical figures, we might still glance at a sample comparison. The figures
for the cities ranked 1 and 32 are shown in Table 14-1.

Table 14-1

City Overall Score	Fukuoka	Phnom Penh
	73	43
Average income U.S.$	37,165	1,529
Educational spending per capita	308	14
Unemployment rate (%)	5	7
Ration of house price to income	11	16
Hospital beds per 1,000 people	19.5	3
Pollution (dust in air)	26	217
Vehicles per kilometer of city road	200	34
Criminal cases per 10,000	345	9
TV sets per 1,000 people	400	200
Inflation (%)	0	5
GDP growth ($)	-1.9	11.6
Average class size (primary school)	32	60
Life expectancy	77	50
Average commuting time	45	15
Phones per 1,000 people	620	29
Mobiles per 1,000 people	374	87
Internet use per 1,000 people	132	30

How curious figures such as these can be is shown in the inverse relation between pollution and density of vehicular traffic. Another telling detail is that most of the latter part of the list is content to measure contentment either through the possession of commodities or virtual goods (such as the price paid in commuting time for access to capital, and the gain in space accomplished by Internet access to virtual space).

DREAM

The metaphorical possibilities inherent to the dream experience fascinated Benjamin through all the stages of the *Arcades Project.* The dream is closely associated with his idea of the dialectical image. In one variation, the phantasmal quality of the commodity fetish is treated as a feature embedded in the collective unconscious of the urban bourgeoisie. This analogy creates certain problems, especially if you wish to be a consistent Marxist, like Adorno.[30] The power of the dialectical image as a notion was weakened for Adorno by the psychologism of the dream and the Jungianism of a collective unconscious. He insisted that the fetish character of the commodity "is not a fact of consciousness," but rather "it produces consciousness . . . in alienated bourgeois individuals."[31] Accordingly, "the dialectical image should not be transferred into consciousness as a dream." Instead, "the dream should be externalized and the immanence of consciousness itself be understood as a constellation of reality."[32] He argued that the failure of industrial societies to achieve the ideal of social emancipation should not be allowed to relegate utopianism back to the realm of myth from which it had been wrested. Instead, society had to square up to the responsibility entailed by the recognition that the metropolitan had become a form of "catastrophe."[33]

UTOPIA

What is true of any modern city applies to the postcolonial city doubly. First, the myth of modernity as a collective instantiation of progress is most often realized in a sense close to Adorno's "catastrophe." Second, the speed with which this phantasm has been pursued in the last three of four decades in Southeast Asia is in inverse proportion to its belatedness. If we do live in cities—and eight of the ten most populous cities in the world today belong to the undeveloped-to-developing regions of the world[34]—the social dialectic between the impulse to privacy and the counter-impulse to betterment (a euphemism displacing the impulse to sociability) has obviously met with a singular resolution. In the interminable dream that began in the nineteenth century, the dialectical tension between desire and its fulfillment continues to find its resolution in the commodity. To the degree that the postindustrial West is the proof of progress, its modes of consumption and culture provide the model for the postcolonial city. In an elaborate comparison between forty years of change in the cultures of Indonesia and Morocco as reflected in two specific cities, Clifford Geertz recently expressed "doubt as to whether the order of life current in the West is really the wave of everybody else's future."[35] He catalogues "the ills attributed to the modern form of life as it has taken shape in the West" as a caveat to aspiring postcolonial nations intent on "joining the ranks of the industrial powers, getting rich, getting healthier, getting skilled, getting armed." The price can entail "secularism, commodification, corruption, selfishness, immorality, rootlessness, general estrangement from the sources of value."[36]

ANTITHESIS

The urban experience as dream colors three relations: first, between solitude and sociability; second, between desire and its fulfillment; and third, between happiness and fear. Each antithesis is a variable compound of make-believe, fantasy, hallucination, delusion, nightmare, and non-being. The intensity of the dreamlike quality to urban experiences grows in direct proportion to the scale of collective living. From Paris to Asia is a transposition of scale. The basic criteria do not change either for the intensity or for the quality of metropolitan experience. Intensity remains a function of the exponential growth in three factors: density of population, heterogeneity of local cultures, and disparity in incomes. Quality remains a function of the relation between the productive capacity of the metropolitan economy to its density, cultural diversity, and economic disparities.

THRESHOLD

This brings us to the second sense in which Benjamin uses the dream as a mode of historical knowledge. The dream is to be cultivated as a "threshold" experience.[37] Falling asleep and getting up become threshold experiences in that each is immanent with knowledge of the adjacent state. The threshold is a cognitive metaphor, in which "the relation of what-has-been to the now is dialectical"[38]—"to pass through what has been, in order to experience the present as the waking world to which the dream refers!"[39] He imaged this new and sudden experience of a present informed by its past as "the caesura in the movement of thought."[40] Time in the city became the progression of "what-has-been" into a "now" of emergent recognition,[41] as of a dream remembered in the moment of awakening, such that the dream remembers a past full of the intimation of a present awaiting realization.[42] It was "the now of recognizability," in which "the dialectic, in standing still, makes an image," giving us "dialectics at a standstill."[43]

DIALECTICS

The notion of the dialectics preoccupied Benjamin throughout the city project. At one point, he toyed with the idea of giving it the subtitle:

"A Dialectical Fairy Play."[44] Later, he reported that it would be organized in a three-part dialectic, in which the presentation of Baudelaire as the allegorist of urban modernity would find its antithesis in sociocritical exemplification. The two movements were to be resolved by "The Commodity as Poetic Object."[45] Benjamin's fascination with the dialectical mode of thought can be extended to a variety of contexts in which the city figures centrally in the relation between nationalism (as the overlap between the colonial and the postcolonial), and globalism (as the translation of the modern into the postmodern). If the nineteenth century was a dream that the twentieth had to get up from, and the study of Baudelaire's Paris was a way of doing it, correspondingly we might speak of the fabric of the postmodern as woven with an antithetical pattern of development. The first direction of this weave mediates the relation of the nation-state to modernity through assimilation into post-Fordist globalization. The other gets woven in as an inversion of the utopian element in the postcolonial. If the dialectical tension were resolved, material prosperity would then subsist under a "philosophy of history that at all points has overcome the ideology of progress,"[46] although it is doubtful if any Asian city has reached the point of that realization.

GLOBALISM

A Benjaminian catechism: The colonial city found out that freedom was an illusion; the global city knows that independence is an illusion; the postmodern city accepts the illusion of infinity. In the nineteenth century, Paris was both capital and the capital for Europe. In the contemporary metropolis in Asia, there is a greater degree of tension between a city's symbolic function as the capital of a postcolonial nation-state, and the economic function of producing, attracting, and disseminating capital. The pattern of uneven growth is endemic within the Asian city and in the relation of the city to its hinterland.[47] The extreme example is Bangkok, "which is some thirty times larger than the second most populous city in Thailand."[48] To the degree that the Asian metropolis draws upon its hinterland for labor and resources, and gives its people opportunities for economic betterment, it fulfills its nationalist function. The case of Singapore is unique in being delinked from its natural hinterland in the moment of its inception as postcolonial city-state so that its subsequent history of tightly prosperous management is widely recognized as untypical and "at variance with other cases" from the region.[49] However, the border of the nation has become porous to the flow of capital, goods, and service through its metropolis. To that degree, the metropolis serves itself insofar as it serves or looks for a part in the global network of economic relationships. The recent attempt by the state to defend the Kuala Lumpur stock market and the nation's capital from international speculation illustrates an extreme situation, in which a nation and its metropolis resist the pull of globalism. The outcome for the nation is still unclear. Meanwhile, Hong Kong provides the opposite extreme, in which a metropolis exists only through its interconnectedness. As a post-colonial city, it is now linked to, and threatened by, its massive hinterland.

In all its diversity, the Asian city remains a type of threshold experience, in which the local negotiates with the global in an antithesis in which the notions of freedom and independence have to be accepted as illusory. Just as the mall mediates—internal to the city—between the interior and the street, on the city's borders the international airports provide a more specifically postmodern inversion of threshold space. The global network of air-traffic creates a regular mass of transit passengers who pass through airports without visiting the cities serviced by such airports or airlines. Ironically, competition for a stake in the global market for travel becomes part of the growth in the reversal of what Benjamin had meant by the threshold experience.

CITY TYPES

Through Benjamin, we see the city of modernity not as the habitation of the bourgeoisie, but as a threshold experience foregrounded by marginal types such as the collector, gambler, prostitute, and flâneur. They share one feature. They resist the notion of the city as home to the burgher. In modernity, the covered arcade provides a dialectical reversal of the traditional antithesis between indoors and outdoors, bourgeois interior and urban panorama. Subsequent architectural developments in the postcolonial city confirm the mall, department store, and the atrium as the site for similar reversals, just as hotels for international travelers are the dialectical inversion of the city as home. Benjamin is salutary in treating the first manifestations of such modernity with irony. Thus, the collector is neither a miser nor a banker. He resists the dispersion to which objects are prone.[50] He rescues them from their functional role in use and exchange value.[51] His habitation corresponds to the museum, which resists the conversion of the street into the market, bazaar, arcade, or department store—all sites for the transformation of objects into commodities. The prostitute takes the infatuation with the commodity form of exchange to its logical extreme by treating her own body as capital in the fetishization of desire.[52] The gambler is the hero who appears to submit to the vagaries of chance by cultivating a divinatory presence of mind. He resists the will to wealth by subverting the principle of accumulation. His propensity to waste is also the gift of prodigality. He finds intoxication in mingling terror with delight. In Adorno's supplement, the gambler is allied to speculation, which "is the negative expression of the irrationality of capitalist ratio."[53] Then there is the flâneur, who combines an assortment of roles in which the hero appears on the stage of the nine-teenth century in the guise of the dandy. The dandy is not a snob. As the observer of the marketplace, he acknowledges the pull of what is resisted. As vocational idler,[54] he resists the work ethic that drives capital. As suspect,[55] he is delinquent from conventional social responsibility; as detective,[56] he treats urbanism as riddle and crime. As journalist,[57] he bears witness; as nostalgist, he is the last incarnation of the sandwich-man.[58] For Benjamin, he is the alienated romantic fascinated by all that horrifies his gaze. He is the trace of an aura close to evanescence.

BACK TO THE FUTURE

What survives as relevance from the *Arcades Project*? The flâneur who could take a tortoise for a stroll[59] now looks dead as a dodo, first jostled and then trampled in the mall he so loved to promenade. Posthumously, he remains the most well-known part of Benjamin's writing on cities, just as flânerie remains the best antidote Benjamin can offer to the fever of living in cities. The most original aspect of his work remains the notion of the dialectical image. The threshold where dream crosses into awakening remains its key metaphor, and the dialectical relation between trace and aura is its most enigmatic preoccupation. These retain the appeal of a unique perspective on urban experience. They also suggest the nature of Benjamin's relevance in a contemporary world aptly described by the lines from Heaney quoted as my epigraph.[60] The contemporary that is not yet past for Benjamin includes the cost paid in local and historical forgetting by the effects of capital and the homogenization of culture through technology. Cities have become bigger, dirtier, richer, and scarier. They are also more exciting and more enervating. Technology and global capital bring futures close to hand, though aura is always being shed, late and soon, and traces steadily accumulate and await recognition. As the Singaporean poet Arthur Yap remarked—ambivalently—in *Commonplace* (1977), "there is no future in nostalgia."[61] The arcades have expanded vastly, and become virtual. They continue to condition consciousness, and invite us to make a fetish of the commodity, on an ever grander scale and in a more truly phantasmal space. The city remains a labyrinth, and a vascular network choked on its own traffic. As time and space shrink, Klee's angel recedes even further into the distance, mourning the decline of mourning.

NOTES

1. Seamus Heaney, "On His Work in the English Tongue," in *Electric Light* (London: Faber, 2001), 61–63.
2. Heinz Paetzold, "The Philosophical Notion of the City," in *The Cities Culture Reader*, ed. Malcolm Miles, Tim Hall, and Iain Borden (London and New York: Routledge, 2000), 216a.
3. Walter Benjamin, *The Arcades Project*, trans. Howard Eiland and Kevin McLaughlin (Cambridge, Mass.: The Bellknap Press of Harvard University Press, 1999), 26.

4. Ibid., 454.

5. Henry Reed, "Lessons of the War," in *Collected Poems,* ed. Jon Stallworthy (Oxford and New York: Oxford University Press, 1991), 50.

6. Theodor Adorno, Walter Benjamin, Ernst Bloch, Bertolt Brecht, and Georg Lukacs, *Aesthetics and Politics,* trans. Ronald Taylor (London and New York: Verso, 1977), 179; Walter Benjamin, *The Correspondence of Walter Benjamin,* trans. Manfred R. Jacobson and Evelyn M. Jacobson, ed. Gershom Scholem and Theodor W. Adorno (Chicago and London: University of Chicago Press, 1994), 581.

7. Benjamin, *The Arcades Project,* 460.

8. Ibid., 458.

9. Theodor W. Adorno, "The Essay as Form," in *The Adorno Reader,* ed. Brian O'Connor (Oxford: Blackwell, 2000), 99, 104.

10. See Robbie B. H. Goh, "Ideologies of 'Upgrading' in Singapore Public Housing: Post-modern Style, Globalisation and Class Construction in the Built Environment," *Urban Studies* 38, no. 9 (2001): 1599, for what he calls "a crisis of 'authorship of place' " in Singapore's housing policies, alluding to a phrase in D. Ley's "Co-operative Housing as a Moral Landscape: Re-examining 'the Postmodern City,' " in *Place/Culture/Representation,* ed. J. Duncan and D. Ley (London: Routledge, 1993), 129.

11. James Donald, *Imagining the Modern City* (Minneapolis: University of Minneapolis Press, 1999), 47.

12. Michel Foucault, "Of Other Spaces," *Diacritics* 16 (1986): 22.

13. Ernst Bloch, "Recollections of Walter Benjamin," *On Benjamin,* ed. Gary Smith (Cambridge, Mass., and London: The M.I.T. Press, 1988), 344.

14. Benjamin, *Correspondence,* 563.

15. Walter Benjamin, *Selected Writings, Volume 2, 1927–1934,* trans. Rodney Livingstone et al., ed. Michael W. Jennings, Howard Eiland, and Gary Smith (Cambridge, Mass.: The Belknap Press of Harvard University Press, 1999), 415. Here the verb is translated as "deconstruction."

16. Benjamin, *The Arcades Project,* 447.

17. Susan Buck-Morss, quoting Adorno, in *The Origin of Negative Dialectics: Theodor W. Adorno, Walter Benjamin, and the Frankfurt Institute* (New York: Free Press/London: Collier Macmillan, 1977), 157.

18. Benjamin, *The Arcades Project,* 907.

19. Proust's *mémoire involontaire,* as discussed in Walter Benjamin, *Charles Baudelaire: A Lyric Poet in the Era of High Capitalism,* trans. Harry Zohn (London and New York: Verso, 1973), 113.

20. Benjamin, *The Arcades Project,* 522.

21. Paetzold, "Philosophical Notion," 218a.

22. Michel Foucault, *Remarks on Marx: Conversations with Duccio Trombadori,* trans. R. James Goldstein and James Cascaito (New York: Semiotext(e), 1991), 121; see also Foucault's *Power,* ed. James D. Faubion, trans. Robert Hurley et al. *Essential Works of Foucault 1954–1984, vol. 3* (New York: New Press, 2000), 274–75.

23. Benjamin, *The Arcades Project,* 207.

24. Margaret Cohen, *Profane Illumination: Walter Benjamin and the Paris of the Surrealist Revolution* (Berkeley: University of California Press, 1993), 24.

25. Cohen, *Protane Illumination,* 10, 21, 25, 26, 116, passim.

26. Benjamin, *The Arcades Project,* 305.

27. Walter Benjamin, *The Origins of German Tragic Drama,* trans. John Osbourne, with an introduction by George Steiner (London: Verso, 1977), 230.

28. Rajnarayan Chandavarkar, *The Origins of Industrial Capitalism in India: Business Strategies and the Working Classes in Bombay, 1900–1940* (Cambridge: Cambridge University Press, 1994), 398.

29. "Best Cities in Asia for 2000," *AsiaWeek.com,* 15 December 2000. http://www.asiaweek/features/asiacities2000/how.html.

30. Adorno et al., *Aesthetics,* 110–33; Benjamin, *Correspondence,* 494–503.

31. Adorno et al., *Aesthetics,* 111, 113; Benjamin, *Correspondence,* 497.

32. Adorno et al., *Aesthetics,* 112.

33. Benjamin, *Correspondence,* 496.

34. Edward W. Soja, *Postmetropolis: Critical Studies of Cities and Regions* (Oxford: Blackwell, 2000), 236.

35. Clifford Geertz, *After the Fact: Two Countries, Four Decades, One Anthropologist* (Cambridge, Mass.: Harvard University Press, 1995), 140.

36. Ibid., 142.

37. Benjamin, *The Arcades Project,* 462.

38. Ibid.
39. Ibid., 838.
40. Ibid., 475.
41. Ibid., 463, 473, 867.
42. Ibid., 463–64.
43. Ibid., 911–12, (compare 917).
44. Benjamin, *Correspondence,* 507.
45. Ibid., 573–74.
46. Benjamin, *The Arcades Project,* 857.
47. David Smith, *Third World Cities in Global Perspective: The Political Economy of Uneven Urbanization* (Boulder, Colo.: Westview Press, 1996), 102ff.
48. David Smith, "Cities in Pacific Asia," in *Handbook of Urban Studies,* ed. Ronan Paddison (London: Sage Publications, 2001), 424b.
49. Leo van Grunsven, "Singapore: The Changing Residential Landscape in a Winner City," *Globalizing Cities: A New Spiral Order?* ed. Peter Marcuse and Ronald van Kempen (Oxford: Blackwell, 2000), 125.
50. Benjamin, *The Arcades Project,* 211.
51. Ibid., 204, 207, 857.
52. Ibid., 325, 361, 511, 861.
53. Benjamin, *Correspondence,* 503.
30. Heaney, "On this Work," 61.
31. Arthur Yap, *The Space of City Trees,* intro. Anne Brewster (London: Skoob Books, 2000), 59.
54. Benjamin, *The Arcades Project,* 427.
55. Ibid., 420.
56. Ibid., 442.
57. Ibid., 446.
58. Ibid., 448, 451.
59. Ibid., 422.
60. Heaney, "On His Work on the English Tongue," 61–63.
61. Arthur Yap, *Commonplace.*

The legacy of colonialism has left many ideological packages in the post-colonial larder. One of the most intriguing and problematic is Christianity, not least because it was often used as justification for and legitimization of colonization. Whether cynically applied or used in the most earnest and steadfast commitment to doing good works, the belief in saving the savage soul in exchange for material wealth runs throughout the history of Western colonization. Similarly intriguing and problematic is how evangelical Christianity has remained and even gained in influence during the postcolonial era in the colonized site, while it has definitely waned, in terms of influence, in the colonizing capital. Evangelical Christianity, in a way, is a transplant of a major institution (rather than an experimental one per se as we see in the pieces by Bishop and Clancey, Adams, Derderian, and Reisz) that took root in the colony while the main tree from which the graft was taken has begun to wither. It is toward some of these concerns and how they manifest themselves in shaping urban life, space, and experience in Singapore that Goh's article turns. In so doing, Goh offers, among other issues, a nexus of geo-cultural-religious products sold through specific media that evokes the alternative mapping strategies for global connections, particularly ones with capital, that Jackson's article also specifically provides.

15

Deus ex Machina: Evangelical Sites, Urbanism, and the Construction of Social Identities

ROBBIE B. H. GOH

It is both helpful, and unhelpful, to regard the city as a machine—
helpful, as part of an analysis of systems of cultural production, and unhelpful as a reductive account of quasi-universal labor and capital processes.
The idea of the city as machine is an awareness of industrial Europe: Many
records of this in the discourses of the mid-nineteenth century might be
adduced, of which Charles Dickens's account of Coketown in *Hard Times*
(1854) might be taken as representative:

> It was a town of machinery and tall chimneys, out of which interminable ser-
> pents of smoke trailed themselves for ever and ever, and never got uncoiled. It
> had a black canal in it, and a river than ran purple with ill-smelling dye, and
> vast piles of building full of windows where there was a rattling and a trem-
> bling all day long, and where the piston of the steam-engine worked monoto-
> nously up and down, like the head of an elephant in a state of melancholy
> madness. It contained several large streets all very like one another, and many
> small streets still more like one another, inhabited by people equally like one
> another, who all went in and out at the same hours, with the same sound upon
> the pavements, to do the same work, and to whom every day was the same as
> yesterday and tomorrow, and every year the counterpart of the last and the next.[1]

The synecdochal logic of this trope is clear: Cities which, from the industrial era, took on increasingly specialized roles in the production of certain commodities, could with some justice be said not only to consist of
machines for such production, but in fact to be themselves large machines
ordered on a logic of production. Marxist-inspired urban theories (such as

the work of the "regulation school") have developed this trope by considering the city as the site of "material practices" rationalizing labor and other
resources for the purposes of capitalist production and consumption.[2]

This synecdoche in which the machine-containing city itself acquires
the formal logic of the machine[3] reveals a process of abstraction through
which apparently disparate objects or orders (the city, city life, the factory,
the machine) acquire equivalences through the "habitual" relations of production and exchange.[4] This habitual abstraction—the set of structural relations and interfaces that become codified by conventional practice, signs,
and value systems—also holds true of the relationship between machinery
and the human agent, as a "fetishized" process of the "reification" of the
human through his or her participation in mechanical production and monetary exchange.[5] It is accordingly possible to see the human agent as an
equivalent of the urban structures within which he or she operates: Cities
"are centres of social and political life where not only wealth is accumulated,
but knowledge (connaissances), techniques, and oeuvres (works of art, monuments). . . . The oeuvre is use value and the product is exchange value."[6]

One problem posed by this somewhat deterministic account of human
equivalence within production and exchange is its tendency to discount or
at least downplay the multiple allegiances and social identities that arise,
particularly in the context of rapid diasporic movements and settlements,
global cities, recently independent and formerly colonized nations, and
politicoeconomic multinational formations (the European Union and the
Euro, the Organization of Islamic Conference or OIC, the Association of
Southeast Asian Nations or ASEAN, or for that matter the Senegalese
national soccer players who play professionally for French clubs). Although
these phenomena do not act on national and social identities with the same
force or impulse, they collectively foster a multiplicity of "work cultures,"
"new claims," "cultural identities, modes of life, and forms of appropriat-
ing urban space," which may operate on denizens of affected cities and
zones.[7] This is particularly true of many of the nations that gained their
independence from colonial control in the first few decades after World
War II, which retained some of the cultural and political institutions of
the colonial masters even as they adapted to the particular conditions of a
multiracial and multilinguistic society, and whose recent economic successes
have brought upon them many of the privileges and problems of globalization and global citizenship. Singapore and Malaysia are good examples, as
well as (to a lesser extent, and *mutatis mutandis*) Indonesia, Hong Kong, the
Philippines, Australia, and New Zealand.

Such "hybrid" and "interstitial" cultural conditions[8] do not totally in-
validate the account of cities as production machines, but they do qualify
the latter by refuting the notion of a homogeneous and universal condition

(of the laborer, the institutional citizen, the culture of global capital) that is produced, and by insisting on local and particular mechanisms of production that add different social identities in different historical and geographical conditions. We are, doubtless, where and how we live; but if this is to be taken seriously, it requires close readings not only of the different conditions of different places[9] but also of the different mechanisms of cultural production at work in any given space.

One such mechanism, which has not yet received adequate scholarly attention, is the set of Christian (and more particularly evangelical) institutions, structures, discourses, and sites operating in Singapore, which originated in the nineteenth century colonial milieu, and thrives in the present context of Singapore's global economic and cultural push. There has been some work on the historical role of Christianity in Singapore's education system,[10] the creation of syncretic local identities, and the geopolitics of religion in Singapore; however, the complex and continuing role of an evangelical cultural machinery remains to be articulated. Christianity came to Singapore around the middle of the nineteenth century with the Anglican, Methodist, and other missionaries who proceeded to establish churches, schools, and other social organizations for the immigrant population. Many of these are not only still extant, but flourishing; so-called mission schools like the Anglican St. Andrew's School (founded 1862) and St. Margaret's School (1842), the Methodist Anglo-Chinese School (1886) and Methodist Girls' School (1887), and others founded by different denominations have a special cachet as quality schools with long and proud scholarly and sporting traditions, and they often attract better pupils than the government "neighborhood" schools.

Mission schools and other such organizations are social mechanisms for the production of specific kinds of identities, affiliations, and value systems, which are not adequately reflected by the religious categories of official census reports and other such quantitative counts. According to the advanced data releases from the 2000 census of population, only 14.6 percent of the population professed Christianity as their religion.[11] This is not an overwhelming proportion, nor even the most rapidly growing sector (which was Buddhism, which jumped from 31.2 percent in 1990 to 42.5 percent in 2000). Yet it is the only growing religion in Singapore other than Buddhism, and the only one to come from other than traditional Asian roots or through Asian trade networks and cultural influences. (Taoism and Islam declined in percentage figures, while Hinduism and other religions held steady over the same period.) Christianity is also most strongly associated with the indices of socioeconomic progress and upwardly mobile class status in Singapore: It is the dominant religion among those with a university education (33.5 percent to Buddhism's 23.6 percent), among those with

English as the language most frequently spoken at home (39.8 percent, to Buddhism's 24.8), and among those who live in the more exclusive private housing as opposed to the predominant public housing (34.3 percent to Buddhism's 30.1).[12]

Even these suggestive census figures may understate the matter, as the evangelical machinery goes beyond the mere positivist data of professed Christianity, extending into a "sequence and set of operations" that constitutes the "social space" of evangelical Christian culture.[13] Many more students pass through the gates of the mission schools than those who formally convert to Christianity; public discourses, texts, and signs may embody Christianity-reinforcing values without requiring conversion or even conscious assent. Christianity in its biblical roots is as much a mechanism for cultural influence as it is a proselytizing force: Injunctions such as the prohibition of work on the Sabbath and rites of offering apply not just to the children of Israel, but also to "the strangers in Israel," the "stranger that is within thy gates" (Leviticus 22:18; Exodus 20:10). Modern evangelical culture and community structures rely on the personal "testimony" or "witness" of the Christian's everyday life and actions, which are meant to attract the nonbeliever—hence the Apostle Paul's description of the believer's life as a "manifestation of the truth commending ourselves to every man's conscience in the sight of God" (2 Corinthians 4:2). The "gates" of the Christian community or institution thus mark the boundaries of a cultural sphere, wherein a variety of mechanisms (praxis, example, symbol, text, ritual, dialogue) seek constantly to display Christianity.

As a former British settlement-colony that is now gearing up for competition as a global city, Singapore's institutional initiatives (in education, media and arts, language policy, urban planning, and other areas) inevitably take on significant elements of the cultural influences of both the historical and contemporary global powers (respectively, Britain and America). Evangelical cultural production is thus inextricably bound with such cultural influences and mechanisms as English as a global language; the values, images, and productions of foreign Anglophone (especially American) film and network companies; the Internet; the business of education; and of course the actual machinery directly concerned with Christianity as a global enterprise. These mechanisms not only produce social identities at odds in various ways with national constructions of "Asian" multiculturalism and a "Singaporean" identity, but also revitalize ideological structures that bear something of the impress of historical colonialism, and are arguably a form of neocolonial influence. Just as Anglophone mission-school education in colonial Singapore was a means for children of immigrant families to tap into the language, networks, values, and habits of the colonial power; so do contemporary evangelical cultures bring with them an inevitable cultural affiliation and ideological pattern. The United States (and to a lesser extent the United Kingdom and Australia) becomes the rising center for a new Anglophone culture of territorial, middle-class materialist, media-savvy progressivism.

MISSION SCHOOLS

Although religious conversion is not required of students during the term of their studies in mission schools, the entire spatial, cultural, and textual logic of these schools is evangelical—aimed at producing an influential climate that, if it does not lead to immediate religious conversion, will abide with the student long after graduation. Some schools have a formal chapel or church structure on their grounds—the Anglican St. Andrew's School, for example, which provides primary and secondary education, has a dedicated church building on its ample grounds, which holds chapel services for the school's students during the week and on Sundays has its own congregation (a significant portion of whom will have alumni and other connections with the school). Other mission schools of more recent construction often have multipurpose halls or theatres that may function as the venue for school religious services and host a church congregation on Sundays, as well as being rented out for commercial purposes when available—the Methodist Anglo-Chinese (Independent) School and Methodist Girls' School being examples.

The architecture and spatial organization of such schools thus serve to convey religious signification to all (not merely the students) who enter their gates. Visitors to the Anglo-Chinese (Independent) School are greeted in the main entrance with the school arms on the wall and above it the legend "To God Be the Glory" in large letters, and below it the school motto "The Best Is Yet to Be." Wall displays of school achievements—the sports triumphs, scholars produced, academic and social honors that are so highly valued in achievement-oriented Singapore society—are thus spatially associated with an ethos of acknowledging God as the giver of all such good things. Schools with an older architecture (especially prior to the postmodernist influences that characterized a considerable part of the rebuilding of Singapore schools in the 1990s and thereafter), which draw on influences such as English ecclesiastical and Palladial-style architecture, display Christian and churchly symbolism in more complex and subtle ways. Thus, St. Andrew's School has a distinctive pink edifice with elements borrowed from the Norman cathedral and Spanish mission architecture; the school has in recent years expanded and built new buildings, elements of the original architecture have been retained.[14] This architecture is redolent with Christian symbolism. For example, the massive buttress-like structures symbolize endurance and permanence (and thus both the enduring Word of God, and Christ as the foundation of the faith); a tower resembles a church spire, and symbolizes both achievements on earth as well as an orientation toward heaven; arches resemble and convey something of the solemnity of cathedral arcades and ambulatories; and, of course, the prominent cross (St. Andrew's features both the traditional crucifix form and the St. Andrew's cross) overlooks main areas like the quadrangle. The grand dimensions of certain cathedral structures, such as high towers, large pediments, and porticoes, and the wide proportions and pillars of the popular Corinthian facade, are often retained (even if in stylized form) in new mission school buildings. These features contribute to the distinctive ambience of the mission school as compared to secular schools, and also constitute a distinct cultural influence: They help to convey an authoritarian structure that ultimately derives from and feeds back into the authority of the church. They also foster an ideology of social, spiritual, and academic "largeness" and grandeur amenable both to worldly and spiritual development; and they accustom students to the feel and design of churches and church rituals. In St. Andrew's Secondary School, for example, it is the custom to welcome new boys in a ceremony in which they march in the main road where the large crucifix and facade of the Chapel of the Holy Spirit awaits them.[15]

The ritualistic elements of such schools is hardly to be overlooked either, and constitute a "disciplining" of students into a set of values and beliefs[16] as well as forming a set of common and everyday practices that bind the student and faculty body into an imaginary community.[17] School rituals such as regular assemblies, social activities, "co-curricular activities," and excursions outside the classroom—all of which feature elements of prayer and the espousing of Christian values such as charity and honesty— establish a normative model of behavior in common for all students. As an alumnus of Anglo-Chinese School, Mr. Ong Kian Min (a lawyer and member of parliament) puts it, "simple things like the ACS roll of honour and school magazine helped students look up to those who brought glory to the school."[18] Where such events involve students' families as well—in parents' meetings and seminars, concerts, dinners, and other activities—the normative model is displayed to this wider community. The reading, writing, and hearing of discourses of Christian development and success—in school magazines and other publications, commemorative speeches, and other organs—also circulate normative value systems to the wider school community, which includes the families of students and of prospective students.

The emphasis on character development and moral behavior in Singapore mission schools also means that the production of social identity is a lifelong process, extending well beyond the physical boundaries of the school and the temporal boundaries of the school years. Mission schools have particularly good mechanisms for the fostering of alumni identity, networks, and connections, enhanced too by Singapore's small physical size and the relatively small circle of Anglophone professionals and university graduates. Regular events in the school's calendar such as sports finals, prize-giving ceremonies, and annual school dinners are given a high profile by holding them in swanky venues such as the best hotels, or having promi-nent alumni (politicians, leading businessmen, top professionals) grace the occasion. Apart from imparting a sense of grandeur and importance to such events, this also reinforces among present students the association between school ties and social and professional aspirations, making the school net-work the locus of personal achievements and their display. Many mission schools also operate a church on their premises as a means of providing a convenient and familiar religious site for graduating students, although, of course, these congregations are not merely made up of former students.

The persistence of these school ties and connections, together with the tendency for Christianity to be the religion associated with Anglophone higher education and, consequently, with material and social success, sug-gests a different kind of mapping of Singapore's urban landscape—one in which specific kinds of socioeconomic identities are produced by special-ized cultural machines. This is perpetuated and corroborated by media dis-courses that often track the school affiliations of politicians and successful businessmen, as if these were contributing factors in their successes. Un-like the more elitist social identities conferred by top universities—Oxford or Cambridge in the United Kingdom, or Tokyo University in Japan—Christian cultural identity in Singapore is not confined to an intellectual elite, or to those with prior social and political connections to ensure admis-sion. Although mission schools in Singapore tend to be held in higher esteem than the average neighborhood (government-run) schools, they are not nec-essarily the very best schools (the elite government schools Raffles Institution and Raffles Girls' School usually claim those honors), and they range in terms of quality of students admitted and scholarly and sporting successes won. Also, the effective perimeters of the mission school cultural identity extend at least to the families and friends of students, if not farther. Elite varsities (or for that matter elite preparatory schools or clubs) are interested in restrict-ing membership so as to enhance their image of exclusivity, but mission schools in Singapore are an example of an "open progressive" cultural mech-anism, which constantly takes in a range of new inductees and processes them in accordance with forward-looking cultural identities and values.

CHURCH.ORG.SG: SITING CHRISTIAN IDENTITY VIA THE INTERNET

The Internet provides all kinds of possibilities and opportunities, not all of them equal or equally effective, for the propagation of Christian social iden-tities.[19] Some of the contextual limitations include (once again) Singapore's small geographical size, which makes physical churches easily accessible (and thus mitigates against the creation of vibrant virtual churches), and a continuing reluctance on the part of Singaporeans (particularly those of the older generations) to engage in web transactions or activities.[20] Yet these conventions of or expectations about the Internet are likely to change in the short to medium term, and it seems likely that more of its opportunities for evangelical activities and connectivity will be exploited.

Already many of the churches in Singapore have at least rudimentary webpages in addition to their brick-and-mortar presences and activities. A number of interesting trends distinguishing Internet evangelical presences begin to emerge, which are indications of the particular characteristics of such sites as cultural mechanisms. Based on existing data, it would appear that church Internet sites are regarded as instruments for attracting young people in particular, for building connections with Singaporeans studying or working overseas, for "broadcasting" church events and activities (i.e., to an unspecific audience assumed to be heterogeneous in tastes and composition), and as a means of transcending the linguistic limitations often faced by physical churches (which, even where they have services in different languages, often have to deal with the problems of split and unequal congregations, space constraints, and slow real-time translations). The main impact of these factors is to reinforce the socioeconomic progressivism latent in evangelical Christianity, to create a set of social values that call forth a young, wired, globally networked Christian identity that is comfortable in an Anglophone and multilingual setting.

Church webpages enhance the networking capabilities evident in mission school structures by allowing a broadcasting of the full range of services, facilities, events, and models of behavior that are an intrinsic part of the evangelical mission. The webpage for the large and dynamic City Harvest Church in Singapore's East Coast area, which reported close to 13,000 attendees (2000 figures), is indicative of this range: its Events Calendar for 2001 included a "Business Breakthrough Dinner" series, a "Manhood Leadership Conference," a "Childrens' Day Celebration," a "Marriage and Parenting Seminar," a "Biblical Economics Seminar," and a "Personal Excellence Conference," in addition to the expected range of church activities such as prayer meetings, Bible studies, and Easter and Christmas celebrations.[21] This clearly allows the church to broadcast "something for everyone" in a way that would not be possible, or would be prohibitively expensive, in other media such as newspaper advertisements, events banners, or by word of mouth. The webpage obviously also allows for more immediate follow-up, with links that provide more detailed information about such events, information about the church (with its sermons online), and other related links such as one to a "men's network," or another to "community service." The (as it were) funneling effect of such a church website is to clutch at the widest possible range of interests and user profiles, and then to channel a specific interest (say, men's concerns such as business, parenting, sexuality, or values) deeper and deeper into the church's discourses and practices.

Notwithstanding this broadcasting of interests, church websites do in addition pay particular attention to the concerns and interests of young people. City Harvest's online video detailing its church history constantly stresses its orientation toward "young people," its focus activities being "fun and fellowship" and "friendship evangelism" through which "many new friends were added."[22] The video features (among other things) images of young people having fun as they participate in dynamic activities such as music, plays and skits, games, and so on. As a narrow-band outlet within the larger broadcast strategy of the church's overall webpage, its youth-oriented pages and links have a similar funneling effect, making initial contact with young people through a wide range of images, activities, and events.

A significant part in this youth connection is the work of pastor Ho Yeow-Sun, the wife of City Harvest founder and senior pastor Kong Hee. Sun (as she is popularly known) has recently entered into a career as a singer of Mandarin popular songs, and has carved out a niche for herself not only in the Singapore music scene, but also in Taiwan and Hong Kong. Several links on the City Harvest page promote her latest CD, invite people to "vote for Sun" (as an indication of her relative popularity as an artist) on their mobile phones, and connect to her webpage (where she talks about youthful interests, such as an episode that happened while scuba-diving, playing with her pets, her favorite foods, and so on). Sun's popular music thus becomes another means of cultural identification for a larger section of the young who may not be Christians or come from Christian families; conversely, Christians who visit the City Harvest webpage and encounter Sun's pages and images are then persuaded that this brand of Christianity has an element of youthful trendiness and fun about it.

Sun's career in Mandarin popular music gives some indication of how churches' web-presences are able (to some extent) to overcome stratifications of social identity according to language spoken. While brick-and-mortar church structures face certain stratifying constraints—mainly the separation in space and time of the events and activities of different language congregations—webpages are to a certain extent able to nurture a common identity across the main languages (English and Mandarin) spoken by most Singapore youths. Web-content, with its emphasis on still images, video clips, and music, and its use of hyperlinks to bring varied material into quick juxtaposition with each other, is structurally predisposed to erode the divisive barriers inevitably set up by brick-and-mortar constraints.

Many churches with multilingual congregations also archive sermon texts in various languages, either as text documents or more commonly as webcast videos. To a certain extent, the unity across different languages that church websites foster is an illusory and simplifying condition: English remains the dominant Internet language, certain demographic imbalances (the fact that Chinese dialects such as Hokkien and Teochew are spoken by older ethnic Chinese in Singapore but hardly at all by younger ones) cannot be corrected, and the incorporation of Mandarin elements is often superficial rather than comprehensive. Yet this air of harmonious unity across different languages, however simplifying, indicates not merely the unifying ideology inherent in such church webpages, but also the significant role of evangelical culture in transforming or at least cutting across some of the existing social divisions.

The emphasis on youthful identities also means that church websites tend to structure themselves as a means for Singaporeans studying overseas to maintain ties and connections with their friends at home. Wesley Methodist Church, for example, has its Ministry to Overseas Graduates and Students (MOGS), which among other things seeks to "maintain a link with students who are currently overseas."[23] Although many of its services are face-to-face activities—"pre-departure talks, returnees fellowships etc."[24]—it is clear that the Internet fosters the church's ability to maintain and nurture contact while the student is overseas. Such websites can thus constitute nodes at the center of far-reaching student networks, effectively creating a globally connected community. As the senior pastor of Faith Community Baptist Church puts it on his church's webpage, the church's mission is "to provide the resources for you to use to enhance your personal Christian growth and your cell ministry, wherever you are in the world."[25]

Such church webpages thus reinforce certain kinds of social identities— in particular, that of the young, media-savvy, wired global citizen, who is likely to study or work overseas and to be receptive to cultural influences and ideas, especially from Anglophone leading nations. Inevitably, Christian evangelical notions of personal development or growth become associated with this set of socioeconomic indicators of growth or progress, and the link is in turn reinforced by the speed, connectivity, and accessibility of the Internet. Like mission schools, church websites are also developmental or progressive in that they are the site of a set of values shared by and propagated among young people through networks based on open "friendship," creating a core group who will in time come to assume leadership and give vital input in the creation and maintenance of such virtual communities and discourses. The efficacy of such a young, media-savvy, networking technology system is not to be underestimated: Even in these relatively early days of the virtual church, City Harvest Church (admittedly one of the leaders in this game) can boast of more than 354,000 hits on its webpage between 2000 and the middle of 2002. Its "Sun" links claim CD sales of more than 100,000 copies in total in Taiwan, Singapore, and Hong Kong.

GLOBAL OPERATIONS, GLOBAL CHRISTIANS

Globally oriented operations are arguably part of the evangelical ideology: The biblical basis often adduced here is the "Great Commission" of Christ in Matthew chapter 28, which commands the disciples to go and teach all nations, and promises that Christ will sustain this enterprise "even unto the end of the world." The structural and ideological resemblances between global capitalist operations and global Christianity are striking, and worthy of separate discussion. For the purposes of the present paper, it suffices to note the coincidence of the development in Singapore of a mature evangelical Christianity intent on extending its operations in other countries with Singapore's regional and global push in its major government-linked industries (banking and financial services, transportation services, and facilities management) and the government's general encouragement of an entrepreneurial ethos of expansion. The coincidence of these ideologies, especially in the 1990s and into the new millennium, means that the idea of Singapore as a Christian hub feeds into, and is reinforced by, secular forces of global capitalism, communications links, and global citizenship.

In some significant ways, Christians and potential converts in Singapore are more inherently predisposed to look "outside" for their cultural influences and affiliations. Quite apart from historical influences—the hymns, liturgies, sermons, rituals, and writings from nineteenth and early twentieth century American and British mission organizations—more recent Christian culture has dovetailed with contemporary media developments, and imported a whole range of texts from the major sources in Britain, the United States, and Australia. In terms of contemporary Christian music, for example, many churches in Singapore rely heavily on the original compositions, soundtracks, minus-one tapes, and scores produced by such groups as the "Hillsongs" organization in Australia, "Kingsway" (in East Sussex, United Kingdom), and U.S.-based "Integrity" (which also produces the well-known "Hosanna" series of music albums and scores), "BMG Songs Inc.," and "Crooked Letter Music." Individual songwriters, worship leaders, and artists like Americans Don Moen and Bob Fitts, and Australians Geoff Bullock and Darlene Zesch, augment their reputations in Singapore with the occasional touring visit, during which they often also conduct worship seminars or talks.

The global Christian children's media also has a significant hold in Singapore, led by products such as the *Arky* series (an animated Noah's Ark) of children's musical tapes and CDs, the *Veggie Tales* videos (featuring animated vegetable characters who comically enact biblically inspired or morally charged stories and skits), and the concerts and videos featuring "Psalty" and "Charity Churchmouse," the musical characters created by the husband-and-wife Retino team. Singapore Christian media output (not including mainstream-crossover acts like City Harvest's singing pastor Sun) is relatively insignificant, confined to occasional small-turnover recordings and limited-run (usually free admission) concerts and musicals from the larger churches. Consequently, most of the Singapore Christian community is predisposed perpetually to look outside for its media products, and consequently derives its images and identities in part from such products.

Furthermore, Christian content and values are not confined to media products from explicitly Christian organizations, and there is a significant output from secular media organizations such as the Hollywood film studios, which also have various kinds of Christian themes and concerns. Texts that have been circulated in Singapore, and that are the closest to orthodox Christian themes and concerns, include television shows like *Touched by an Angel* (CBS, 1994–) and *7th Heaven* (Warner Brothers, 1997–), and films like *The Third Miracle* (1999, dir. Agnieszka Holland). Of course, the range of popular film and television texts that include some kind of reference to Christianity would include the trivial, unorthodox, or (from a Christian perspective) outright blasphemous, ranging from popular comedies like *Sister Act* and *Sister Act II,* to the plethora of horror films that ransack Christian culture for their incidentals (*Stigmata, End of Days,* and the *Omen* series are just some examples). Notwithstanding these texts at the more trivializing end of the spectrum, it remains true that some secular media productions contribute significantly to the popularization of Christian values and tropes; the highly successful *Touched by an Angel* series, for example, is in its ninth season, while *7th Heaven* is in its sixth. Both have attracted fans through their uplifting and affirming storylines and their willingness to take moral positions on complex contemporary issues.

There are no data to correlate the popularity of such shows in Singapore with specifically Christian viewing households, but there are structural reasons to regard such shows as part of a significant Christian cultural influence in foreign media productions: the sensitivities of race and religion in multiracial Singapore mean that its domestic media output usually skirts around, or simply ignores, the values, cultures, and rituals of the different religions in Singapore.[26] The fact of multireligious Singapore becomes represented in most domestically produced television programs as a religious absence or neutrality. Singapore Christians thus only receive images and representations addressing and affirming Christian values, concerns, and social identities (i.e., Christian religious observances in a permissive contemporary society, attitudes to premarital sex and abortion, moral parenting, belief and faith, Christianity in the workplace and in human relations, and so on) from foreign media producers in Anglophone countries with Christian cultures such as the United States and Britain. In much the same way, Singaporean Buddhists are likely to receive most of the media images pertaining to their faith from texts produced by Far East producers in Hong Kong, Taiwan, and (to a lesser extent) Japan. Singaporean Hindus will likewise be influenced by the media productions of India, and Singaporean Muslims by Malaysian and Indonesian productions.

Language is only part of the picture, rather than the fundamental cause of such divided affiliations. Many Chinese Christians in Singapore can also speak some Mandarin, while Christians of Indian descent might speak both English and Tamil and thus have their choice of media texts. The issue is not so much language and access to different media productions, as it is the geocultural stratification of social identities as dictated by religious affiliations.[27] Singapore Christians, by this geocultural logic, are conspicuous for having the most other-oriented and transformative affiliations to the images, cultures, and texts of Anglophone media nations. In contrast, Hindus, Buddhists, and Muslims arguably have regional cultural affiliations that reinforce Asian traditions, languages, and social identities.

In terms of geophysical orientations, the Christian cultural machinery predisposes adherents to a more far-flung, more arguably global perspective than do the faiths originating in Asia. An Anglophone education and linguistic facility clearly have something to do with this, but the cultural influences and affiliations are much deeper than that. Singaporean Muslims go on pilgrimage to Saudi Arabia and watch largely Malaysian television programs (either in addition to or instead of English-language shows), and Singaporean Buddhists may go on religious-themed trips to Thailand or China and watch HongKong dramas. However, Singaporean Christians, who think of going to Rome for (the Catholics or) the great cathedrals of Europe, or even for studying in the seminaries of the United States and Britain, consume the literary and media productions from Anglophone countries, concern themselves with current affairs and socioeconomic developments in these countries, and get advice from each other about which of the vibrant large churches they should visit on their holidays in the United States, Australia, the Philippines, Korea, England, or New Zealand.

The Christian cultural machinery and network production is thus predisposed toward a certain brand of global identity—comfortably Anglophone (although not confined to it) but also exposed to the historical and social contexts, media, values, and ideological systems of Anglophone countries and those with strong Christian traditions. Such a global identity and network system has its problems, most significantly its tendency to follow the lines of historical colonialism and to reinforce neocolonial cultural domination by contemporary centers like the United States. Singaporean Christians who use their "Christian" first names exclusively, speak mostly English, and are more concerned with events happening in Chicago or Boston than with Kuala Lumpur, Beijing, or Jakarta may with some justice be accused of being deracinated individuals who lack some of the recognizably or prominently "Asian" characteristics. Yet for the very same reasons these are likely to be individuals who are more comfortable working in multinational companies based in North America or Europe or being posted to those regions, or working in most of the foreign media companies with offices in Singapore. The government has recognized and promoted the importance of a good Anglophone education in the creation of this class of global "cosmopolitans" who (it is believed) will lead Singapore's global entrepreneurial charge.[28] What it has not explicitly acknowledged (and what may be impolitic to acknowledge) is that this Anglophone education has to be reinforced by a suitable geocultural familiarity and orientation as well, and that these are closely intertwined with the Christian cultural machinery and networks.

Global Christianity in the Singapore context does not merely mean a fundamental orientation toward "Western" cultures and identities, of course. The globalizing thrust of the Great Commission involves many Singapore churches and Christian organizations in a twofold international flow (of capital, manpower, organizational structures, and cultural influence) in which there is influx from centers rich in Christian resources and outflow again in the direction of "mission fields" where Christianity is relatively weak. Such a flowchart naturally means that Singapore is the recipient of (various) expertise, administrative guidance, funding, and manpower from Christian organizations, especially those in America such as Operation Mobilization (a missionary organization), Disciple, and Bible Study Fellowship (BSF) International (training and scriptural resources organizations), and Sword of the Spirit (an ecumenical organization). However, Singaporean churches and Christian organizations are at the same time dispensers of various resources to countries like Vietnam, Thailand, Indonesia, Cambodia, Nepal, the Philippines, India, and elsewhere. This outflow most typically takes the form of mission trips to preach the gospel and win converts, but this is often intertwined with a whole range of other activities and services: medical aid, teacher training in English and other subjects, infrastructure assistance (repairs, building works), "tent making" endeavors involving all kinds of business contacts and projects, and so on. Not coincidentally, such movements often mirror or reinforce secular flows of capital and labor: The Singapore–India Christian connections, for example, are based in part on the Singapore churches' activities among the many

Indian migrant workers who come to work in Singapore for a number of years, some of whom then return to their villages as Christian converts and with connections to Singapore churches and organizations. The provision of services and supplies by Christian networks to countries in the region like Vietnam and Cambodia parallels the attempts by Singaporean business interests to establish footholds in these new markets; both projects may reinforce each other by contributing to a stronger "Singaporean" presence and influence in each of these countries.

CONCLUSION

Several consequences follow from, and certain issues are raised by, such Christian cultural mechanisms. In the first place, they stress the essentially mixed, dialogical, and hybrid nature of social identities in many of the urban centers of Asia's new and rapidly developing nations. Christian cultural machines are significant, not necessarily in terms of the sheer numbers of professed adherents, but because of the element of a sociohistorical "unconscious" at work in these mechanisms, linked as they are to such forces as historical colonialism, globalization, linguistic factors, communications, and media technology. Unconscious cultural forces also imply the reality of multiple and split (and at times conflicting) social identities, ideological impulses, and affiliations. While the manifestations of such divisions to date have been at the intercommunity level (for example, clashes between Muslims and Christian tribes in Indonesia), or between generations (for example, the conspicuous bunching of Christianity as a cultural force and professed religion among the young in Singapore), it is likely that more intense divisions will develop as global communications and networks strengthen. Once again, it will be the developed urban centers, particularly those competing as "global cities," that will be the hot spots of such split demands and loyalties. In the case of Singapore, the next crisis point is likely to arise if and when data accounting systems become capable of recognizing the prominence of Christian culture (in its broad sense) and its inextricable link to the educated and successful global identities privileged by the government and the public.

The operation of Christian cultural mechanisms in Singapore also suggests the ways in which urban cultural landscapes will increasingly become sites for overdetermined signs and overlapping networking systems. This is no doubt exacerbated by the sheer small size of Singapore's physical landscape, its population density, its multilingual and multiracial composition, and the relatively high degree of governance and governmental intervention in social transformations and cultural policy. Similar conditions exist in other major cities in the region and elsewhere, and are likely to intensify in the next few decades. Evangelical Christianity's flexible and adaptive uses of space and its symbolisms, media texts, Internet resources, international networking systems, and other strategies in the Singapore context are merely exemplary instances of what is in reality an implosion of information and influences in major urban centers. If Christianity seems inherently suited to adapt to this exploitation and manipulation of shared spaces and discourses—the Apostle Paul's hint that "I am made all things to all men" (1 Corinthians 9:22) might be taken as one basis for this strategy—this only reiterates the ways in which Christian culture corresponds with some of the significant ideological and technological currents of the present era.

NOTES

1. Charles Dickens, *Hard Times* (Harmondsworth: Penguin, 1969), 65.
2. David Harvey, *The Condition of Postmodernity: An Enquiry into the Origins of Cultural Exchange* (Oxford: Basil Blackwell, 1989), 27, 121–22.
3. Le Corbusier, *The City of To-morrow and Its Planning* (London: The Architectural Press, 1929), 13.
4. Karl Marx, *Capital: A Critique of Political Economy,* vol. 1, ed. Frederick Engels (New York: International Publishers, 1967), 71.
5. Ibid., 77–81.
6. Henri Lefebvre, *Writings on Cities,* trans. and ed. Eleonore Kofman and Elizabeth Lebas (Oxford: Blackwell, 1996), 65–66.
7. James Holston and Arjun Appadurai, "Cities and Citizenship," in *Cities and Citizenship,* ed. James Holston (Durham: Duke University Press, 1999), 9; Saskia Sassen, "Whose City Is It? Globalization and the Formation of New Claims," in *The Urban Movement: Cosmopolitan Essays on the Late-Twentieth-Century City,* ed. Robert A. Beauregard and Sophie Body-Gendrot (Thousand Oaks, Calif.: Sage Publications, 1999), 100.
8. Homi Bhabha, *The Location of Culture* (London: Routledge, 1994), 2.
9. Sassen, "Whose City Is It?," 100.
10. See Lily Kong, "Ideological Hegemony and the Political Symbolism of Religious Buildings in Singapore," *Environment and Planning D: Society and Space* 11 (1993): 23–45; Jean DeBernardi, "Lim Boon Keng and the Invention of Cosmopolitanism in the Straits Settlements," in *Managing Change in Southeast Asia: Local Identities, Global Connections,* ed. Jean Debernardi, Gregory Forth, and Sandra Niessen (Canada: CCSEAS XXI, 1995), 173–87; Robbie B. H. Goh, "Composing the Modern Nation: Mission School Magazines, Narrative Modes and Cultural Typologies in Colonial Singapore," *Journal of Commonwealth Literature* 36, no. 1 (2001): 59–74.
11. Census of Population Office, "Advance Data Release No. 2: Religion" (Singapore: Department of Statistics, November 2000), http://www.singstat.gov.sg. Date accessed: 18 May 2001.
12. Ibid., 6–8.
13. Henri Lefebvre, *The Production of Space,* trans. Donald Nicholson-Smith (Oxford: Blackwell, 1991), 73.
14. The landmark "Woodsville" campus of St. Andrew's School was decommissioned when the contiguous new secondary school premises were completed in 1986, but the Woodsville buildings are still on display, and function as the campus of the Tung Ling Bible College. Moreover, many of the architectural features of the Woodsville campus were incorporated into the design of the new school.
15. St. Andrew's School. "Welcoming the New Sec Ones." http://www.saints.com.sg/webpage/events2000/SEcOne2000.htm. Date accessed: 5 July 2002.
16. Michel Foucault, *Discipline and Punish: The Birth of the Prison,* trans. Alan Sheridan (New York: Vintage Books, 1979).
17. Benedict Anderson, *Imagined Communities: Reflections on the Origin and Spread of Nationalism* (London: Verso, 1991), 76–82.
18. Anglo-Chinese School, *ACS Echo* (published by the Board of Governors of the Anglo-Chinese School), February/March 2002, 11.
19. For the data and fieldwork in this section, I am greatly indebted to my researcher Ms. Tiffany Tsao.

20. The recent furor over an incident in which a hacker made unauthorized online withdrawals from twenty-one Development Bank of Singapore (DBS) accounts brought to light once again Singaporean fears and ignorance about the Internet; these are particularly pronounced in the case of "older people." See Ignatius Low, "Online Banking: Not Foolproof, but You Can Avoid Danger," *The Straits Times,* 3 July 2002, 6.

21. City Harvest Church, "Events Calendar 2001." http://www.chc.org.sg/version3/event_calendar.htm. Date accessed: 13 July 2001.

22. City Harvest Church, "City Harvest Church History." http://www.chc.org.sg/version3/main.htm. Date accessed: 4 July 2002.

23. Wesley Methodist Church, "Ministry to Overseas Graduates and Students (MOGS)." http://www.wesleymc.org/Ministries/MOGS/index.htm. Date accessed: 13 July 2001.

24. Ibid.

25. Faith Community Baptist Church, "A Word from Senior Pastor, Apostle Lawrence Khong." http://www.fcbc.org.sg/homepage3.htm. Date accessed: 11 July 2001.

26. The logical exceptions are the documentaries or other factual or descriptive accounts, for example, a program on heritage buildings that may include footage of a Hindu temple and its activities.

27. There is arguably also a significant ideological difference between the tolerance shown by religions like Hinduism and Buddhism to other faiths (or for that matter to the lack of a professed faith), and evangelical Christianity's tendency to regard such religions as serious errors standing in the way of salvation. Although different denominations and theologies within Christianity have varying degrees of tolerance of other faiths, this crux (the term is used advisedly) of Christian fundamental faith in general means that there tends to be a greater demand for "acceptable" media products of the faith.

28. Goh Chok Tong, "First-World Economy, World-Class Home." National Day Rally speech delivered 23 August 1999. Text reprinted in Ministry of Information and the Arts webpage. http://www.gov.sg/mita/pressrelease/99082202.htm. Date accessed: 24 February 2000.

List of Contributors

Kathleen M. Adams is an Associate Professor of Anthropology at Loyola University Chicago and an Adjunct Curator at the Field Museum of Anthropology. Her research interests include identity politics, art, tourism, and cultural displays in Indonesia and San Juan Capistrano, CA.

John Armitage is head of Multidisciplinary Studies in the School of Social, Political and Economic Sciences, University of Northumbria, United Kingdom. He is an associate editor of *Theory Culture & Society* and a member of the editorial board of the *Journal of Visual Culture.*

Ryan Bishop is associate professor in the American Studies Program and the Department of English at the National University of Singapore. Among his publications are works on international sex tourism in Thailand, critical theory, rhetoric, and the history of technology in relation to the university, the military, and aesthetics.

Gregory Clancey received his Ph.D. from the Program in the History and Social Study of Science and Technology at M.I.T., and currently teaches in the Department of History at the National University of Singapore. He is the co-editor of *Major Problems in the History of American Technology* (with M. Roe Smith) and *Historical Perspectives on Science, Technology, and Medicine in East Asia* (with Alan Chan and Loy Hui Chieh). His recent research centers on constructions of science and nature in modern Japan.

Richard Derderian is assistant professor in the Department of History at the National University of Singapore. His research has centered on multiculturalism, memory, and second-generation North African artists in France. He has published in *Contemporary French Civilization, Post-Colonial Cultures in France,* and has a forthcoming article in the *Radical History Review.*

Angela Rivas Gamboa is a doctoral candidate in the Department of Anthropology at Rice University.

Robbie B. H. Goh is associate professor in the Department of English Language and Literature at the National University of Singapore.

Peter A. Jackson is fellow in Thai History in the Australian National University's Research School of Pacific and Asian Studies. He specializes in modern Thai cultural history, with particular emphases on the history of Buddhism and the history of gender and eroticism, and is the author of numerous books on these topics.

Anthony D. King is Bartle Professor of Art History and Sociology at Binghamton University and is the author of many books on the social production of building form, colonialism and urbanism, social and spatial theory, postcolonial theory and criticism, and transnational cultures.

Shirley Geok-lin Lim is professor of English and Women's Studies at the University of California, Santa Barbara, and chair of English at the University of Hong Kong. She is a prize-winning poet and has published widely on Asian-American literature, feminist literature and theory, and postcolonial literature.

George E. Marcus is chair of the Department of Cultural Anthropology at Rice University. He is the editor of *The Late Editions* series of annuals (1993–2000), co-editor with James Clifford of *Writing Culture,* and co-author with Michael M. F. Fischer of *Anthropology as Cultural Critique.*

Rajeev S. Patke is associate professor of English at the National University of Singapore whose many research interests include postcolonialism, critical theory, and modernism.

John Phillips is associate professor of English at the National University of Singapore. He has published widely on continental philosophy, critical theory, visual culture, psychoanalysis, modernism, and aesthetics.

Steve Pile is senior lecturer in the Faculty of Social Sciences at the Open University. He has published widely on issues concerning place and the politics of identity. He is author of *The Body and the City* (1996), editor of several other books, and is currently preparing a book on city life.

Emma Reisz is a research student at Christ's College, University of Cambridge. She writes on the economic and agricultural history of the British colonial empire.

Joanne Roberts lectures on international business at the University of Durham Business School, United Kingdom. She is the author of *Multinational Business Service Firms,* and co-editor and contributor to *Knowledge and Innovation in the New Service Economy.*

James N. Rosenau is widely known for his research on the dynamics of change in world politics and international relations. The author or editor of over thirty-five books, he is the University Professor of International Affairs at George Washington University in Washington, D.C. His most recent book on "fragmegration" is called *Distant Proximities: Dynamics beyond Globalization,* which will be published by Princeton University Press.

Diane Wildsmith is an architect practicing with an international design consultancy in Jakarta for the past ten years. She is a visiting assistant professor at the University of Indonesia in the Department of Architecture, whose research interests concern the effects of globalization on the design of cities.

Wei-Wei Yeo is assistant professor of English at the National University of Singapore, whose research interests include Victorian literature, urban processes, and Dante.

Index